International Political Economy Series

Series Editor
Timothy M. Shaw
University of Massachusetts Boston
Boston, MA, USA

Emeritus Professor
University of London
London, USA

The global political economy is in flux as a series of cumulative crises impacts its organization and governance. The IPE series has tracked its development in both analysis and structure over the last three decades. It has always had a concentration on the global South. Now the South increasingly challenges the North as the centre of development, also reflected in a growing number of submissions and publications on indebted Eurozone economies in Southern Europe. An indispensable resource for scholars and researchers, the series examines a variety of capitalisms and connections by focusing on emerging economies, companies and sectors, debates and policies. It informs diverse policy communities as the established trans-Atlantic North declines and 'the rest', especially the BRICS, rise. NOW INDEXED ON SCOPUS!

More information about this series at
http://www.palgrave.com/gp/series/13996

David Monyae · Bhaso Ndzendze
Editors

The BRICS Order

Assertive or Complementing the West?

palgrave
macmillan

Editors
David Monyae
Centre for Africa-China Studies
University of Johannesburg
Johannesburg, South Africa

Bhaso Ndzendze
Centre for Africa-China Studies
University of Johannesburg
Johannesburg, South Africa

ISSN 2662-2483 ISSN 2662-2491 (electronic)
International Political Economy Series
ISBN 978-3-030-62764-5 ISBN 978-3-030-62765-2 (eBook)
https://doi.org/10.1007/978-3-030-62765-2

This Palgrave Macmillan imprint is published by the registered company Springer Nature Switzerland AG
The registered company address is: Gewerbestrasse 11, 6330 Cham, Switzerland

Acknowledgements

This book stemmed from a research seminar held within the auspices of the University of Johannesburg Centre for Africa-China Studies in partnership with the SARChI Chair for African Diplomacy and Foreign Policy at the University of Johannesburg and sponsored by Oxfam's Pan Africa Programme under the title 'BRICS-Africa Cooperation: Progress, Prospects and Challenges' on the 29th of August in 2017. We sincerely thank the scholars for availing themselves on the occasion of the proceedings, and presenting their papers on the day, and subsequently working very hard over the course of the next year to channel them into chapters which form much of this book. In the same vein, we sincerely appreciate the efforts of those who were not active participants in the seminar but were rather recruited into the project in the book production stage and delivered impressively.

We wish to thank Oxfam particularly the Pan Africa Programme, which has been a visible and leading organisation on the emerging countries and the implications their different rises carry has on Africa. Always with a finger on the pulse of the issues, their Africa-China Dialogue Platform has churned out relevant and timely research. More than this, their investment in this work, and the incredible cooperation, leadership and efficiency displayed by their team has allowed us to produce this work in the face of many obstacles. Special recognition in this regard is owed to Joab Okanda, Peter Kamalingin and Wing Lam for showing continuous commitment to the project. Similarly, we are thankful for the funding provided by the Department of Higher Education and Training under the BRICS Studies ITG framework.

The authors also thank Ms. Monica Seeber our copyeditor, for working with us in ensuring that the book was as polished as possible, and that all the groundwork was complete before we could send the manuscript to Palgrave Macmillan. Likewise, we would like to thank the Political Economy Series Editor, Professor Tim Shaw for his commitment to not only this work, but the entire series. These works are growing understanding around emerging issues, and, moreover, the series has given platform to fresh new voices from the Global South in these critical debates concerning the Global South (a phenomenon that is all too rare in the publishing world).

We would also like to thank the anonymous reviewers who complied with our deadlines and offered insightful comments and direction on all of the chapters to ensure that the end product was as proficient, comprehensive and factual as possible.

Sincere appreciation also goes to colleagues at the Centre for Africa-China Studies, including Mr. Charles Matseke, Ms. Lebo Masebua, Zizipho Masiza, Ms. Smangele Zwane, Dr. Westen Shilaho (who was very helpful in the proposal phase), Dr. Emmanuel Matambo and Mr. Bongane Gasela, along with past and present colleagues at the University of Johannesburg Centre for Africa-China Studies, including Co-Director Professor Peng Yi, Ms. Gugulethu Nkosi, Ms. Hellen Adogo and Mr. Gibson Banda and our team of Mandarin lecturers. Without their patience and proactive closing of many gaps necessitated by the editing of this work, it never would have reached completion. Finally, the authors would like to thank each other for seeing the project through.

July 2020

David Monyae
Bhaso Ndzendze

Contents

Notes on Contributors

Bruno De Conti is a Lecturer at the Institute of Economics, University of Campinas (Brazil). He holds a Ph.D. in Economics from the University of Paris 13 (France) and the University of Campinas (Brazil). He has been a Visiting Fellow at HTW Berlin (Germany) and a Visiting Professor at the University of Paris 13 (France), Universidad Autónoma de Madrid (Spain), Moscow State Institute of International Relations (MGIMO, Russia), Free University of Berlin (Germany), Universidad Nacional de Colombia and Southwestern University of Finance and Economics (China). At the University of Campinas, he is currently Coordinator of the Graduate Programme in Economics at BRICS Network University (BRICS NU) and Director of the Confucius Institute.

Bongane Gasela is a researcher at the Centre for Africa-China Studies at the University of Johannesburg.

Oscar van Heerden is a scholar of International Relations, where he focuses on International Political Economy, with an emphasis on Africa, and SADC in particular. He completed his Ph.D. and Masters studies at the University of Cambridge (UK). His undergraduate studies were at Turfloop and Wits. He is an active fellow of the Mapungubwe Institute for Strategic Reflection (MISTRA).

Célio Hiratuka is a Lecturer at the Institute of Economics, University of Campinas (Brazil) and a Researcher at the Centre of Industrial and Technology Economics and at the Brazil-China Studies Group at the same university. He is also Researcher of the South American Network of Applied Economics. Currently he is the coordinator of Graduate Studies at the Institute of Economics. His research interest includes the Brazilian Industrial Structure, International Trade and Foreign Direct Investment, Economic Development and Brazil–China Economic Relations. Prof. Hiratuka has several papers published in national and international peer-reviewed journals in his research areas.

Prof. Maxim Khomyakov is a Vice Director of St Petersburg Campus of Higher School of Economics (St Petersburg, Russia) and a director of the BRICS Studies Centre at Ural Federal University (Ekaterinburg, Russia). He was a Vice President (international affairs) at Ural Federal University, Ekaterinburg, Russia from 2009 until 2017. Prof. Khomyakov was a visiting scholar at a number of universities, including Texas A&M University (2002) and European University Institute (2007–2008; Florence, Italy). Between 2002 and 2013, he organised a number of transnational research and teaching projects in political philosophy and religious studies. Since 2015, Prof. Khomyakov has been actively involved in establishing university collaboration in BRICS countries, and especially in establishing the BRICS Network University. His research interests include theory of modernity, theory of toleration, Russian philosophy of the nineteenth century and higher education theory. His works include several books and more than 60 scholarly articles.

Wynand Lambrechts SMIEEE, obtained his B.Eng., M.Eng., and Ph.D. degrees in Electronic Engineering from the University of Pretoria (UP), South Africa. He achieved his M.Eng. with distinction. He has authored two publications in peer-reviewed journals and has presented at various local and international conferences. Wynand is the lead author on two books; in the fields of sustainable energy and in microelectronic engineering, published by international publishers. He has co-authored four contributing chapters in other books in the fields of green energy and technology and the fourth industrial revolution. He previously held a position as an electronic engineer at Denel Dynamics, a state-owned company in South Africa. He is currently employed by SAAB Grintek Defence (SGD) and is also serving as a part-time research associate at the University of Johannesburg (UJ), South Africa.

Chris Landsberg is a professor and an NRF SARChI Chair for African Diplomacy and Foreign Policy at the University of Johannesburg.

Tshilidzi Marwala is Vice-Chancellor and Principal of the University of Johannesburg.

Emmanuel Matambo holds a Ph.D. from the University of KwaZulu-Natal, with his work focused on China–Zambia relations from a constructivist theoretical perspective. His work has appeared in numerous international peer-reviewed journals. He is a Senior Researcher at the University of Johannesburg Centre for Africa-China Studies.

David Monyae is the Executive Director of the University of Johannesburg Centre for Africa-China Studies and lectures a postgraduate course on the International Political Economy of Africa–China Relations. He has previously served as Section Manager: Research in the Parliament of South Africa and as Senior Analyst at the Development Bank of Southern Africa.

Bhaso Ndzendze is Research Director of the University of Johannesburg Centre for Africa-China Studies and a Lecturer in the Department of Politics and International Relations at the University of Johannesburg on Technology Dynamics in International Relations.

Garth Shelton is an associate professor of international relations at the University of the Witwatersrand and the director of its East Asia Project.

Westen K. Shilaho, Ph.D. (Wits), is a research fellow at the Centre for Africa-China Studies at the University of Johannesburg.

Saurabh Sinha is Deputy Vice-Chancellor: Research and Internationalisation, University of Johannesburg.

Bob Wekesa is in the Department of Journalism and Media Studies and the African Centre for the Study of the United States at the University of the Witwatersrand.

Arthur Welle has an Undergraduate Degree in Anthropology and Economics, and a Master's Degree in International Relations, all of them from the University of Campinas (Brazil). He is currently a Ph.D. candidate in Economic Theory at the same university and his main research focus is on international economy and labour economics.

List of Figures

List of Tables

CHAPTER 1

Introduction: The Genealogies, Elements and Implications of a 'BRICS Order'

David Monyae and Bhaso Ndzendze

Introduction

This volume discusses aspects required for the advancement of the BRICS, foremost being infrastructural development and the production of knowledge relevant to these countries. The book highlights infrastructure—hard and soft—as the nerve centre of development. Ports, airports, road and rail networks, are central to economic activity, backed by soft infrastructure—health, education and capacity development.

The setting up of the New Development Bank (NDB) and subsequently the launching of its African Regional Centre in Johannesburg, South Africa, in August 2017, illustrated the importance that the BRICS

D. Monyae · B. Ndzendze (✉)
University of Johannesburg Centre for Africa-China Studies, Johannesburg, South Africa
e-mail: bndzendze@uj.ac.za

D. Monyae
e-mail: dmonyae@uj.ac.za

D. Monyae and B. Ndzendze (eds.), *The BRICS Order*, International Political Economy Series,
https://doi.org/10.1007/978-3-030-62765-2_1

countries attach to the quest for an alternative financial regime to underwrite its development projects. The Shanghai-headquartered NDB is one of the tangible achievements of the BRICS since inception, and is proof of its quest to reorder the post-Cold War financial order. The NDB is poised to play a major role in the development of Africa and the emerging markets. The World Bank, a symbol of the Western hegemonic influence in global financial affairs, often bypasses certain ventures in Africa for lack of immediate returns. Once the NDB expands beyond the BRICS member states it will complement China's established engagement with Africa: investing in Africa's infrastructural development. The NDB shows that the global South has staked its claim to play a role in its own development and financial institutions. The bank affords the global South an alternative to the domineering Western-leaning financial order manifested through the World Bank and International Monetary Fund (IMF).

The book also teases out the nexus between knowledge and economic activity. It shows that besides trade pacts, the BRICS countries must accent collaboration in research by universities to reduce dependence on the Western canon.

The contributors explore the emergence and evolution of the BRICS countries in relation to each member, and teases out the place, role and unique contribution of each one of them to the bloc. It highlights the indisputable influence of BRICS in international relations without glossing over inherent challenges that militate against the bloc operating as it should. The BRICS is composed of countries which, although strategic in their respective regions, differ in power and influence owing to economic size, military capability, skills and level of poverty. South Africa, despite being the smallest on almost all indices, has for long punched above its weight through soft power. However, as Africa's representative in the bloc South Africa does not enjoy unanimous endorsement across Africa as the continent's leader. India and China are yet to resolve the Himalayan border dispute, and have competed for economic and political interests in the Asian region, in Africa and even globally. The chapters in this volume show that whereas the BRICS has the potential to reconfigure the global power distribution, and chip away at the monolith presented by the United States and the EU, it is imperative that it addresses its inherent fault lines.

The chapters flag out normative inconsistencies within the BRICS bloc. The BRICS countries are at different stages in the democratisation process. Questions of progression and evolution are also gaining momentum with unparalleled perturbation. In particular, the fourth industrial revolution is a theme the book explores: specifically how the

BRICS will contribute to this technological age defined by artificial intelligence, big data and the Internet-of-things, among others. The advantages and disadvantages to the BRICS bloc of this rapid technological age are worth explaining. The impact of new technologies in medicine, mining and the manufacturing sector is phenomenal. But the flipside of artificial intelligence is that it has the potential to exacerbate unemployment and inequalities. The book will seek to nuance this subject.

This introductory chapter will preface the book by exploring the background to the formation of the BRICS and briefly detailing the global economy since 2000, and then tracing the origins of the BRICS from Bandung through IBSA, the emergence of the BRICS within the post-2000 global economy, and the subsequent rise and outcomes of BRICS summitry.

A Brief Portrait of the Global Economy Since 2000: Locating the BRICS Rise

Various elements and indeed key events in the global economy of the twenty-first century have their origins in the middle of the century which preceded it—in particular, the end of the Second World War in Allied (United States, Soviet, French and British) victory in 1945, and the ensuing Cold War between the two dominant coalition partners and their slew of satellites. The need for reconstruction and mutual isolation and containment between Washington and Moscow, representing competing versions of the world order, led to the foundation of a number of international political and economic institutions and determined their trajectories for the remainder of the period between the late 1940s and the early 1990s, with consequent legacies reverberating well into the present—and, moreover, with important patterns remaining intact.

Widely seen as the moment in which globalisation would take hold, the post-Cold War era, and the subsequent twenty-first century produced economic crises which, while vindicating predictions of increased economic integration, also gave rise to contagious economic crises. The 2008–2009 global recession and the subsequent euro debt crisis were to also mark a new moment in history as they were contrasted by the continued, if uneven, rise of the BRICS countries.

The Great Recession and Its Aftermath, 2008–2018

In the year 2009, global GDP growth was low, low enough to be 5.8 percentage points behind what it had been in 2007. 'The downturn in emerging and developing countries was almost the same as in developed countries' (Dullien et al. 2010: 1). Countries in Eastern Europe and Central Asia were the most severely affected, their GDP growth rates declining by a combined average of 15.2 percentage points between 2007 and 2009. Latin America and Sub-Saharan Africa saw declines of 7.6 and 4.8 percentage points respectively for the same period. 'Even in developing Asia growth rates dropped by 4 percentage points between 2007 and 2009' (Dullien et al. 2010: 2). The 2008–2009 global financial crisis was rooted in financial mismanagement. Andre Roux (2014: 171–3) breaks down the 2008 crisis to a series of five stages: (1) global imbalances and liquidity build-up, (2) bursting of housing bubble (3) consumer panic, (4) global recession and (5) policy attempts at a cure. These will be examined in turn.

Following the crisis, especially between 1999 and 2009, there was an almost exponential growth in the foreign exchange reserves held by the developing world; they grew from US$500 billion in 1999 to about US$4.5 trillion in 2009. As a consequence, there was a 'sea of liquidity and, by and large, interest rates … were very low in many parts of the world' (Roux 2014: 171). Secondly, as a consequence of the low interest rates consumers borrowed extensively in order to acquire residential properties and there developed a housing boom. The world's major banks started to give loans through the sub-prime market to households that could not afford the loans. Soon, the bubble burst. By 2007 and 2008, many families defaulted on their mortgages ('especially since interest rates started rising again amid inflationary concerns' (Roux 2014: 172)). The demand for new houses soon declined, as did the prices—the banks incurred huge losses and hence the financial meltdown in late 2008.

The third phase of the crisis was the resultant panic. By the end of 2008, millions of consumers 'suddenly' realised that they were in a financial predicament; they were heavily indebted and the value of their assets—especially residential properties—had plummeted. As a result, many began to take individual austerity measures, and this fed into the fourth stage of the crisis with the banks' reluctance to lend and consumers' equal reluctance to get into further debt—this led to a domino effect that had a deepening effect on the recession.

The demand for consumer goods fell, and manufacturers produced fewer goods; for example, the number of automobiles assembled in the United States in January 2009 was 60 per cent below that of January 2008, whereas in Germany, machine-tool orders were 40 per cent lower than a year earlier (*The Economist* 2009). Economic growth consequently fell in these countries. Investment in capital declined, and workers lost their jobs. The process became cyclical. Because of the integration of world economies, the effects became internationalised. A slowdown in one country's demand for a particular good led to a slowdown in the amounts of that good imported from another country. Imports fell, unemployment rose and the crisis deepened. The impact was catastrophic.

For the first time since the 1980s, the global economic growth rate was negative.The final stage entailed policy attempts aimed at curbing the process. Because the economic recession was rooted in the rapidly slowing consumer demand for goods and services (and no prospect of consumer demand increase was in sight), in 2009 governments adopted expansionary fiscal policy programmes. Governments in the United States, the UK and elsewhere increased their spending and lowered taxes, in order to improve the buying power of consumers. This coincided with an aggressive lowering of official interest rates (to below one per cent in the case of the United States) in the hope that the lower cost of borrowing would make consumers borrow to finance spending on consumption, and producers borrow to finance investment in productive capacity and inventory (Roux 2014: 173). Soon, there were signs of recovery, and in 2010 the global economy grew by some four per cent, although—as even the IMF conceded—the recovery pattern was uneven as the developed states were outpacing most of their underdeveloped and developing counterparts. But the consequences of the crisis have not dissipated. Two of its most persistent remnants were in different interfaces; the first was in the developing world, and the other was the euro debt crisis.

> ... it was only when the crisis turned into a global economic recession that developing and emerging market economies were affected, mainly through the trade channel, and in some cases through workers' falling remittances. In many developing countries, the economic consequences of these indirect effects were as severe as the direct effects were on developed countries. (Frieden and Walter 2017: 1)

Countries in the Eurozone borrowed particularly heavily, largely to finance current consumption, 'as financial institutions in the rest of Europe were eager to lend' (Frieden and Walter 2017: 2). Large current account imbalances developed, as capital and goods flowed out of countries with current account surpluses into countries with current account deficits. Borrowing fed economic expansion, which grew into a boom, then a bubble, largely in housing markets. 'When the bubble burst, lending dried up' and soon those heavily indebted states were unable to service their debts, 'unable to make up for the collapse of domestic demand by exporting, and unable to borrow additional funds in order to cover their continuing payments deficits' (Frieden and Walter 2017: 2).

The Eurozone debt crisis materialised into a decade-long nine-year struggle as it took almost a decade for Europe 'simply to return to pre-crisis levels of per capita output' (Frieden and Walter 2017: 2). Further, dynamics of inequality showed themselves in this ostensibly united supranational body.

> One set of countries, the creditor states, have been exceptionally successful in shifting most of that burden onto the debtor states. It is not surprising that the Eurozone debt crisis has led to huge bailout programs combined with strong conditionality that have forced the crisis countries to implement harsh austerity measures (e.g., spending cuts and tax increases) and pushed those countries into deep recessions; this is a commonplace of debt crises. (Frieden and Walter 2017: 2)

In its gravity, the crisis is matched (if not, indeed, exceeded) only by Britain's 2016 referendum vote to leave the EU. The details of this have proved particularly difficult to determine. and the consequences of a British exit from the EU, should it indeed take place, are still to be felt across the political, economic and labour landscapes for many years to come. Some of the most consequential economic trends in the twenty-first century, however, took place outside the traditional centres of global economic activity. This was the rise of the BRICS countries' economies, which is discussed below.

New and Re-Emerging Actors in the Global Economy, 2000–2008

Brazil

The average annual growth rate of Brazil was marked by growth in the period 1995–2003, averaging at 2.2 per cent. Admittedly, this was lacklustre by international standards for this period, but substantial growth took place from 2004 to 2008, with the yearly GDP growth reaching 4.8 per cent. 'There was a slump in 2009 as a result of the world crisis', with its growth declining to -0.6 per cent (Amann and Baer 2012: 413). However, in 2010 growth jumped to 7.5 per cent. Compared to the growth experiences of many Asian countries this is not a spectacular achievement. However, the acceleration in growth has helped unemployment rates to decline. At the end of 2010, formal unemployment in Brazil hit a historic low of 5.7 per cent. Production also began on new offshore oilfields. Brazil has become renowned for its export prowess in such fields as soya, steel, cotton, oil, biofuels and regional aircraft. The growth was meaningful to the Brazilian people as 'the resurgence of the Brazilian economy has been associated with declines in income inequality and the incidence of extreme poverty. In other words, Brazil is touted as an example of the compatibility of growth and equity' (Weyland 2016: 165). Brazil has also pushed for greater regional cooperation in the form of institutions. The Common Market of the South (MERCOSUL) particularly stands out. By enhancing trade and investment within South American states in the 1990s, 'this integration scheme furthered Brazil's goal of using economic exchanges to gain political influence' (Weyland 2016: 165). 'Even after economic crises undid these concrete payoffs, Brazil kept promoting this trade pact as a major foreign policy initiative in South America' (Cason and Power 2009: 133).

Russia

Russia's post-USSR economic trajectory can be studied in three discernible phases. The first ran from 1989 to 1998, wherein there was a rapid and noticeable decline in the country's GDP per capita. Indeed by 1998, its GDP per capita was at 56 per cent of its 1989 levels (in annual terms, this meant that there had been a continuous 5.6 per cent reduction in GDP per capita for the past decade) whereas, comparatively, global

GDP per capita increased by 10 per cent in that entire ten-year period. The second phase was between 1998 and 2008. During this time, the country's GDP per capita increased dramatically. In 2007, it exceeded its 1989 level for the first time, with GDP per capita seven per cent above what it had been in 1989. Finally, since 2008, the Russian economy has undergone a slowdown since the Great Recession such that its GDP per capita has not seen much improvement. 'The collapse of world prices for oil and other commodities in 2008 exposed the downside of Russia's dependence on the production and export of oil, gas, and other natural resources' (Cooper 2009: 1). Thus, until recently Moscow presided over one of the world's fastest growing economies, and the living standards of the Russian people improved after undergoing the shocks of the austerity measures which were a result of the post-Soviet reforms.

This strong economic performance had been a major factor in the popular support that the Russian leadership enjoyed and was also arguably a factor in the boldness with which that leadership reasserted Russia's status as a world power, challenging the United States, Europe, the neighbouring former Soviet states in economic and national security areas (Cooper 2009: 1).

India

Since its moment of independence in 1947, India appeared set for one of two destinies: 'on one side lay greatness; on the other, collapse' (Cohen 2000). The probability of collapse is no longer a subject of serious analysis— 'India is emerging as a major Asian power, joining China and Japan' (Cohen 2000). Like China, India was growing during the crisis, never once registering a quarter of negative growth throughout the 2008–2009 period, its GDP reaching growth levels of more than six per cent throughout this period, making it, after only China, the second-fastest grower in the global economy (Joseph 2009: 3). In addition to its soft power status on account of its being the world's largest democracy, the country has at its disposal the world's second-largest army and also maintains 'a strategic position at the crossroads of the Persian Gulf, Central Asia, and Southeast Asia' (Cohen 2000). Its population is set to pass China's by 2024 (Chaubey 2017).

China

The rise of China, prognosticated Ikenberry (2008), 'will undoubtedly be one of the great dramas of the twenty-first century'. That this prediction could be made in 2008 is telling, for while much of the world was steeped in economic malaise and a recession in the following year, China's economy was rather buoyant, registering 9.6 per cent in 2008 and 9.2 per cent in 2009. The size of its economy would quadruple since the launch of market reforms in the late 1970s which were a major boost to the country's GDP from an annual average of six per cent between 1953 and 1978 to 9.4 per cent between 1978 and 2012, and from a US$50 billion economy to a US$6 trillion economy. The country also saw its domestic savings-to-GDP ratio grow from 48.84 per cent in 1980 to 53.47 per cent (*The Guardian* 2016). This process of market liberalisation led to the establishment of China as a major global exporter. It eventually allowed for the reopening of the Shanghai Stock Exchange in 1990 (for the first time in over 40 years) and, ultimately, to China's entering the World Trade Organisation (WTO). The country emerged as 'one of the world's major manufacturing centres' while simultaneously over one billion people in that country came to '[consume] roughly a third of the global supply of iron, steel, and coal' (Ikenberry 2008). Further, it accumulated massive foreign reserves, worth more than $1 trillion at the end of 2006, and US$3 billion by 2018 (Babones 2018). China's military spending has increased at an inflation-adjusted rate of over 18 per cent a year, and its diplomacy has extended its reach not only in Asia but also in Africa, Latin America and the Middle East. As early as 2008, when China was still the third-largest economy in the world, this led to numerous comparisons with the United States, always with one of two conclusions: for some, 'China is emerging as both a military and an economic rival – heralding a profound shift in the distribution of global power' (Ikenberry 2008), whereas for others, echoing Chinese President Hu Jintao's notion of peaceful development, the country was not eager to outgrow and initiate rivalry with the United States, or indeed any other signposts of the West (Sun 2017: 426). More recently, other scholars (for example, Wang, 2017) have seen China as representing a middle way between these two extremes, being seen as carrying out a 're-globalisation' of the world economic order through its economic activity, thereby dislodging the prevalent Western order without recourse to military action. How much China can do this on its own is questionable, however. And, as seen, it is not the only player eager for international reform.

South Africa

Having inherited an economy characterised by vast inequality from the disintegrating apartheid government, by 2005, a decade into the new South Africa, the democratic South African government presided over an impressive 87 straight months of growth (currently running at about five per cent a year), low budget deficits and low inflation. The Johannesburg Stock Exchange (JSE), riding the wave of the commodities boom, has been making record gains. Consumer demand has been buoyant, with the signs of conspicuous consumption all around, from the gaudy new gated housing estates to the increasing numbers of sleek European sports-cars on the roads. House prices rose by 21 per cent in 2005 (a welcome slow-down from 32 per cent in 2004), and new-car sales in January this year were 22 per cent up on a year earlier. For 2006 as a whole, the National Association of Automobile Manufacturers of South Africa expects them to be even higher than last year's 617,500 (*The Economist* 2006). 'Based on the international poverty line of US$1.90 per day, (2011 Purchasing Power Parity (PPP), exchange rates), 18.8% of South Africans were poor in 2015, following a decline from 33.8% in 1996' (World Bank, 2015). The country, however, was among those adversely affected by the Great Recession—declining by 6.10% in the first quarter of 2009 and saw eight years of mild recovery before entering another technical recession in 2018. Importantly, however, the economy has grown by very minimal figures and underperforming even its own intended growth rates of 6% or higher (RSA 2013). The country's central difficulty is its inequality—with a Gini coefficient of 0.63; and 50% of the income accruing to only 10% of the population (World Bank, 2015). The World Bank assesses that 'given population growth, gross domestic product (GDP) per capita growth has been close to nil since 2014, leaving little room to reduce poverty', and prescribed that 'strengthening investment, including foreign direct investment, will be critical to propel growth and create jobs'. At the same time, the country remains the most industrialised in the African continent, and retains numerous prospects on account of the nascent African Continental Free Trade Area (ACFTA), and the ascendance of a more global investor-friendly President as of 2018.

Together, BRICS represent 26 per cent of the planet's land mass and are home to some 46 per cent of the world's population. Regarding economic growth, BRICS are ahead of the projection made in 2001 (South Africa not included): 18 per cent of the world's GDP—above

Goldman Sachs's forecast of 14.2 per cent. According to the World Trade Organization (WTO) statistics, the participation of BRICS in global exports doubled between 2001 and 2011, from eighte per cent to 16 per cent. In those eleven years, their total exports grew by more than 500 per cent, while their total global exports grew by 195 per cent in the same period. Between 2002 and 2012, intra-BRICS trade increased by 922 per cent, from US$27 billion to US$276 billion. Between 2010 and 2012, BRICS international trade rose by 29 per cent, from US$4.7 trillion to US$6.1 trillion. Within BRICS, China and India have the biggest GDPs. The rise of these BRICS countries can also be noted in their successful bids to host major international sports events. China hosted the 2008 Olympics, whereas South Africa, Brazil and finally Russia hosted the FIFA World Cup in rapid succession in 2010, 2014 and 2018.

The History of the BRICS

The post-Second World War order produced a stratified world order in which there were dominant and peripheral players (Waterlow 1977: 17). From the rubble of the most destructive conflict in world history emerged two new major powers, the United States and the Soviet Union, whose rivalry with one another was to give the period its name—the Cold War—and whose desire to outplay one another was to set the future trajectories of many states.

The order coincided with the oncoming of independence for scores of countries in Africa and Asia. These newly independent states, coming as they did into an unequal order which was, moreover, unreceptive to their voices and interests, developed, over time, patterns of mutual identification, and attempted, with mixed successes, to act collectively. In these processes, they met in frequent intervals, developed plans and produced critiques of the world which in many ways still ring true in contemporary international relations. The BRICS can be seen as being the latest—as well as the most powerful—such incarnation. Two factors make the BRICS different: the grouping is composed of highly motivated states who are slighted by an international status quo not adjusting to their emergence. Secondly, the group also represents a growing alternative centre of power outside the West and is thus capable of real impact in transforming the global stage.

The Global South, from Bandung to NIEO

The idea of a 'Third World' came about in the setting of an intensifying Cold War. 'While the First World referred to the advanced capitalist countries, the Second World was the communist alternative, though China's position was ambiguous, not least after the breakdown of close relations with the Soviet Union in 1958' (Kiely 2015: 152). The term 'appears to have been used by some members of the French left to refer to a third force, independent of both capitalism and official communism' (Kiely 2015: 152). This notion of a third force, 'nonaligned between hostile capitalism and official Communism', gained adoption by a litany of anti-colonial and recently independent statesmen. Some of the leaders included Jawaharlal Nehru of India and Josip Broz Tito of Yugoslavia (independent of Soviet influence since at least 1961).

> The post-war context was in some respects a favourable one, with both superpowers supporting the end of empire and conditionally supporting independence and the extension of sovereignty to new nation states. The Atlantic Charter of 1942 and the United Nations' Universal Declaration of Human Rights of 1948 both laid down the normative basis for decolonization, and the defeat of the Nazi regime served to undermine, in official circles at least, some of the most extreme forms of racism, colonialism and empire. On the other hand, the liberal international order promoted by the United States was one in which power was still exercised through vetoes at the UN Security Council, and through weighted voting at (admittedly weak) international financial and development institutions like the IMF and World Bank. (Kiely 2015: 153)

In addition to this, international aid, from the United States as well as the USSR, was often tied to conditionalities as well. 'In this respect then, the Third World referred to non-alignment, but its usage was wider than this. It usually referred to countries that had been colonized and were relatively poor in the world economy' (Kiely 2015: 153). Therefore, from the onset, economics was never far removed from the proceedings of this grouping as the collective were pursuing development, often seen as a necessary basis if political sovereignty was to be maintained (Worsley 1967: 9). But norm entrepreneurship was also at the heart of the project. 'The "spirit of Bandung" marked the process of liberation of the colonial world and defined the path for the international insertion of those countries that formed the Non-Aligned Movement, with an explicit condemnation of racism, colonialism and imperialism' (Bissio 2015).

Against this background, the non-establishment was founded 'as an international principle' by a number of states, principally at the Bandung Conference held in Sukarno-led Indonesia in 1955 and then in Belgrade, Serbia in 1961. In addition to Indonesia, the conference was arranged by Burma, Ceylon, India and Pakistan. Delegates came from Afghanistan, Cambodia, the Peoples' Republic of China, Egypt, Ethiopia, the Gold Coast, Iran, Iraq, Japan, Jordan, Laos, Lebanon, Liberia, Libya, Nepal, the Philippines, Saudi Arabia, Sudan, Syria, Thailand, Turkey, the Democratic Republic of Vietnam, the State of Vietnam and Yemen. This made the conference the first major Afro-Asian summit. The core issues in the conference were cooperation, sovereignty, nationalism and the anti-colonial movement. Bandung was an important milestone which set up the countries for the formulation of the Non-Aligned Movement (NAM) in the Belgrade Conference six years later. Among the Belgrade Conference attendees were repeat participants from the earlier Bandung meeting. New participants, however, included newly independent African states; Ghana, Guinea, Mali as well as Morocco. Brazil and Ecuador were accorded observer statuses.

Importantly, the focus in Bandung was non-alignment, 'which was emphasised even more at the conference in Belgrade, which took place against the background of the construction of the Berlin Wall and thus rising geopolitical tensions between First and Second Worlds' (Kiely 2015: 152). In addition to this 'geopolitical vision', an economic variant of 'Third Wordlism' persisted:

> The Non-Aligned Movement did not ignore this more explicitly developmental approach, but it was through the United Nations Conference on Trade and Development (UNCTAD), that this economic approach was emphasised. UNCTAD was founded in 1964, alongside what remains the largest intergovernmental organisation of developing countries, the Group of 77 (which retains the name G77 but now has over 130 countries as members)'. (Kiely 2015: 153)

The G77 'is the largest intergovernmental organisation of developing countries in the United Nations, which provides the means for the countries of the South to articulate and promote their collective economic interests and enhance their joint negotiating capacity on all major international economic issues within the United Nations system, and promote South-South cooperation for development' (Kiely 2015: 153). The G77 took up the UNCTAD agenda, particularly in the 1970s when calls were made through the UN General Assembly for a New International Economic Order (NIEO). Championed in 1974, against the backdrop of successful oil diplomacy by the OPEC countries in 1973, the New International Economic Order was brought forward by the United Nations Conference on Trade and Development (UNCTAD) to institute fairer trade relations between developed and underdeveloped states through the reduction of trade restrictions such as tariffs and a higher commitment to developmental assistance by the developed nations. The NIEO largely failed, as some of its demands such as the right to nationalise multinational corporations operating in their territories, were deemed impractical. Nevertheless, economic historians acknowledge it as 'an important signpost in the push for international reform by actors who see themselves as disadvantaged in the north-south dichotomy' (Ndzendze 2017: 141).

Various factors characteristic of the challenges of the Global South limited the scope of the NIEO. 'While the rise of neoliberalism was undoubtedly a factor in the undermining of Southern solidarity, there is equally good reason for questioning the extent of such solidarity in the first place. Nonalignment was always compromised by the fact that in practice, most Third World states were aligned to either one of the superpowers, even if this often changed over time' (Kiely 2015: 153). Already in the 1960s, scholars could write of 'a paucity of interaction and cooperation in the Third World' (Miller, 1966: 16). Nationalisms and individualised outlooks, he wrote, were the fundamental weakness of the Third World. Voting within the UN for example saw little joint execution. African states only voted with each other 60 per cent of the time, while Afro-Asian identical voting happened one out of three times (Miller, 1966: 16–17). If the peripheral states were to forge a united front and then pursue their interests collectively, they could perhaps attain concessions and improve the trade relations. The actions of the OPEC in the 1970s proved that the oil-producing states, though mostly poor, could use their numbers and the West's demand for their oil as a tool (Duncan and Goddard 2003: 17).

> In the post-Cold War world, nonalignment became an even more problematic idea. Moreover, there was significant economic differentiation among

> the countries of the South, and this was particularly clear by the late 1970s and early 1980s. There were the rapidly growing first tier East Asian newly industrializing countries, the industrializing countries of Latin America which went into severe recession by 1982, some of the poorest countries in parts of sub-Saharan Africa and South and West Asia, and the oil exporters. (Kiely 2015: 153)

On account of this heterogeneity, scholars were of the view that the 'end of the third world' (as previously forecast by Harris in 1986) had arrived. Yet, the BRICS presents a potential rebuke to this view. In some ways, the group represents a reinvigoration (though, as will be seen, the sources of divergence and even confrontation have by no means been entirely put to rest). One more platform, the IBSA forum, played a crucial surrogate role in this regard.

From IBSA to BRICS

To be sure, the G77, UNCTAD and indeed even the Non-Aligned Movement are still extant in the post-Cold War setting, 'but to some degree these have been displaced by new alliances, and a new context' (Kiely 2015: 153). The India–Brazil–South Africa Dialogue Forum (IBSA) is one of these. Emerging from the ideological battleground that was the Cold War, the 1990s were characterised by new, centre-left governments in the United States and the UK, along with other countries in the developing world. While this took shape in the Clinton and Blair governments, it also held sway for the early years of the twenty-first century—the Republican candidate for president of the United States, George W. Bush campaigned on the basis of 'compassionate conservatism'. The democracies of Brazil and South Africa were also maturing at this point, with the latter recently emerging from apartheid rule.

It was in this climate that the IBSA forum emerged. Formalised in 2003, it placed emphasis on the countries' democratic credentials. It also touted the fact that it was composed of countries who were middle powers, regional leaders, as well as developing countries. Specifically, they intended to 'contribute to the construction of a new international architecture; bring their voice together on global issues; deepen their ties in various areas' as well as opening itself up to 'concrete projects of cooperation and partnership with less developed countries' (IBSA 2013).

As of 2019, IBSA has met seven times. The first three summits happened in consecutive years between 2006 and 2008. The grouping only met again in 2010 (in Brazil simultaneously with the BRICS summit). While the 2011 summit took place, the next summit, which was supposed to be held in 2013, was cancelled. The lack of steam behind the IBSA in some ways marks a shift in concentration from the trilateral IBSA to the multilateral BRICS—a transition that took place quietly, the latter swallowing the former. This is in large part due to the commonality of membership, and the effectiveness of BRICS summitry.

BRICS Summitry (so Far), 2009–2018

Composed of the developing states of Brazil, Russia, India, China and (belatedly added) South Africa, the BRICS association was formed in 2009 upon being benchmarked in 2001 by the Goldman Sachs economist Jim O'Neill to be set, caeteris paribus, to match the level of industrialisation and economic standing of the developed nations. It was therefore, at the very least, to bring about some level of multilateralism and a shift away from the historically globally dominant US and the EU countries and 'their' international financial institutions, primarily Bretton Woods, as well as ratings agencies such as Moody's, Fitch and Standard and Poor's. In the successive summits since 2009, the BRICS countries have discussed and enacted various mutual positions and common policies and have sought to build institutions indicating a shift away from the West-dominated order, including a development bank and a 'BRICS ratings agency'.

1st Summit (2009)

The inaugural summit took place in Yekaterinburg, Russia, on 16 June 2009 and included only Brazil, Russia, India and China. The four countries could boast some 15 per cent of the global GDP. More than this, they held about 40 per cent of gold and hard currency reserves. Further, between 2003 and 2007, these states represented some 60 to 65 per cent of all new growth in the global GDP. While China was the largest economy, Brazil also shone as a country which had seen its economy become more and more integrated into the global economy, especially with the other three BRIC states, as between 2003 and 2008, Brazil's trade with these countries had grown by some 380 per cent, from US$11 billion to US$51.7 billion.

2nd Summit (2010)

Taking place on 16 April 2010, this was hosted in Brasília, Brazil, and was noteworthy for the inclusion of South Africa into the BRICS at the behest of China. Another item on the agenda was the Iran nuclear deal, marking the BRICS countries' serious commitment to multilateral solutions to security matters. The summit statement also saw the declaration that 'We underline our support for a multipolar, equitable and democratic world order, based on international law, equality, mutual respect, cooperation, coordinated action and collective decision-making of all States'. Nevertheless, these emerging powers were not ready to fundamentally discount the role to be played by the pre-existing, perhaps Western-dominated, forums. Point 3 of the statement clearly expressed:

> We stress the central role played by the G-20 in combating the crisis through unprecedented levels of coordinated action. We welcome the fact that the G-20 was confirmed as the premier forum for international economic coordination and cooperation of all its member states. Compared to previous arrangements, the G-20 is broader, more inclusive, diverse, representative and effective.

Nevertheless, the countries declared that they would 'strive to achieve an ambitious conclusion to the ongoing and long overdue reforms of the Bretton Woods institutions', and thereby urged that

> 'the IMF and the World Bank urgently need to address their legitimacy deficits. Reforming these institutions' governance structures requires first and foremost a substantial shift in voting power in favor of emerging market economies and developing countries to bring their participation in decision making in line with their relative weight in the world economy. We call for the voting power reform of the World Bank to be fulfilled in the upcoming Spring Meetings, and expect the quota reform of the IMF to be concluded by the G-20 Summit in November this year. We do also agree on the need for an open and merit based selection method, irrespective of nationality, for the heading positions of the IMF and the World Bank.'

Apart from protesting the longstanding tradition of World Bank and IMF leadership being taken by the United States and Europe respectively, the BRIC countries also urged that the general personnel of these institutions needed 'to better reflect the diversity of their membership'.

3rd Summit (2011)

The third summit was hosted by China in 2011 under the theme 'Broad Vision, Shared Prosperity'. Among the core agenda items for the BRICS, who were all on the United Nations Security Council, were the NATO air strikes targeted at Libya. Internally, the countries were eager for procurement diversity with Brazil and India, especially, urging China to do more to purchase Indian pharmaceutical products and Brazilian aircraft. Similarly, South Africa voiced its own intentions to diversify its product base. China's fellow BRICS members also pressed the country on its currency practices, but nevertheless the yuan was not itemised for discussion. Rather, more emphasis for economic reform was made on a global scale, and particularly in terms of financial institutions.

All BRICS countries called for 'comprehensive reform of the UN, including its Security Council'. Beijing reassured its Indian, Brazilian and South African counterparts that China would back their UNSC aspirations. The meeting further saw the countries make it known that they intended to make payments to one another in their own currencies henceforth, as opposed to the US dollar.

4th Summit (2012)

The main item on the agenda for the fourth BRICS summit was the creation of a new development bank. Hosted in New Delhi, the summit concluded with the Delhi Declaration, containing the announcement of a 'BRICS-led South-South cooperation bank'. A set of feasibility studies were the prerogative of the finance ministries of the countries which were to present reports in the subsequent summit. The summit also echoed the sentiments expressed in the first, namely that the leaders of both the IMF and the World Bank ought to be selected from other countries outside European and the United States.

5th Summit (2013)

Hosted in Durban, South Africa, the fifth BRICS summit was still centred on the formation of the 'development bank'. More details trickled from the summit regarding this envisioned institution, as did some disagreements; the main points of divergence were centred on what the bank would do, and how it would be profitable enough to make a return on investment for its initial investors.

6th Summit (2014)
The sixth BRICS summit, hosted for the second time by Brazil in 2014, resulted in the announcement of the New Development Bank. Member states came to an agreement to all contribute to the funding of this new financial institution for an initial US$100 billion. The NDB was designed to incorporate all five of the member states, both functionally as well as symbolically. Thus while its official headquarters would be in Shanghai, its first president would be Indian, its first board chairmen would be Russian (board of governors) and Brazilian (board of directors), and its first regional office was to be opened in Johannesburg. In turn, the presidency of the bank is to rotate among the BRICS members for a period of five years each.

7th Summit (2015)
The seventh BRICS summit, held in Russia, saw the bank come into force, as well as the US$100 billion BRICS Contingent Reserve Agreement (CRA). The main goal of the latter was to serve as a form of insurance against global liquidity pressures. As a result, it was seen as an 'alternative IMF' (Desai and Vreeland 2014). The CRA is unevenly funded by the five member states, with China contributing 41 per cent, India, Brazil and Russia 18 per cent each, and South Africa five per cent.

8th Summit (2016)
In the eighth BRICS summit, once again held in India, the member states announced their intentions to create a ratings agency. The NDB was also called on to have a priority criteria for investing. In addition, the group statement denounced terrorism, as well as made a pronouncement on enhancing research centres, especially in agriculture and in rail.

9th Summit (2017)
In the ninth BRICS summit, held in Xiamen, China, the BRICS leaders convened under the theme of 'Stronger Partnership for a Brighter Future'. The leaders declared, inter alia, that:

> We emphasise the importance of an open and resilient financial system to sustainable growth and development, and agree to better leverage the benefits of capital flows and manage the risks stemming from excessive cross-border capital flows and fluctuation. (BRICS 2017)

Further, there was consensus on security issues. The BRICS countries welcomed the outcomes from the BRICS High Representatives for Security Issues which had met on 27 and 28 July in Beijing, 'and commend[ed] the meeting for having discussion and deepening our common understanding on global governance, counter-terrorism, security in the use of ICTs, energy security, major international and regional hotspots as well as national security and development' (BRICS 2017). They also welcomed Brazil's proposal for the establishment of a collective BRICS Intelligence Forum, while making it known that they 'deplore[d] the nuclear test conducted by the DPRK'.

10th Summit (2018)
Convened in South Africa, the tenth BRICS summit saw the leaders reaffirm

> commitment to fully implementing the 2030 Agenda for Sustainable Development and the Sustainable Development Goals (SDGs), to provide equitable, inclusive, open, all-round innovation-driven and sustainable development, in its three dimensions— economic, social and environmental—in a balanced and integrated manner, towards the ultimate goal of eradicating poverty by 2030 (BRICS 2018).

Climate change also featured on the agenda, with the leaders 'welcoming the progress towards finalising the Work Programme under the Paris Agreement and express[ing] their willingness to continue working constructively with other Parties' in the final preparations for the discussions at the UN Framework Convention on Climate Change (UNFCCC) in the then-upcoming 24th Conference of the Parties (UNFCCC COP24). The leaders also emphasised 'the importance of an open world economy, enabling all countries and peoples to share the benefits of globalisation, which should be inclusive and support sustainable development and prosperity of all countries' (BRICS 2018).

Literature Review

Gilpin (1981: 232) argues that American governance of the international system is in decline, but he notes that the United States 'continues to be the dominant and most prestigious state in the system'. This dominance and prestige have become especially pronounced in the post-Cold War era. Arguments have been made that the BRICS represent a potential threat to the US's unipolarity and Western hegemony.

Such an outcome, however, is not guaranteed. Ikenberry (2008) argues that 'the rise of China does not have to trigger a wrenching hegemonic transition. The US-Chinese power transition can be very different from those of the past because China faces an international order that is fundamentally different from those that past rising states confronted'. This, Ikenberry argues, is because 'China does not just face the United States; it faces a Western-centered system that is open, integrated, and rule-based, with wide and deep political foundations'. Against the backdrop of mutually assured destruction on account of nuclear weaponry by both players, 'today's Western order, in short, is hard to overturn and easy to join'.

Prashad (2013: 12) argues that

> '... the BRICs do not promise any kind of revolutionary transformation of the world order; they are modest in their ambitions. Nevertheless, they are the first formation in thirty years to challenge the settled orthodoxy of the Global North. What the BRICS have enabled is the opening up of some space, allowing a breath of air to oxygenate the stagnant world of neoliberal imperialism. The BRICS states have their own commitment to neoliberal policies, but they are no longer willing to bend before imperial power. It is in this gap between neoliberal policy and imperial power that an opportunity presents itself for the bloc of the South.'

Such questions are at the centre of the present debate and, indeed, serve as the impetus for the present book.

Theoretical Underpinnings

From assessing the literature, we can conceive of the BRICS phenomenon's interaction with theory on two main fronts. The first is in attempting to account for the rise of the BRICS; the other is in formulating an interpretation of the implications of the BRICS phenomenon. In this way, the relevance of dependency theory is called into question, with at least some revisions needed, on the one hand, and, on the other, for a broader reading of the BRICS beyond their impressive economic figures and to appreciate some of the transformations it is already bringing about. Wedded into this is the impact their actions are already yielding—not only in the global arena, but also their impact in the domestic politics of the West itself (from the probe into Russian interference in the 2016 US presidential election, to the debates over whether to adopt 5G technology as developed by Huawei in Britain, Germany, Australia and New Zealand, to the trade war between the United States and China).

Accounting for the Rise

The global South is underrepresented in international relations scholarship. Further, the main theoretical framework conceived in the global South 'reinforced this tendency of questioning developing countries' capacity for agency' (Weyland 2016: 144); such is dependency theory, which depicts the countries of the global South as 'objects of Northern pressures – dominated and constrained'.

> 'However, dependency theory was criticised heavily because this bleak picture did not conform to the developmental achievements of increasing numbers of Asian and Latin American countries. The success of East Asia's 'tigers' and the rise of regional great powers like Brazil and India, not to mention China, have been especially striking. Developing countries have done much better than expected by the theorists of dependency and even by 'dependent development'... Nations in the global South do have considerable agency; their states can engage in active 'dependency management' and advance in the global system, despite First-World predominance. Brazil, for instance, created a sophisticated computer industry and started to export airplanes to the United States'. (Weyland 2016: 144)

The dependency school of thought saw 'Third World' is being intentionally underdeveloped, and that in line with this it was best to enact autarky and pursue self-sufficiency. Leftist scholars who argued this included Raul Prebisch and Andre Gunder Frank. These analysts never took into account the importance of population size, which have been the strengths of the BRICS. But the experience of the BRICS—especially China and India—has been such that this orthodoxy is turned on its head. China and India, and Brazil under President Cardoso, have developed precisely on the basis of opening up their economies—applying the same principles on which the EU and the United States pontificated but never fully practised.

Dependency theory can be defined as a way of seeing the global trade system as unbalanced towards the global North and biased towards the global South. That is, 'it is a way of understanding historically embedded, political-economic relations of peripheral capitalist countries within the broader context of the global economy' and the kind of world these come to create in terms of commerce (Conway and Heynen 2014: 111). The principal proponents of this line of thought (Raul Prebisch, Paul Singer, Celso Furtado, Osvaldo Sunkel) argued that Latin America's (and the rest of the global South's) historical marginalisation and resultant underdevelopment were perpetuated by unequal commercial arrangements. Further, they noted what the basic premises of dependency theory now are; the heterogeneity of states in the international system (the international division of labour) as well as the class distinction within countries. For the sake of brevity, here we will only delve into the former, for it is more pertinent to the subject matter.

States, according to this theory, have different standings in the international system. There are four different types (or perhaps tiers) (Ghosh 2001). The first isthe centre core (CC) states such as the United States, the UK and France which dominate international trade through international institutions such as the World Bank and the International Monetary Fund. They are the wealthiest. At the periphery of the core (PC) are states such as the Netherlands, Japan and Canada, and below these are the states at the centre of the periphery (CP) such as South Africa, Brazil and India. Lastly there are states which are at the periphery of the periphery (PP), these are the poorest states and examples may include the Democratic Republic of Congo (DRC), Cambodia and El Salvador. The theory also claims that as a result of the structure of the system, the CC states have their interests served by the PP, CP and PC states; while the PC have their interests served by the PP and CP, and the CP states likewise exploit the PP states. Perhaps the clearest exemplar of this is the imbalance of trade within the North American Free Trade Agreement (NAFTA). For many, NAFTA has been a mechanism through which the United States and Canada attain access to cheap Mexican labour in their backyards. They have imposed few labour safety standards; resulting in massive injuries and the loss of limbs (Ghosh 2001). In its gruesome and graphical way, this speaks directly to the 'international division of labour' claimed by the dependency theorists.

The international division of labour can be seen in the way in which some states are essentially dependent on minerals while others are sufficiently diversified. This is attested to by the fact that most PP states such as the DRC are purely resource extractive and others such as Ghana are mainly agricultural, whereas France, the UK and their ilk have fledging automotive, manufacturing and financial markets. How this came to be so (or, rather, how this remains to be so) is largely based on the structures put in place by the CC countries. For example, the structural adjustment policies (SAPs) implemented by Sub-Saharan states have had the net effect of trapping the region in what has been an ongoing (and seemingly perpetual) cycle of stagnation and dependence. For some, the spread of the Ebola virus in West Africa in 2014 was as a result of the neoliberal orthodoxy imposed on Liberia which championed privatisation of health services. The outcome, in a situation where there was a lack of state capacity with regards to health and no will on the part of the private interests to invest in a 'clientele' which could not afford the treatment, was the transnational proliferation of what could have been a containable outbreak.

With the advent of neoliberalism in the 1980s, the dependency theory discourse, which painted trade as something of a zero-sum game, fell out of favour. But even the briefest analysis of the contemporary international trade system will reveal the extent to which the dependency theory literature still has a great deal to explicate, perhaps now more than ever. Still today, scholars write of there being obvious connections between the divergent trajectories of capitalism's expansion in the global North vis-à-vis the global South (Duncan and Goddard 2003; Conway and Heynen 2014). Also obvious and pertinent is the unequal competition that remains 'an extremely powerful, dependency relationship in globalisation's transformative, disciplinary, and destructive influences' (Conway and Heynen 2006). In fact, for some, exploitation of many global South countries by colonial and neocolonial core countries intensified following their achievement of political independence, further increasing the aggregate (Jha and Wilkinson 2012: 8).

There are several salient features to the modern, post-1980s neoliberal international order. The most obvious is perhaps the manner in which there is a perpetuating and reinforcement of imbalance. As Conway and Heynen (2014) put it, the international system seems as though it is bent on encouraging and stimulating growth for 'winners' (core and peripheral core countries), and not the 'losers' (poor, weak,or failed states). In other words, there is a continuously growing gap between the world's rich states and their poorer counterparts (Glennie and Hassanaien 2012). In many ways, then, dependency theory is still relevant. The evolving world system of core–periphery relationships has entered a new advanced phase of 'modernity' in which there are new dependency relationships, ecological uncertainty, rapid technological change and a multiplicity of cross-cutting flows of information, cultural messages and knowledge exchange (Ghosh 2001).

The BRICS countries, initially peripheral states, act as a kind of repost to dependency theory's claim that there are structures which perpetuate an order which favours the West/core. In essence, they point out that the historically peripheral states can shift their standing in the global economy. But that some countries seem to be breaking out of the dependency trap 'does not mean that a trap never existed' (Glennie and Hassanaien 2012: 2). In fact, the trap continues to exist in many ways. In ironic fashion, these emerging states may come to form a new core, or at least periphery core. South Africa has a 1:10 trading ration with the countries of the southern African subregion.

Implications

The other side of the theoretical engagement of the BRICS is also in terms of its implications of the BRICS' rise. In many ways, Jim O'Neill (2001), who came up with the grouping for the purposes of an investment index, never fully appreciated the political significance of the rise of the then BRIC countries. Paying attention only at the economic dimension (as 'emerging markets'), his analysis, either in the paper or in subsequent interviews (Tett 2010), did not take into account the political equation of the rise of the BRIC countries. However, this superficial reading of the formation underappreciated their collective capacity. Despite these divergences, especially in the India–China nexus (see Chapter 7of this volume), they are afflicted by the same issue: the collective slights they have endured at the behest of the West. In other words, they have a collective motivation to change the global order in some way. Indeed, we are seeing these countries seek to transform the global economy. Importantly, this is coinciding with an American and European retreat and protectionism. Indeed, American and European populism (on the left and the right) has been on the basis that low-skilled jobs in manufacturing and (to some extent) in telecommunications have gone to China and India, respectively, and that their governments have to do something to reverse this. In this way, then, we could be seeing a situation in which these BRICS countries are causing a shift not only in the global system but—even more so—in the domestic politics of the developed states. In previous years, the countries on the periphery complained (and indeed some still complain, with justification) of Western meddling in their internal systems; recently an FBI investigation was convened with the task of looking into Russian influence on the 2016 American presidential election; likewise the EU is of a mind that Russia funded media activity aimed at promoting a 'yes' vote during the Brexit referendum.

Of course, the BRICS countries are not the first underdeveloped countries to break out of that mould. But what lies at the root of their protestations against the present order is that theirs are different histories and outlooks. Whereas post-War Japan, West Germany, Taiwan, South Korea, Singapore and others have risen through their alignment with the West (in a Cold War context), these countries have risen in large part owing to their own internally engineered programmes of growth, with little to no clemency from the West. They owe very little to the West and, indeed, see themselves as having numerous legitimate causes for disgruntlement towards it.

This goes back to the work of Gilpin (1981) who argued that 'an international system is stable if no state believes it profitable to attempt to change the system', and subsequently argued that a state, or in this case a coalition of states, would only attempt to change the international system 'if the expected benefits exceed the expected costs'. The question at the centre of this work is therefore whether these states have begun exhibiting patterns of behaviour which render them assertive or, alternately, complementing the West.

Impetus for, and Outline of, the Book

A cursory look at the BRICS shows China's pre-eminence within the group as well as the broader global South. Equally noteworthy is the development of trade relationships between various parts of the South, with China playing as the principal import partner of all four of the BRICS countries. This would seem to imply, then, that any rearrangement of the present order would lead to ushering in a 'Chinese order'. But, as this volume makes evident throughout, China could never 'go at it alone'. As Nye (1990) observed after the end of the Cold War, the United States (and by extension any would-be superpower) needs to wield a great deal of legitimacy—both to grow and to sustain its position of leadership. In other words, the very idea of a new order relies on cooperation.

We can expect multilateralism because the other BRICS players are themselves not too far behind and are leaders—or set to be leaders—in their own regions and specific key sectors. If the question is whether the BRICS countries are assertive or whether they are complementary to the West, the answers must be varied as there are many perspectives and attendant methodologies through which both to ask this question and to answer it—as this volume has set out to do.

In Chapter 2, Bhaso Ndzendze ponders this from the perspective of the BRICS countries domestic polities and systems of governance. Asking whether the politically democratic countries among the BRICS (Brazil, India and South Africa) have their democratic system as a result of the West, the chapter concludes that the countries are democratic not because of the West but in spite of it. In this way, the configuration of their systems of governance is not only in contrast to much of what Western literature has to say on the subject, but has also come about as a result of autochthonous routes, owing very little to the West, which has rather posed obstacles than enabled their democratisation trajectories. Whereas in Brazil the United States had sponsored a coup in 1964, and subsequently had cordial relations with Brazil's military regime, in India the British created social stratifications which would pose the greatest strictures against democratisation; the caste system. The failure of the British to create trajectories to democratisation are further explicated in Pakistan and Bangladesh, which have experienced repeated military coups.

Five chapters, looking at each BRICS country, channel the book's central question to bilateral relations. In Chapter 3, Bruno De Conti, Célio Hiratuka and Arthur Welle look at Brazil's economic relations with Africa. The chapter discusses the monetary–financial dimension, and then the productive dimension, with a particular focus on Brazil. Secondarily, the chapter presents the economic relations between Brazil and Africa in the recent period, allowing us to analyse the role the BRICS have (or may have) on that continent. Clearly drawn from this chapter is the conclusion that the relationship between Brazil and Africa was influenced heavily by the discovery of offshore oil in Brazil, thereby rendering the country less reliant on Angola for its energy needs—thus any growth in the relations between the two will rely strongly on product diversification by both. De Conti et al. show that emergence of the BRICS is fundamental to the quest for a new international order, but it has to deal with the risk of creating (or reproducing) asymmetries within and outside the bloc; moreover, this is happening at a time when a new leadership has been elected in Brazil, rendering the next decade of the BRICS particularly noteworthy.

Leadership change and its impact on BRICS-facing foreign policy is also a major theme in Chapter 4, wherein Bongane Gasela assesses India's objectives in being a part of the BRICS formation. The country, the chapter argues, is playing a balancing act between the West and the apparent alternative, China, while it still bolsters its own economic standing. This has particularly become clear since Narendra Modi took office as Prime Minister in 2014. Meanwhile, the growing relevance of India to a post-Brexit Britain, with much of the previous asymmetries now reversed (India now outranking its former colonial metropole in terms of economic size), is key to understanding broader Indian foreign policy.

In Chapter 5 Garth Shelton pays attention to China. Given the size and continued rapid growth of China's economy, it is unquestionably the core of the BRICS grouping and is expected to shape the form and content of BRICS cooperation as it evolves. China's very significant financial reserves and industrial capacity underpin the potential success of the BRICS process; therefore China's continued interest in and commitment to BRICS, is crucial. To the extent that BRICS advances China's national interests, it will become more effective and relevant in the global system. The chapter makes the case that China has a number of compelling reasons for participation in BRICS and has specific national interests which can be advanced through BRICS.

In Chapter 6, Chris Landsberg and Oscar van Heerden question one of the earliest BRICS puzzles: South Africa's entry. The chapter illuminates the role of South Africa and Africa within BRICS. Among the questions the chapter responds to is the significance of South Africa's membership in the light of its contested leadership in Africa and its modest influence in comparison with the other BRICS countries. South Africa's relations with the rest of the African continent is also analysed. South Africa's own misconceptions are also examined in this chapter.

Picking up from the foundation laid in Chapter 4, in Chapter 7 Bhaso Ndzendze and David Monyae look at the longevity and coalition-building capacity of the BRICS in light of China's and India's strategic rivalry in border disputes, exacerbated by two apparently conflicting alliances with Pakistan and Bhutan. Crucial to this chapter are the dilemmas brought on by British-drawn borders on the Tibet, Kashmiri and Bhutanese frontiers. Realism wins out, the authors argue, as the two players are confined from going to war not only by their regional responsibilities and India's economic dependence on China, but also by their nuclear arsenals, and a pragmatism which seems to have won out in both Beijing and New Delhi, at least for the moment. The sustainability of the BRICS is further consolidated by the political and economic attachments between the other countries to China and India, as well as to one another; the BRICS transcends India and China, and any crack in its formation would be a result of disintegration not only between these two players, but also of their relations with Brazil, Russia and South Africa, and of these states among each other.

In Chapter 8, Westen Shilaho looks at the BRICS international standing through the prism of a continent that often acts as a crucible for judging any major actor on the international stage. This chapter broadly analyses the cooperation between BRICS countries and Africa without minimising the role that Africa's traditional trading partners from the West still play on the continent. It specifically zeroes in on the China–Africa partnership, using Kenya, the East African region and the Horn as the entry point. China, the most noticeable among BRICS countries in investments in Africa, naturally takes up much attention in this chapter.

In Chapter 9, Bob Wekesa looks at the central theme of the book from the perspective of media and mutual understandings (and misunderstandings). This chapter tangentially moves away from the bulk of previous analyses that have zeroed in on the Africa–BRICS relations from the perspective of the BRICS, directing their policies and deal-making towards the continent. Instead, the chapter is interested in looking at perceptions of the BRICS from the continent—an understudied area in the fledgeling field of BRICS scholarship and a potential contribution to Afro-based studies. The question that the chapter seeks to shed light on is whether Africans are optimistic, pessimistic or pragmatic in their perceptions of the BRICS and, by extension, what this says about BRICS soft power capital on the continent. These perceptions, potentially leading to an assessment of the image of the BRICS in Africa, are tracked by undertaking a textual media content analysis of two leading business news and analysis publications. With the common adage that media is the first draft of history and even the 'fast' draft, media content can help us to understand perceptions in lieu of a more extensive survey of African public opinion on the BRICS. By analysing media reporting, we can make provisional conclusions as to whether the BRICS are perceived in a manner that boosts their soft power (optimism) or in a manner that diminishes their soft power (pessimism).

An important aspect of the BRICS formation is interdependence not only in economic terms, but also (in relation to this) in transfers of information and knowledge creation. In Chapter 10 Maxim Khomyakov writes from the perspective of higher education and knowledge sharing. Importantly, looking at the BRICS from this aspect highlights that it need not be merely a political grouping the affairs of which are confined to summits by heads of state, but it has to also involve the citizens of the member states—a practical application of the bottom-up approach. This chapter focuses on the role of Russia within BRICS as well as Russia's import in Africa. Drawing on Russia, the chapter also demonstrates the role of the BRICS universities in concretising the BRICS group through sharing of knowledge. It is time the global South designed its developmental models, as opposed to recycling Western models which are inappropriate to developing countries.

In Chapters 11 and 12, Wynand Lambrechts, Saurabh Sinha and Tshilidzi Marwala look at the BRICS through the lens of technological development. Chapter 11, which serves as historical background for Chapter 12, details the global transformation of industry towards an innovative, sophisticated and autonomous technology-driven environment in the form of the fourth industrial revolution with special relevance to the BRICS and the global South. Chapter 12 focuses on the challenges and opportunities in Brazil, Russia, India, China and South Africa in integrating Industry 4.0 to transform and grow their local economies. In anticipation of the emergent Industry 4.0 and its significance, the chapter presents the changing social, political and economic fortunes of Africa that can boost economic growth through technology and industrialisation. On the theme of the book, these chapters are prescient; in developing towards Industry 4.0, the BRICS will for a number of years and even decades have to enact some form of bandwagoning and pragmatically transmit the experiences and technological and innovating edges of the western states. This is already taking place, as Germany is working closely with Brazil to underscore the importance of partnership among countries in several aspects of manufacturing. The BRICS also have comparative advantages; demography in particular is a significant reason for growth in China, India and the African countries. The chapter also presents a timely analysis of the technology-related rivalry between China, the United States and Canada.

In Chapter 13, David Monyae and Emmanuel Matambo's perspective is that of international finance. This chapter discusses the NDB as a pragmatic indication that BRICS has the capacity to underwrite its own development projects, specifically infrastructure, and to reduce reliance on the WB, IMF and other Western donors. The developing world, particularly Africa, has accused the Bretton Woods institutions of burdening them with debt that has stifled rather than contributed to the advancement of the global South. Although its bias is towards the BRICS and Africa, the chapter also maps out the Asian Infrastructure Investment Bank (AIIB), a Chinese initiative, which funds development projects in the Asia-Pacific. The chapter also reviews the ties between the BRICS and the global North and seeks to show that despite the quest to break from Western hegemony, the global South cannot operate in isolation as it still maintains links with the Western-dominated financial system, and has trade pacts and engagements with the West in the spirit of globalisation and free trade. How the BRICS bloc has to maintain these links with the West while at the same time advancing the cause of the global South is at the core of this chapter.

Overall, the following chapters portray an uneven picture, with varying degrees of complementing the West by the BRICS, but at the same time there are some discernible patterns of international order adjustment. This is perhaps to be expected; short of open conflict, changing global order takes time, and is bound even to be denied by some of the emerging powers themselves. But, perhaps naturally, there are areas and aspects of the BRICS which have been touched on only in passing. These are important areas of future research and will be detailed in the Conclusion to this volume.

Bibliography

Amann, E., & Baer, W. (2012). Brazil as an Emerging Economy: A New Economic Miracle? *Brazilian Journal of Political Economy, 32*(3), 412–423.

Associated Press. (2019, 1 March). Canada Says It will Allow the U.S. Extradition Case Against Huawei Executive Meng Wanzhou to Proceed. https://www.washingtonpost.com/world/the_americas/canada-says-it-will-allow-the-us-extradition-case-against-huawei-executive-meng-wanzhou-to-proceed/2019/03/01/3c776642-3c54-11e9-b10b-f05a22e75865_story.html?noredirect=on&utm_term=.98d1483f6093. Accessed 1 March 2019.

Babones, S. (2018, May 24). China Is Sitting On $3 Trillion In Currency Reserves, But Is That Enough? *Forbes*. https://www.forbes.com/sites/salvatorebabones/2018/05/24/china-is-sitting-on-3-trillion-in-currency-reserves-but-is-that-enough/#e95c7145fce8. Accessed 1 March 2019.

Bissio, B. (2015, May). From Bandung to BRICS: Two Styles One Objective. *América Latina en movimiento*. https://www.alainet.org/en/print/170350. Accessed 22 February 2019.

BRICS. (2009, January 16). Joint Statement of the BRIC Countries' Leaders. http://en.kremlin.ru/supplement/209. Accessed 19 January 2019.

BRICS. (2017, 4 September). BRICS Leaders Xiamen Declaration. https://www.brics2017.org/English/Documents/Summit/201709/t20170908_2021.html. Accessed 1 March 2019.

BRICS. (2018). BRICS Summit 2018: Johannesburg Declaration Adopted. https://www.jagranjosh.com/current-affairs/brics-summit-2018-held-1532510234-1. Accessed: 1 March 2019.

Cason, J., & Power, T. (2009). Presidentialization, Pluralization, and Rollback of Itamaraty. *International Political Science Review, 30*(2), 117–140.

Chaubey, S. (2017, 21 June). India Likely to Surpass China's Population by 2024. *Times of India*. https://www.indiatoday.in/india/story/india-china-population-984014-2017-06-21. Accessed 1 March 2019.

Cohen, S. P. (2000, 1 June). India Rising. *Brookings*. https://www.brookings.edu/articles/india-rising/. Accessed 1 March 2019.

Conway, D., & Heynen, N. (2006). *Globalization's Contradictions: Geographies of Discipline, Destruction and Transformation*. New York: Routledge.

Conway, D., & Heynen, N. (2014). Dependency Theories: From ECLA to Andre Gunder Frank and Beyond. In V. Desai & R. B. Potter (Eds.), *Companion to Development Studies (3rd Edition)* (pp. 111–115). London & New York: Routledge.

Cooper, W. H. (2009). *Russia's Economic Performance and Policies and Their Implications for the United States*. Washington, D.C.: Congressional Research Service.

Desai, R. M., & Vreeland, J. R. (2014, 17 July). What the New Bank of BRICS is all About. *Washington Post*. https://www.washingtonpost.com/news/monkey-cage/wp/2014/07/17/what-the-new-bank-of-brics-is-all-about/?utm_term=.9a6fde68e0bc. Last accessed 1 March 2019.

Dullien, S., Kotte, D. J., Márquez, Alejandro, & Priewe, J. (Eds.). (2010). *The Financial and Economic Crisis of 2008–2009 and Developing Countries*. New York and Geneva: United Nations Conference on Trade and Development.

Duncan, R., & Goddard, J. (2003). *Contemporary America*. New York: Palgrave Macmillan.

Frieden, J., & Walter, S. (2017). Understanding the Political Economy of the Eurozone Crisis. *Annual Review of Political Science, 20*(19), 1–19.

Ghosh, B. N. (2001). *Dependency Theory Revisited*. Burlington, UT: Ashgate.

Gilpin, R. (1981). *War and Change in World Politics*. New York: Cambridge University Press.

Glennie, J., & Hassanaien, N. (2012). Dependency Theory—Is It all Over Now? *The Guardian*, 1 March, http://www.theguardian.com/global-development/poverty-matters/2012/mar/01/do-not-dropdependency-theory. Last accessed on August 29 2018.

Ikenberry, J. (2008). The Rise of China and the Future of the West. *Foreign Affairs, 87*(1), 23–37.

India-Brazil-South Africa Dialogue Forum (IBSA). (2013). Available at http://www.ibsa-trilateral.org/. Accessed 12 July 2013.

Jha, S., & Wilkinson, S. (2012). Does Combat Experience Foster Organizational Skill? Evidence from Ethnic Cleansing During the Partition of South Asia. *American Political Science Review, 106*(4), 883–907.

Joseph, M. (2009, September 3–4). Global Financial Crisis: How was India Impacted?, prepared for the InWEnt-DIE Conference on Global Financial Governance – Challenges and Regional Responses, September 3-4, 2009 in Berlin, Germany. https://www.die-gdi.de/fileadmin/_migrated/content_uploads/Global_Financial_Crisis_and_Impact_on_India_Berlin030909.pdf. Accessed 22 January 2019.

Kiely, R. (2015). *The BRICs, US 'Decline' and Global Transformations*. London: Palgrave Macmillan.

Miller, J. D. B. (1966). *The Politics of the Third World*. London: Oxford University Press.

Ndzendze, B. (2017). *Beginner's Dictionary of Contemporary International Relations*. Pretoria: NLSA.

Nye, Joseph. (1990). *Bound to Lead: The Changing Nature of American Power*. New York: Basic Books.

O'Neill, J. (2001). *Building Better Global Economic BRICs*. Goldman Sachs. https://www.goldmansachs.com/insights/archive/archive-pdfs/build-betterbrics.pdf. Last accessed 6 December 2020.

Prashad, V. (2013). *The Poorer Nations*. London: Verso.

Prebisch, R. (1950). *The Economic Development of Latin America*. London: New Left Review.

Roux, A. (2014). *Everyone's Guide to the South African Economy* (11th ed.). Cape Town: Zebra Press.

RSA. (2013). *National Development Plan 2030*. National Planning Commission. https://www.gov.za/issues/national-development-plan-2030#:~:text=The%20NDP%20aims%20to%20eliminate,leadership%20and%20partnerships%20throughout%20society. Last accessed 6 December 2020.

Sun, J. (2017). Growing Diplomacy, Retreating Diplomats—How the Chinese Foreign Ministry has been Marginalized in Foreign Policymaking. *Journal of Contemporary China, 26(*105), 419–433.

Tett, G. (2010, January 15). The Story of the Brics. *Financial Times.* https://www.ft.com/content/112ca932-00ab-11df-ae8d-00144feabdc0. Last accessed 6 December 2020.

The Economist. (2006, 8–14 April). Chasing the Rainbow. *The Economist*, 54–57.

The Economist. (2009, February 19) The Collapse of Manufacturing. *The Economist.* https://www.economist.com/leaders/2009/02/19/the-collapse-of-manufacturing. Accessed 22 January 2019.

The Guardian. (2016). China GDP: How it Has Changed Since 1980. *The Guardian.* https://www.theguardian.com/news/datablog/2012/mar/23/china-gdp-since-1980#data. Accessed 22 January 2019.

Wang, D. (2017, 2 May). Re-Globalization: When China Meets the World Again. New Zealand Institute of International Affairs. http://www.nziia.org.nz/portals/285/images/Events/2017/Christchurch/2017-05-02percent20Wangpercent20Dong.pdf. Accessed 27 February 2019.

Waterlow, C. (1977). *Superpowers and Victims: Outlook for World Community.* Englewood Cliffs, N.J.: Prentice-Hall.

Weyland, K. (2016). Realism Under Hegemony: Theorizing the Rise of Brazil. *Journal of Politics in Latin America, 8*(2), 143–173.

World Bank. (2015). *The World Bank in South Africa.* The World Bank. https://www.worldbank.org/en/country/southafrica/overview. Last accessed 6 December 2020.

Worsley, P. (1967). *The Third World* (2nd ed.). London: Weidenfeld and Nicholson.

CHAPTER 2

Autochthonous Routes to Democracy: Assessing the Brics Polities

Bhaso Ndzendze

Introduction

In July 2018, during the BRICS Summit taking place in Johannesburg, three of the five heads of state and government who lead the countries which make up the association brought with them not just their delegations but also some anxieties. One (Michel Temer of Brazil) would be facing elections in just three months, and the other two (Narendra Modi of India and Cyril Ramaphosa of South Africa) in less than a year. Many among their constituents were surely watching. With the economies of the first two in conditions of stagnation, pressures to deliver tangible outcomes were palpable. On the other hand, their Chinese and Russian interlocutors felt no such anxieties, and had no re-election worries in sight. Vladimir Putin of Russia had recently been re-elected (as this had been universally expected, it seemed only an official confirmation), and Xi Jinping of China had in the eyes of many been declared a president for life

B. Ndzendze (✉)
University of Johannesburg, Johannesburg, South Africa
e-mail: bndzendze@uj.ac.za

D. Monyae and B. Ndzendze (eds.), *The BRICS Order*,
International Political Economy Series,
https://doi.org/10.1007/978-3-030-62765-2_2

(or as long as he desired) due to a constitutional revision earlier that year which removed the presidential limit of two five-year terms. Yet their lack of electoral anxieties may not by any means be equated as carte blanche or absence of pressure; much of the legitimacy they seemed to wield rested on their own embodying of the economic and security prospects of their constituents. This, then, is the crux of the BRICS often overlooked—they are not only international actors but are also five countries, of diverse histories, polities and systems of governance and with varied domestic pressures (but the fulcrum of which is economic growth).

Insofar as this volume's central focus is the extent to which the BRICS countries are assertive of their own identities or complementary to the West, a review of the countries' domestic political systems is appropriate. Western influence, or lack thereof, is to be gleaned most distinctly from a country's incorporation of or imperviousness to the Western origins of the political system it takes up.

Two axioms inform this chapter: firstly, the West has, at least ostensibly, sought to impart systems of governance complementary to its own in the world through various instruments (in a long history that begins with colonialism, proceeding to Bretton Woods institutions, and culminating in the International Criminal Court). Secondly, the BRICS countries have, at various points and to varying degrees, been the subject of attempted norm permeation at the behest of the West. Thus, it would be appropriate to assess the extent to which these countries are bulwarks against Western hegemony, not only in the international arena but also in their domestic political arrangement.

The chapter's findings have indicated that, to varying degrees, the BRICS countries have proven to be impervious to the influence of the West in their political systems. Those countries which are widely regarded as democratic—Brazil, India and South Africa—have obtained their democratic dispensations despite and not because of the West. In Brazil, the United States backed the 1964 coup and had very cordial relations with the military regime. Further, the democratisation of Brazil was the result of an internal compromise between the generals and the pro-democracy movement (such that remnants of the old regime are still present). The democracy of India was also the result of domestic actions taken by the early postcolonial government at the behest of prudent measures taken by the Prime Minister Jawaharlal Nehru—including balancing the right-wing and left-wing extremists in his own party, enacting federalism and subordinating the military (which had been very prominent under British rule). The British legacy in India was in many ways quite opposed to democracy, not only in the prominent role previously given to the military but also in the crystallisation and instrumentalisation of caste. Thus, any claims of India's being a democracy due to the British rule are readily dismissed by the fact of Pakistan and Bangladesh (themselves part of Britain's India) having experienced repeated military coups while the Republic of India has had none.

In South Africa, the West showed a lacklustre posture towards the democratisation movement, largely continued to ignore or act against United Nations resolutions against the regime, and continued to avert calls for sanctions against the regime up to the mid-1980s.

The non-democracies, though not studied in this chapter, would seem equally impervious to Western influence. Firstly, the democratisation experiment attempted in Russia at the behest of the West after the fall of the USSR was unsuccessful because it had no moorings within Russian society (Shleifer and Treisman 2005; Monyae 2017). Secondly, China, though predicted to democratise by the criteria of most modernisation theorists (Schumpeter 1942; Dahl 1971; Lipset 1994; Huntington 1991; Linz and Stepan 1996), has remained a centralised society run by the Communist Party of China with no democratisation prospects despite the growth of the middle class. Further, the niche which China has carved out for itself in the world means that essentially the regime has fortified itself against external pressures for democratisation.

Democracy: A Brief Conceptual Definition

In this chapter, we understand 'democracy' in its political terms rather than in economic, cultural or social manifestations. Democracy, termed by Dahl (1971) as 'polyarchy', is characterised by the presence of political procedures that facilitate (or at least 'provide opportunities' for) universal adult participation in the political process through competitive elections where there is a likelihood that those in power could be removed (Dahl 1971: 38). Further, these rights of participation must be enshrined in the legal and constitutional framework of the country in question. Thus, throughout this chapter we proceed with a minimalist conception of political (rather than 'cultural' or perhaps even 'economic') democracy.

The remainder of the chapter works towards problematising the seemingly natural West-democracy exclusivity through the prism of the BRICS; by highlighting the idiosyncratic nature of the countries' systems—arguing that the democracies among the BRICS (Brazil, India and South Africa) assume characteristics unique to themselves. The methodology for doing so is in line with the requirements of the research question: to what extent, if at all, did the West shape the domestic political systems of the BRICS as they are in the present? Describing the political systems of these three democracies and ascertaining Western influence in shaping them is fulfilled through a research protocol that makes use of a combination of quantitative and qualitative methods with case study (within-case) analysis and comparative (time-series and vertical) analyses, drawing from numerical indicators such as polls and surveys as well as qualitative indicators such as memoirs, congressional resolutions and reportage (first and second person accounts and statements).

BRICS Countries' Autochthonous Political Systems

The BRICS countries' rankings in the Freedom House index have remained fairly consistent for the better part of a decade. Their latest (2018) scores are listed in Table 2.1 below.

According to the ranking, three of the five countries qualify as free, and by implication their populations may be considered citizens of democracies. As will be seen in their individual case studies, about four decades previously (with the exception of India) they would not have made such a qualification. Their democratisation projects began in different points around the 1980s and, for South Africa, culminated in 1994. The time period coincides with the so-called third wave of global democratisation (Huntington 1991: 13). India's coincided with the second wave after the

Table 2.1 Freedom House scores of the BRICS countries, 2018

Country	*Freedom House score*
Brazil	2.0 (Free)
India	2.5 (Free)
South Africa	2.0 (Free)
Russia	6.5 (Not free)
China	6.5 (Not free)

Source Freedom House Report 2018 (https://freedomhouse.org/)

Second World War.[1] This has led to considerably distorted historiographies over-emphasising external role-players. For many scholars, it has been due to the role of the West, primarily the United States. To be sure, in an insightful model, Seva Gunitsky (2018: 117) links democratisation in the domestic spheres of many countries with occurrences in the international sphere. Firstly, the model proposes that 'domestic change during the twentieth century often cannot be explained by the specifics of local revolts from below or elite concessions from above'.

> Instead, contention was often embedded in a broader global process – a decades long confrontation between hegemonic rivals who embodied and promoted competing regime types. In this way, domestic party realignments and coalitional shifts often became reflections of broader geopolitical dynamics rather than of internal forces or party intrigues. Transformations of the international system, not just the internal attributes of states, have been major and often under-examined drivers of globe-spanning regime change.

This is true for a great many countries, and in many ways this argument is a follow-up to the work of John Dunn (2005: 13–14), who argued that

> the story of a word of casual origins, and with a long and often ignominious history behind it, which has come quite recently to dominate the world's political imagination ... [Democracy] began as an improvised remedy for a very local Greek difficulty two and a half thousand years ago, flourished briefly but scintillatingly, and then faded away almost everywhere for all but two thousand years. It ... came back to life as a real modern political option ... in the struggle for American independence and with the founding of the new American republic. It ... then returned, almost immediately ... if far more erratically, amid the struggles of France's Revolution. It ... [had a] slow but insistent rise over the next century and a half, and ... triumph[ed] in the years since 1945 ... Within the last three-quarters of

[1] 'The first wave of democratisation took off in the nineteenth century, starting with the United States and France. This soon spread to other countries such as the UK, Switzerland, Italy, Argentina, Ireland and Iceland. Democratic institutions and norms slowly took shape including extending the right to vote to the majority of the population' (Khoo 2014: 11), while 'The second wave started in the 1940s and lasted approximately 20 years. 'During this period, West Germany, Austria, Japan, Brazil, Turkey and Greece were democratised. The third tide of democratisation resumed in the 1970s and swept 30 countries, including Spain, Philippines, South Korea, Taiwan, Ecuador and Peru into its democratising wave' (Khoo 2014: 11).

> a century democracy has become the political core of the civilisation which the West offers to the rest of the world.

In this view, then, there is a natural lineage of democracy stemming from the West; as Dunn would have it, all present-day democracies are to attribute their having this system to the West. It is interesting to examine how much Brazil, India and South Africa, classified as democracies, can be said to be democracies due to Western influence. The following sections will put this assumption to the test by conducting in-depth case-study analyses with this very question under assessment.

Brazil

Having undergone numerous and tumultuous shifts in governments between 1889 and 1964, Brazil would be regarded as an 'unconsolidated democracy', but with the democratisation project beginning in the 1980s and culminating in the 2000s this was no longer the case:

> 'With the passage of time, Brazilian democracy has come to be viewed relatively favourably in regional perspective, having managed to avoid some of the more spectacular ills that have afflicted several neighbouring countries (e.g., financial default, party system collapse, populism, secessionism, and replacement of presidents by dubious constitutional means). The post-1985 regime is defined positively not only by what it is but also by what it is not.' (Power 2010: 218)

The country has similarly 'passed more conventional tests of democratic consolidation', including Samuel Huntington's (1991) 'two-turnover rule (two successfully handled alternations in partisan control of the government)', and Linz-Stepan threshold of 'whether relevant actors accept democracy as "the only game in town"' (1996).

> In sharp contrast to the 1980s, when analysts fretted over various potential veto players that might truncate or undermine democracy (e.g., the armed forces, right-wing landowners, organised business groups, the Globo television network), one of the most outstanding features of Brazilian democracy today is the absence of any major antisystem actor with political clout. (Power 2010: 219)

The road to such a state of affairs, which in contemporary terms, with the election of Jair Bolsonaro, appeared under threat once more (Spector 2018), was a long one. With the exception of the contemporary dispensation, Brazilian people have had a single previous democratic order. That previous era had lasted between 1946 and 1964 when it was upended in a military coup. However, the present system far outperforms its post-Second World War precursor. As Power (2010: 220) asserts, 'when contrasted with the vigour of the current regime, the democracy of the immediate post-war years appears rather limited'. A major difference, and a key one, is the reach of democracy. The democratic 1946–1964 regime could best be described as only a formal one, and 'would best be defined as an elites' democracy' (Bresser-Pereira 2000: 1–2). As will be seen, the present system is riddled with its own elite problem, but since 1985 the common people have played a larger role, thanks to the vibrant party plurality system. Interviews among senior citizens from Sao Paolo, Brasilia and Rio de Janeiro, along with contemporaneous literature, highlight that following twenty years of military rule, the people of Brazil have gone on to gain political freedom, with violations of their rights by the state having decreased considerably (Hagopian and Mainwaring 1987; Freedom House 2018). Previous blockades to full participation by the population have subsequently been removed: for example, 'in 1985, illiterates, making up over one-fourth of the country's adult population, were enfranchised' (Hagopian and Mainwaring 1987: 1). This was consolidated in 1987 when the Brazilian Congress wrote a new constitution replacing the previous one which had been brought into formulated by a declaration by the junta in 1967 (Hagopian and Mainwaring 1987: 1). In the subsequent era, despite the first two presidents (José Sarney and Fernando Collor) being 'oligarchic clients of the 1964–1985 military regime', those who formed their careers by taking stands against the military rule 'have governed Brazil uninterruptedly since 1992' (Power 2010: 221). This trend was only bucked in 2018, with the emergence of Jair Bolsanaro, nonetheless with a diverse legislature to enact checks and balances on his tenure in the executive.

This has paid off economically as well. It was economic crisis which helped bring the dictatorship down, but the democratic dispensation began 'with a roaring start': GDP growth was in the range of 7–8 per cent in the first year. 'However, the period also saw mounting inflation and currency devaluation, and the collapse of the Cruzado Plan in late 1986 inaugurated a long period of stagflation' (Lisboa and Latif

2013: 2). Worse was still to come, as in 1987 through 1992 average GDP growth was at -0.14 per cent and hyperinflation averaged at 1 300 per cent annually, nearly hitting 2500 per cent in 1993 (Bresser-Pereira 2000: 1-2). But, 'after the Plano Real ended hyperinflation and instituted a fiscal adjustment' Brazil registered an average annual rate ranging from some 3.2 per cent in 1994 and 2008, 'a far cry from the 1930–1980 period when growth averaged 7 per cent annually but still quite respectable' (Lisboa and Latif 2013: 2). Further, under President Lula da Silva (2003–2010) through the first term of Dilma Rousseff (2010–2015), the country was estimated to have lifted some 36 million people from extreme poverty and created 15 million jobs between 2003 and 2010 (Gonçalves and Machado 2015).

In light of the progress and indeed the shortcomings which the country has registered, it is worth assessing the historical role played by the West (if primarily the United States) in the domestic affairs of Brazil, up to and including its system of governance, and what results they have yielded.

Brazilian Democracy and the US

Western influence on Brazil goes back to its colonial era (from roughly the sixteenth century to 1822) as a Portuguese possession. But even in its postcolonial dispensation, the country, after its elite deposed Emperor Pedro II for abolishing slavery by decree in 1889, introduced a constitution in 1891 that sought to craft the newly established republic along the same lines as the United States. The Constitution of 1891 designated a federal arrangement that resembled that of the United States, but if American actions over its constitutional doctrines are what matters, then US involvement in Brazil—when it did come about—was, if anything, counter-democratic. The reasons for the backing by the American administration for the coup against João Goulart (who had been elected vice president and succeeded Jânio Quadros when the latter resigned) in 1964 remains a controversial subject, but the fact of the United States in the overthrow is documented—historians nowadays are likely to debate motives, but its occurrence is historical fact.

Bandeira (1978 [2001]: 13) understands the United States' role in the coup as stemming from the interest of the American business community as being in standing in the way of 'an autonomous, nationalist and industrialised Brazil'. Read this way, the divergence between the United

States and the Goulart's administration could be seen as being somewhat inevitable and was hastened 'by the increasing lack of complementarity between the two national economies, once Brazil began to industrialise in the mid-twentieth century' (Fico 2014: 31). Indeed, against the backdrop of the Cuban Revolution in 1959, according to Bandeira (1978 [2001]: 13), the Kennedy administration already showed signs of intent to get rid of Goulart as early as 1963. Fico, 'distinguishing between US destabilisation of the Goulart government and the conspiracy to topple him' finds that the American government had contemplated 'many options and engaged in different types of actions in 1961 and 1962, but only began to move to overthrow Goulart in 1963' (Fico 2014: 31). Publicly, Kennedy spoke of respecting Brazilian sovereignty, but privately, he discussed ways to destabilise Brazil (Pereira 2018: 11).

> On 30 July 1962, Kennedy spoke with some of his advisors about the situation in Brazil. The meeting was secretly recorded. The US Ambassador to Brazil Lincoln Gordon, was present. Gordon said: I think one of our important jobs is to strengthen the spine of the military. To make it clear, discreetly, that we are not necessarily hostile to any kind of military action whatsoever if it's clear that the reason for the military action is ...

The United States was at this period dominated by Cold War rationales that aimed at containing the spread of communism in Latin America; indeed, the coup followed earlier strikes against democracy—which the United States stood for—in other parts of the world. Clandestine activities were carried out against democratically elected leaders in far-flung parts of the world such as Iran (1953), Guatemala (1954) and the Democratic Republic of the Congo (1960), and many more were still to take place in the future. American foreign elites often conflated communists with nationalists, 'and increasingly endeavoured to transform Brazil into a bulwark against Cuban influence rather than a functioning democracy' (Bandeira (1978 [2001]: 1).

United States–Brazil relations were 'very close and cooperative from the Second World War until the mid-1970s', upon which there was some divergence (Gordon 2001: 1). Importantly, the United States continued sustained relations with the military regime despite its well-known human rights violations. A change came in the latter half of the military era (1975–1985), but this is owed only due to an alliance that was formed 'between extreme nationalists and romantic socialists, promoting the idea of Brazil as "leader of the Third World," presumably in some sort of crusade against a capitalist First World' that was presumably American led (Gordon 2001: 1). At this time, the country also began to entertain the possibility of developing atomic weaponry (Gordon 2001: 1).

Brazil's democratisation process was therefore wholly domestic in its engineering and consolidation—and in its flaws. Following a period of 21 years of military rule, the country acquired the status of a political democracy on 15 March 1985 (Power 2010: 218). The transition towards democracy in Brazil did not come out of a vacuum, however, and it therefore did not mean a total dismissal of those who had been part of the dictatorial government (Power 2010: 219). 'Key civilian figures in the authoritarian regime, after a certain point, did not resist the regime change but joined the opposition bandwagon in order to retain their positions and influence in the new government' (Hagopian and Mainwaring 1987: 3). In addition, unlike in Argentina (whose military government (1976–1983) fell apart following a tactical loss in the diversionary war against Britain over the Falklands Islands, or Islas Malvinas as known in Argentina), 'the Brazilian military government was able to manage the regime transition until the very end' (Hagopian and Mainwaring 1987: 3). They were also pragmatically let into the fold, as the would-be architects of the democratic system solicited their contributions in carving the new republic.

From these earlier years through the contemporary era, critics have claimed that the system was still too associated with the old guard (indeed, in 2009 *The Economist*, referring to the appointment of former president José Sarney as president of the senate of by the left-leaning President Lula, spoke of Brazil as a country where 'dinosaurs still roam'). Every cabinet has had ministerial-level positions filled by high-ranking officials of the dictatorship era or their associates. This level of continued power is even stronger in the provinces. The recent election of Jair Bolsonaro is therefore only the latest, if more impactful, node of the military's continued relevance; buttressed in many ways by the failings and corruptibility of the Workers' Party. Only time will tell what is to come in the Bolsonaro era. But his rise, and the nature in which it took place, points to an important fact; being entirely Brazilian in its creation, the democratic system in Brazil has flaws and perforations that are Brazilian in nature.

India

Fascination with and speculation about India's democracy began soon after the strike of midnight on 15 August in 1947, and has led to India's polity being among the closely watched in the world. For close to eight seven decades, India's democracy has stood as a major 'intellectual puzzle' (Kohli 1987; Lijphart 1989; Lalvani 2002). 'As a single territory commanded by a state, India has long posed something of a puzzle: even the British, who had possessed it as an empire, marvelled at its oddity. As an independent democratic state since 1947, India remains defiantly anomalous' (Khilnani 1997: 2).

In this regard, Indian history, 'as well as the contingencies of its unity', did not go a long way in preparing the country for the form of its polity it sought to create; a democratic and secular society. This, all the while being one of the two most populous countries in the world. 'Huge, impoverished, crowded with cultural and religious distinctions, with a hierarchical social order almost deliberately designed to resist the idea of political equality, India had little prospective reason to expect it could operate as a democracy' (Khilnani 1997: 3). Sunil Khilnani draws a parallel to the United States and France who, like India, had become democratic societies 'without really knowing how, why, or what it meant to be one'. Political historians of India are now always appreciative of this, hanging onto 'nationalist myths, enamoured of immemorial "village republics"' (Khilnani 1997: 3). 'Nor', and centrally to the thesis of this chapter,

> was democracy a gift of the departing British. Democracy was established after a profound historical rupture. The experience, at once humiliating and enabling, of colonialism, which made it impossible for Indians to regard their own past as a sufficient resource for facing the future and condemned them, in struggling against the subtle knots of the foreigner's Raj, to struggle also against themselves. But it also incited them to imagine new possibilities: of being a nation, of possessing their own state, and of doing so on their own terms in a world of other states. (Khilnani 1997: 4)

Another majorly debated issue is the degree to which the British invented systems of governance in India or made careful use of pre-existing social norms and hierarchies, including the caste system in particular. In this regard, punctilious research by Dirks in *Castes of Mind* (2001: 1), finds that 'Indian society was highly fragmented into communal groupings that served as centres for social identity', but at the same time:

> In trying to make sense of these groupings, the Portuguese first suggested caste identities. The British expanded on that idea to promote order in Indian society. Thanks to them, the discipline required for census counts helped establish a clear hierarchy of caste categories.

Although both during and after colonialism, Indian people of all classes, and with the political elite specifically, found the caste categories anathema to the categorisation, 'caste has now become a factor in India's competitive politics' (Pye 2002). Those who are classified in the upper caste are more prone to voice protest to India's 'affirmative action' policies which they may see as giving unfair advantage to lower castes. Therefore, Dirks' work demonstrates that one of the more explicit legacies of the British is not democracy as some have argued but rather the social stratification which they consolidated and promoted for instrumental reasons. Indeed the author positions the work as a response to 'Western experts who have associated caste with traditional India' (Dirks 2001; see Pye 2002).

Another aspect of Indian politics which has been argued to be as a result of the British tradition is its lack of coup attempts, and the fact that 'even [Indira] Gandhi's months of emergency rule, which many thought perilously close to a dictatorship, [were] ended by the electors' verdict in 1977' (Alikhan 2015). But any association of this with British rule is undermined by Pakistan, which has a history marked by repeated military dictatorships. By 2010, the country had lived more under military rule than civilian government (Mukherjee 2010). 'It might be noted in passing that Bangladesh, the former East Pakistan, has also had its full share of military coups since its own independence' (Mukherjee 2010: 67). This was due to Nehru's strong belief that independent India 'needed to rethink the role of the army', and his commitment to this belief through policy, which saw him undertake measures 'that would firmly subordinate it to the civilian authority' (Alikhan 2015). Indeed,

'One of the first things that happened after Independence [was] that Teen Murti House, traditionally the grand residence of the army chief, was assigned instead to the prime minister: A small matter by itself, perhaps, but a clear indicator of the way the wind was blowing.' (Alikhan 2015)

Indian Democracy

Though India obtained independence in 1947, the first election held under universal male suffrage took place in 1951, a watershed moment in the history of a country which had seen a kaleidoscope of watershed moments in its recent memory. Indian people's rights draw legitimacy from the constitution of 1950, that is the basis for India's politics:

> by allowing and encouraging (within limits) popular participation in the political system within a framework of rules, rights, structures and processes which must be broadly respected by both rulers and ruled. Here probably lies the strength of India's democracy, which has developed a different mode of legitimacy to consolidate itself in the context of challenges from within and outside its boundaries. (Chakrabarty 2008: 61)

Between 1947, the year of India's independence, and 1964, with the death of Jawaharlal Nehru, however, the Indian National Congress party would maintain its position as the preeminent 'political institution sustaining India's democracy' (Chakrabarty 2008). Prime Minister Nehru, sought to convey, and succeeded in conveying, the INC as 'the central fact of India', prevailed in protecting the independence-winning movement 'against tendencies undermining its democratic structure' (Chakrabarty 2008). In these early years, the party proved so strong and present in Indian people's lives, that it could be conceived as the only party capable of governing. It is for this reason that Morris-Jones (1974) could realistically describe the situation as 'one party dominance' or 'the Congress system'. The party could indeed preserve India's democracy, by some accounts despite itself, because it was 'a huge, hierarchically structured party, broadly rooted throughout the country side, [that] apparently provided the mechanism whereby a plurality of elites, sub elites and groups could both voice their claims and attempt to [realise] them' (Manor 1981).

> At the same time, the Congress could adequately mediate and settle these multiple and often conflicting claims. If necessary, it could count on the extreme faith in the constitutional and legal system and also the fact that the ruling party, which had fought for independence, was held in high esteem and therefore what was decided by the Congress Party and its leadership was accepted by the masses at large. (Chakrabarty 2008: 58)

This is not to assert that the party was incapable of taking up the various complains of other sections of the populace: '"the principle of consensus" helped the Congress system work so smoothly for the first two decades after independence' (Chakrabarty 2008: 58). Thus, under Nehru the party proved capable of both absorbing new demands, and taking measures to satiate them (Chakrabarty 2008: 58). This was a tricky balancing act, for 'despite the pronounced socialist tilt of both Nehru and Indira Gandhi, the fact that the party never identified itself with the left shows the extent to which the centrist ideology prevailed over other considerations. Similarly, the argument that the right-wing elements found in the party an effective instrument to champion their goals also reveals the careful handling of the party's centrist image' (Chakrabarty 2008: 61).

India's image of being 'a robust, non-Western democracy' stems not only from electoral practices, which have also been refined over decades and onto which India has innovated but just as well 'the tenacious persistence of that system' against the context of numerous other regions where democracy has made only 'cameo appearances' (Sen 2005: 13). In this regard, this includes 'the comprehensive acceptance by the armed forces (differently from the military in many other countries in Asia and Africa) as well as by the political parties (from the Communist left to the Hindu right, across the political spectrum) of the priority of civilian rule—no matter how inefficient and awkward (and how temptingly replaceable) democratic governance might have seemed' (Sen 2005: 3). Moreover,

> The decisive experiences in India also include the unequivocal rejection by the Indian electorate of a very prominent attempt, in the 1970s, to dilute democratic guarantees in India (on the alleged ground of the seriousness of the 'emergency' that India then faced) The officially sponsored proposal was massively rebuffed in the polls in 1977. (Sen 2005: 13)

In the end, 'even though Indian democracy remains imperfect and flawed in several different ways ... the ways and means of overcoming those faults can draw powerfully on the argumentational tradition' (Sen 2005: 13).

Another BRICS country, with similarly British colonial legacies and by many accounts deemed just as ill-prepared for autonomous democratic consolidation, has gone on to prove relatively resilient, if also flawed, in its democratic system of governance. This country is examined in the following section.

South Africa

South Africa, though since 1652 characterised by racial segregation and the political exclusion of the non-European populations, formally codified this policy in 1948, three years after the Second World War, and three years after it had been a principal signatory to the Charter of the United Nations. The route to apartheid's declaration was by the vote; already largely reserved to the whites, the elections were held on 26 May 1948 and resulted in the defeat of the incumbent United Party and its leader Jan Smuts. Only approximately 900,000 people voted and the United Party actually won over 49 per cent of the vote compared to the Reunited National Party's securing just under 38 per cent of the vote. However, in South Africa's 'Westminster' style constituency politics this resulted in the Reunited National Party taking 70 seats, five more than the United Party. Beginning in 1948 and for much of the next four decades, the South African government's legislative programme was aimed primarily at racial separation, with the introduction of an avalanche of legislation designed to codify white hegemony and consolidate already self-evident white control—not only of the levers of political power but also of the economy. South Africa's institutions, 'based on legally entrenched and violently enforced segregation and white privilege, looked formidably strong at the time, and its leaders were determined to perpetuate apartheid. South Africa's coffers were brimming with mineral revenues, boosting their confidence' (French 2019: 1). Moreover, 'there was little pressure for change from Western governments' against the apartheid regime (French 2019: 1).

The Winning of South African Democracy

For much of the US–USSR clash that defined the latter half of the twentieth century, events in South Africa were not much of a central concern in Washington's foreign policy. Indeed, Pretoria 'remained largely at the periphery of US strategic calculations' (Thomson 2008: 372). Nonetheless, in comparison to the rest of the region, however, South Africa was the subject of far greater focus. Thomson (2008: 372) surmises that this is due to the fact that 'the issue of apartheid demanded an ongoing response from US decision makers', and beginning with Eisenhower, successive administrations gradually reacted owing to 'the occurrences of the 1960

Sharpeville shootings, the 1976 Soweto revolt, and the township uprisings of the mid-1980s' (Massie 1997; Thomson 2008).

Between 1984 and 1986, owing to media reporting straight from the ground in South Africa, apartheid became a more pronounced issue for the United States. 'The result was a package of federal sanctions imposed on the Republic underwritten by the Comprehensive Anti-Apartheid Act (CAAA) of 1986' (Thomson 2012: 371-372). The Act essentially placed sanctions on the apartheid regime, intended to remain in place until such a time as racialised rule was struck down. But this was followed by yet another period of silence on South Africa; after the coming into being of the Act in 1986, 'South Africa was almost immediately dropped from the US political agenda' (Thomson 2012: 372). As Lonie (1992) puts it, it was as if the United States felt 'satisfied that it had "done something" about apartheid' and that it could now 'move on to other concerns'.

More than this, however, there were several ways in which the Reagan administration, having vetoed the bill in 1986 (later to be overridden by Congress), went against its provisions. Particularly questionable were its interpretations of the 1986 Act; these were to do with uranium procurement and the acquisition of credit. 'Although the CAAA unambiguously proscribed the importing of South African "uranium and uranium ore" into the United States, the Treasury Department was to classify the compound of uranium hexafluoride, a fuel used in nuclear reactors, as *exempt* from this embargo' (Thomson 2012: 372 [italics added]). Additionally, although this Act banned American financial institutions from issuing new loans to South Africa, Reagan continued to allow short-term credits (Mills 1988). Moreover, the United States continued to use its veto power in the United Nations Security Council (UNSC) to stand in the way of such multilateral stances intended against apartheid South Africa for the remainder of the Reagan administration. Tellingly, the United States was not alone in slow-walking heavy-handedness against the apartheid regime. By comparison to, for example, the UK, the United States was doing better: 'the African National Congress (ANC) ... privately acknowledged this shift in approach, comparing it favourably against the UK's unchanged position under Margaret Thatcher' (Thomson 2012: 375; see also Munthali 1992).

Though imperfect, the bill allowed for a platform for Reagan's successors, 'to play a minor, but significant role in supporting the negotiations process which began after Nelson Mandela was released from prison in 1990' (Thomson 2012: 375). In particular, 'it was to be George [H.W.]

Bush's White House meetings with Nelson Mandela and [South African president] F.W. de Klerk ... that proved most significant' (Thomson 2012: 375). Showing backing for the talks between the two leaders and the two sides they represented and overall goal they sought after, the (still unofficial) president of the ANC received an invitation to the White House in June of 1990. Three months later, De Klerk followed suit. Mandela would spend nearly two weeks in the United States, primarily fundraising for his party, and recruiting prospective post-apartheid investors. Yet both men, in their White House appointments, wanted guarantees on the same matter: sanctions (Thomson 2012). For his part, De Klerk assured his US counterpart that the talks had reached an 'irreversible' stage (De Klerk 1991). Bush agreed, but the sanctions were not to be lifted in 1990. A number of crucial issues still needed attention: De Klerk was yet to release all the political prisoners, the State of Emergency still held, as did the Group Areas and Population Registration Acts.

This mooting of the end of the sanctions debate made neither the Bush nor Clinton administrations lose interest in the issue, however. For example, in its reappraisal of US policy towards Pretoria in December of 1992, the US State Department asserted that 'South Africa continues to require special attention. The end of apartheid and the creation of a new, multiracial South African society will continue to be a high US priority and therefore warrant a special activist policy' (Thomson 2012: 380). The Bush administration had also made the proposal, for instance, 'that the high regard of the US held by all elements in that country will be a great asset'. Clinton administration held the same view, seeing the United States playing the role of a key facilitator. 'Yet, the assessment of this impact should remain proportionate. The only other accounts addressing US policy at this time, the memoirs of US diplomats, have, however tentatively, overstated Washington DC's role' (Thomson 2012: 380).

In reality, South Africans (both the government and the anti-apartheid parties) were not very eager on the prospect of direct involvement by the United States in their talks.

> Washington's advances in this respect were rebuffed. Herman Cohen (US assistant secretary of state for African affairs from 1989 to 1993) later recounted how, at a White House diplomatic reception, President Bush

> and Secretary of State Baker had been engaged in "cornering and button-holing" their South African guests, saying "you've got to have a mediator, we really want to help." (Cohen 1992: 24)

The American president followed soon with a telephone call to Mandela. These instances got only 'polite rejection' (Thomson 2012: 380). These sentiments were shared by the government; De Klerk also turned down the administration's offer—just as politely but just as effectively. As he wrote to President Bush: 'it cannot be expected that South Africans should surrender responsibility for determining their own future' (Thomson 2012: 380). He was to later recall that 'one of the strengths of the South Africa's transition to non-racial constitutional democracy is precisely the fact that ours was a "home-grown" solution. We did not seek—or require—international mediation of any kind' (De Klerk 2012).

To be sure, numerous US experts made their way to South Africa for purposes of offering advice (Lyman 2002: 92–95), and after the shocking assassination of South African Communist Party (and key ANC ally) Secretary General Chris Hani, the United States trained the security detail of Mandela and other ANC leaders (*The Star* 26 August 1993). But assistance from the outside was confined to this and not much else. 'In terms of the available advice, "supply outran demand"... Some of this "surplus" help, however, can also be accounted for by negotiators resisting too much outside influence' (Thomson 2012).

The aim was an indigenous, South African constitution. This was accomplished. One example may suffice here—that of the role of traditional authorities. The institution of traditional authority and the great import it has had on the South African experience has been the subject of intense study. From this scrutiny, traditional leaders have emerged as 'decentralised despots' (Mamdani 1996) and as the compromisers of democracy (Ntsebeza 2011), while at the same time as not wholly irrelevant or anathema to the process of democratic consolidation in post-1994 South Africa (Williams 2004). Moreover, that they have been seen as indispensable role players in rural development by the South African government makes it clear that the institution of traditional authority, to the surprise and chagrin of many analysts, has in some ways gained more power in the wake of the democratic transformation, despite their historical role. They have emerged, in some sense, stronger. What is clear is that in the successive eras of colonialism and latter-day apartheid, London (through Cape Town), and then Pretoria, were the dominant partners (Davenport 1977: 277) in the exchange since they wrenched away a great deal of the autonomy which the traditional rulers had once had (Hendricks and Ntsebeza 1999: 100). Leading up to 1994, their days of legislative power had seemed to be numbered (Ndzendze 2018: 26)— for example, most rural residents of South Africa anticipated that land allocation, 'in keeping with the democratic principles proclaimed in the constitution' (Ntsebeza 1999: 15), would fall into the hands of the then-incoming, newly elected councillors.

Nevertheless, rural South Africans, in line with the substantive-redistributive perception that they hold about democracy, have come to embrace the traditional leadership institution because of its linkage with the delivery of development. Traditional communities 'seldom believe that they must make an either/or choice concerning democracy and the chieftaincy, but instead search for ways to combine the two' (Williams 2004: 115). A 1996 survey found out that 61 per cent of rural citizens (or perhaps subjects) believed that the chieftaincy 'had a role to play in the new South Africa' while only 41 per cent believed that there was a 'conflict' between the chieftaincy and democracy (Africa and Mattes 1996: 16). As a result, the chieftaincy continues to exercise direct authority over about 40 per cent of the population of South Africa (see Williams 2004). The central government officially recognises over 1600 chiefs and headmen (RSA 2003: 39). The chieftaincy does not appear to threaten the durability of the democratic regime; in some instances even fostering democracy by, for example, facilitating elections; as seen in a rural KwaZulu-Natal village with intense African National Congress (ANC) and Inkatha Freedom Party (IFP) rivalries (which could turn violent—historically, they have done) where one chief worked tirelessly to ensure that the 2000 elections were undertaken in a manner that was free, fair and smooth. This is a South African phenomenon with no signs of design or provenance from the halls of either the White House or Capitol Hill.

Certainly, the United States, as early as 1992, held the view that the future of the post-apartheid state should have a federal constitution. US-sponsored seminars were made available to the negotiators on the topic of federalism, providing opportunities for delegates to work through ideas away from formal negotiating forums (Lyman 2002: 93–94; Cohen 2008). In his memoirs, Ambassador Lyman speaks of 'enriching the dialogue' and 'lending weight' to these negotiations on federalism. 'It would, however, be easy to overstate the US influence in this instance' (Thomson 2012: 382). Ultimately, the (semi-federal) nature of the final South African constitution was a result of the compromises reached among the negotiators themselves and, as we have seen, has been evolving through idiosyncratic and South Africa-specific realities. De Klerk's (2012) recollection on this issue points to such a conclusion: 'if the US helped to persuade the ANC to accept the degree of federalism that we finally achieved, it would have been a positive contribution. However, I would not over-emphasise the US role in this regard'.

This re-evaluation truthfully portrays the influence of Washington in the gaining of South African democracy; along with its role in propping up the apartheid regime in the late Cold War. Washington did take measures meant to show its stance against apartheid, but there is little to no evidence of its having played a greater role than any other state in the world. Indeed, the United States was one of many other actors. 'In short, the primacy of South Africa's internal political dynamics should be acknowledged when seeking to explain this country's transition from apartheid, even if foreign actors were closely in attendance' (Thomson 2012: 384).

Further, it would overlook the role played by other actors, particularly those in Africa. More than to any single country in the West, the fall of apartheid is to be attributed to the frontline states as well as others in the rest of the continent for giving crucial support to the liberation movements operating in exile. Many of them were put under enormous strain by the United States itself for doing so. After going into exile in 1961, ANC Deputy President Oliver Tambo established anti-apartheid missions all over the continent, basing the movement in Tanzania. Northern Rhodesia (present-day Zambia) was a critical transit point for South Africans on their way there to be trained as Umkhonto we Sizwe (MK) militants. The route, traversed through the 'Freedom Ferry', moved from Botswana across the Zambezi River. After the ANC was banned in South Africa, from 1969, Zambia became its headquarters. 'It was from Lusaka that the ANC operated and coordinated the activities of MK in various parts of Southern Africa. Recruits who left South Africa via Lesotho or Mozambique ended up in Lusaka before they were sent for military training' (SAHA 2011).

Since the advent of the democratic dispensation after the dismantling of apartheid in 1994, South Africa positioned itself as a representative of the global South, while also pursuing economic growth through relations with the West. To the latter end, Pretoria 'chose foreign policy that met the stringent criteria of Brenton Woods institutions', with such measures as liberalising its markets, privatising certain sectors in the economy as well as corporate-friendly taxation levels (Saule 2014). At the onset, '[the] relationship with the United States was ... negatively impacted by the hangover of Cold War politics and the US's relationship with the apartheid government', and indeed 'the new government also considered Russia and other American enemies like Cuba, Iran and Libya allies' (Saule 2014: iii). Indeed, the South African government is argued to have 'never fully trusted the US's intentions and was wary of agreeing too often with the country for fear of being called a puppet of the US' (Saule 2014: iii). Over time, however, owing to the personal rapport between presidents Nelson Mandela and Bill Clinton 'the two countries managed to find common ground and continue to trade with each other successfully' (Saule 2014: iii). Importantly, trade relations were always ahead of the political relations, which always tended to vacillate:

> Under the presidencies of both Mandela (1994-1999) and Thabo Mbeki (1999-2008) there was strong American enthusiasm for South Africa's democratic breakthrough, but a number of policy differences surfaced between Pretoria and Washington to create tensions in the relationship. Under Mandela these included disputes over trade and aid, the future of peace operations in Africa, and South Africa's close relationship with states the U.S. sought to isolate as 'rogues': Iran, Libya and Cuba. Under Mbeki the issues included differences over Zimbabwe, HIV/AIDS and the direction of then-US President George W. Bush's post-9/11 foreign policy, culminating in the 2003 US invasion of Iraq, which South Africa strongly opposed. (Hamill 2013: 1)

A symbolic though telling testament to the suspicion and contempt with which the United States regarded the struggle for democracy in South Africa, is the fact that Mandela would be on the US international terrorist list as recently as 2008 (French 2019).

Towards a Non-Western Democratic Framework: A Growing Literature

With democracy in political terms having been defined, and the autochthonous nature of the democratic dispensations of Brazil, India and South Africa subsequently discussed, it is important to now explore the nexus between the two and the argument that democracy is nominally a Western phenomenon (as seen in Dunn [2005: 13]). In this way, then, the chapter is a contribution to a growing body of work which seeks to delink the ostensibly natural link between democracy and the West.

In the view of many scholars (for example Dunn 2005; Huntington 1991), 'democracy has a clear trajectory that can be traced from ancient experiments with participatory government in Greece and to a lesser extent in Rome, through the development of the British parliament, the American Declaration of Independence and the French Revolution, and then finally onto the triumphant march of the liberal model of democracy across the globe over the last 200 years, particularly under Western tutelage' (Isakhan 2016: 57). Among the leading scholars in the new train of argument are Isakhan and Miller. Miller (2018: 138), notes that 'the history of the relationship between liberalism and Western history is just that—history. It is not a deterministic blueprint for the future of liberalism, nor its prospects outside of the West'. Indeed, non-Western democracy is an empirical and conceptual reality 'and it is demonstrably possible to have a democracy in a place that did not experience Western history or produce Enlightenment philosophers', as there have been 'authentically indigenous pathways to open societies and accountable governance that have arisen in the non-Western world' (Miller 2018: 138).

Isakhan's argument rests on several counterarguments, but one of the stronger is a focus on 'the etymology of the word itself' which is also as a result of 'the deeply Eurocentric roots of the study of democracy's past embedded in the canon of Western political thought' (Isakhan 2016: 59).

> By focusing on the use of the word 'democracy' we therefore miss the fact that many of the people who have practiced or lived under or fought for democracy have not used the Greek-derived word 'democracy' to describe their government. It is little wonder that ancient Assyrians or Israelites, medieval Muslims or Scandinavians, or pre-colonial Africans or Maoris did not use a Greek word to describe their best governmental arrangements. This does not mean that these people did not practise democracy, only that they did not use the word. (Isakhan 2015: 8–12)

This has several implications: continuing to insist on understanding the origins of this system through this word association 'means that because this word has not been used in other linguistic traditions to describe their models of inclusive governance, the practice of democracy can be dismissed as being foreign to their respective history and culture' (Isakhan 2016: 59). The opposite is just as likely:

> '... if we were to insist on only including those who use the word 'democracy' to describe their governmental arrangements before they can be included in the history of democracy, then we are forced to include some very un-democratic regimes. As an example, Saddam Hussein frequently referred to himself as the 'shepherd of democracy' and claimed to be creating a democracy compatible with Arab and Iraqi culture.' (Isakhan 2012: 105–109)

At a time when democracy is undergoing major threats, including in the West itself (Freedom House 2019; Monyae 2019), the fact that there is democracy also in other soils freely from Western inculcation of it also means that democracy can find sustenance and preservation from others across the world, and not necessarily in the West. '[E]ven if American power recedes or Eastern European democracy backslides, there are other centres of liberal power in the world' (Miller 2018: 138-139).

Conclusion

In an attempt to review the extent to which the emerging powers are compliant of the West or asserting their own forms of global governance, this chapter assesses the role played by the West in the political systems of the BRICS (Brazil, Russia, India, China and South Africa). It argues that, to varying degrees, the BRICS countries have proven impervious to the influence of the West in their political systems. Those countries which are democratic—Brazil, India, and South Africa—have obtained their democratic dispensations in spite of and not because of the West. Further, that the democratisation experiment at the behest of the West attempted in Russia after the fall of the USSR proved unsuccessful because it had no moorings with Russian society and that China (though predictable to democratise by modernisation theorists) has remained a centralised society run by the Communist Party of China with no democratisation prospects, is some indicator of the BRICS' autochthonous domestic systems of governance. The niche which China has carved out for itself in the world means that essentially the regime has fortified itself against external pressures for democratisation. Thus, not only do the BRICS countries owe very little to the West in terms of their systems of governance, they have also proved to operate outside the ideas of progress posited by Western scholars.

This has many implications, including crystallisation of the literature pointing to the lack of an inherent genealogy of democracy within the West, as the democratic countries in the BRICS largely democratised without much influence from the West. Indeed, as seen, these countries democratised in spite of the hurdles placed in front of them by the West; from colonialism and caste-moulding in India, to support and acquiescence to undemocratic dispensations in Brazil and South Africa. A more domestically focused analysis of each of the BRICS systems of governance may yield findings in terms not only of the motives and pressures their leaders have to deliver continued economic growth, but also possibly of their capacity for norm and ideational entrepreneurship (Öniş and Gençer 2018) and what form of new global order they may yet introduce in the world, should the opportunity arise.

Bibilography

Africa, C., & Mattes, R. (1996). 'Building a democratic culture in KwaZulu Natal: The present terrain. *IDASA: Public Opinion Service, 9*(1), 1–23.

Alikhan, A. (2015, 3 June). Why India has Never Seen a Military Dictatorship. *Quartz India*. https://qz.com/india/418468/whyindiahasneverseena militarydictatorship/. Accessed 2 February 2019.

Arat, Z. F. (1989). Democracy and Economic Development: Modernization Theory Revisited. *Comparative Politics, 21*(1), 21–36.

Bandeira, L. A. M. (1978 [2001]). *O Governo João Goulart: as lutas sociais no Brasil 1961–1964*. Brasilia: Editora Revan/Editora UnB.

Béja, J.-P., & Goldman, M. (2009). The Impact of the June 4th Massacre on the Pro-Democracy Movement. *China Perspectives, 2*(78), 18–28.

Bell, D. A. (2015, May 29). Chinese Democracy isn't Inevitable. *The Atlantic*, 1–10.

Borstelmann, T. (1993). *Apartheid's Reluctant Uncle: The United States and Southern Africa in the Early Cold War*. New York, NY: Oxford University Press.

Bresser-Pereira, L. C. (2000, August 1–5). *After the Elites, Civil Society's Democracy in Brazil*. Paper presented to the panel 'The Evolution of Democracy in Latin America' at the IPSA-International Political Association Congress, Quebec.

Bristow, M. (2011, March 10). Chinese Leader Rules Out Democracy. *BBC*. https://www.bbc.com/news/world-asia-pacific-12697997. Accessed 26 February 2019.

Chakrabarty, B. (2008). *Indian Politics and Society Since Independence: Events, Processes and Ideology*. New York, NY: Routledge.

Chitalkar, P., & Malone, D. M. (2011). Democracy, Politics and India's Foreign Policy. *Canadian Foreign Policy Journal, 17*(1), 75–91.

CNN. (2005, January 24). Purported Al-Zarqawi Tape: Democracy a Lie. http://edition.cnn.com/2005/WORLD/meast/01/24/iraq.zarqawi/index.html. Accessed 26 February 2019.

Cohen, H. J. (1992). United States Congress. House. Committee on Foreign Affairs. Subcommittees on International Economic Policy and Trade, and on Africa. *The termination of economic sanctions against South Africa: Joint hearing*. Washington DC: US Government Printing Office.

Cohen, H. J. (2008). *Assistant Secretary of State for African Affairs, 1989–1993*, interviewed by Alex Thomson in 2012, Washington DC, 17 April 2008.

Dahl, R. A. (1971). *Polyarchy*. New Haven, CT: Yale University Press.

Dallmayr, F. (1996). *Beyond Orientalism: Essays on Cross-Cultural Encounter*. New York, NY: State University of New York Press.

Dallmayr, F. (2010). *Comparative Political Theory: An Introduction*. Basingstoke: Palgrave Macmillan.

Davenport, T. (1977). *South Africa: A Modern History* (2nd ed.). Johannesburg: Macmillan South Africa.

De Klerk, W. (1991). *F. W. de Klerk: The Man in his Time*. Johannesburg: Jonathan Ball Publishers.

De Klerk, F. W. (1998). *The Last Trek—A New Beginning*. Basingstoke: Macmillan.

Dirks, N. B. (2001). *Castes of Mind: Colonialism and the Making of Modern India*. Princeton, NJ: Princeton University Press.

Dreifuss, R. A. (2006). *1964: a conquista do Estado*. Petropolis: Vozes.

Dunn, J. (2005). *Setting the People Free: The Story of Democracy*. London: Atlantic.

Fico, C. (2008). *O Grande Irmão*. São Paulo: Civilização Brasileiro.

Fico, C. (2014). *O golpe de 1964: momentos decisivos*. Rio de Janeiro: Editora FGV.

Freedom House. (2018). *'South Africa,' Freedom House*. https://freedomhouse.org/country/south-africa/freedom-world/2018. Last accessed 7 December 2020.

Freedom House. (2019). *Democracies in decline, Freedom House*. https://freedomhouse.org/issues/democracies-decline. Last accessed: 7 December 2020.

French, H. W. (2019, February 7). Notes from Underground. *New York Review of Books*. https://www.nybooks.com/articles/2019/02/07/nelson-mandela-prison-notes-underground/. Accessed 10 February 2019.

Goel, R. K., & Nelson, M. A. (2001). Government Fragmentation Versus Fiscal Decentralization and Corruption. *Public Choice, 148*(3/4), 471–490.

Gonçalves, S. L., & Machado, A. F. (2015). Poverty Dynamics in Brazilian Metropolitan Areas: An Analysis Based on Hulme and Shepherd's Categorization (2002–2011). *EconomiA, 16*(3), 376–394.

Gordon, L. (2001, April 2). Brazil-US Relations: A New Chapter? *Brookings*. https://www.brookings.edu/opinions/brazil-u-s-relations-a-new-chapter/. Accessed 1 February 2019.

Gunitsky, S. (2018). Democracy's Future: Riding the Hegemonic Wave. *The Washington Quarterly, 41*(2), 115–135.

Hagopian, F., & Mainwaring, S. (1987). *Democracy in Brazil: Origins, Problems, Prospects*. Notre Dame, IN: Helen Kellogg Institute for International Studies.

Hamill, J. (2013, August 2). U.S.-South Africa Relations in the Obama-Zuma Era: Part I. *World Politics Review*. https://www.worldpoliticsreview.com/articles/13136/u-s-south-africa-relations-in-the-obama-zuma-era-part-i. Accessed 1 December 2019.

Hendricks, F., & Ntsebeza, L. (1999). Chiefs and Rural Local Government in Post-Apartheid South Africa. *African Journal of Political Science, 4*(1), 99–126.

Hobson, J. M. (2004). *The Eastern Origins of Western Civilisation*. Cambridge: Cambridge University Press.

Hodge, N. (2018, September 27). Vladimir Putin is not Invincible. *CNN*. Available at: https://edition.cnn.com/2018/09/26/europe/putin-pension-protest-analysis-intl/index.html. Accessed 10 January 2019.

Huntington, Samuel. (1991). *Democratization in the Late Twentieth Century*. Norman, OK: University of Oklahoma Press.

Isakhan, B. (2012). *Democracy in Iraq: History, Politics, Discourse*. London: Routledge.

Isakhan, B. (2015). 'Democracy: Critiquing a Eurocentric history,' pp. 1–14, *APSA 2015: Proceedings of the 2015 Australian Political Studies Association Conference*, Canberra, Australia.

Isakhan, B. (2016). Eurocentrism and the History of Democracy. *Politische Vierteljahresschrift, 51,* 56–70.

Khilnani, S. (1997). *The Idea of India*. New York, NY: Farrar, Straus and Giroux.

Kohli, A. (1987). *State and Poverty in India*. Cambridge: Cambridge University Press.

Lalvani, M. (2002). Can Decentralization Limit Government Growth? A Test of the Leviathan Hypothesis for the Indian Federation. *Publius, 32*(3), 25–45.

Lijphart, A. (1989). *Democracy in Plural Societies: A Comparative Exploration.* Mumbai: Popular Prakashan.

Linz, J., & Stepan, A. (1996). *Problems of Democratic Transition and Consolidation.* Princeton, NJ: Johns Hopkins University Press.

Lipset, S. M. (1994). The Social Requisites of Democracy Revisited, *American Sociological Review, 59*, 1–12.

Lisboa, M., & Latif, Z. A. (2013). *Brazil: Democracy and Growth.* London: Legatum Institute.

Lyman, P. N. (2002). *Partner to History: The US Role in South Africa's Transition to Democracy.* Washington, DC: United States Institute of Peace Press.

Manor, J. (1981). Party Decay and Political Crisis in India. *The Washington Quarterly, 4*(3), 25–40.

Markoff, J., & Herrera, A. (2014). Another Chapter from Democracy's Secret History: A Research Program on Some Small Spanish Towns. In B. Wejnert (Ed.), *Voices of Globalization (Research in Political Sociology)* (Vol. 21, pp. 31–49). Bingley: Emerald Group Publishing.

Markoff, J. (1999). Where and When Was Democracy Invented? *Comparative Studies Society and History, 41*(4), 660–690.

Mamdani, M. (1996). *Citizen and Subject: Contemporary Africa and the Legacy of Late Colonialism.* Princeton, N.J.: Princeton University Press.

Massie, R. K. (1997). *Loosing the Bonds: The United States and South Africa in the Apartheid Years.* New York, NY: Doubleday.

Miller, P. D. (2018). Non-'Western' Liberalism and the Resilience of the Liberal International Order. *The Washington Quarterly, 41*(2), 137–153.

Mills, M. (1988). South Africa's Critics Renew Bid for Sanctions. *Congressional Quarterly Weekly Report, 46*(13), 811.

Mitra, S. K. (2013). How Exceptional is India's Democracy? Path Dependence, Political Capital, and Context in South Asia. *India Review, 12*(4), 227–244.

Monyae, D. (2017). *The US, Russia, China and Africa in the Evolving Global Order.* University of Johannesburg Centre for Africa-China Studies Policy Brief Series Issue 3. http://confucius-institute.joburg/category/policy-briefs/. Accessed 3 November 2018.

Monyae, D. (2019, February 6). Diplomats Dropped the Ball. *Pretoria News.*

Moore, B., Jr. (1966). *Social Origins of Dictatorship and Democracy.* Boston, MA: Beacon Press.

Morris-Jones, W. H. (1974). *The Government and Politics of India.* New Delhi: BI Publications.

Mukherjee, K. (2010). Why has Democracy Been Less Successful in Pakistan than in India? *Asian Affairs, 41*(1), 67–77.

Ndzendze, B. (2018). *Dictionary of Contemporary of International Relations.* Pretoria: NLSA.

Noer, T. (1985). *Cold War and Black Liberation: The United States and White Rule in Africa, 1948–1968*. Columbia, MO: University of Missouri Press.

Ntsebeza, L. (1999). Democratization and traditional authorities in the new South Africa, *Comparative Studies of South Asia, Africa and the Middle East, 19*(1), 83–93.

Ntsebeza, L. (2011). *Democracy Compromised: Chiefs and the Politics of Land in South Africa*. Leiden: Brill.

Öniş, Z., & Gençer, A. S. (2018). Democratic BRICS as Role Models in a Shifting Global Order: Inherent Dilemmas and the Challenges Ahead. *Third World Quarterly, 39*(9), 1791–1811.

Parker, P. (2011). *Brazil and the Quiet Intervention, 1964*. Austin, TX: University of Texas Press.

Pereira, A. (2018). The US Role in the 1964 Coup in Brazil: A Reassessment. *Bulletin of Latin American Research, 37*(1), 5–17.

Power, T. J. (2010). Brazilian Democracy as a Late Bloomer: Reevaluating the Regime in the Cardoso-Lula Era. *Latin American Research Review, 47*(Special Issue), 218–247.

Republic of South Africa, Department of Provincial and Local Government. (2003). *White Paper on Traditional Leadership and Governance*. Pretoria: Government Printer.

Pye, L. W. (2002, May/June). Capsule Review: Castes of Mind, *Foreign Affairs*. https://www.foreignaffairs.com/reviews/capsule-review/2002-05-01/castes-mind-colonialism-and-making-modern-india. Last accessed 7 December 2020.

Saule, A. (2014). *The Impact of the United States (US) and South Africa's (SA) Trade Relationship on Botswana, Lesotho, Namibia and Swaziland (BLNS) [1999–2013]*. MA Thesis, University of the Witwatersrand.

Schumpeter, J. A. (1942). *Capitalism, Socialism and Democracy*. New York, NY: Harper & Brothers.

Sen, A. (2005). *The Argumentative Indian*. New York, NY: Farrar, Straus and Giroux.

Spector, J. B. (2018, November 2). As BRICS Democratic Impulses Vanish at an Alarming Rate, South Africa Must Rethink its Priorities. *Daily Maverick*. https://www.dailymaverick.co.za/article/20181102asbricsdemocraticimpulsesvanishatanalarmingratesouthafricamustrethinkitspriorities/? Accessed 20 January 2019.

Shleifer, A., & Treisman, D. (2005). A Normal Country: Russia After Communism. *Journal of Economic Perspectives, 19*(1), 151–174.

Soboul, A. (1975). *The French Revolution 1787–1799*. New York, NY: Vintage.

South African History Online (SAHA). (2011). *Frontline States*. https://www.sahistory.org.za/article/frontline-states. Accessed 3 February 2019.

The Economist. (2009, February 5). Where Dinosaurs Still Roam: A Victory for Semi-Feudalism. https://www.economist.com/the-americas/2009/02/05/where-dinosaurs-still-roam. Accessed 3 February 2019.

Thomson, A. interview with H.J. Cohen, Assistant Secretary of State for African Affairs, 1989–1993. Washington, DC, 17 April 2008.

Thomson, A. interview with M. Munthali, Southern African campaigns, *TransAfrica*, Washington, DC, 13 October 1992.

Thomson, A. interview with D. Lonie, Principal Foreign Affairs Aide to Representative Gerald Solomon, R-NY, US Congress, Washington, DC, 29 September 1992.

Thomson, A. interview with F. W. de Klerk, President of the Republic of South Africa, 1989–1994, Personal Correspondence, 28 March 2012.

Thomson, A. (2008). *US Foreign Policy Towards Apartheid South Africa, 1948–1994: Conflict of Interests*. New York, NY: Palgrave Macmillan.

Thomson, A. (2012). A More Effective Constructive Engagement: US Policy Towards South Africa after the Comprehensive Anti-Apartheid Act of 1986. *Politikon, 39*(3), 371–389.

Williams, J. M. (2004). Leading from Behind: Democratic Consolidation and the Chieftancy in South Africa. *The Journal of Modern African Studies, 42*(1), 3–136.

CHAPTER 3

Brics, Brazil and Africa: Economic Potential and Challenges

Bruno De Conti, Célio Hiratuka, and Arthur Welle

The acronym BRIC was coined in 2001 by Goldman Sachs and was used by financial market analysts as a reference to a group of countries that offered opportunities for highly profitable investments. The use of the acronym was spread in the media and finally encouraged a meeting of these countries' governments to enable discussions about the world economy. The first summit was held in Yekaterinburg, Russia, in 2009, with a focus on the necessity of reforms in the international financial system, but other topics such as international trade, food security and renewable energy were also discussed.[1]

We see therefore that this group, created as an object, and envisaged by global investors as a source of high-yielding assets, has been gradually structuring itself as a subject, an important player in international dialogues, with a very clear message: we will not accept the role imposed on us by the world economy; we want to be protagonists in the international economic stakes. This claim is justified by the fact that

B. De Conti (✉) · C. Hiratuka · A. Welle
University of Campinas, Campinas, Brazil

D. Monyae and B. Ndzendze (eds.), *The BRICS Order*, International Political Economy Series,
https://doi.org/10.1007/978-3-030-62765-2_3

the BRICS countries jointly hold 42.6 per cent of the world's population, 22.5 per cent of global GDP,[2] and around 25 per cent of the world's land. The group was initially organised around a programme of refusing the status quo; the current challenge is therefore to build a positive economic agenda, with proposals regarding the international order and also the relationships between the five countries.

The first aim of this chapter is to explore the possibilities and challenges for the establishment of this network of economic relations among the BRICS countries. The chapter shows that these economic relations are increasing very rapidly, but are mainly due to the importance of Chinese trade and investments in the other four countries. The construction of BRICS is fundamental to the quest for a new international order, but it has to deal with the risk of creating (or reproducing) asymmetries within the bloc. First, the chapter discusses the monetary-financial dimension, and then the productive dimension, with a particular focus on Brazil. As a second aim, the chapter presents the economic relations between Brazil and Africa in the recent period, allowing us to analyse the role the BRICS have (or may have) on that continent.

BRICS Challenges and Potential: The Monetary-Financial Dimension

With regard to the monetary-financial dimension (such as portfolio investments, loans, presence of banks and usage of currencies) the relationship between the BRICS countries is still weak. Nevertheless, the potential of the group to implement—or to accelerate—significant changes in the world arena is enormous.

The post-war international monetary and financial system arose from the Bretton Woods Agreement and the multilateral institutions it created—especially the International Monetary Fund (IMF) and the World Bank (WB).[3] These institutions were created by all the countries gathered at the conference, but despite the discourse of multilateralism they are based on a strong asymmetry, which reflects the geopolitical stakes and the balance of power at the moment of its creation.

In the second decade of the twenty-first century, the Bretton Woods Agreement is no longer followed and the international economy has changed. Nowadays, in addition to the importance of BRICS in terms of GDP and international trade, the financial markets of these countries are increasingly important at the international level—notably a lavish source of income for international investors. The process has been gradual, as the integration of these countries into financial globalisation has taken place since the 1990s (in the case of China, even later).[4] Currently, because of very high interest rates, gains in stock markets (related to economic growth, but also to speculative movements) or changes in exchange rates, the BRICS financial markets offer international investors returns they don't normally get in their home countries. Hence, the BRICS countries are the destination of an increasing amount of foreign capital, especially in times of low profitability in central countries[5] such as that arising post-2008. Additionally, the BRICS themselves are also gradually becoming major investors at the international level.

Nevertheless, the institutions created in the post-war period did not accompany these changes in the world scenario, retaining the aforementioned power asymmetry. Two concrete examples are sufficiently illustrative: by a tacit agreement, the managing director of the IMF is always European and that of the WB is almost always a North American. In the IMF, the votes of each signatory country have different weights, deriving from its quota; however, the votes of the United States have a weight equivalent to about 17 per cent of the total and for the most important decisions it is necessary to reach 85 per cent of the votes, which virtually gives the US veto power. In 2016, after years of negotiations—with hard opposition by the Republican Party in the US Congress[6]—the IMF implemented a reform to increase the BRICS voting power, but the veto power of the US was not affected.

It is obvious that beyond the rhetoric of multilateralism these institutions are still attached to a reality that no longer reflects the contemporary international economy. The perception among the BRICS countries is that the dialogue within these institutions is less than harmonious. The Russian foreign minister, Sergey Lavrov, has expressed it very clearly, stating in 2015 that the BRICS bloc had to 'actively push' for reforms in these institutions, and claiming that reforms in the international monetary and financial system as a whole 'to make them more equitable' remained 'high on our list of priorities within BRICS'.[7]

With regard to the international monetary and financial System (IMFS), the emergence of the BRICS group is a means of facing a situation in which these countries (and their financial markets) are merely a hunting ground for international capital. The possibility of a coordination among BRICS countries to exercise some (even if minor) control over the dynamic of international financial capital flows would be really important for the bloc. This is the dimension in which the BRICS group may possess the strongest potential for change.

The BRICS want to improve their control over the dynamics of the IMFS. For this, the sixth BRICS Summit of 2014 decided on two very important initiatives. First is the BRICS contingent reserve arrangement, through which the BRICS share a volume of international reserves (the initial amount was US$100 billion), and which appears to be an important precaution for countries on the periphery against the tendency of the international economy to alternate moments of abundance with periods in which liquidity is lacking ('international liquidity cycles'). Conceivably, in a moment of lack of international currencies affecting one of the BRICS countries, the arrangement will make it easier to access the reserves available to be shared instead of requesting a loan from the IMF.

Secondly, and most importantly, the BRICS have created the New Development Bank (NDB), jointly financed and administered by the five BRICS countries. The central objective of this bank is to finance investments related to infrastructure and sustainable development. Its initial authorised capital is US$100 billion. Unlike that of the IMF, the governance structure of this bank is equal (the five countries having the same voting power) and its presidency rotates. Despite the source of resources, funding will not be restricted to the BRICS. It is a very audacious initiative, assembled with impressive speed—the intention was declared in 2012, and four years later the bank was already in operation.[8]

Although the official rhetoric states that these new institutions are complementary to those of the Bretton Woods, it is difficult to avoid the perception of their potential to replace, in a sense, the roles of the IMF and the WB, but there is one essential difference: the IMF and the WB impose very severe conditions on the borrowing countries which constrain their autonomy of economic policy, whereas the access of the BRICS to shared reserves, and also to a source of low-cost funding through the NDB, are not subject to the same conditions.

In addition to these two initiatives, which are already in place, there is a third interesting idea. The dynamics of financial capital flows at the international arena are such that nowadays there is a new protagonist group, constituted by the 'rating agencies'. These agencies give notes for securities issued by international economic agents (companies, but also the public sector national treasury and/or central bank). However, it is very inappropriate that companies, and especially BRICS governments, are judged by the rating agencies located in the central countries, mainly because they are not neutral—in their notes there is an implicit judgement on the economic policies and the role of the state in each country.[9] This has given rise to the idea of creating a BRICS rating agency.

All are connected to one goal: BRICS wants to change its role from that of a passive to an active player on the international financial scene. Here, again, there are important difficulties. One of the main obstacles emanates from the monetary sphere. Money, like language, is only useful if it is also used by others. This explains why the BRICS meetings are, paradoxically, still carried out in English and the economic operations between the BRICS are notably in US dollars (after all, the dollar is the most internationally accepted currency, which reinforces its own acceptability by all agents). The share of international exchange markets relative to BRICS currencies is still very low at 8.2 per cent—much less than the share of their economies in the world GDP.[10] There is nothing abnormal about this, as there is a component that prolongs the strength of currencies whose use is already widespread on the international scene and makes it difficult for agents to use the currencies of the peripheral countries—explained by the fact that the usefulness of a currency comes from its acceptability by others and, therefore, from the confidence the community places in it and the network of use already established.[11]

The association of the BRICS countries aims therefore to accelerate this process through these new institutions, mainly because the NDB credit can be offered in the national currencies of each one of the BRICS countries. This may spread the use of BRICS currencies among BRICS agents, and also in other countries that will eventually take funding from the NDB. In addition, it will stimulate the settlement of international trade between the BRICS in their own currencies. Finally, the 'reserve agreement' will make the BRICS currencies appear more reliable to international investors because it reduces the risk of a currency crisis in the BRICS.[12] In short, the monetary-financial integration of the BRICS will be enormously stimulated by the increase in the use of their own currencies for their economic activities. This is not easy, but efforts in this direction can accelerate a process that would otherwise be too slow and uncertain.

BRICS Challenges and Potential: The Productive Dimension

Thanks to the first ministerial meeting held in 2006, the institutionalisation of an annual summit from 2009 onwards and the official incorporation of South Africa in 2010, the BRICS bloc has gradually deepened and broadened its cooperation mechanisms.

The way BRICS has affected its members can be analysed from a dual perspective (Fonseca 2013). The first aspect concerns the influence that the BRICS can have on the international order, linked to its coordination capacity in the main multilateral institutions. The second comes from the interaction of the BRICS countries with each other, which implies a variety of areas where there is significant potential for intra-BRICS cooperation.

With regard to international trade—as in other multilateral cases—the importance of BRICS has greatly increased since the origin of the bloc and the BRICS members seek to amplify their influence on the discussions within the World Trade Organization (WTO). Despite the different weight that foreign trade has in the development strategies of this group of countries—reflected in the different degrees of economic openness and the diversity of products exported by each—it has been possible to perceive in the Doha Round coordination of positions in the negotiations, particularly in the area of agriculture. The positions of Brazil, India, South Africa and China (Russia joined the WTO later) have been important in the face of the interests of the United States and the EU (which sought to maintain selective protection policies in their agricultural markets) and to conserve space for less developed countries to protect their agricultural markets in view of food security problems. Similarly, in the non-agricultural market access (NAMA) negotiations, BRICS coordination has helped to maintain the defence of their markets for industrial goods and their bargaining power to advocate for more tariff reduction in developed countries (Thorsteinsen and Oliveira 2014). It can be said that the coordination of actions has brought this group of countries to a new level in terms of bargaining power within the WTO, as they have managed to reconcile the particular interests of each country and to exert considerable influence on important negotiations. This is a result of the group's organisational capacity, but also its growing importance in international trade. Table 3.1 shows that the group's share of global exports increased from 7.5 per cent in 2000 to 19 per cent in 2015.

Here we come however to a crucial point in the analysis of BRICS: the asymmetries involved within this group. Table 3.1 shows that the increase in the world trade participation mainly reflects the growth in China's trade, since its share in the world exports has grown from 3.9

Table 3.1 BRICS countries' shares in world trade (%)

	Brazil (%)	*China (%)*	*India (%)*	*Russia (%)*	*South Africa (%)*	*BRICS total (%)*
2000	0.9	3.9	0.7	1.6	0.4	7.5
2005	1.1	7.3	1.0	2.3	0.4	12.1
2010	1.3	10.3	1.4	2.6	0.5	16.2
2015	1.2	13.7	1.6	2.1	0.4	19.0

Source UNCTAD

per cent in 2000 to 13.7 per cent in 2015. For the total BRICS trade, China's share was 52.3 per cent in 2000 and reached 72.4 per cent in 2015.

Yet, Table 3.1 also shows that from 2000 to 2010 all BRICS countries increased their shares of world exports. This period includes the global economic growth cycle before the international financial crisis, characterised by a favourable cycle of international prices for agricultural and mineral commodities. The period 2010–2015 corresponds to the years following the outbreak of the global financial crisis, causing a sharp decline in global economic activity, the reduction of commodity prices and the slowdown in world trade. In this latest period, China and India have managed to sustain growth in their share of global exports, while Brazil, Russia and South Africa have been more directly affected by the crisis. Among BRICS countries, Brazil and South Africa are those with the lower participations and which saw a decline of 0.1 per cent each between 2010 and 2015.

To a large extent this divergent export performance in the post-2008 period is associated with the export profile of the different BRICS countries. Exports from Brazil, Russia and South Africa are mostly primary products (agricultural and mineral), whereas those from China and India include large quantities of manufactured goods. Only in China is the participation of manufacturers greater than that of primary products. Even India, although gaining increasing importance in global industrial production, retains a greater share of primary goods (mainly petroleum products) (Table 3.2).

Table 3.3 shows the trade values among BRICS. It shows that the volume of intra-BRICS trade has had a significant growth rate between 2000 and 2010 (around 28 per cent per year) and an increase from 3.7

Table 3.2 BRICS countries' shares in world trade: manufactured and non-manufactured products (%)

	Brazil (%)	*China (%)*	*India (%)*	*Russia (%)*	*South Africa (%)*	*Total BRICS (%)*
Non-manufactured						
2000	1.5	2.0	1.1	4.5	0.7	9.8
2005	2.0	2.2	1.5	6.4	0.8	12.8
2010	2.7	2.2	2.1	6.4	0.9	14.4
2015	2.6	2.9	2.3	5.8	0.8	14.4
Manufactured						
2000	0.7	4.7	0.6	0.5	0.3	6.7
2005	0.8	9.5	0.8	0.6	0.3	12.0
2010	0.7	14.8	1.2	0.5	0.4	17.5
2015	0.6	18.6	1.4	0.6	0.3	21.4

Source UNCTAD

Table 3.3 Intra-BRICS trade and its participation in total BRICS exports and total world exports

Year	*US$ billion*	*% of BRICS exports*	*% of World exports*
2000	17.71	3.7	0.3
2005	72.24	5.7	0.7
2010	210.70	8.5	1.4
2015	242.30	7.7	1.5

Source UNCTAD

per cent to 8.5 per cent of total BRICS exports. Compared to total world exports, the share rose from 0.3 per cent in 2000 to 1.4 per cent in 2010. Between 2010 and 2015, the growth rate (around 3 per cent per year) was much lower and intra-BRICS trade fell to 7.7 per cent of total BRICS exports and 1.5 per cent of world exports.

Finally, Table 3.4 shows the trade matrix between the BRICS countries in 2015. The data show that the largest flows are China's exports to India, Russia and Brazil; and from Brazil and Russia to China. These flows represent seven per cent of the total.

It is possible to notice therefore that despite the recent growth of intra-BRICS trade there is still potential for further increase in bilateral trade between the group countries, since they are still at a low level. For example, Brazilian trade—whether as a source or as a destination for

Table 3.4 Intra-BRICS trade in 2015 (%)

Destination	*Origin*					*Total (%)*
	Brazil (%)	*China (%)*	*India (%)*	*Russia (%)*	*South Africa (%)*	
Brazil	–	11	1	1	0.2	14
China	15	–	4	12	2	33
India	1	24	–	2	1	29
Russia	1	14	1	–	0.1	16
South Africa	1	7	2	0.1	–	9
Total	18	56	7	14	4	100

Source UNCTAD

goods—is still very focused on relations with China, and negligible with the other BRICS countries. Table 3.4 showed that Brazilian trade with all other BRICS countries (besides China) results in no more than 5.2 per cent of the total BRICS intra-trade (two per cent with India, two per cent with Russia and 1.2 per cent with South Africa).

Given the level of development of these countries and the importance of industrial activity for all of them, it would also be important to implement efforts to increase intra-industry trade. Returning to the example of trade between Brazil and China, despite the increasing importance of flows it is still a trade with a typical cross-sectorial profile—that is, Brazilian exports to China are concentrated on unmanufactured goods and those from China to Brazil are mainly composed of manufactured goods.

Concerning direct investment, the BRICS bloc is also increasingly important for the global economy. In terms of investment stocks, BRICS accounted for 8.5 per cent of the world total in 2015. For inward flows, the total for 2005–2015 was 16.1 per cent. In the case of outward investments, the volume is smaller, but similarly important, reflecting the strategy of a few companies based in BRICS countries to become global companies (Table 3.5).

Nevertheless, the BRICS investments within the group of countries are still incipient. It is not easy to obtain bilateral flows between countries, and the only year with available data for all countries is 2012 (see Table 3.6). This year, the intra-BRICS investment stock was only 3 per cent of the total foreign investment stock and accounted for only 0.2

Table 3.5 Direct investments received and held by the BRICS. The stock in 2015 and the accumulated flows in the period 2005–2015 (% of the world total)

	Stock 2015		*Accumulated flows 2005–2015*	
	Inward (%)	*Outward (%)*	*Inward (%)*	*Outward (%)*
Brazil	2.2	0.7	3.7	0.5
China	3.2	1.8	7.4	4.9
India	0.8	0.4	2.1	0.8
Russia	1.6	1.3	2.5	3.0
South Africa	0.7	0.4	0.4	0.2
BRICS total	8.5	4.6	16.1	9.4

Source UNCTAD

Table 3.6 Stocks of investments held abroad in 2012 (US$ millions)

Outward	*Total*	*Brics*	*Brics/Total (%)*	*Brazil*	*China*	*India*	*Russia*	*South Africa*
Brazil	266.252	364	0.1	–	364	–	–	–
China	531.941	12.282	2.3	1.450	–	1.169	4.888	4.775
India	79.857	2.384	3.0	88	275	–	1.841	180
Russia	406.295	1.524	0.4	4	234	1.251	–	35
South Africa	111.780	24.639	22.0	718	20.284	203	3.434	–
Total BRICS	1.396.125	41.193	3.0	2.260	21.157	2.623	10.163	4.990

Source UNCTAD

per cent of the global total. At the country level, only South Africa has a significant share of its outward foreign investment in other BRICS countries (concentrated in China, however).

This means that compared to bilateral investment between BRICS, the challenges and opportunities are even greater than in trade flows. It is important to highlight that investment flows have a greater capacity than trade flows to consolidate integration between countries because they imply a long-term commitment, requiring closer relationships with the environment, business and even the culture of the partner countries. The impacts of investments are also greater because they can contribute to capital formation and job creation in the countries receiving them. For some sectors, technology transfer can also be stimulated. Finally, the investments and activities of BRICS multinational companies in another country of the group will also encourage increased trade flows.

The potential problem concerns the acquisition of enterprises in strategic sectors by the foreign capital. In Brazil, Chinese companies are buying companies in the sector of energy, taking advantage the current economic crises in the country. Moreover, the government of Michel Temer rushed to privatise public companies, including those related to oil and electricity—which may seem to be a good thing for international investors (mainly Chinese), but is in reality a questionable strategy when one thinks about the importance of these sectors for Brazilian development.

Apart from these investments related to strategic sectors, this path towards a situation of greater maturity in economic relations between the BRICS should therefore involve mechanisms to encourage increased trade flows and, in particular, investments between the countries of the group. This is a crucial issue and should be a priority for BRICS because of its potential to strengthen integration and cooperation between countries.

Besides analysing the importance of BRICS for world trade and external investments, and economic relations within BRICS countries, this chapter also aims to evaluate economic relations between Brazil and Africa. The next section will therefore present these discussions, starting with Brazilian foreign policy regarding Africa and scrutinising economic relations over the last 20 years.

Brazil-Africa: Economic Relations (1997–2017)

Brazilian foreign policy has always had a deep interest in relations with the African continent, due in large part to the historical and cultural relationship that they share on both sides of the Atlantic and to the mutual desire for economic development—mainly with countries that, like Brazil, were Portuguese colonies in the past. In general terms, however, this foreign policy cannot be considered monolithic, varying between two poles: relations with the central countries versus relations with the peripheral countries.

In some contexts, Brazil sought to deepen its relations with the peripheral countries—first in the early 1960s, with the so-called 'independent foreign policy' of presidents Jânio Quadros and João Goulart, and a second moment during the military governments, especially that of Medici, promoting an approximation and identification policy with the Third World (Miyamoto 2011). An example of this was the recognition in 1975, of the independence of the Lusophone countries Mozambique and Angola before most countries did so. With the serious external debt crisis that Brazil passed through in the 1980s, the country turned inwards, trying to deal with internal affairs. In the 1990s, the neoliberal government of Fernando Henrique Cardoso sought closer ties with the central countries.

Brazilian foreign policy has revived its international relations with Africa since 2003, with the government of Luis Inácio Lula da Silva, which has made the South–South relationship one of its priorities. In fact, Brazil was trying to act on several fronts in order to change the configuration of world power, aiming to give greater weight to peripheral countries and consequently to highlight its own role in the international arena. Brazil has therefore claimed leadership positions in the most important world organisations such as the Food and Agriculture Organization of the United Nations (FAO) and the WTO; has suggested proposals to solve shared world problems; has presented itself as a mediator of conflicts (as in the case of the negotiations regarding nuclear technology involving Iran, in 2010); has participated in peace missions (the largest engagement in these activities in Brazilian history, with up to 2200 troops in Haiti); and has called for changes in the international structures of power (Miyamoto 2011).

In addition to seeking this greater weight in multilateral institutions, Brazil sought to deepen its bilateral relationship with several peripheral countries, with particular reference to the African countries, especially the large economies of South Africa and Nigeria, and the Portuguese-speaking countries Angola, Mozambique and Guinea-Bissau. In this sense, the Brazilian government has initiated initiatives to stimulate not only an increasing trade with Africa, but also to magnify direct investments in African countries, concentrated in Angola, South Africa, Mozambique and Ghana. The data below shows that the initiatives—connected to the economic boom in Brazil—were largely successful.

Trade relations between Brazil and Africa may be divided into three different periods. Between 1997 and 2002 we notice a period of stability of Brazilian exports at around US$2 billion per year. The second period is from 2003 to 2011, when there was a strong increase in both exports and imports. The third is from 2012 to 2017, when we see a strong decrease in both commercial flows (see Fig. 3.1).[13]

Imports went through a period of significant increase between 2001 and 2009, from an average level of US$4 billion a year to a peak of US$18 billion in 2009. As we will discuss below, imports are highly concentrated in oil and its derivatives, mostly from Nigeria.

On the other hand, Brazilian exports to Africa rose from US$2 billion (average of the years 1997–2002) to US$12 billion in eight years (2001–2009), an increase of 500 per cent in the period. There is a 20 per cent drop shortly after the outbreak of the financial crisis (2008), but exports were growing again between 2010 and 2012, peaking in 2012 at around US$14 billion. After this period, Brazilian exports to Africa were on a slow and steady decline until the end of 2016, returning to a level of US$8 billion per year at the end of this period. The years of 2016–2017 break this trend, as we see a significant increase of 25 per cent in total exports, reflecting a devaluation of the Brazilian currency (mostly in 2015).

From the Brazilian point of view, the trade with Africa represents a sizeable portion. Africa's share in Brazilian total imports reached 10 per cent between 2005 and 2009, but has declined to less than four per cent in recent years (Fig. 3.2). Africa's share of Brazilian exports has come

Fig. 3.1 Import and Export Brazil–Africa (12 months accumulated value US$ FOB) (*Source* Brazilian Ministry of Industry, Foreign Trade and Services, deflated to 2017 prices by US CPI)

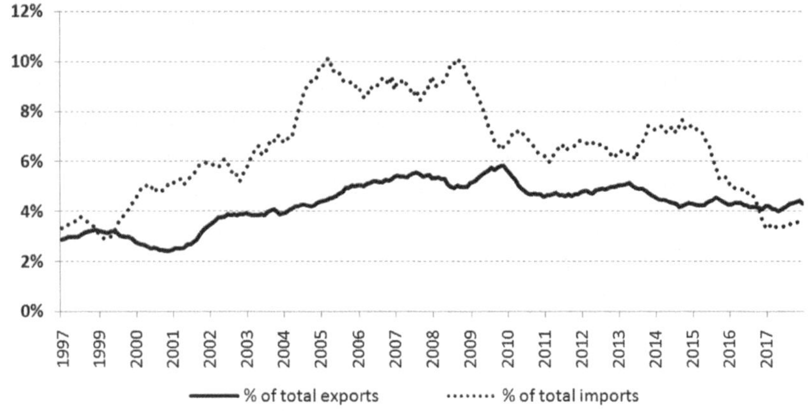

Fig. 3.2 Africa's share in Brazil–World total trade 1997–2017 (12 months rolling average) (*Source* Brazilian Ministry of Industry, Foreign Trade and Services)

from three per cent in 1997 to about 6 per cent at the end of 2009, and in 2017 is closer to four per cent.

However, the technology content of both imports and exports was overall very low, in spite of the wishes of both sides of the Atlantic (Fig. 3.3). Brazilian imports from Africa are highly concentrated in petroleum and petroleum derivatives, representing the astonishing share of 84 per cent of all imports from 1997 to 2017. They are followed by chemical nitrogenous fertilisers (also a petroleum derivative) and phosphates, representing seven per cent of all imports in the last 20 years. Other relevant products are coal (one per cent) and cocoa (one per cent).

The African countries with the highest level of exports to Brazil in this period were Nigeria (48 per cent), Algeria (24 per cent), Morocco (seven per cent), South Africa (6 per cent) and the group of Portuguese-speaking countries (Angola, Cape Verde, Guinea-Bissau, Mozambique, São Tomé and Príncipe with 4.5 per cent).

There was a major change in Brazil's internal production of petroleum with the discovery of oil reservoirs below deep-sea water on the Brazilian shore (also known as pre-salt oil). Although the discovery itself was made by the state-owned company Petrobras in 2006, the difficulties of drilling in such conditions, and the investments required, delayed production for a few years. With this, Brazil has become a self-sufficient producer of

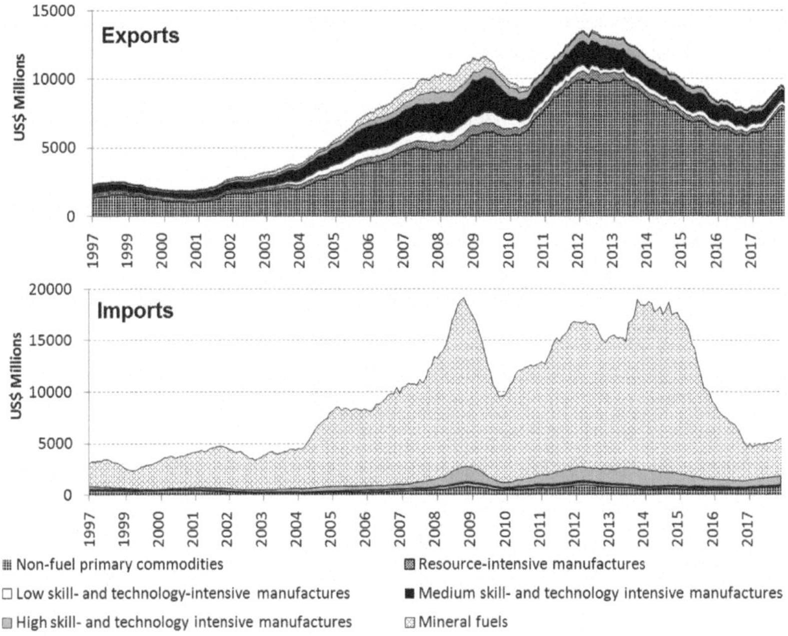

Fig. 3.3 Technological content of Brazilian imports and exports from/to Africa (12 months accumulated value US$ FOB) (*Source* Brazilian Ministry of Industry, Foreign Trade and Services, deflated to 2017 prices by US CPI)

oil since 2016. The association of the oil supply investments with the recession of the whole economy from 2015 to 2017 have led to a rapid decrease in petroleum imports by Brazil.[14]

The most striking figure comes from Nigeria. From 2009 until mid-2016, the Nigerian mineral fuels alone represented more than 50 per cent of all Brazilian imports from Africa of any kind of product, but fell to less than 15 per cent in one year (July 2016 to July 2017). In value, it dropped from more than US$10 billion per year in 2013 and 2014 to US$0.7 billion in 2017.

It is therefore clear that this declining importance of petroleum for bilateral trade is a permanent change in Brazilian imports of African products. The commercial balance that was in most of the recent years (Fig. 3.3) in favour of the African continent has turned, in the middle of 2016, in favour of Brazil. In this new standard, looking only at 2017 we can see that, although petroleum is still the most important product, the share of fertilisers has grown to 20 per cent, as Brazil has not created a local industry in this sector.

Brazilian exports to Africa are not as heavily concentrated as are imports, but nonetheless we can see that agricultural commodities combined reach half of the total. The most important products in the sum of all Brazilian exports to Africa in the whole period (1997–2017) were sugar (30 per cent), meat (13 per cent), tractors and other vehicles (10 per cent) and cereals (6 per cent). In the last four years there was an increasing concentration in sugar (35 per cent), meat (16 per cent) and cereals (eight per cent)—again, primary commodities.

If we aggregate these products in sectors we can see (Fig. 3.4) that prepared foodstuffs (86 per cent) is the leading product group, followed by animal products. But we also see products such as aircraft, cars and machinery in the Brazilian exports—different from the imports from Africa.

A considerable part of technological export is tied up with the agricultural sector. The Brazilian government has a direct influence in promoting this flow by financing it through the international programme More Food International (MFI), an initiative begun in 2010—under Lula da Silva's

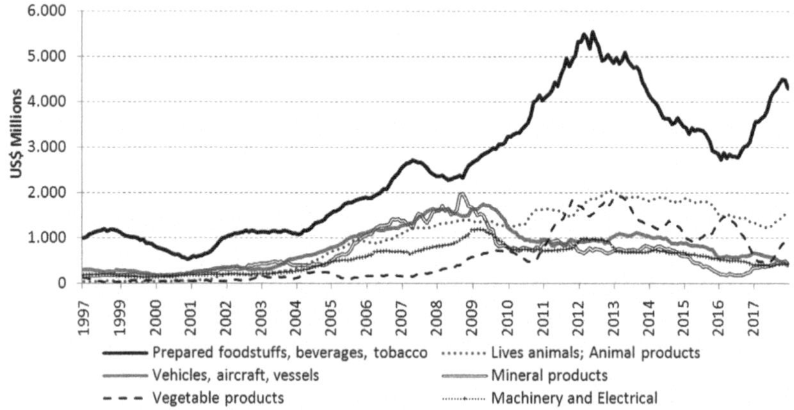

Fig. 3.4 Relevant sector exports Brazil-Africa (12 months accumulated value US$ FOB) (*Source* Brazilian Ministry of Industry, Foreign Trade and Services, deflated to 2017 prices by US CPI)

government—which aims to support the interchange of agriculture technology and its products. Its members in Africa are Mozambique, Ghana, Zimbabwe, Senegal and Kenya. The initiative contemplates three areas of work: (a) technical cooperation aimed at supporting agrarian development programmes based on family farming; (b) financing for exports of agricultural machinery and equipment; and (c) training of technicians and family farmers in the use of agricultural machinery and equipment sold through the programme. This programme has financed more than US$500 million of machinery exports between 2010 and 2014 (Pinto et al. 2015), but it has also been criticised for prioritising the interests of industry over those of family farmers (Cabral et al. 2016).

For the purposes of this chapter, in addition to the general figures of international trade between Africa and Brazil, we have selected two cases for analysis: the trade between Brazil and South Africa (one of the most developed countries on the continent and a member of BRICS); and the trade between Brazil and the Portuguese-speaking countries of Africa, given the historical and political ties they maintain.

Brazil has had a favourable trade balance with South Africa since 1999 (Fig. 3.5). The initial growth of exports between these two countries follows the general trajectory of Brazilian exports to the whole world, rising from US$0.5 billion annually until 2002 to a level of US$2 billion annually between 2007 and 2014; between 2015 and 2017, exports

Fig. 3.5 Import and Export Brazil–South Africa (12 months accumulated value US$ FOB) (*Source* Brazilian Ministry of Industry, Foreign Trade and Services, deflated to 2017 prices by US CPI)

stabilised at approximately US$1.5 billion per year. In the last four years, Brazil has exported US$5.6 billion to South Africa, representing 16 per cent of total exports to Africa. The most relevant products exported from Brazil to South Africa were vehicles (US$1.5 billion, or 26 per cent of the total, in which US$820 million were trucks or tractors), machinery and its parts (US$750 million or 13.3 per cent of the total), meat (US$650 million or 11.5 per cent of the total) and sugar (US$400 million, seven per cent of the total).

Meanwhile, Brazilian imports from South Africa have been falling since 2011, when they peaked at US$1 billion per year, then reaching half of that amount in 2016. In the last four years, imports totalled US$2.3 billion, with considerable technological diversity (Fig. 3.6). Out of this total, coal accounted for 14 per cent (US$310 million), pesticides 11 per

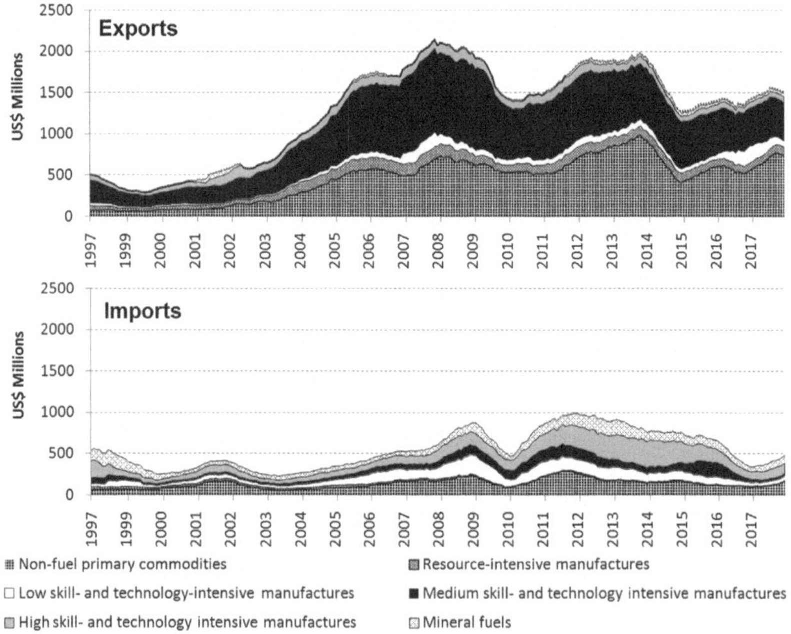

Fig. 3.6 Technological content of Brazilian imports and exports from/to South Africa (12 months accumulated value US$ FOB) (*Source* Brazilian Ministry of Industry, Foreign Trade and Services, deflated by US CPI)

cent (US$240 million), platinum used in the auto industry 10 per cent (US$215 million), and cars nine per cent (US$199 million).

Trade relations with Portuguese-speaking African countries are guided by the diplomatic efforts addressed to deepen cooperation among its member states. The main result of such efforts is the Community of Portuguese Language Countries (CPLP is the Portuguese acronym), an international forum whose members are Brazil, Angola, Cape Verde, Guinea-Bissau, Mozambique, São Tome and Principe and, since 2014, Equatorial Guinea.

The trade flows between Brazil and African Lusophone countries show a period of steady growth from 2003 up to 2009 (Fig. 3.7). In this last year, both exports and imports peaked at about US$2.5 billion annually (more than 20 per cent of the total exports to Africa). After the start of the world crisis, exports remained at US$1.5 billion per year until 2015, when they again fell to about US$750 million per year (eight per cent of total exports to Africa). Exports to this group are highly concentrated (more than 90 per cent) in a single country, Angola, because of the relatively small size of the other economies.

Such concentration is even stronger in the imports from African Lusophone countries. Once again, Angola is the major exporter among these countries. Mineral fuels, in this case, petroleum, account for virtually everything that Angola exports to Brazil (Fig. 3.8).

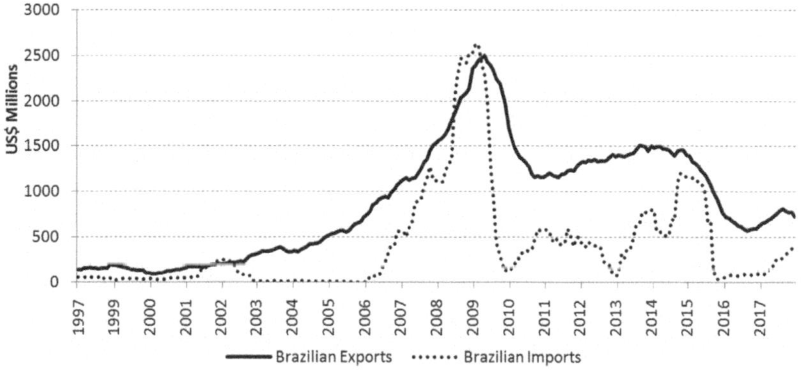

Fig. 3.7 Import and Export Brazil–Portuguese-speaking countries (12 months accumulated value US$ FOB) (*Source* Brazilian Ministry of Industry, Foreign Trade and Services, deflated to 2017 prices by US CPI)

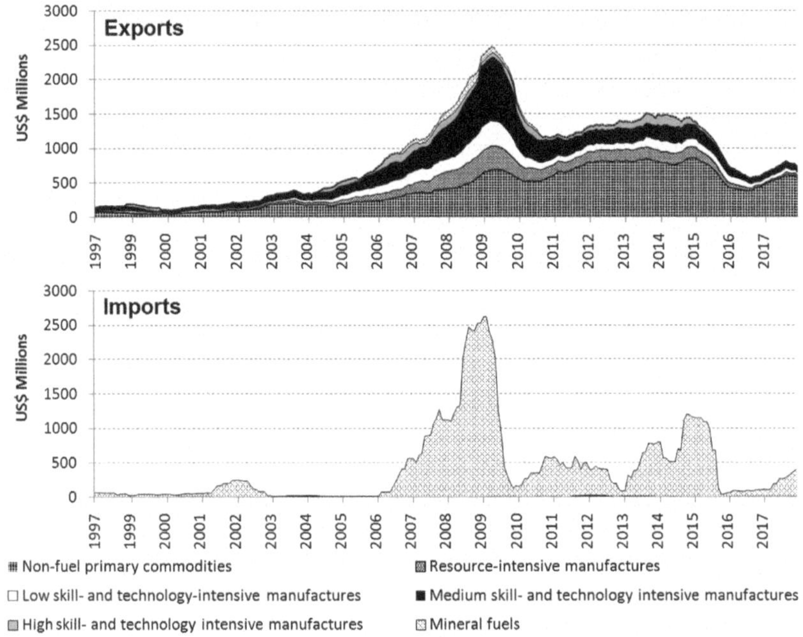

Fig. 3.8 Technological content of Brazilian imports and exports from/to the Portuguese-speaking countries of Africa (12 months accumulated value US$ FOB) (*Source* Brazilian Ministry of Industry, Foreign Trade and Services, deflated to 2017 prices by US CPI)

Angola is by far the largest recipient in Africa of foreign direct investments from Brazil, accounting for almost 50 per cent of the stock of outward investment positions of Brazil, followed by South Africa, Mozambique and Ghana (Fig. 3.9). Nonetheless, the whole African continent represents only a small fraction of all Brazilian outward investment (1.1 per cent in 2012 and 0.5 per cent in 2016). In values, the stock of Brazilian investments in Angola peaked in 2012–2014 with a mean of US$1.4 billion. In 2016, this figure had dropped to US$0.5 billion.

The investments in Angola had two main destinations: oil production and civil construction. Actually, the sectors are intertwined because the main drive of the rapid growth of Angolan economy was the oil sector, and as a consequence the construction sector was also in high demand. Petrobras and the largest Brazilian construction companies

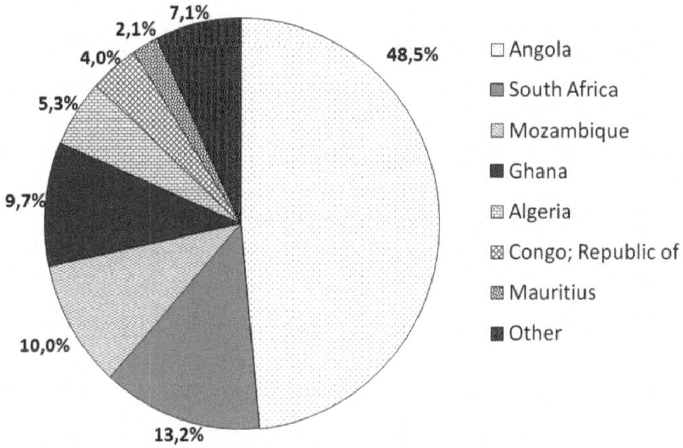

Fig. 3.9 Brazilian outward direct investment positions (Stock) 2016; US Dollars (*Source* Authors' elaboration based on data from the IMF Coordinated Direct Investment Survey [CDIS])

established themselves, or strengthened their positions, in Angola in this period, often with government support, predominantly in financing (especially through the Brazilian development bank, BNDES) (Rodrigues and Gonçalves 2016). The scale of Brazilian investment was very significant from an Angolan perspective: at one point, the Brazilian construction firm Odebrecht was the largest private employer in Angola.[15] At a second level, South Africa, Mozambique and Ghana are also recipients of important flows of direct investment from Brazil.

Since 2015, however, the same Brazilian economic actors present in Africa (Petrobras, the construction companies and BNDES) are suffering in the domestic market. A change in the federal government imposed an orthodox view of the economy and BNDES's role in national development. The bank had its loans reduced to a third of the 2014 level. At the same time, the economy entered into a recession that destroyed the interest for investments and consequently eroded the construction sector's demand base. A wide range of corruption allegations arose, involving politicians and, among others, the biggest Brazilian construction companies. Finally, in the oil sector Petrobras was also involved in the corruption scandals and started a strong deleverage period, selling assets in Brazil and abroad. The extent of the retraction of the Brazilian companies in Africa is still not clear. The investments of African companies in Brazil are quite low.

This section has shown that economic relations between Brazil and Africa are still lower than the importance of their economies, and therefore represent abundant opportunities for increasing integration. Nevertheless, it would be important to take a more horizontal approach, notably through the diversification of the goods traded on both sides, and collaboration in technological development. This can not, however, be obtained as a natural result of deeper economic integration—that can lead to even higher asymmetries[16]—but has to be politically oriented. In this sense, the dialogues within BRICS are important.

Conclusions

The importance of BRICS in the contemporary international economy is unquestionable. Despite the recent crises in Russia, South Africa and Brazil, the regional role of these countries, the size of their consumer markets and their natural wealth mean that global economic agents cannot ignore them. Nevertheless, attention directed by international investors—and also by central governments—at these countries does not necessarily mean changing the international order to a more inclusive one. On the contrary, the history of the creation of the acronym BRIC illustrates a point of view that sees these countries as an object: as a source of raw materials and industrial products at low prices; as a source of cheap labour; and as a source of highly profitable financial assets.

Instead of accepting this passive role, the BRICS governments have decided to move in the direction of changing their positions in the international arena—but this is difficult within already existing multilateral institutions, since they tend to perpetuate the hierarchy of power already established. The BRICS therefore decided to: (i) synchronise their demands within the 'old' institutions (notably the WTO, the IMF and the WB); and (ii) create new institutions. Thus, the BRICS have structured themselves as a subject, which stands against the status quo and is fighting for a new order.

The difficulties are considerable, since the central countries do not accept these demands easily and because the complexity of the international economy does not allow rapid changes in certain dimensions (for example, money). Nevertheless, the potential for deepening the integration of BRICS is enormous; in the dimension of trade, investment, finance and money (as discussed in this chapter) but also in science and technology, agriculture, food security, cybersecurity and so on.

Finally, it is important to refer to a very important challenge: despite the efforts to build a stronger governance structure in the BRICS institutions, it is clear that there are some hierarchies even among BRICS countries. China is the most powerful country. This power—economic, but also political—inevitably creates the risk of asymmetry among the BRICS that would be at odds with its original purpose. It may be seen for instance through the standard of trade that has been established among BRICS countries, having China as the exporter of industrial goods and the importer of mineral and agricultural goods from the other countries. In any case, it is better for Brazil, Russia, India and South Africa to actively participate in this construction and face the risk than to passively accept the existing hierarchies.

Concerning economic relations between Brazil and Africa, the chapter shows up some important features. First of all, it is clear that this relationship also involves some asymmetries since, in this case, Brazilian exports tend to be in more dynamic sectors whereas African exports tend to be concentrated in petroleum and derivatives. Brazilian investments in Africa are much higher than the other way round. We see therefore that in this case the concept of 'semi-periphery' is quite useful to designate the Brazilian role in the international division of labour, since its total external trade is dominated by exports of commodities and imports of industrial goods, but with Africa the standard trade is different. Moreover, Brazilian investments in Africa are much higher than the other way round.

Secondly, the chapter shows that the deepening of economic relations between Brazil and Africa in the twenty-first century has been mainly due to: (i) the economic boom (in the world, but particularly in Brazil, from 2004 to 2010); and (ii) political choices made during Lula's government, which defined relations Brazil–Africa as a priority. In this sense, it is not quite correct to say that the constitution of BRICS enhanced these relations. Actually, the involvement of the Brazilian government with the initiatives that led to the constitution of BRICS must be also understood in the light of the priority given to South–South relations. It does not mean, however, that the inclusion of South Africa in the BRICS bloc is not welcome in the sense of deepening this Brazil–Africa economic relations. The chapter has revealed that the most important economies in Latin America and Africa still do not have economic relations compatible with their economic sizes, showing significant potential for future collaboration. Moreover, their productive structures are not so asymmetrical, allowing economic relations that may be not based in the concentration of low added value on one side and high added value on the other side.

One possible problem is that after the institutional breakdown in Brazil,[17] its foreign policy changed substantially and the current government (under president Michel Temer) is explicitly in favour of more collaboration with the Western countries and less with the Southern countries.[18] Even so, Brazilian civil society (including the universities, but also the entrepreneurs) knows how important it is to enhance economic relations with BRICS countries. In this sense, we expect that the economic recovery in Brazil, South Africa and Russia will be interconnected to a new phase of strengthening the BRICS bloc.

Notes

1. This summit involved the heads of governments of Brazil (Luís Inácio Lula da Silva), Russia (Dimitri Medvedev), India (Manmohan Singh) and China (Hu Jintao).
2. Data for 2015.
3. For interesting analyses regarding the Bretton Woods System, see Eichengreen (1998) and Helleiner (1994).
4. The insertion of peripheral countries in the financial globalisation is analysed in Chesnais (1996).
5. Following the framework proposed by the United Nations Economic Commission for Latin America and the Caribbean (ECLAC), this chapter will mention 'central countries' when referring to the global North and 'peripheral countries' when referring to the global South.
6. The discussions about this reform began in 2010, but the US Congress only approved it in December 2015.
7. Declarations made at the seventh summit in Ufa, 2015.
8. This attests to the importance that has been given to BRICS by all governments at that time. In Brazil, this is no longer the case after the institutional breakdown that deposed the elected president Dilma Rousseff and conducted Michel Temer to office. Temer's government gave explicit priority to the relationship with the United States and Western Europe (for details, see his political party's document 'Ponte para o futuro').
9. The most important rating agencies (Fitch, Standard & Poor's and Moody's) reduced the rates of the Brazilian public bonds in 2014–2015 taking part in a campaign of the market agents against Dilma Rousseff's governments that was not necessarily related to the level or trajectory of the Brazilian public debt. For details, see De Conti (2015).

10. Data for 2016. For an analysis of the usage of currencies at the international level, see De Conti and Prates (2016).
11. For instance, the pound sterling kept its role as the key currency of the IMS for a long time after the US economy had already become the most important.
12. The access to the reserve arrangement gives the BRICS countries' central banks more power to defend their currencies against sudden over-depreciations.
13. All values shown in the figures below are in American dollars, Free on Board (FOB), and deflated to 2017 by the consumer price index (CPI) of the US.
14. In 2015 and 2016, Brazilian GDP fell 3.8 per cent and 3.6 per cent respectively.
15. http://africanbusinessmagazine.com/uncategorised/the-brazilian-companies-in-africa/, *African Business Magazine*, 10 December 2012 [accessed 19 September 2018].
16. Due to the trend of specialisation in the international trade.
17. In 2016, the Brazilian president Dilma Rousseff suffered an impeachment process that was quite controversial and is considered by an important part of the Brazilian population as a *coup d'état*.
18. A document published by Michel Temer's political party (namely, 'Ponte para o futuro') declares that his government would give priority to the collaboration with the United States and Western Europe.

Bibliography

Cabral, L., Favareto, A., Mukwereza, L., & Kojo, A. (2016). Brazil's Agricultural Politics in Africa: More Food International and the Disputed Meanings of 'Family Farming'. *World Development, 8*, 47–60.

Chesnais, F. (Ed.). (1996). *La mondialisation financière: genèse, coût et enjeux*. Paris: Syros.

De Conti, B. (2015). A disciplina imposta à periferia: do FMI às agências de rating. In L.G.M. Belluzzo & P.P.Z. Bastos (Eds.), *Austeridade para quem? Balanço e perspectivas do governo Dilma Rousseff*. São Paulo: Carta Maior: Friedrich-Ebert-Stiftung.

De Conti, B., & Prates, D. (2016). *The International Monetary System Hierarchy: Current Configuration and Determinants*. Manchester: 28th Annual EAEPE Conference.

Eichengreen, B. (1998). *Globalizing Capital: A History of the International Monetary System*. Princeton: Princeton University Press.

Fonseca, G. (2013). BRICS: Notes and Questions. In J. V. S. Pimentel (Ed.), *Brazil, BRICS and the International Agenda*. Brasilia: Fundação Alexandre Gusmão.
Helleiner, E. (1994). *States and the Reemergence of Global Finance: From Bretton Woods to the 1990s*. New York: Cornell University Press.
Miyamoto, S. (2011). 'A política externa brasileira para a África no início do novo século: interesses e motivações'. XI Congresso Luso Afro Brasileiro de Ciências Sociais - Diversidade e (Des)igualdades. Salvador 7 a 10 de agosto de 2011.
Oliveira, G. Z. (2015). Política africana do Brasil: mudança entre Lula e Dilma? *Revista Conjuntura Austral*, Porto Alegre, *6*(29), 33–47.
Pinto, G. L., Belmonte, Í., & Pádua, C. D. A.. (2015). Padua 'Exportações brasileiras de máquinas e equipamentos agrícolas para a África: análise da situação atual e do ambiente de negócios'. *BNDES Setorial, 41*, 5–42.
Rodrigues, P. C. S., & Gonçalves, S. D. (2016, January/June). Política externa e investimentos brasileiros em Angola. *Austral: Revista Brasileira de Estratégia e Relações Internacionais, 5*(9), 249–273.
Thorsteinsen, V., & Oliveira, T. M. (2014). *BRICS in the World Trade Organization: Comparative Trade Policies*. Brasília: IPEA.

CHAPTER 4

Ambiguity or Strategic Play? Distilling India's BRICS Relations

Bongane Gasela

Introduction

India is the second fastest growing economy in the developing world. It forms part of the coalition of the developing world countries that seek to challenge the current global order and offer less developed countries an alternative to maladies such as underdevelopment, poverty and unemployment. The BRICS grouping, of which India forms part, has grown in stature as evidenced by the establishment—in which India played an instrumental role, and which it chairs—of its New Development Bank (NDB). This chapter argues, however, that New Delhi finds itself at crossroads by being in the same group of developing countries as its Asia-Pacific competitor, China. Its participation in BRICS is perceived as a means of counterbalancing China's increasing influence and power in Asia. India also seeks to catch up with China on the global stage, hence

B. Gasela (✉)
Johannesburg, South Africa

D. Monyae and B. Ndzendze (eds.), *The BRICS Order*,
International Political Economy Series,
https://doi.org/10.1007/978-3-030-62765-2_4

its forming partnerships with countries that are wary of China's development, and which foresee a future dominated by China and in which the West's influence would be reduced.

The first segment of this chapter is a historical overview of India's economy from the eighteenth century, with the coming of the British during the reign of the Mughal Empire. The argument here is that the arrival of the British marked a watershed, as it ushered in India's modern economic history and its present-day challenges. The subsequent segment details India's contemporary economic performance in a globalised world, and its takeoff between 2008 and 2018. An assessment is made of India's principal exports and imports as well as its major trading partners. The next part discusses India's position and aims within the BRICS coalition vis-à-vis its retention and heightening of alliances with the West. Some scholars detect ambiguity, insofar as New Delhi's involvement in BRICS is an attempt to challenge the West's dominance in the world, but in reality, the chapter argues, India also has relations with the US (its principal export market) and with the European Union. This move is seen as India's endeavour, while it is growing, to balance China and buy time.

India's Economic Profile

A number of significant events took place in the world during the eighteenth century. The Industrial Revolution began in England and spread to other parts of Europe. The discovery of the sea and trade routes by the Portuguese explorer Vasco Da Gama in the sixteenth century had paved the way for the English, Portuguese, Dutch and French to go and do trade in India; the India they dealt with was in the throes of an internal power struggle during the eighteenth century, leading to the dissipation of power of the Mughal Empire. The unfolding conflict afforded the British an opportunity for a stronghold in India. British rule in India was characterised by coercive means to cultivate the land for agricultural produce as well as the export of raw materials to Britain to feed its industries.

India owes its economic success to the economic reforms of 1991 instituted during the time of Prime Minister Narasimha Rao, based on the socialist ideologies initiated by its first prime minister after independence, Jawaharlal Nehru. However, although the causes of India's growth manifested after the economic reforms of 1991, they could be traced to the 1980s and early 1990s when there was an increased accumulation of physical capital, labour productivity and land expansion.

The causes of India's current growth stretch back to the first term in office of Prime Minister Indira Gandhi (1966–1977). Under her leadership, the government adopted the approach which saw the nationalisation of commercial banks; they were expanded into branches which opened in both rural and urban areas according to the requirements of the Reserve Bank that prescribed a branch licensing policy.

India's status among the fastest growing economies in the world and one of the most attractive destinations for foreign direct investment. It is also the largest democracy in the world in terms of population, and the second most populous country in the world after China. Its population is divided along lines of religion, ethnicity and caste, with 14 languages (excluding English), 250 minor languages and various dialects. According to statistics provided by Worldometers (2019), the population of India in 2017 was estimated at 1,339,180,127, accounting for 17.74 per cent of the world's population.

Despite its growing economy, India is a poor country with persistent unemployment rates. Its lowest rate of unemployment was in 2014 when it recorded a low of 3.14 per cent. The highest rate of unemployment was in 1983 when it reached 8.3 per cent. In 2017, the rate increased to 3.52. The highest rate of unemployment for the ten-year period 2008–2018 was in 2008 when it reached 4.12 per cent.

According to the projections of the International Monetary Fund, India is likely to overtake Germany as the fourth largest economy in the world by 2022, with a projected GDP of US$10 trillion (Nag 2017).

The notable thing about India's rise is not that it is new, but that its path has been unique. Rather than adopting the classic Asian strategy of exporting labour-intensive, low-priced manufactured goods to the West, India has relied on its domestic market more than exports, consumption more than investment, services more than industry and high-tech more than low-skilled manufacturing (Das 2006). This approach has meant that the Indian economy has been largely insulated from global downturns, showing a degree of stability that is as impressive as the rate of its expansion. The consumption-driven model is also more people-friendly than other development strategies.

India's Trade

India's Aggregate Exports for One Year (September 2017–August 2018)

India's exports were US$27.84 billion in August 2018, as compared to US$23.36 billion in August 2017, illuminating a growth of 19.21 per cent. The exports were improved by petroleum exports which account for 31.8 per cent followed by the sale of jewellery and gem at 24 per cent, engineering products at 21.2 per cent and pharmaceutical and drugs accounting for 18.2 per cent.

At 16.5 per cent of total exports, India's largest trading partner for the year 2017 was the US. Of Indian exports to the US, pearls, precious stones, metals and coins valued at US$7.43 made up 21 per cent, the largest segment. The second largest were pharmaceutical products (9.9 per cent of India's exports to the US, to the value of US$3.44 billion). The third largest comprised machinery, boilers and nuclear reactors (5.9 per cent of the exports to the value of US$2.07 billion).

The second largest destination is the United Arab Emirates, which receives 9.7 per cent (at US$20.8 billion) of India's total exports. The exports comprise pearls, precious stones and metals, making up 39 per cent of New Delhi's exports to Abu Dhabi. The second largest group of export products to the UAE are mineral fuel, oils and distillation products (15 per cent with a value of US$3.04 billion). Clothing exports account for 6 per cent of the exports to the UAE.

India's third largest destination for exports is Hong Kong. The share of exports from India to Hong Kong is 5 per cent, valued at US$10.8 billion, with the lion's share attributed to precious stones, pearls and metals accounting for 44 per cent of India's total exports to Hong Kong.

China, the fastest growing economy in the BRICS grouping, and India's competitor for power in the Asia-Pacific region, is India's fourth largest exports destination at 4.3 per cent of India's total exports and with a value of US$9.1 billion.

In recent years, India's exports have largely been made up of pearls, precious and semi-precious stones and jewellery, and accounting for 16 per cent of New Delhi total's aggregate consignments. The next most exported goods (at 12 per cent of total exports) comprise oils, mineral fuels, wax and bituminous substances. The value share of vehicle parts and accessories is similar to that of machinery and mechanical appliances, which accounts for 5 per cent of India's aggregate exports.

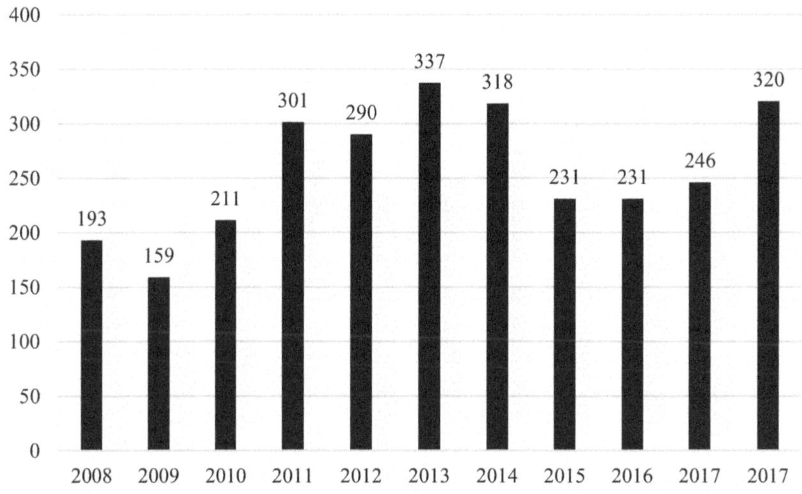

Fig. 4.1 India's exports for the ten-year period from 2008 to 2018 (in billions of USD) (*Source MIT Observatory of Economic Complexity*)

The figure below projects India's trade trajectory for a ten-year period, from 2008 to 2018. It is a positive growth trajectory. The lowest number of exports recorded by New Delhi was in 2009, after the 2007–2008 global financial crisis. Since then, India's exports have been on the rise, with 2011 showing the highest level (Fig 4.1).

Imports

In August 2018, imports to India increased 25 per cent year on year to US$45.24 billion. India's highest purchases comprise gold, petroleum, crude and machinery, accounting for 92.6 per cent, 51.6 per cent and 46.2 per cent, respectively. India's major import partners are China, the US, UAE, Saudi Arabia and Switzerland (Fig 4.2).

India's growth trajectory is likely to see it surpass Japan in 2030 as the third largest economy in the world. Given India's rise, and what many scholars have written about emerging economies, it is possible that India might want a place in the world concomitant with its economic

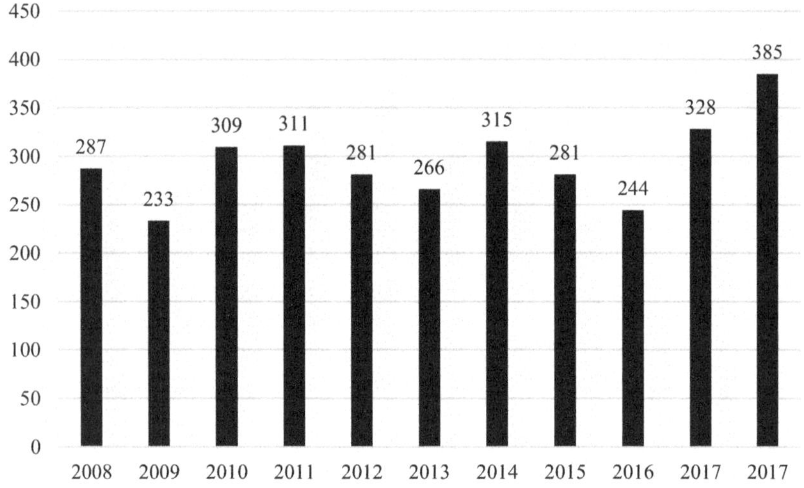

Fig. 4.2 India's aggregate imports from 2008 to 2018 (in billions of USD) (*Source: MIT Observatory of Economic Complexity*)

status. The following sections of this chapter seek to address this question, couched in a discussion of the broader determining factors of Indian foreign policy, eventuating into the question of what India wants from the BRICS.

Indian Foreign Policy

The foreign policy of India is a by-product of a number of factors. New Delhi's approach to international relations is conditioned by the history of the country, geographical factors, its national interests and ideological elements.

The history of India plays a role in past and present foreign policy under different leaders since its independence in 1947. When India gained independence from Britain—which led to the partitioning of the country into two (India and Pakistan) on a religious basis—the country was experiencing modest growth rates of about 3 per cent per year coupled with high levels of illiteracy (14 per cent) and a life expectancy average of 26 years. From these domestic realities, India's government under the leadership of Nehru (1947–1964) was faced with the task of building the nation from the ruins of years of colonialism and the partitioning, which led to the mass movement of people and disruptions of the social fabric. Bringing back socio-economic normalcy to India at this period had to contend with the Cold War between the US and the Soviet Union. Prime Minister Nehru adopted the non-alignment policy which meant that India chose not to belong to either side of the ideological bipolar world, between the two superpowers. The non-alignment ideology was the blueprint for India's foreign policy under the Nehru administration; belonging to either side was perceived by Nehru as defeating India's hard-fought independence by forming part of an ideological grouping of states and, by default, being pitted against states on the opposite side.

However, India's resolve to stay faithful to non-alignment was put to a test insofar as its neighbouring states were belonging to either side of the conflict between superpowers. Its immediate neighbour, Pakistan, was in an alliance with the US while China was in a (sometimes troubled) alliance with the Soviet Union. India's objective in not aligning to either side was because it believed peaceful coexistence was an elixir to remedy its socio-economic problems and would enable the country to adopt an inward-looking approach so as to pay attention to its development.

Neither of the two conflicting superpowers indicated interest in India at the onset of the Cold War (Ganguly and Pardesi 2009). The Soviet Union did not have any vested interest in India. Although India received $255 million of the US$5.9 billion given by the US to Asian countries in 1953 (during but separate from the time of the Marshall Plan for post-war recovery in Europe) while Pakistan obtained around US$98 million, the US showed scant interest in a nation which was in the process of building itself up in the wake of colonialism and partitioning (Ganguly and Pardesi 2009).

India cashed in on the lack of interest from the US and the Soviet Union by affording itself the opportunity to assert its peace-intended non-alignment ideology to the poor countries of the time, most of which belonged to the African continent. New Delhi hosted the Asian Relations Conference in 1947, and played a leading role at the Bandung Conference of 1955 which India used for asserting its view on the unfolding global socio-economic events characterised by Western domination of the international political economy.

The non-aligned policy brought about improvement in India. New Delhi experienced considerable growth of 3.5 per cent per annum, and the nation's institutions such as the military were strengthening—this strength was manifest in the 1971 war against Pakistan for the eventual independence of East Pakistan (Bangladesh) and the testing of its nuclear weapons in 1974.

Geographical Factors

Geography is another great determinant of a nation's foreign policy. In analysing the strengths and weaknesses of a nation's external posture, therefore, we must also take into consideration the geographical realities with which that country is faced (Alam 2015). Geographical aspects such as demographics, the size of the territory, accessibility to the territory from outside its frontiers and natural resources play a key role in formulating a country's standpoint in relation to its neighbours and peers in international relations.

Since its independence, the geographical position of India has played a central role in the formulation of the foreign policy as indicated by Nehru when he said:

> Look at the map. If you have to consider any question affecting the Middle East, India inevitably comes into the picture. If you have to consider any question concerning South-East Asia, you cannot do so without India. So is also with the Far-East. While the Middle-East may not be directly connected with South East Asia, both are connected with India. Even if you think in terms of regional organizations in India, you have to keep in touch with the other regions. And whatever region you have in mind, the importance of India cannot be ignored. (Sharma 2016)

India is situated in the middle of Asia and is the largest littoral state in the Indian Ocean, which is of geo-economic relevance to the world economy. More than 60 per cent of the world's oil and petroleum is conveyed through the Indian Ocean. Economic activities around the Indian Ocean are critical for the stability and security of India, as the ocean is home to vast deposits of oil and gas. In this regard, India has a role to play in ensuring peace and stability in the Indian Ocean. India's policy framework towards the territories in the Asia-Pacific hinges on forging cooperation through the Indian Ocean Rim Association (IORA) with the help of a strong navy.

The size of the Indian territory plays a crucial role from a security standpoint as it would be difficult for any other country to invade it. However, size alone cannot be a determinant in the formulation of a foreign policy in terms of security. For example, Britain with its small territorial size (in relation to other states) colonised many countries, including India (before it was partitioned). Size has to be coupled with other factors such as natural resources. Despite its size, India's military defeat in the Sino-Indian war of 1962 (over the Aksai Chin and Arunachal Pradesh border regions claimed by both countries) was a watershed in the structure of its foreign policy from the viewpoint of security. Nehru became a supporter of defence spending and reconsidered India's security policies, and India started a military modernisation programme which saw the strengthening of its air force and the expansion of its navy.

Foreign Policy Making

India's process of making foreign policy is usually unaffected by the general elections that frequently take place. The non-alignment policy of India since its independence was a constant presence in the formulation of foreign policy as its sought to continue its multi-alignment approach in the interest of its domestic socio-economic realities such as poverty—which India seeks to alleviate by economic development through partnership with strategic countries under the auspices of platforms such as the United Nations (UN) and the World Trade Organization (WTO).

India's priorities and patterns have been in flux since its independence in 1947. After the adoption of the new constitution on 26 November 1949, under the leadership of Jawaharlal Nehru, the economy was to be a centrally planned one, with the government seeking to promote the welfare of the people by affording a conducive economic and political environment. The Nehruvian vision of a prosperous India was envisioned through three five-year plans extending from 1951 to 1966. The first five-year plan (1951–1956) put emphasis on food security through increased agricultural production as an introductory phase for industrial development in the subsequent five-year plans. During this phase, India's economic policy was inward-looking as the world was divided into the two spheres of influence during the Cold War. This plan yielded considerable outcomes, achieving a GDP of 3.6 per cent against a target of 2.1 per cent (Sumitra 2015).

The second five-year plan (1956–1961) was constructed around self-reliance and growing India's heavy industry, with the aim of reducing the importation of producer goods. In adherence to the state's socialist economic arrangement, the plan recommended the installation of goods-producing industries in the government-controlled sectors of the economy. The growth trajectory during this phase was laudable, as the economy achieved a growth rate of 3.9 per cent per annum against an ambitious objective of 4.5 per cent (Sumitra 2015).

The third five-year plan (1961–1966) was a continuation of the preceding phase. Emphasis was placed on heavy industry and a signficant level of attention was paid to agriculture. This phase revealed widening gaps between the targets and the achievements of the phases and it is on these gulfs that the third five-year plan was based: the implementation of strategies for increased production and human resource development. This phase was dealt a blow as a result of a border dispute between China and India which led to the Sino-India War of 1962, won by China.

The policies mentioned above reflect India's economic priorities in that period. In contemporary times India has found itself at a crossroads. It is advocating for the recognition of Third World countries as significant players internationally, and it is on a search for world recognition as a global power, possibly using the BRICS grouping to challenge the current global order. At the same time, however, India maintains relations with countries that champion the current global order, particularly the US and the European Union.

BRICS, India and the Current Global Order

India is a strong voice within BRICS. It is against any proposal that may impede the growth of the coalition, and it turned down China's proposal to invite Pakistan, Sri Lanka and Mexico into BRICS because it believed that the focus should be on developing the current members of the group and that a large membership would present the bloc with too many differences.

India has attached more significance to the BRICS than other multilateral groupings. For example, when the UN imposed sanctions on Russia, India continued trading with Russia, signing a US$400 billion military defence deal. India is playing a leading role within the BRICS by challenging the global status quo in multilateral institutions. New Delhi aspires to challenge the US dollar as the international currency, calling for a diversified international monetary system, and has begun advocating for intra-BRICS trade with members using their own currencies. Doing away with the US dollar as the international currency would be a step towards crumbling the world economic order in which powers is concentrated in the Western countries. The creation of cryptocurrency for the BRICS is likely to be perceived as a huge blow to US dominance. Although this may seem ideal, it is highly likely that China, the second largest economy in the world and the largest in the BRICS grouping, would seek to close the gap left by the US, and advocate for the use of the yuan as the denominator currency. Efforts to displace the US dollar have already begun, with China announcing a crude oil futures contract that would be denominated by the Chinese yuan and could be converted to gold using the Shanghai and Hong Kong exchange rates (Garrie 2017). While India may be in support of de-dollarisation, it may also reject China's move towards filling the void by giving the Chinese yuan a leverage over other currencies. This may put further strains on the unstable friendship between India and China.

The establishment of the BRICS Development Bank is an achievement of great proportions in the light of challenging and offering an alternative to the International Monetary Fund (IMF) Western-dominated financial institutions which dictate economic reforms to the borrower. The establishment of the Bank illuminated Indo-Sino rivalry when the location of the headquarters was being discussed. India proposed New Delhi, a proposition challenged by China, which wanted Shanghai. China garnered the most votes to be the host country of the New Development Bank, and to pacify India an Indian national got the presidentship of the bank (Mishra and Roche 2014).

Counterbalancing China

The growing influence of China is another factor that informs India's foreign policy. India has expressed opposition to the unipolarity in multilateral institutions and BRICS is not insulated as China's influence is growing; it is the largest economy in the grouping and seeks to use the BRICS to enhance its Belt and Road Initiative (BRI), a flagship of its foreign policy and a pedestal of power in the Asia-Pacific, the developing world and the world. New Delhi sees China's BRI as a threat to the development of other BRICS nations because the BRI stands to benefit China substantially at the expense of other members. India showed its opposition to the BRI by not attending China's Silk Road forum but instead announced a proposal to establish its silk road with the US, in the form of a highway to Thailand. Behind the scenes of the Silk Road forum, India also announced the proposal of a north–south corridor with Russia.

As India's economy continues to grow, India will most probably continue attaching great importance to BRICS and will work to ensure stability within BRICS to ensure the smooth flow of trade with fellow BRICS members. India's efforts at promoting peace have expanded beyond BRICS as evidenced by its peacekeeping activities in North Africa, the Mediterranean and the Indian Ocean. New Delhi has also been aiding the Tibetan fight for independence, and providing assistance and refuge to the Rohingya people. By helping Tibetans and the Rohingyas, India seeks to counterbalance China's influence in the Asia-Pacific as it is wary of China's assertive role. Championing peacekeeping in North Africa would present India with favourable terms in its relations with Africa's economic powerhouse, South Africa.

India's approach to the BRICS has been put in the spotlight with reference to its role in other multilateral groupings. The significance of BRICS to India has generated varied opinions from its scholars and policymakers. In the pecking order, the G20 is perceived as more important to India than the BRICS. The erstwhile director of the Indian Council for Research on International Economic Relations (ICRIER), once argued that BRICS is not of significant importance to most Indians as it does not have an effect on solving social woes or foreign policy objectives. With regard to the latter, Wulf and Debiel (2015) argue that India's foreign policy changed between 1990 and 2010 owing to changes in government.

The nature of BRICS as a non-alliance grouping affords the member states the latitude to pursue their interests, whether fostering cooperation or entrenching competition with rivals and fellow BRICS members. With this being said, in its quest for global power status India has used the latitude afforded by the BRICS to take an ambiguous stance vis-à-vis China in the sense that it cooperates with China on one hand and competes with it on the other.

The efficacy of the BRICS coalition depends on all its member states and more so on China. India should tread with caution and circumvent disputes that could lead to friction and fragmentation within BRICS (Nataraj 2016). An example would be the growth in animosity between India and China over the South China Sea, as well the trade deficit between the two countries, which would divide the BRICS grouping as the two disputing countries would seek to enlist the support of fellow BRICS members.

In terms of the trade deficit between India and China, the former cautioned the latter at the WTO—after China reiterated that it would increase its imports from India—that the US$63 billion trade deficit was indefensible and bridging the gap needed much more than lip-service (Sen 2018). The Indian government argued that China needed to put effort into lowering the trade barriers for its products such as pharmaceuticals, rice, meat and IT products, so as to balance the trade differences.

While BRICS may be conceived as trying to undermine the Western-dominated global order, this may not be so, as all BRICS countries, and in this case India, have cordial relations with the West.

India and the West

India, the UK and the EU

The relationship between India and the EU has a complex historical context: the connection between Europe and South Asia. From as far back as the 1960s, India was one of the countries to establish relations with the developing EU (or European Economic Community as it was then called). The legal framework of the ties between India and the EU was formulated in 1994 (the delay in formulating a legal framework is owed to the exclusion of India from the Lomé Convention of 1975, after France, Italy and Belgium advocated for a regional approach to forming a partnership with Third World countries, and the European Commission opted to establish relations with African countries instead of India). India later signed an agreement for commercial and economic cooperation with the EU which restricted bilateral relations to no more than economic relations. This is reflective of the narrow relationship that forms the basis of present-day relations between India and the EU (Kavalski 2015).

Present-day relations between New Delhi and Brussels are founded upon the aforementioned 1994 EU-India Cooperation Agreement which provided a legal framework for EU–India relations. However, the free trade agreement for which negotiations started in 2007 has yet to materialise. Relations between India and the EU have been hit by complications insofar as the UK voted to exit the EU, which has painted a murky picture of future relations. The future of economic relations between India and the UK will only be clear when UK is officially out of the EU and facing restricted movement of goods, services and people—and would seek to foster ties with India as New Delhi could offer investment opportunities. Currently, there is a large number of Indian companies operating in the UK, coupled with a significant Indian diaspora. The UK has realised the strategic importance of India to its economy and has negotiated free trade agreements (shelved until the UK is officially out of the EU).

India and the EU have a partnership on Foreign Policy and Cooperation which seeks to address security issues at various summits including at the G20, where New Delhi and Brussels have forged a macroeconomic dialogue for discussing and exchanging economic experiences and structural reforms. The EU has extended support to India in developing plans for sustainable development, water and waste management, transport, industry and city to city cooperation.

With regard to research and innovation, a field growing to greater prominence in the context of the 4th Industrial Revolution, the EU is India's leading partner in publications. New Delhi also participates in the European Commission's innovation and research programme known as the Horizon 2020, which the Indian Department of Science and Technology and the Department of Biotechnology joined in 2016, and the Ministry of Earth Sciences which started participating in 2018. Indian students are the largest beneficiaries from Third World countries of the EU's Erasmus Programmes on Higher Education, and the number of Indians studying in Europe increases every year owing to the EU scholarships.

There are uncertainties over India's investments in the EU (and vice versa), as the EU is the second largest investor in India and accounts for one-quarter of all investments flowing into India which are instrumental in creating employment. The exit of the UK from the EU will have a negative impact on India's investments in the EU because Indian companies in the UK have employees from various EU countries and the restriction of people's movement would affect their productivity (Nair 2018).

The Indian Prime Minister Narendra Modi's visit to the UK, after the invitation from the British government to attend the Commonwealth meeting, signalled the growing desire on the UK's part to form economic ties with India. While the UK invited India to the Commonwealth so as to form economic ties for the post-Brexit era, India could not have rejected the invitation as it would present India with a chance of augmenting its role in the Commonwealth (Roy-Chaudhury 2018).

India and the US

India has good relations with the US despite its misgivings about America's dominance in institutions such as the UN, the WB and the IMF.

A clear strategic coming together of India and the US is hinged on balancing China's rise in the international system in the case of the US, and in the Indo-Pacific region in the case of India (Tourangbam 2018). The relations between India and the US are also described as a 'global strategic partnership' on the basis of democratic values, India being the oldest democracy in the world and America perceived as the most democratic country and the voice for democratic principles and good governance in multinational institutions such as the UN and the IMF. The two countries' bilateral commitments are based on the mottos 'Forward Together We Go' and 'Shared Effort, Progress For All' which were adopted in 2014 and 2015, respectively, between India's Prime Minister Narendra Modi and former US President Barack Obama. In the following year, the two countries' relations were labelled the 'Enduring global partners in the twenty-first century'. Indo-America cooperation is strategic insofar as it hinges upon an array of areas of common interest to the two countries. There are over 50 dialogue mechanisms between India and the US, on political issues, trade and economics, defence, civil nuclear cooperation, environmental issues, energy and climate change, science and technology. The countries interact with each other more than they do with other countries.

The establishment of the BRICS has ramifications for the US. The New Development Bank uses the US dollar as its monetary denominator but its goal is to create a new currency and denounce the use of the US dollar—which will depend on whether the IMF will work together with the US in creating projects for the developing countries and grant rising economies such as India the status they deserve. Unless the US pushes for reforms in the IMF the BRICS coalition will continue advancing the New Development Bank and will seek not to use the US dollar as the denominator currency (Rohde 2015).

The relations between India and the US are aligned on issues that, inter alia, involve China's growing global influence and Belt and Road Initiative, and the China–Pakistan economic corridor that stretches across Kashmir a territory that India calls 'Pakistan-occupied' because illegally occupied (Pant 2017). The Indo-America partnership has taken on a military characteristic as the two countries are now involved in army and naval activities as part of the 'Framework for India-US Defence Relations' that was signed in 2005 and renewed for a further ten-year period in 2015. New Delhi's relationship with Washington defeats the purpose of India's role in the BRICS as well as the principle it stands for: that of a fair and peaceful world. The foreign policy goals of India are ambiguous in this regard, with no clear stance on India's role in the BRICS. India wants a reformed world, but not one reformed along Chinese lines. As a middle power caught between a system it does not think ideal, and a system dominated by its principal rival, its position of ambiguity is appreciable. India may also be using the West to buy some time against China, as it builds up its own power bases (economic, political and even military).

Conclusion

The chapter gave an account of India's position in the global political economic system, a sphere where India and fellow members of the BRICS coalition seek to challenge the West's dominance; this unipolarity of power does little to help the countries of the developing world disentangle themselves from the shackles of underdevelopment and poverty. As part of the BRICS grouping, India plays a rather calculated role, as it uses BRICS to advance its national interests: to grow its economy by integrating with the affluent countries of the global South as well as to keep check and balance on the meteoric rise of China's influence in both the developing world and the world at large. On the other hand, India has relations with the same countries whose unfair dominance in the international economic and political system the BRICS seeks to diminish. There could not be a clearer indication of India's double-pronged approach than its stance of both asserting and complementing the West by keeping tabs on China's growth and by using the West to grow its own economy.

India's latitude in practising its multipronged foreign policy suggests that BRICS is not an anti-West alliance but one that complements the West. What BRICS seeks to achieve is to play a role in advancing the needs of the developing countries which are marginalised in the current global order institutions.

Bibilography

Alam, Z. (2015). Geo-Strategic Dimensions of India's Foreign Policy. *International Journal of Science and Research, 4*(1), 819–822.

Das, G. (2006). The India Model. *Foreign Affairs, 85*(4), 2–16. https://doi.org/10.2307/20032037.

Ganguly, S., & Pardesi, M. S. (2009). Explaining Sixty Years of India's Foreign Policy. *India Review, 8*(1), 4–19. https://doi.org/10.1080/14736480802665162.

Garrie, A. (2017, September 7). BRICS for Gold: A Dollar-Smashing Monetary Revolution. *Asia Times*. http://www.atimes.com/brics-gold-dollar-smashing-monetary-revolution/.

Kavalski, E. (2015). The EU–India Strategic Partnership: Neither Very strategic, nor Much of a Partnership. *Cambridge Review of International Affairs, 29*(1), 192–208.

Mishra, A. R., & Roche, E. (2014). Brics Bank: Can India Counter China's Ambitions? *Live Mint*. https://www.livemint.com/Politics/X2uUr1PwXujyW4Y3yXxU8H/Brics-bank-Can-India-thwart-China-ambitions.html.

Nair, S. S. (2018, June 20). Post Brexit World—India's Trade Relations with the EU and UK. *RSA*. https://www.thersa.org/discover/publications-and-articles/rsa-blogs/2018/06/post-brexit-world—indias-trade-relations-with-eu-and-uk.

Nag, A. (2017). India to Overtake Germany in 2022, Oust Britain from Top 5 Economies After 2017. *Live Mint*. https://www.livemint.com/Politics/isicV1nvsRrnVJpcFgZ1CL/India-to-overtake-Germany-in-2022-oust-Britain-from-top-5-e.html.

Nataraj, G. (2016, September 27). India can't Use BRICS to Raise Stature Till Interests with China Converge. *Financial Express*. https://www.financialexpress.com/opinion/india-cant-use-brics-to-raise-stature-till-interests-with-china-dont-converge/392831/.

Pant, H. V. (2017). India Challenges China's Intentions on One Belt, One Road Initiative. *Yale Global Online*. https://yaleglobal.yale.edu/content/india-challenges-chinas-intentions-one-belt-one-road-initiative.

Rohde, V. (2015). *BRICS and the New Development Bank: Impact on the US Economy and the Dollar*. A with Honors Project 145. https://spark.parkland.edu/ah/145.

Roy-Chaudhury, R. (2018, April 17). India's New Political Interest in the Commonwealth. *IISS*. https://www.iiss.org/blogs/analysis/2018/04/india-interest-commonwealth.

Sen, A. (2018, July 12). India Tells China: $63-b Trade Deficit Untenable. *The Hindu Business Line*. https://www.thehindubusinessline.com/economy/macro-economy/63-b-trade-deficit-untenable-india-tells-china/article24401094.ece.

Sharma, S. (2016). India's Foreign Policy Since Independence. *International Journal of Research in Social Sciences, 6*(10), 394–398.

Sumitra, G. C. W. Bhodiakhera. (2015). Analysis of Five Year Plan in India. *International Journal of Management and Social Sciences Research (IJMSSR), 4*(7), 53–57.

Tourangbam, M. (2018, July 10). What's Next for India-US Relations? *The Diplomat*. https://thediplomat.com/2018/07/whats-next-for-india-us-relations/.

Worldometers. (2019). http://www.worldometers.info/world-population/india-population/.

Wulf, H., & Debiel, T. (2015). India's 'Strategic Autonomy' and the Club Model of Global Governance: Why the Indian BRICS Engagement Warrants a Less Ambiguous Foreign Policy Doctrine. *Strategic Analysis, 39*(1), 27–43.

CHAPTER 5

China, Economic Partnership, Common Development and BRICS

Garth Shelton

Introduction—The BRICS Vision

Jim O'Neill's year 2000 prediction that over time the BRIC grouping of countries would surpass the G7 in terms of combined GDP and consumer expenditure is rapidly becoming a reality. Indeed, the BRICS (Brazil, Russia, India, China and South Africa) economies originally grew faster than O'Neill's (2011: 4) prediction, and are now set to dominate the top ten economies in the world. Today, the BRICS cannot accurately be defined as 'emerging markets'; in reality they are the 'new growth markets' which over time will come to dominate the global economy based on combined population size and industrial capacity (O'Neill 2018). Despite recent slower growth in some BRICS countries, Goldman Sachs projects that by 2030 the BRICS economies will form the foundation of the global economic system (Wilson and Purushothaman 2003). The market capitalisation of BRICS economies is expected to total

G. Shelton (✉)
Wits University, Johannesburg, South Africa

D. Monyae and B. Ndzendze (eds.), *The BRICS Order*, International Political Economy Series,
https://doi.org/10.1007/978-3-030-62765-2_5

US$80 trillion by 2030, making up over 55 per cent of global equity capitalisation.

There are many challenges and opportunities for advancing intra-BRICS trade and investment. Arguably, the 'S' in BRICS represents not only South Africa, but also Africa as a whole, which needs to be integrated into the BRICS development process (Satheakge 2017b: 2). The immense hydrocarbon and mineral wealth of the African continent could be mobilised to promote long-term urbanisation and economic growth in BRICS economies. At the same time, well-managed African economies can benefit from the BRICS relationship, bringing mutually cooperative beneficial development to both Africa and BRICS countries. Building a stronger domestic economic environment would have advantages for BRICS investors, and would thus create a 'win-win' situation ensuring benefits for both BRICS and Africa.

China's economic rise and participation in the BRICS grouping provides the African continent with a range of new development partners and opportunities unmatched in its postcolonial history. China's strategic engagement with BRICS offers a unique opportunity to promote a new and innovative development path. BRICS investments and infrastructure development programmes are expected to underpin and promote continued economic growth in BRICS countries, as well as in other developing countries, through a process of expanded South–South collaboration, policy coordination and economic cooperation. The New Development Bank (NDB) is well positioned to facilitate accelerated economic development in BRICS countries, Africa and the global South as a whole (Satheakge 2017a: 3).

Following the 10th BRICS summit in Johannesburg in 2018, the BRICS system is expected to be strengthened and expanded through the participation of other developing countries via the BRICS dialogue system and BRICS-Plus process. Moreover, BRICS is expected to advance industrialisation, infrastructure construction and to promote full participation in the fourth industrial revolution. Other issues where progress is expected include BRICS cooperation over peacekeeping in Africa, promotion of gender equality, intra-BRICS tourism, intra-BRICS investment and improved healthcare mechanisms. It is also hoped that increased BRICS interaction with Africa will support and advance South Africa's National Development Plan (NDP) and the AU's Agenda 2063 development programme.

Mutual respect and shared learning through the BRICS process form the basis for cooperation in a multipolar world, at the same time promoting peace and global harmony. Africa is expected to increasingly look to BRICS as its key development and geopolitical partner. Over time, the global financial, economic and political systems will be restructured through a constructive evolutionary process as the balance of economic capacity becomes more evenly distributed in the global system. BRICS collaboration, cooperation and strategic solidarity can advance and hasten this process, with positive outcomes for developing countries (Yu 2017). Within the next few years, global economic governance institutions, as well as the UN, are expected to transform themselves to reflect the new distribution of economic strength within the international system (Pillai 2014: 66). Without inviting more direct BRICS participation in the global economic policy-making institutions, these institutions will risk losing legitimacy and relevance.

The development of BRICS is likely to be slow and incremental, but, underpinned by solid economic growth in the emerging economies, it is expected to provide a new and positive contribution to the evolution of the international system. BRICS bases its policy on partnership and historical solidarity and seeks a 'win-win' relationship within BRICS and in terms of BRICS interaction with other developing countries. The key to advancing a BRICS 'win-win' relationship is to ensure both international and national cooperation.

The Drivers of China's BRICS Engagement

Given the size and continued rapid growth of China's economy, it is unquestionably the core of the BRICS grouping and is expected to shape the form and content of BRICS cooperation as the organisation evolves. China's very significant financial reserves and industrial capacity underpin the potential success of the BRICS process—thus, China's continued interest in and commitment to BRICS is crucial for the success of the BRICS organisation and process. To the extent that BRICS advances China's national interests, it will become more effective and relevant in the global system. China's motivation for participation in BRICS is therefore a key concern in understanding and assessing the BRICS process. It will be argued below that China has a number of compelling reasons for participation in BRICS, and has specific national interests which can be advanced through BRICS.

Trade and Investment

Intra-BRICS trade has grown from US$567 billion in 2010 to US$744 billion in 2017, confirming the potential for BRICS's economic cooperation (Davies 2018). Trade linkages among BRICS countries suggest that intra-BRICS commercial cooperation is strong, but there is still significant potential for expansion and growth. The challenge for BRICS countries themselves is to expand intra-BRICS trade and investment in order to ensure continued long-term growth, sustainable economies and continued progress towards achieving the sustainable development goals (SDG) (Han 2016). As it is the leading trading nation, an expansion of global trade would be immensely beneficial to China. Moreover, as the BRICS Sanya Declaration (2011) stated:

> Accelerating sustainable growth of developing countries is one of the major challenges for the world. We believe that growth and development are central to addressing poverty and to achieving the MDG goals (now SDG goals). Eradication of extreme poverty and hunger is a moral, social, political and economic imperative of humankind and one of the greatest global challenges facing the world today, particularly in the Least Developed Countries (LDCs) in Africa and elsewhere.

China's economic growth has been largely driven by the export of manufactured products, thus undoubtedly China sees BRICS as a strategic opportunity to expand its export network. At the same time, the importation of oil and commodities remains important for China and underpins trade cooperation within the BRICS framework. International Monetary Fund (IMF) studies confirm China's critical role in generating global economic growth through its increasing prominence as an importer of commodities, goods and services. BRICS and developing countries benefit directly from increased exports to China and are able to generate new growth as a consequence of expanding demand in China.

While China has benefited significantly from trade under the Bretton Woods system, reform and modernisation of that system is in China's long-term interest. Reform of the global trading system (Wang and Tao 2004) (as outlined by the Group of 77 and China in Geneva on 22 August 2003), aimed at improving the access of developing countries to the markets of the developed industrialised economies and strengthening programmes to eradicate poverty, underdevelopment and economic vulnerability on the world's LDCs, could be the road map for China to promote trade reform through BRICS.

There is clearly significant potential for expansion and growth in trade among BRICS countries. China is seeking a mechanism to unlock that potential; at the same time, China expects South Africa to ensure that its BRICS diplomacy is broadly supported by African countries. South Africa's role as a representative (or promoter) of the African continent within BRICS is critically important. BRICS could be decisive in advancing African regional integration which, in turn, will open the way for faster economic growth on the continent—which would benefit China's overall engagement with Africa. Through expanded interaction, the challenges of the developing countries can be debated, and possible solutions for the future outlined (Ai Ping 2013). Reform of global financial institutions could make a major contribution to improving conditions for developing countries to address urgent development needs. BRICS can play a key role in promoting the necessary reforms for a more open global trading system and fairer access to wealthy markets for the developing countries (Ren 2017).

Economic Growth and the Chinese Dream

The 'Chinese Dream' demands continued economic growth to lift its living standards to a higher level. To achieve the Chinese Dream of rejuvenation and prosperity, China needs further to integrate into the global economy, to increase exports and to continue to attract foreign direct investment (FDI). The Communist Party of China (CPC) has identified 2035 as the target date for the establishment of a 'moderately prosperous society', while by 2049 China is expected to become a 'modern socialist country that is prosperous, strong, democratic, culturally advanced, harmonious and beautiful'(Zou 2017: 17). Creating a better life for the Chinese people demands a continued strong growth rate and increased international commercial engagement. Participation in and the strengthening of BRICS would certainly contribute positively to China's efforts to advance economic development and prosperity. China's past four decades of rapid development require another three decades of strong growth to ensure escape from the middle-income trap. A 5–7 per cent annual economic growth for the next 30 years is required to ensure that China reaches its goal of a modern developed country. Economic growth thus remains the focus of China's domestic economic policies and the focus of China's engagement with the world.

Many Chinese scholars contend that BRICS can make good progress if it is based on 'seeking common grounds, while reserving differences' (Hu 2012: 55–56). For China, the priority is to use BRICS to promote continued economic development for the foreseeable future. China is expected to use BRICS to identify new trade and investment opportunities, both within the BRICS grouping and more broadly in the developing world. Increased cooperation among BRICS countries is expected to build a more balanced world economy, improve global economic governance and promote democracy in international relations. Significant changes in the global economic landscape demand that the representation and the voice of emerging markets and developing countries should be increased in the UN, World Bank (WB), IMF and World Trade Organization (WTO). BRICS provides a unique mechanism through which developing countries can advance a global governance reform agenda and a transformation process to implement that agenda (Jain 2017: 8).

Over the last 40 years, China has lifted 700 million people out of poverty and created a modern urbanised and industrialised society. This remarkable achievement offers encouragement to other developing countries and suggests a road map for poverty reduction and increased material prosperity. Inspired by China's success, it is now possible to believe in a world without extreme poverty by the year 2040. Technological progress enables humanity to meet basic human needs throughout the global system and ongoing advances in science have improved health, education and infrastructure to the benefit of many. The world is now capable of sustained social progress and continued poverty reduction. Systematic change in the global structure will create greater stability in the international system and over time all participants will benefit. BRICS, with China at its core, can play a key role in advancing the struggle against poverty (Ji 2012).

Common Development

President Xi Jinping has made it clear that China, BRICS and the developing countries share a common interest in promoting industrialisation and economic growth. He has promised continued engagement with BRICS, despite slowing global growth. Moreover, President Xi has confirmed that 'China will unswervingly follow the path of peaceful development', while it is China's hope that 'all countries in the world will pursue peaceful development' Xi Jinping (2018). China's foreign minister, Wang Yi, has also stressed the importance to China of links with developing countries. Wang has confirmed that 'the developing countries are always the basis of China's diplomacy'. China is committed to continuing to enhance cooperation with other developing countries, and to uphold the rights and interests of the developing countries at the UN, G20, APEC and other platforms. Wang also emphasised that 'China will forever be a reliable friend and sincere partner of the developing countries' (Wang 2013).

China has undertaken to link its own development closely with the economic progress of developing countries, while providing them with support in line with China's own capacity. China shares a natural affinity with the developing countries and thus cooperation within BRICS and the global South is China's preferred form of international engagement. In addition, Chinese leaders have stressed that even when China becomes stronger and more prosperous, it will remain a committed member of the developing world because China and fellow developing countries have a similar past, common development task and shared national interests. BRICS thus serves as a very valuable mechanism for China to advance its conception of common development and shared prosperity.

South–South Cooperation

As a key partner within the BRICS framework, China has confirmed its intention to accelerate South–South cooperation and mutual economic development (Wang 2017). BRICS is being transformed into a global forum to advance South–South cooperation and the G20's role in promoting a global transformation of economic power distribution (Thomashausen 2018). Increased China–Africa trade will advance the development of the African continent and give substance to BRICS objectives to strengthen South–South commercial interaction. Expanded Chinese interaction with BRICS offers significant opportunity for long-term economic growth. In China's view, countries of the global South have a common interest to expand South–South cooperation (Liu 2018).

In the context of advancing South–South cooperation, China promotes appropriate business-to-business dialogues and information-sharing processes to accelerate intra-BRICS trade and investment. This will help to counter the destabilising trend towards antiglobalisation and protectionism. Accelerating sustainable growth in developing countries should be driven by a moral imperative to address poverty and achieve the SDGs as soon as reasonably possible (Hou 2017). BRICS should thus strengthen its philosophy of cooperative development and the commitment to accomplish the SDG targets.

China supports enhanced South–South cooperation in the spirit of the 1955 Bandung Conference's programme for African-Asian solidarity and collaboration to address global injustice, discrimination and the marginalisation of developing countries, as outlined in the New African–Asian Strategic Partnership (NAASP) which underpins China–Africa engagement and forms an overarching framework for the BRICS process in the context of South–South cooperation.

Transforming the Global System of Governance

Originating with the non-aligned movement (NAM), the roles and influences of developing countries in the global arena have steadily grown. The 1955 Bandung Conference asserted the independence and sovereignty of developing countries, while clearly articulating separate interests from the dominant industrialised economies—it was since then that economic growth in the developing countries has increased significantly, resulting in the emergence of the 'global South'. China has led the way among countries of the South with an impressive and sustained growth rate for many years, and a number of other countries, notably India and Brazil, have become important drivers of economic growth. Characterised by impressive growth trajectories, these states have also become more important on the global stage. They are economic centres of gravity within their own regions and have increasing political influence regionally and globally.

United by a common interest to transform the international economic and political system, these emerging markets represent a new shift in the global balance of power (Brookings Institute 2007). The term 'market BRICS' was coined by the corporate sector to identify emerging markets and promising export opportunities, while 'political BRICS' constitutes an informal political grouping focused on promoting common development goals and crafting a new global agenda. BRICS was originally constituted to identify and advance specific economic goals, but political reform has been added to the group's longer-term vision. China is driving the BRICS agenda to suggest a process which can transform global governance towards a more just, democratic and fair system.

President Xi Jinping (2018) has pointed out that 'cooperation among BRICS countries can help build a more balanced world economy, improve global economic governance and promote democracy in international relations'. In terms of reform of global governance, President Xi stressed that it must reflect the very significant changes in the global economic landscape, which demands that the representation and the voice of emerging markets and developing countries should be increased. Moreover, as China's overall national strength is improving, it should follow Chairman Mao Zedong's advice when he stated that 'China ought to make a greater contribution to mankind'.

Over time, the global financial, economic and political system and decision-making processes are expected to be restructured through a constructive evolutionary process as the balance of economic power is distributed more evenly in the system. BRICS collaboration, cooperation and strategic solidarity can advance and hasten this process (Hou and Yu 2017). Within the next ten years, the IMF and the WB (and, later, the UN) will be required to transform themselves to reflect the new distribution of economic power within the international system. Without inviting more direct BRICS participation in the global economic policy-making institutions they will risk losing legitimacy and relevance. Institutional restructuring is inevitable in response to the dominant changes taking place in the global economy, but it will take time.

Through BRICS, China supports and advances global governance reform to reflect the new realities of global power distribution and economic development. Restructuring the UN, in line with the Group of 77 and China's UN Programme for Reform (A/51/950) as well as the Declaration of the Twenty-Seventh Annual Ministerial Meeting of the G-77, would bring strong permanent African and possibly South African, representation to the UN Security Council. Thus BRICS, with strong support from China, could be a key driver for UN reform to the benefit of Africa, South Africa and China itself.

Yu Keping, professor and director of the China Center for Global Governance and Development, points out that reform of global governance lags behind the process of globalisation and is now becoming more urgent. Given the pace and impact of globalisation, global governance needs change, improvement and reorientation. The goal is a democratic, fair, transparent and equitable global governance system which provides adequate space for both big and small international participants. Improving global governance and enhancing the opportunities and positive outcomes of this process, requires the commitment and participation of all countries. Along with its peaceful rise, China has an increasing responsibility to contribute to improvements and changes in global governance.

Huang Renwei (2012), Special Council Member of the China Center for Contemporary World Studies (CCCWS) has suggested that there is now a significant opportunity to reform the global governance system. He proposes that BRICS institutionalises cooperation and transforms a forum into a mechanism to produce joint action and specific policy outcomes. If BRICS countries agree on the form and content of the reform of international institutions, significant progress can be made in transforming the existing global order. Current global governance amounts to 'Western governance', which is not widely supported in the global South. Adjustments and systems changes are required to address the shortcomings of the current system. In the short term, BRICS is expected to form the core of new global governance as the international system evolves.

In China's vision, BRICS is advancing the requirements for a more equitable international order and a broad consensus on a road map for comprehensive reform. Within the new order, both China and developing countries are expected to play a more direct and constructive role in international rule-making and global governance. According to Chinese scholars, in advancing global governance reform, BRICS should focus on mechanism building based on the positive outcomes of recent summits and meetings of high-level officials. Other contributing factors could include: a clear road map and timetable for cooperation which would be helpful in advancing the process; expanding the content of cooperation with a focus on areas where progress can be swift and meaningful; encouraging NGOs and think tanks to conduct research and provide suggestions and ideas for the expansion of BRICS cooperation; cooperating at UN and G20 conferences, where members can advance policy synchronisation; establishing regular dialogue mechanisms with the G8, the OECD and important regional organisations; and strengthening cooperation with second-tier emerging economies and middle powers to build BRICS-associated partnerships and a broader cooperative framework. In seeking to promote the development of a new global governance system, BRICS is advancing new values and new cooperative ideas, offering new strategic thinking, providing new models for global problem solving while advancing global peace, stability and collaboration (Yang 2012).

International Stability

China will remain focused on peaceful development for many more years, as the country needs another 30–40 years of global peace and stability to grow its economy and promote prosperity for all its people. Many rural people are still to receive the benefits of economic growth, thus China must remain focused on promoting overall growth and prosperity.

China's participation in BRICS is motivated by a desire to advance international stability, creating suitable conditions for accelerated economic interaction. Many Chinese scholars have pointed out that China's peaceful rise underpins and promotes BRICS engagement and cooperation. Professor Xia Liping, dean of the School of Political Sciences and International Relations at Tongji University, for example, points out that during the 1980s Deng Xiaoping suggested that 'with regard to the overall international situation, it is possible to strive for more long-term peace and war can be avoided'. Deng believed that the international community should always focus on advancing human development and should at the same time oppose hegemonism and war. In March 1985, he pointed out that 'the world is facing two globally strategic issues ... One is an issue of peace and the other an issue of economy, or development'.

In September 2011, the State Council Information Office released the White Paper entitled *China's Peaceful Development* in which China confirmed its strategic choice of peaceful development to advance economic prosperity and the well-being of its citizens. With increased economic growth, China's international status is expected to change further, facilitating a greater role for China in international affairs. As the Asia-Pacific region is becoming the centre of world economic growth, increased BRICS interaction with this region would significantly benefit all BRICS members. At the same time, the balance of international forces is shifting towards a multipolar world within which China will play a more prominent role and BRICS is expected to be the institutional framework within which proposals for a new global multipolar order will be crafted.

To this end, China is seeking to make contributions in advancing a set of Chinese-style theories of globalisation and contributing more to the debate on global governance reform. Western values need not be accepted as universal values—through globalisation a new international value system should be developed; China seeks to participate directly in the reconstruction of world order, advancing the interests of developing countries and smaller powers; as current rules of global governance have been largely formulated by Western nations they may not conform to the interests and objectives of international society as a whole.

The Belt and Road Initiative (BRI)

President Xi Jinping has proposed the building of a Silk Road Economic Belt and a twenty-first-century Maritime Silk Road to advance increased economic cooperation and international exchange, among other goals. The BRI is also intended to guide the global governance system towards a more fair and equitable system with a bigger role for China and developing countries in international rule-making and decision-making (Shaoshi 2016).

The post-Second World War wave of globalisation, advanced by the US, has created economic dividends mainly for the developed countries, with disadvantages for developing countries. The BRI seeks to advance a new wave of globalisation, to create new opportunity and economic growth options for the developing countries. The global financial crisis undermined the US-led globalisation model, but the BRI offers a new phase of mutually beneficial globalisation and cooperation. The BRI's philosophical foundation is one of 'sharing and inclusiveness' with a view to transforming the global economy (Zhang et al. 2017: 146).

The BRI focuses on the coordination of economic development policies and is driven by transportation and communication linkages which advance the opening and strengthening of trade routes. New networks of maritime, road and rail connections can transform global trade and advance economic cooperation to unprecedented levels. In addition, the BRI offers diverse platforms for cooperation and will focus on green development, economic partnership and the promotion of peace to advance economic development. Through BRI, China intends to fully open its economy to the world and will focus its own efforts on maintaining economic growth towards national rejuvenation.

But in addition to advancing China's economic prosperity, the BRI is designed and intended to offer significant opportunity to all participants. Based on Eastern wisdom and historical experience, the BRI aims at creating the conditions for common prosperity and development in participating countries and more broadly. Through this initiative, China offers a mechanism to build a community of shared future for all of humanity. BRICS as well as other China-inspired diplomatic mechanisms, such as the Forum on China–Africa Cooperation (FOCAC), the Asia Infrastructure Investment Bank (AIIB) and the Shanghai Cooperation Organisation (SCO) all support and complement the BRI in advancing a new phase of globalisation and economic prosperity.

Professor He Wenping, a leading scholar at the Chinese Academy of Social Sciences (CASS), has outlined the strategic framework of China's international engagement referring to the complementarities between, BRICS, the BRI, SCO, AIIB and FOCAC. All of these mechanisms advance China's economic development, new globalisation and international peace (He 2018: 20). The mechanisms are based on a broad concept of economic partnership and mutual benefit and not on old Cold War alliance systems. China's foreign policy is expected to be increasingly advanced through these partnerships. The increased synergy between BRICS and the BRI is thus expected to become a priority and will help to strengthen and consolidate the BRICS process.

Strengthening BRICS Cooperation and Global Governance Reform

A key objective of BRICS cooperation is to promote a new global order in which the needs of developing countries are more adequately addressed. In China's view, globalisation needs to be reshaped and redesigned to stimulate economic growth and job creation in developing countries, thus moving away from the perpetuation of wealth accumulation in developed countries. In practice, the Washington Consensus has placed little emphasis on equity, the assumption being that trickle-down economics will over time, benefit the poor. However, it is now clear that more active government interventions are required to promote development and to combat poverty. Markets remain at the core of any successful economy, but governments and global economic institutions need to create an appropriate climate to allow commerce to flourish and jobs to be created.

Dr. Hu (2012: 58), deputy director-general and research fellow at the CCCWS, argues that 'global governance must go parallel with the democratisation of international relations'. He points out further that 'global governance does not equal hegemony ... Major powers must listen to and consider the opinions of developing countries and minor countries'. Thus, international organisations should adopt principles and procedures of democracy in the process of formulating and implementing international resolutions and programmes. The interests of smaller countries should not be ignored in the process, as this will result in a perpetuation of narrow power politics. Emerging economies, such as the BRICS grouping, should participate in global governance and seek to reform systems to create a more even balance and a more equitable system. BRICS engagement should be in the form of constructive and positive participation.

The long-term goal is improving the representation of developing countries and shaping a more inclusive and creative global development agenda. Global governance reform should provide for every member of the international community to make their voices heard on issues of national concern. Within the G20, discussions have led to consensus on a wide range of issues. The BRICS structure offers a major platform for consensus building on these issues among key players of the global South. Ai Ping, executive president of the CCCWS, has suggested that a broadened intra-BRICS dialogue among both officials and think tanks can make a major contribution to crafting a cooperative agenda for global governance reform.

According to China's perspective, the road map to advance BRICS cooperation and development should be guided by the following: upgrade trade and investment links; build cooperative but flexible relations; advance BRICS through an incremental approach; be pragmatic in developing areas of mutual interest; build a new type of South–South system of consultation and cooperation; expand areas where cooperation is possible; quickly move forward on areas of consensus; shelve differences for later; initiate closer think-tank cooperation to identify future areas of cooperation; coordinate consultation and cooperation in the UN and G20; strengthen policy synchronisation and develop constructive links with other non-BRICS developing countries (Yuan 2018: 22). The development of BRICS is likely to be slow and incremental, but underpinned by solid economic growth in emerging economies, it is expected to provide a new and positive contribution to the evolution of the international system (see Besada et al. 2013).

In advancing BRICS, China has suggested a focus on promoting BRICS as a key South–South multilateral cooperation forum; BRICS should focus on reforming global (Western) governance; BRICS countries could form an effective pressure group within the G20 to advance the development agenda of the global South; BRICS cooperation should be focused in practical and achievable results, while trade and investment should be the focus of BRICS. The short-term assignment is to develop appropriate business-to-business dialogues and information-sharing processes to accelerate intra-BRICS trade and investment (Mthembu 2018). At the same time, as the BRICS Sanya Declaration emphasised, accelerating sustainable growth in developing countries should be driven by a moral imperative to address poverty and achieve the SDGs as soon as reasonably possible.

In this context, China's economic rise and the strengthening of BRICS provides the African continent with a range of new development partners and opportunities unmatched in its postcolonial history. Africa's strategic and concerted engagement with BRICS offers a unique opportunity to promote a new development path, along with existing development and trade processes. Cooperative trade agreements with the EU and the US, complemented by BRICS investments and infrastructure development programmes, are expected to underpin and promote continued economic growth in Africa.

Conclusion—China and BRICS

Chinese officials and scholars argue that one of the key objectives of BRICS is to reform the system of global governance in accordance with new economic and political trends in the international system. The major powers should take into consideration the opinions and interests of developing countries and seek to accommodate the emerging powers. The key trend in current international affairs is the rise of emerging countries and the growing economic influence of these states. Moreover, as an organised group such as BRICS emerging powers can influence and shape global affairs. Currently, global governance is in effect Western governance, while BRICS aims to democratise the global system to reflect the views and aspirations of developing countries. For the sake of stability and harmony, global governance should include the views and interests of developing countries.

The progress of BRICS is expected to be slow, but calculating and effective, in the years ahead. Through BRICS, China is expected to seek a readjustment in the global governance system through a process of gradual reform, rather than confrontation (Phaahla 2018). Confrontation will create uncertainty, undermine economic confidence and slow global growth. At the same time, BRICS will provide the global community with new ideas and new solutions to current problems. Creative thinking and common objectives within the BRICS group could open the door for constructive progress on a wide range of issues.

The democratic deficit in international institutions prevents market access for developing countries and has undermined their economic progress. The globalisation process is affecting the world in different ways and in differing intensity. Global institutions should focus on areas that represent opportunities for benefiting the entire global system and not merely the wealthy economies. A focused reform agenda with the potential for maximum overall benefit is the first goal, while measured and balanced policy implementation is the second. BRICS should encourage global institutions to promote the well-being of all states through the provision of appropriate public goods which benefit all systems participants. Over time, the world will become more globalised, offering increasing opportunity for cooperation and joint action (Stuenkel 2012). A number of global public goods should be promoted to provide a stronger foundation for growth and development in poor countries. In China's perspective, these public goods include global peace and stability, health, the environment and knowledge dissemination. All are vital for the uplifting and future prosperity of the developing countries and the world as a whole.

Chinese officials have indicated that the evolving BRICS system at the multilateral level and the bilateral level serves as a model for South–South cooperation. Continued cooperation and collaboration based on the past augurs well for a continued warm friendship and a long-term BRICS strategic partnership. Over the longer term, reforms of global financial institutions are required to reduce the democratic deficit and fully to integrate global markets for the benefit of all participants. BRICS can play a key role in driving this process. Without appropriate changes, the global system will continue to undermine development in the global South and prevent effective poverty reduction programmes.

The bonding of the BRICS member states in a common goal to eliminate the iniquities of the existing outdated economic and political system of global governance provides hope and inspiration to developing countries (Wang 2018). BRICS is expected to be successful to the extent that it accepts and advances China's national interests for promoting the BRI, and increased trade and global governance reform. As the core economy within BRICS, China is expected to strongly influence the group's evolution and success. If BRICS can accept and embrace China's concepts of economic partnership and common development, the organisation is expected to prosper and provide the momentum to transform the global political and economic system.

Bibilography

Ai Ping. (2013). Pooling Wisdom and Efforts for Further Co-operation Among BRICS. In H. Hu & X. Jin (Eds), *Yearbook of Contemporary World Studies*. Beijing: Central Compilation and Translation Press.

Besada, H., Tok, E., & Winters, K. (2013). South Africa in the BRICS. *Africa Insight, 42*(4), 1–15.

BRICS Sanya Declaration. (2011, April 14). Sanya, Hainan, China.

Brookings Institute. (2007, February). *Rise of New Powers*. Brookings Global Economy and Development.

Davies, R. (2018, July 6). Importance of the BRICS Trade and Investment Agenda. *Business Report*.

Han, L. (2016, October). BRICS Still Relevant. *Chinafrica*.

He, W. (2018, July). A Synergy in Motion. *Chinafrica*.

Hou, W., & Yu, L. (2017, October). Bigger for Better—BRICS Plus. *Chinafrica*.

Hou, W. (2017, September). New Bank on the Block. *Chinafrica*.

Huang, R. (2012). The Emergence of BRIC Countries and the Global Governing System. In *Yearbook of Contemporary World Studies 2011/12*. Beijing: Central Compilation and Translation Press.

Hu, H. (2012). The Evolution and Future Development of Global Governance. In *Yearbook of Contemporary World Studies 2011/12*, Beijing: Central Compilation and Translation Press.

Jain, P. (2017, March). The BRICS Agenda: Functional Co-operation Between Competing Logics. *Global Dialogue*.

Ji, P. (2012). When the Balance of History Swings to the Asia-Pacific Region. In *The Changing World and China's Development*. Beijing: China Center for Contemporary World Studies.

Liu, X. (2018). China's Common Interest Theory in the Context of International Strategy. *Contemporary International Relations, 28*(2), 26–34.

Mthembu, P. (2018, March 1). The Strategic Imperative of South Africa's 2018 BRICS Presidency. *The Star*.

O'Neill, J. (2018, July 20–26). Time for BRICS to Ponder Road Ahead. *China Daily*.

O'Neill, J. (2011). *The Growth Map—Economic Opportunity in the BRICS and Beyond*. London: Penguin.

Phaahla, E. L. (2018) From IBSA to BRICS: The Coming of Age of an Alliance? *BRICS Journal, 2*(5).

Pillai, M. (2014). The Formation of the BRICS Think Tank Council. *The Thinker, 62* 18–20.

Ren, X. (2017, 28 July–3 August). BRICS to Play Key Role in Safeguarding Free Trade. *China Daily*.

Satheakge, B. (2017a, September 4). BRICS in Bid to Expand Footprint. *New Age*.

Satheakge, B. (2017b, November 22). BRICS Bank Steps Up Lending. *New Age*.
Stuenkel, O (2012, December). *Can the BRIC Co-operate in the G20? A View from Brazil* (SAIIA Occasional Paper, No. 123).
Thomashausen, A. (2018, July 25). Is BRICS Emerging as a Global Forum? *Pretoria News*.
Vanyna, E. (2018, July 5). BRICS Making Headway Despite West's Scepticism. *The Star*.
Wang, H. (2017, September 8–14). Summit Paves Way for New Globalization. *China Daily*.
Wang, H. (2018). Global Development and China's Mission. *Contemporary International Relations, 28*(2), 38–46.
Wang, X, & Tao, Z. (2004). WTO Competition Policy and its Influence in China. *Social Sciences in China, 25*(1), 43–53.
Wang, Y. (2013, September 26). *As a Member of the Developing World, China Will Always Speak up for Developing Countries*. PRC Ministry of Foreign Affairs, New York, NY. www.fmprc.gov.cn. Accessed 26 July 2018.
Wilson, D., & Purushothaman, R. (2003). *Dreaming With BRICs: The Path to 2050* (Goldman Sachs Global Economics Paper, No. 99).
Xi, J.(2018). BRICS Co-operation Benefits World Economy, Beijing, China.
Xu, S. (2016, April-June). The Belt and Road Initiative: A New Model for Regional Co-operation. *Qiushi*.
Yang, J. (2012). On the Tenets, Orientation and Mechanisms of the BRICS. In *Yearbook of Contemporary World Studies 2011/12*. Beijing: China Center for Contemporary World Studies.
Yu, K. (2012). Global Good Governance and the Rule of China. In *The Changing World and China in Development*. Beijing: Central Compilation and Translation Press.
Yu, L. (2017, September 1). The Power of Five: Building a Stronger Partnership. *Newsweek*.
Yuan, P. (2018). China's International Strategic Thought and Layout for a New Era. *Contemporary International Relations, 28*(1), 28–36.
Zhang, Y., Huang, Y., Liang, J., & Si, W. (2017). On New Missions of the Belt and Road Initiative. *Contemporary International Relations, 27*(6), 15–22.
Zou, C. (2017, November). The 19th CPC National Congress *Chinafrica*.

CHAPTER 6

Manna from Heaven! South Africa's Search for Relevance in the BRICS Constellation

Chris Landsberg and Oscar van Heerden

Introduction

All states, however big or small, have foreign policies. They therefore harbour goals vis-à-vis external state and non-state actors. Some of these goals are to join alliances and coalitions that would help them to pursue their political, economic and social interests. They also seek to transform the world in images that would advance their perceived interests, and they also defend their political, economic and ideological friends (Landsberg 2018).

The Brazil, Russia, India, China, South Africa forum as we know it now has its genesis in 2006 (Dirco 2017a). During the 2006 Brazil, Russia,

C. Landsberg (✉)
South African Research Chair in African Diplomacy and Foreign Policy, University of Johannesburg, Johannesburg, South Africa
e-mail: clandsberg@uj.ac.za

O. van Heerden
Mapungubwe Institute for Strategic Reflection, Johannesburg, South Africa

D. Monyae and B. Ndzendze (eds.), *The BRICS Order*, International Political Economy Series,
https://doi.org/10.1007/978-3-030-62765-2_6

India and China (BRIC) leaders' meeting at the G8 Outreach in St Petersburg, and the subsequent foreign ministers' meeting on the margins of the UN General Assembly in New York, the BRIC leaders had informal engagements with former South African President Thabo Mbeki, who was there as part of the Africa Outreach group.

The first BRIC summit was held in Yekaterinburg, Russia, on 16 June 2009, and South Africa's membership was discussed in earnest. The Mbeki government was fully aware of the interest in it to join, but was concerned about issues of equality among members, and that such a formation should not become another neoimperialist one in Africa. South Africa was invited to join the grouping in 2010 at the Sanya Summit, a year after Yekaterinburg. Soon after South Africa joined, the group added an 'S' to its acronym and BRIC became BRICS. It was invited on the basis that the political purchase of each member was its status as some great power in its subregion.

From the onset, South Africa celebrated the invitation to this illustrious, albeit amorphous, emerging constellation, even though the country had no clear strategy for joining this club. The invitation was in line with South Africa's search for 'prestige', its anointment as an important player in world affairs, and its perceived role as a pivotal state in Africa.[1] The 2014 Twenty-Year Review by the Presidency reinforced South Africa's purported prestige and global gravitas when it stated that 'South Africa's standing in BRICS and other groupings indicates that the country is regarded as a significant emerging power'; the country therefore declared itself as belonging to the premier league of world affairs, such as the United Nations Security Council (UNSC) and the Group of 20 (G20). While South Africa at times tries to understate its hegemonic ambitions in Africa, it clearly harbours ambitions of a pivotal or anchor role on the continent. BRICS membership is a means and a tool to help it to realise this ambition, at least in part. It certainly sees itself as an African 'great' power.

The invitation for South Africa to join BRICS was also in line with a key goal of South Africa's foreign policy, one that it has in common with many states: that of playing a transformational role in world affairs (Holsti 1995). Post-settlement governments have long harboured the idea of South Africa as a 'bridge-builder' in global affairs.[2]

The Zuma government regarded the invitation to join the Brazil–Russia–India–China (BRIC) constellation its greatest foreign policy achievement. In July 2011, the minister of international relations and cooperation in the Zuma-led government, Maite Nkoana-Mashabane, articulated the view that South Africa's membership of BRICS formed part of 'progressive forces globally working for a better and just world order'.[3] South Africa's engagement with BRICS was also seen as the quest to 'transform the western-dominated global order' and in particular the global governance architecture. South Africa therefore saw BRICS as a potential countervailing force in a Western-dominated world order, and it thus looked at BRICS not solely through geoeconomic, but also geopolitical and geostrategic lenses.

The BRICS is not as cohesive as is often assumed. The BRICS countries all belong to varying and multiple common denominations, as well as playing leadership and active roles in different multilateral denominations and structures. But South Africa did see BRICS as an attempt to weave BRICS into, and promote the formation of, a constellation of like-minded states, focusing on restructuring the global economic, political and security architecture dominated by the West, and the 'establishment of an equitable, democratic and multi-polar world order'. The idea of like-mindedness is interesting here, as not all BRICS members are democracies, in the classical Western sense, for example.

For Pretoria-Tshwane, BRICS membership was further justified as 'the formation of a more balanced world economy, more reasonable international relations, more effective global governance and more durable world peace'.[4] But the idea that BRICS represents some countervailing balance of power and alternative constellation is not as straightforward as is assumed. BRICS started off as an economic constellation with the major intention of boosting economic interactions among the member states. BRICS should be viewed as a major coalitional actor which started off as an economic constellation, and increasingly adopted political economic and global power political ambitions. BRICS was searching for a common cause. By 2018, BRICS was still searching for a clear political role and identity, and pushed very hard by Pretoria in the quest to contribute with some true value-adding as the smallest BRICS member. This assumption of BRICS as a political and strategic balancer in world affairs therefore needs further probing and analysis.

BRICS and South African Agency in World Affairs

There is no doubt that the invitation to join BRICS greatly boosted South Africa's agency in world affairs, and its prestige as a pivotal player. South Africa had long felt under pressure to justify its BRICS membership as beneficial to Africa. South Africa also saw this invitation as an opportunity to diversify its economy and to help it reinforce its status as a pivotal, or anchor state in Africa that would pursue an 'African agenda'.[5] In this regard, Nkoana-Mashabane (2016: 7) said:

> … our cooperative partnerships with emerging economies complement other existing platforms which we utilise to pursue the African Agenda. Since we joined the Brazil, Russia, India, China and South Africa (BRICS) formation, Africa's developmental needs and aspirations have been fully incorporated into the BRICS agenda.

So South Africa saw itself as both the spokesperson and the defender of African interests in BRICS, and did so beyond mere economic interests.

Clayson Monyela (2012), at the time spokesperson for the ministry of international relations and cooperation (Dirco) also portrayed South Africa's presence in BRICS as beneficial for Africa:

> … if South Africa could also lead the rest of the continent in the search of its own standards where these are high, Africa would be on an accelerated path to greater economic might. By exploring cross border expansion in trade and infrastructure, as well as improvements in domestic productivity, South Africa will have more than justified its role as a BRICS member.

The assumption of policy is clear: South Africa is there to defend African interests, and Africa's interests will be naturally served. But assumptions could easily be cloaked as presumptions. The idea that what is good for South Africa is automatically good for the rest of Africa could backfire in a major way, as other Africans would take umbrage at this idea.

In this regard, the Centre for Conflict Resolution (CCR) in Cape Town properly cautioned in 2014 that Pretoria should not assume that its own selfish interests and those of the African continent are inherently competitive. As the 2014 CCR report put it,

> Tshwane [Pretoria] has sought to advance a broader African peacebuilding and development agenda within the BRICS. However, the extent to which the BRICS countries' interests in Africa converge with the continent's own interests is still uncertain.

The report went further and asserted that

> a key challenge for Tshwane relates to how it can navigate tensions between its 'African Agenda': promoting security and development on the continent

> and ensuring that Africa has a strong global role, its ambitions to play a leading role on the continent, and its ability to wield influence within the BRICS, of which it is the smallest member, accounting for only 2 per cent of the bloc's economic might.

But given that South Africa is a member now, it must continue to fight for relevance and a role, and one way of doing so is to insist that the other BRIC members must seek to prioritise African peace, security and development instead of merely craving the continent's mineral riches. As Vincent Malunga (2018) put it:

> The range of areas of cooperation appears to be expanding as well, with South Africa proposing the following:
>
> 1. A working group on peacekeeping;
> 2. The establishment of a vaccine research centre;
> 3. The establishment of the BRICS gender and women forum;
> 4. BRICS strategic partnership towards the advancement of the Fourth Industrial Revolution; and
> 5. The establishment of the BRICS Tourism Track of cooperation.

This point by Malunga is an example of South Africa's trying to push the raison d'être of BRICS beyond the strictly economical. As the dwarf among the BRIC giants, it was also searching for a role and unique value proposition.

These efforts by Pretoria are also born out of South Africa's experiencing a myriad frustrations and challenges in BRICS. Kudrat Virk (2018) poignantly observed that 'for South Africa, membership in the BRICS is replete with challenges, not least which are posed by the grouping's still ongoing attempts to craft a distinct and shared identity for itself on the global stage'. Virk is correct in also asserting that 'while the BRICS may have accepted South Africa as an interlocutor for Africa "by default", it is highly questionable that the continent has done the same'. It should not be assumed that other African countries simply buy into the idea that South Africa is there as the African champion. As Chris Landsberg and Candice Moore (2013: 10) have argued, 'several countries have questioned South Africa's claim to fairly represent the interests of African states within BRICS and the G20', going further to caution that 'many countries like Nigeria and Senegal also take umbrage at the fact that external powers look to South Africa as Africa's representative'.

The portrayal of South Africa as Africa's legitimate representative is not a view shared across the board. South Africa has never been mandated to be Africa's permanent representative, or even spokesperson on the world stage. Hence, South Africa is battling to navigate multiple interests and conflicting agendas, and is struggling to convince fellow Africans that it is acting on their behalf. It is for this reason that Pretoria felt the need in 2013 to start a BRICS-Africa Outreach Dialogue in order to make other African states feel accommodated. In 2018, the government of Cyril Ramaphosa continued with this practice when the new president also hosted the BRICS-Africa Outreach Dialogue and the BRICS Plus Initiative during the Summit—attended by the leaders of Rwanda, Ethiopia, Angola, Zambia, Senegal, Gabon, Togo, Uganda, Jamaica, Argentina, Turkey, Botswana, DRC, Lesotho, Madagascar, Malawi, Mauritius, Mozambique, Seychelles, Tanzania and Zimbabwe (Dirco 2017a). The South African government offered the rationale for both the Outreach Dialogue and the Initiative on the basis that they '… were held simultaneously to reflect the broad partnerships BRICS has engendered with the African continent and the global South'.

It should be remembered that for many years since the onset of democracy in 1994 South Africa expressed multiple identities in its international role: an African state pursuing an Africa first policy; a state that is non-aligned; a country of two economies, walking on two legs, one in the South and the other in the North; and a country pursuing a policy of universality, choosing its friends independently without much dictation from the West or anyone else. When Thabo Mbeki became president, South Africa clarified the country's identity more sharply as an African state that would pursue a pro-African and pro-South strategy, based on an African Renaissance, and a vigorous global governance strategy, in search of global political and economic transformation. (see Maloka 2018: 293). Indeed, the concentric circles of the Mbeki government went: Africa bilateral and multilateral; South–South cooperation; North–South dialogue and economic and political governance—and the Zuma government built on this, protestations to the contrary notwithstanding (Maloka 2018: 302).

The 2011 White Paper, 'The Diplomacy of Ubuntu', reaffirms its commitment to the spirit of Bandung and commits South Africa to 'South-South cooperation and opposition to colonialism as a natural extension of our national interest' (Dirco 2011: 3). The governing party, the African National Congress (ANC), retained ideological closeness to groups such as the Non-Aligned Movement that were instrumental in championing decolonisation as part of 'third world' solidarity; also participating actively in the G77 and for historical sentimental reasons linked to earlier calls for a New International Economic Order in the early 1970s to challenge the dominance of Western countries in multilateral economic arrangements (Pahad et al. 2012: 138). In many of its official policy documents, for example, the ANC still describes South Africa as championing a 'non-aligned' foreign policy posture. In this sense, it still makes constant throwbacks to the heydays of the Cold War, apartheid era discourse.

Beyond the purported non-aligned posture, South Africa carved a role for itself as a system stabiliser or 'bridge-builder' between the developing and the developed countries (a role that was expressed most obviously in the context of multilateral trade negotiations) and worked hard to cultivate an African identity through participation in informal clubs such as the Africa Group at the UN in New York, and in the World Trade Organization (WTO) and World Intellectual Property Organization (WIPO) in Geneva. On this score, the idea of South Africa 'walking on two legs' with one leg in the North and the other in the developing South is one that has been around since the Mandela years (Landsberg 2010a). Today, South Africa is challenged to prove that its two legs are rooted in Africa and abroad, and that it is committed to advancing African interests.

South Africa's Attraction to BRICS?

While the BRIC countries, notably Russia and China, were very clear about their intentions behind their overtures to Pretoria, South Africa was never clear what role, precisely, the BRICS would play in its foreign policy calculus. These countries regarded South Africa as the 'gateway' to Africa; the African 'hegemon' that would come to deliver the continent on the BRICS altar in the age of the commodity-driven 'Africa rising'.[6] BRICS needed a capable partner that would secure acceptance for the club in Africa, and it looked to South Africa as that African 'giant' that would make it possible. Kudrat Virk (2018: 450) put it succinctly: 'In March 2013, the South African port city of Durban hosted the BRICS summit under the theme "BRICS and Africa: Partnership for Development, Integration and Industrialisation"'. She reminded us that officially the African focus of the Durban summit was characterised as 'a testimony to the consensus that exists among the BRICS countries on the importance of forging a true and effective partnership with the African continent'. 'Yet', she cautioned, 'while the summit theme reflected South Africa's prioritisation of Africa's need for infrastructure development, regional integration and industrialisation, the degree and nature of the individual BRICS countries interests on the continent are more complex and driven by individual agendas that may not necessarily converge with Africa's expectations, stoking fears of a new "scramble for Africa" among critics'. This talk of 'Africa rising' could just be cover for a 'new scramble' for Africa's resources (see Landsberg 2018). The BRIC members were all interested in Africa's role in the global supply chain of resources and commodities, and looked to South Africa to help them to access this 'hottest frontier' in the global resources war.[7]

What compounds the situation is that 'neither Africa as a whole (in the form of the African Union (AU)), nor South Africa in particular seems to have a clear detailed strategy in place for engaging the BRICS' (Virk 2018). While for Russia BRICS is mainly a geopolitical instrument to help challenge the West, for China, BRICS is an avowedly geoeconomic instrument. China and India have their eyes firmly set on the industrialisation of their states, and have insatiable appetites for the continent's resources, and it was hoped that the purported 'lead nation' of Africa, and self-confessed spokesperson for the continent, South Africa, would deliver Africa.

South Africa was a 'pivotal state' in Africa and it bought into this idea of being the 'gateway' to Africa.[8] In June 2011, President Zuma referred in Parliament to the BRICS membership as bolstering 'our position as a gateway to Africa', uncritically and unapologetically endorsing the notion. In the words of Gerrit Olivier and Maxi Schoeman, 'what particularly counted in South Africa's favour becoming a BRIC member, was its "gateway to Africa" credentials based on its location, its status as a regional power in the continent, and most importantly that it would represent the "whole of Africa" in the power club'. Indeed, the 'gateway to Africa' label was used as a very strong trump card in support of South Africa's inclusion in BRIC, support particularly from China, as Beijing expected South Africa to promote its well-known ambitions and externally imposed ambitions in Africa. M.J. Khan (2011) and Patrick Bond (2013) depicted South Africa's inclusion into BRICS as inauspicious, claiming that as so-called gateway, it will act as sub-imperialist power and assume the role of 'deputy-sheriff' as it looks after the interests of other BRICS powers in Africa.

So why the attraction and interest in South Africa as the supposed 'gateway' to Africa? Elsewhere, Landsberg, Kornegay and Qobo (2017: 2) have asked: '... especially once BRIC became BRICS with the addition of South Africa, was the global geopolitical impetus that brought the initial quartet together as a grouping intent on reshaping the international political landscape in order to accommodate their individual and collective economy?'. They suggested, further, that 'there is also the importance of the commercial diplomacy of the BRICS countries on the African continent as part of pursuing their national economic interests'. BRIC countries, at least some of them, were attracted by South Africa's considerable mineral wealth, and by the time of the invitation it was valued at US$2 trillion. Economic diplomacy was again at play.

South Africa was investing some US$40 billion in infrastructure development. Its market development and sophistication was a major attraction. Its excellence in science technology innovation, compared to other African states, was considerable. Its exports to BRIC countries rose from R5.7 billion in 2008 to R22. 8 billion in 2011, considerable from a South African point of view (Nkoana-Mashabane 2012). Its bridge networking role in the UN, the Group of 77 Plus China, IBSA Dialogue Forum, the G20 and others was a major attraction for BRIC, as its vote-pulling and bandwagoning potential were regarded as attractive (Landsberg 2010b).

South Africa's agency role in Africa, especially during the Mbeki years—from its role in creating the African Union (AU), crafting NEPAD, the African Peer Review Mechanism (APRM) and engaging the G8 and other powers—gave it lustre and a sense of gravitas, and BRICs members interpreted this as South Africa's being some special pivotal state. As Maite Nkoana-Mashabane (2012) asserted, 'South Africa, together with other African countries, initiated the dialogue with the Group of 8 in 2000, which led to the subsequent endorsement of the AU's New Partnership for Africa's Development [NEPAD] by the international community at large'. Engaging the G8 and others was regarded as a key rationale for involving South Africa in the BRICs, and it is noteworthy how South Africa continuously stressed the apparent benefits for the rest of Africa, thereby elevating itself to spokesperson for Africa. An ANC International Relations National General Council document made the link explicit between its UN Security Council ambitions and its BRICS membership when it recommended that 'Africa receive at least two permanent seats', and that the country should 'approach our BRICS partners who are Permanent Members of the Security Council to lobby for South Africa's inclusion as one of the two seats' (ANC 2015).

Many external powers, BRICs countries included, were attracted by the idea of South Africa as the spokesperson for Africa on the world stage. There is no gainsaying that South Africa's foreign policy is genuinely committed to placing the 'voice and participation' issues of Africa and the South on the agenda of multilateral and bilateral actors (DTI 2009), including BRICS. Even since the Monterrey Consensus of 2002, South Africa has been committed to 'contin[ing] to enhance the participation of all developing countries and countries with economies in transition in decision-making' (DTI 2009). South Africa has been adamant that the structural concerns related to substantive imbalances and skewed balances of power in world affairs needed to be addressed.

'Careful what you wish for' goes the Chinese saying! Apart from its elation at the invitation to join the BRICS club, and the shot in the arm that this invitation gave its grandiose ambitions as an African lead nation, South Africa was at first confused about what to do with the invitation. This was especially so in view of the fact that South Africa, Brazil and India had forged a common Thabo Mbeki-inspired platform characterised as IBSA to consolidate a 'Southern' agenda in the twenty-first century (Masters and Landsberg 2015). But this IBSA Trilateral initiative soon lost its focus and leadership and the Zuma government saw BRICS as an opportunity to come up with its own anti-Mbeki initiative. What complicated matters were that IBSA had a clear agenda that included the reform of the United Nations Security Council and international financial institutions; engagement in a productive North–South dialogue that would yield a shared development consensus; and pursuit of projects that generate shared benefits in more concrete policy areas such as health, education, science and technology, trade and defence cooperation (Dirco 2010). BRICS could certainly take a leaf out of IBSA's book. IBSA countries were natural partners for a number of reasons: they had a long history of working together in realising a world order that was just and equitable. In the case of South Africa, this may not have been the case before the democratic breakthrough, but the ANC in exile shared similar ideological attributes as other Third World movements.

The three IBSA countries had a deep commitment to multilateralism, both as a substantive quality that places emphasis on international law, equality of sovereigns and a rules-based system of governing public goods through intergovernmental organisations (Masters and Landsberg 2015).

They also shared similar perspective with respect to realising the gains of procedural multilateralism to increased participation and the voice of developing countries in key multilateral institutions. Most importantly, the three countries were all democracies, and had more in common normatively that made it relatively easier for them to work together.

BRICS could learn much from IBSA's coherence and common positioning. Those close to earlier developments within IBSA have suggested that China had sought membership of IBSA, a move that was blocked by India.[9] The reason for this had to do largely with unresolved territorial disputes between India and China, and general antipathy in India's foreign policy towards China. The two could work fairly well within the BRICS, since commitments there were not as deep, and there tended to be less emphasis on normative issues. When China failed to join IBSA, it then encouraged and supported South Africa's bid for BRICS membership. A 2017 official document by the Dirco observed in this regard that 'the formation of the IBSA forum in 2003 illustrated an appetite for mini-lateral partnerships and enhanced co-operation amongst countries of the global South'(Dirco 2017b). Even with Russia as a member, South Africa officially regards BRICS as a South–South constellation. Ironically, though, while IBSA helped to inspire BRICS, certainly from India and Brazil's perspective, and later on that of South Africa, in a sense, South Africa's joining of the BRICS eroded IBSA's relevance.

Why Is South Africa so Committed to the BRICS? What Is in It for Pretoria?

The Zuma government was looking for an international raison d'être after the change in government from Mbeki-Motlanthe to Zuma. It was interested in building its own international legacy and, while it was out of the starting blocks slowly, BRICS provided this rationale and South Africa did develop in incremental fashion a BRICS strategy. South Africa liked the idea of being in the company on an association of leading emerging economies. With the possible exception of Russia, the BRICS members are all developing or newly industrialised states, albeit all differing in size, influence and growth potential, with South Africa the slowest of them. They all also hold different geostrategic positions in their regions. One of the most significant aspects of BRICS was that these countries together represent almost three billion people, a vast market indeed, with a combined nominal GDP of US$13.7 trillion, and an estimated

US$4 trillion in combined foreign reserves. South Africa therefore liked to be in a company of an emerging power coalition that could bolster its global gravitas and stature. The minister of trade and industry, Rob Davies, bought into this narrative of massive capital injections into Africa and South Africa in particular: he asserted in 2010, looking at foreign direct investment, that China had US$28.7 billion investment in Africa, followed by US$25 billion from India, US$10 billion from Brazil and even Russia at US$ 9.3 billion direct investment (Davies 2010: 8). According to Malunga, Mminele contends that 'South Africa's trade with BRICS countries has expanded in recent years, as exports to BRICS countries grew from R20 billion in 2005 (EUR1 billion), to R154 billion (EUR9 billion) in 2013 although this slowed to EUR8.5 billion in 2015. Imports have similarly increased from R48 billion (EUR2.8 billion in 2005 to R277 billion (EUR16 billion) in 2015' (Malunga 2018: 16). An uncompromising drive for foreign direct investment continues to register as a major strategic objective of the former Zuma government.

Three Key South African Policy Rationales

There are at least three discernible assumptions, and three policy drivers that incrementally developed behind South Africa's BRICS activism. Writing in 2012, Garth Shelton suggested that 'South Africa should advance a comprehensive look east policy, based on an economic focus intended to boost South Africa's trade and investment profile and thus take full advantage of the commercial opportunities offered in the region' (Shelton 2012: 235–6). The South African government had hoped that by joining the BRICs it would be enabled to build a stronger relationship with China, in line with its 'look East' policy. Indeed, South Africa, too, had a 'look East policy'. In the words of Scarlett Cornelissen (2015: 190), 'in general, this period in South African foreign policy saw the extension of cordiality towards East Asian states driven by a number of strategic motives'. 'The establishment of closer ties with the East Asian region was, in the first instance, part of a "go out strategy" pursued by South Africa in its wider efforts to bolster reintegration with the international community', argued Cornelissen. She proceeded to assert that in turn it was hoped that this would lead to growth in commercial relationship (trade and investment opportunities that benefit South Africa) between the two countries. It is difficult to link any commercial activity between

South Africa and China to the BRICS, since it is bilateral relations that are structured largely for that purpose.

At least two of the key BRICS members had clear strategic calculations for establishing and joining BRICS: China and India, for example. Mzukisi Qobo, Francis Kornegay and Landsberg have written (2017: 4) that 'China has decided to engage fully in the realities of the global order rather than take a victim posture. It may not necessarily view the global system as benign, but it positions itself strategically to maximise gains, including how it participates in multilateral forums or negotiate bilateral relations with other countries'. We went further, to observe that 'other countries such as India are more calculative and pragmatic about their choice of bilateral relations, and would not allow a quasi-ideological alliance, as is the case with the BRICS formation, to determine their approach to international relations'. From the start, these and other BRICS countries approach BRICS with clear strategic calculations, and those are economically driven, in the main.

Initially at least, South Africa saw the BRICS grouping as a geopolitical mechanism among five countries whose influence in the global system has been growing, and it could challenge the existing global order. A careful reading of the ANC's much talked about 2015 International Relations document reveals that South Africa saw China and Russia through the old Cold War lens as representing a bulwark against US 'imperialism'. In that discussion document, South Africa in Africa comes across as a spokesperson for China and Russia, and goes out on a limb, attacking Washington and the West of fermenting a strategy of destabilisation towards these countries. In her first Budget vote as minister of international relations and cooperation, Nkoana-Maite Mashabane framed the BRICS as a grouping of countries of the South arrayed against the North. There is still a view in South African government circles or the ruling party that regard the BRICS as almost an extension of the struggles that were waged by the Non-Aligned Movement or the G77 (Nkoana-Mashabane 2012: 35). South Africa has much work to do to convince other BRIC members that it should also have a clear political agenda of advancing multilateralism and ensuring that Africa and the South has voice in these fora.

What South Africa fails to grasp is that each of the BRIC countries is occupied with furthering their own interests, with geopolitical matters playing a secondary role. Many of the BRICS countries, including China, India and Brazil, are pragmatic in their foreign policies. They hardly antagonise the West, but seek mutually beneficial relations with the US and Europe. On the other hand, rhetoric in the South African governing party is decidedly anti-Western, and uncritically views the BRICS as a counterweight.

Third, South Africa sees the BRICS as holding promise to create an alternative world order, an emerging global suborder, and to yield institutions that are substitutes of the existing Bretton Woods institutions. South Africa sees BRICS as an emerging global suborder today—it is unclear whether as a disrupter in global affairs, or merely an interrupter in the status quo ante. This view is born of lack of appreciation of how deep the roots of the existing institutions go, and that their longevity is in part due to (soft) hegemonic incorporation of developing countries. Over a third of the countries that were part of designing the current multilateral economic architecture (notably the World Bank and the IMF) were developing countries—including India, China, El Salvador, Mexico, Brazil, Chile, the Philippines, Egypt and Ethiopia. The intellectual, normative and hard power resources possessed by leading Western countries that have championed the liberal multilateral order may take many years to replicate. Countries such as China and India seek not to replace the US multilateral order but want greater representation and voice in decision-making processes. Even new institutions such as the Asia Infrastructure Investment Bank and Belt and Road Initiative are characterised by commitment to open, liberal markets, and are inclusive in their expression.

South Africa has thus failed to make a sensible reading of the ways in which the world is changing today, and that the decline of US power and leadership does not equate to a decline in the liberal internationalist order that it created. China is increasingly projecting itself as a new champion of that order rather than creating an alternative order, but the notion of a China devoid of self-interest and even neoimperialist aims in Africa may yet come to disappoint South Africa. Russia seems bent on exploiting America's confusion and hyperactive, skittish behaviour. Africa does not features prominently in the strategic calculations of these two; but Russia operates with clear geopolitical and geostrategic calculations. For Brazil and India, market access to Africa's vast mineral riches appears to be the overriding considerations in Africa. It is now up to South Africa to insist on, and articulate, a clear engagement strategy and agenda for BRICS in Africa beyond mere resource exploitation. The onus is on Pretoria to ensure that BRICS become more legitimate, and that its credibility grows on the continent.

Three Key Policy Drivers for South Africa

Four months after joining BRICS officially, we saw the early signs of an emerging coherent BRICS policy by South Africa. In April 2011, Zuma led a powerful South African delegation to the BRICS leaders' meeting in the Hainan Province of China under the theme 'Broad Vision, Shared Prosperity' (Dirco 2017b). South Africa joined the new organisation with the objectives to:

1. Consolidate South Africa's BRICS membership and commit to processes and related mechanism;
2. Identify and leverage opportunities for South Africa's development agenda;
3. Enhance the African agenda and sustainable development;
4. Promote and broaden cooperation in the multilateral arena; and work for cooperation with other emerging markets.

In line with its foreign policy objectives, South Africa was happy that this summit also committed to exploring cooperation in the areas of security, central banks and agriculture expertise and to establishing a network of research centres and development banks.

By 2012, greater clarity and confidence emerged by South Africa, and the government released a Cabinet-approved 'BRICS strategy' boldly stating that South Africa's membership of BRICS is based on three fundamental goals (Monyela 2012: 10):

1. Advancing national interests;
2. Promoting regional integration programmes and related continental infrastructures and
3. Partnering key players of the South on issues related to global governance and its reforms.

South Africa deserves credit for having pushed BRICS on issues of multilateralism, including global political governance reform, UN Security

Council reform included (Monyela 2012). These three primary goals were unpacked on three levels of engagement: domestic or national, regional-cum-continental, and international.

It was in 2013 that South Africa had a real spring in its BRICS step as it hosted the BRICS summit in Durban. It felt under pressure, and needed to make good on its promise of being the 'gateway to Africa', and it invited the AU and a host of African countries to attend the summit (Landsberg and Moore 2013). It insisted that BRICS summit pledge support to Africa and help to forge a new funding model in Africa where regional projects spanning a number of African countries are favoured for finance. South Africa was adamant that the continent's link to BRICS and the BRICS link to African countries offered a window of opportunity to African countries to boost trade and to industrialise. But it is fair to say there does not exist a common African position vis-à-vis BRICS, or even a coherent South African-Africa position in relation to BRICS.

In line with its 'open for business' plug, the country tried hard to put socio-economic challenges on the agenda; that summit saw the establishment of the BRICS Business Council, with business magnate Patrice Motsepe named chairman of this body. Here was a clear example of trade and investment following the flag, and corporate South Africa and government having their strategies in sync. It reinforced the cargo cult syndrome of looking for, and relying on, foreign largesse as the way out of South Africa's domestic challenges.

It is during this summit that clarity emerged on the promissory note to establish a BRICS-led New Development Bank (NDB) and the Contingent Reserve Arrangement (CRA). Progress was made with regard to negotiating the capital structure, membership, shareholding and governance of the NDB. The Durban summit agreed that the CRA will have an initial size of US$100 billion, and South Africa committed US$5 billion. South Africa can claim that it has benefited from BRICS while also contributing to it. It is therefore both benefactor and recipient.

Between 2013 and 2018, South Africa was losing its lustre on the international stage and, with doubts regarding the character of the investment climate in the age of a junked economy, the South African government hopes that Western companies losing confidence in the country could be replaced by companies from the BRICS. South Africa showed particular interest in all the talk of a BRICS credit rating agency that would, presumably, offer a positive rating of sovereign risk profile. The putative BRICS rating agency and the BRICS Development Bank are true manna from heaven. Malunga (2018) appeared to be backing this 'manna from heaven' analogy when he stated that South Africa has gained from project funding from the BRICS. He asserted that, 'for its part, South Africa has benefitted from the 2016 approved BRICS project funding when it was granted US$180 million for renewable energy, which helped stabilise grid electricity during difficult times when load shedding was a problem'. There were even more largesse coming South Africa's way. Said Malunga: 'An additional loan of US$200 million has been granted by the NDB in May 2018 for the expansion of the Durban port.' While a contributor, South Africa was also a beneficiary of the NDB and, given the 'cargo cult'-like obsession with foreign direct investment by the Ramaphosa government, we can safely expect South Africa to approach the NDB for further support.

Conclusion

The BRICS countries' economic resources are not boundless. BRICS states face their own social and economic constraints. But despite the resource limits of the BRICS group, and deeply entrenched protectionist elements in some of these countries, South Africa hopes that, in line with the then Zuma government's policy of 'open for business ... in a big way', this initiative would on its own create vast economic opportunities for the country first and foremost, and to the continent, secondarily. For the new Cyril Ramaphosa-led government we should perhaps rephrase the mantra: South Africa is 'open for BRICS business with BRICS ... in a big way'.

Although it is important to engage in the BRICS for reasons largely to do with knowledge sharing, drawing lessons on development strategies, cultural exchanges and increasing contact between the people of these countries, South Africa needs to develop a clear perspective of its interests in the BRICS—but, but above all, as former minister in the Presidency Essop Pahad (2017) suggested, an African continental interest paradigm for BRICS. Such a perspective should be grounded in a pragmatic view of what the BRICS represents and what its limits are. Without a clear identification and articulation of interests, including Africa's interests broadly, it will be difficult for South Africa to notch any meaningful gains from the BRICS grouping. This may just be a lost opportunity in foreign policy. Its relationship with the BRICS countries should not be at the expense of other important relations with Western countries and other developing and emerging economies that are outside of the BRICS.

In the final analysis, BRICS offers South Africa an opportunity to think through and develop a strategic agenda for the continent that integrates it into the global economy, provided that South Africa can link the BRICS agenda to the imperative of African integration. If it applies itself in terms of policy it could emerge with an independent African approach to engage all external partners in the interest of the continent's development.

Thus far, the South African government's view of BRICS has not evinced much clarity of focus on what BRICS is and isn't. There has been a tendency to conflate it with the second coming of the Cold War and therefore of the BRICS as an anti-imperialist alliance—which it is not, given the unmistakable example of the only recently defused Sino-Indian confrontation at Doklam in the Himalayas—just in time to have a semblance of harmony at the then upcoming BRICS summit in Xiamen in September 2017.

There has even been a tendency to misuse it as a proxy in South Africa's domestic factional politics wherein it has been depicted as a reason for the West punishing South Africa (and former president Jacob Zuma) because South Africa became a member of BRICS when, in fact, BRICS does not feature as a threat perception in Western geopolitical and economic calculations.

Looking back at 2018, when it took over the chair of BRICS, under the leadership of new President Cyril Ramaphosa, South Africa must focus its energies in developing a BRICS African agenda that can help it regain leadership momentum on the African continent via the NDB Bank while offering its own vision of BRICS as a semi-alliance in global economic governance within the club governance framework of the G20. The Ramaphosa government has articulated a pro-economic diplomacy foreign policy strategy since coming into office. It is imperative that in future South Africa ensures that this strategy speaks to the continent's broader development needs and agenda. South Africa has to be careful, in BRICS and other forums , not just to use Africa for selfish political and economic ends. It should be genuine about promoting Africa's interests as eagerly as it does its own. Self-interests, thinly disguised as African interests, will only come to expose South Africa in BRICS and other forums.

Notes

1. For a perspective on the idea of 'prestige', see Holsti 1995, p. 19.
2. For the idea of South Africa as a 'bridge builder', see Landsberg 2010: 98.
3. Remarks by minister of international relations and cooperation, Maite Nkoana-Mashabane on the occasion of the OR Tambo Dinner, Heads of Missions Conference, Velinere Conference Centre, 14 July 2011.
4. *Business Day*, 28 March 2012.
5. For an assessment of what constitutes the 'African agenda', see Landsberg and Kondlo 2007.
6. For the notion of South Africa as a purported hegemon, see Adebajo and Landsberg 2003.
7. 'Investing in Africa: the hottest frontier', *The Economist*, 6 April 2013.
8. For the idea of South Africa as a pivotal state see Habib and Landsberg 2003.
9. See the example in Masters and Landsberg 2015.

Bibliography

Adebajo, A., & Landsberg, C. (2003). Nigeria and South Africa as Regional Hegemons. In M. Baregu & C. Landsberg (Eds.), *From Cape to Congo: Southern Africa's Evolving Security Regime*. Lynne Rienner: Boulder, CO.

African National Congress (ANC). (2015, October 11). A Better Africa in a Better World, ANC International Relations National General Council, Luthuli House, Johannesburg.

Bond, P. (2013). Sub-imperialism as Lubricant of Neo-liberalism: South African 'Deputy-Sheriff' Duty Within BRICS. *Third World Quarterly, 34*(2), 2013.

Cornelissen, S. (2015). South Africa's Relations with China and Japan. In L. Masters, S. Zondi, J-A. van Wyk, & C. Landsberg (Eds.), *South African Foreign Policy Review*, Volume 2.

Davies, R. (2010). Another Trade is Possible: Compliments of the Emerging Nations. *New Agenda*, Issue 38, Second Quarter, 2010.

Department of International Relations and Cooperation (Dirco). (2010). *South African IBSA National Focal Point, The Diplomat, May 2010*. Pretoria: Dirco.

Department of International Relations and Cooperation (Dirco). (2011). *The Diplomacy of Ubuntu, The White Paper on Foreign Policy*. Pretoria: Dirco.

Department of International Relations and Cooperation (Dirco). (2017a). Outcomes of the Tenth BRICS Summit, Johannesburg, 25–27 July. Pretoria: Dirco.

Department of International Relations and Cooperation (Dirco). (2017b). Presentation on BRICS, BRICS Chief Directorate, Pretoria.

Department of Trade and Industry (DTI). (2009). ITEDD: Global Economic Strategy, 2009 (Pretoria: DTI). www.dti.gov.za.

Habib, A., & Landsberg, C. (2003). Hegemon or Pivot? Debating South Africa's role in Africa, Centre for Policy Studies, Sheraton, Pretoria, August.

Holsti, K. J. (1995). *International Politics: A Framework for Analysis* (4th ed.). Englewood-Cliffs, NJ: Prentice Hall.

Khan, M. J. (2011). The BRICS and South Africa as a Gateway to Africa. *Journal of the Southern African Institute of Mining and Metallurgy, 111*(7), 493–96.

Landsberg, C. (2010a). *The Diplomacy of Transformation: South African Foreign Policy and Statecraft*. Basingstoke: Macmillan.

Landsberg, C. (2010b). South Africa's Transformational Approach to Global Governance. *Africa Insight, 39*(4), 2010.

Landsberg, C. (2018). Afro-centric Diplomacy: The Golden Decade 1998–2008 and Pan-African Agency in world Affairs. In C. Landsberg (Ed.), *Africa Rise Up! Perspectives on African Renewal*. Johannesburg: Real Africa Publishers.

Landsberg, C., & Kondlo, K. (2007). *South Africa and the 'African Agenda', Policy Issues and Actors*. Johannesburg: Centre for Policy Studies.

Landsberg, C., Kornegay, F. A., & Qobo, M. (2017). BRICS Studies: Some Suggested Themes, UJCI Africa-China Policy Brief 1, July 2017.

Landsberg, C., Qobo, M., & Kornegay, F. (2017b). Reflections on the ANC NEC International Relations Sub-Committee Discussion Document. *Guiding Discussing Document, FES South Africa, 2017*, 4.

Landsberg, C., & Moore, C. (2013). BRICS and South African Cooperation, and the Durban Summit: What's in it for South Africa? *Portuguese Journal of International Affairs*, No. 7, Spring/Summer 2013.

Landsberg, C., & Smith, R. (2015). South Africa's Foreign Policy for sale'. *The Thinker*, Vol. 65, Quarter 3, 2015: 24–8.

Maloka, E. (2018). South Africa and the African Union. In A. Adebajo & K. Virk (Eds.), *Foreign Policy in Post-Apartheid South Africa, Security, Diplomacy and Trade*. London: Tauris.

Malunga, V. (2018). BRICS and South Africa: 10-year Anniversary Dividends or Endless Dialogue? *The Diplomatic Informer*, Issue 3, Spring Edition, 2018.

Masters, L., & Landsberg, C. (2015). IBSA's tri-lateral Constellation and Its Development Fund: Valuable Partners in Development Cooperation? *South African Journal of International Affairs, 2*(3), 2015.

Monyela, C. The editor's Note, Let's Talk SA's Foreign Policy *Ubuntu. Diplomacy in Action*, Issue 1, 2012.

Nkoana-Mashabane, M. (2016). Letter from the Minister, *Ubuntu. Diplomacy in Action: Issue, 1,* 2016.

Nkoana-Mashabane, M. South Africa: An important building BRICK within BRICS'. *Ubuntu, Diplomacy in Action*, Issue 1, 2012.

Pahad, E. (2017). Speech at the BRICS Governance Seminar, Quanzhen, China, 17 August 2017.

Pahad, E., Landsberg, C., & Maloka, E. (2012). The Fourth Pillar: A Century of Solidarity in ANC Politics. In B. Ngcaweni (Ed.), *The Future We Chose: Emerging Perspectives on the Future of the ANC*. Africa Institute: Pretoria.

Shelton, G. (2012). South Africa and East Africa, Missed Opportunities. In C. Landsberg, & J-A. van Wyk (Eds.), *South African Foreign Policy Review*, Volume 1. Pretoria: Africa Institute.

The Presidency, Twenty Year Review, South Africa 1994–2014. Pretoria-Tshwane, 2014.

Virk, K. (2018). South Africa and the BRICS. In A. Adebajo & K. Virk (Eds.), *Foreign Policy in Post-Apartheid South Africa, Security, Diplomacy and Trade*. London: Tauris.

CHAPTER 7

China–India Strains: Whither the BRICS?

Bhaso Ndzendze and David Monyae

Introduction

The relationship between China and India is a crucial one. As they are two of the world's most populous states, and as both are rising powers and key players in the nascent BRICS association, the complexities between them are potentially implicative for the future of the association, for regional peace and for stability in Asia and the geo-economically important Indo-Pacific—as well as for the economic development of both parties and their global partners; within BRICS, and generally, China is India's largest import partner, with a US$52-billion deficit in favour of the former (a fact commonly used to fan populist sentiment in India) as of 2018. This chapter will unpack the significance of India and China within the BRICS and then delve into the history of the relationship between these two

B. Ndzendze (✉) · D. Monyae
University of Johannesburg Centre for Africa-China Studies, Johannesburg, South Africa
e-mail: bndzendze@uj.ac.za

D. Monyae
e-mail: dmonyae@uj.ac.za

D. Monyae and B. Ndzendze (eds.), *The BRICS Order*, International Political Economy Series,
https://doi.org/10.1007/978-3-030-62765-2_7

major countries. The chapter will then give an account of some of the ongoing issues and potential flashpoints in the relationship—including boundary disputes, the ongoing tightening of alliances with one another's rivals, and disparate visions of world order—and show how it could be argued that they may threaten the bilateral relationship and therefore the BRICS group of which the two countries are so elemental. The fourth section of the chapter will detail the prospects of the key bones of contention between the two regional giants.

Sino-Indian Relations in Historical Perspective

After he took control of the government in New Delhi, Nerandra Modi wasted little time in trying to strengthen ties with Beijing. Within days of taking office, he promptly invited Chinese President Xi Jinping to India. But by the time Xi arrived in September 2014, the tricky nature of the India–China relationship was in full display as the Chinese president conducted a state visit in India while, simultaneously, troops from both countries squared off in Ladakh. This complexity in the India–China relationship, which has seen no less than half a dozen standoffs in the past 30 years alone, goes back to the colonial era, when Britain produced opium in the north of India and then subsequently forced it into Chinese territory—an issue which led to the so-called Opium Wars of the 1830s to the 1850s and subsequently led to loss of territory (and prestige) for China.

But the first modern and direct source of discord in the China–India relationship was China's decision to invade Tibet in October 1950—an act which eliminated a major buffer zone, and birthed border disputes between the two states. India's decision to grant asylum to the exiled young Dalai Lama after he fled Tibet in 1959 further drove a wedge between them. These soured relations resulted in the 1962 border war between the two Asian giants, in which India was soundly defeated within a month; nevertheless, the war resolved nothing, as territorial disputes along the 3225 kilometre-long Himalayan border continue to strain relations (and may have planted the seeds for future cataclysm, as India subsequently made a prodigious effort to modernise its army and acquire nuclear weapons to exact a deterrence against Beijing). For its part, India says Beijing is occupying 33,000 square kilometres of its territory in Jammu and Kashmir, while China claims the whole of Arunachal Pradesh. As will be discussed later in the chapter, this is further compounded by

India's self-perceived duty to protect Bhutan from Chinese encroachment, as well as China's cordial relationship with India's traditional enemy, Pakistan.

Diplomatic ties between India and China were re-established in 1976 and, despite an Indian upgrade in border securitisation infrastructure in the 1980s under Indira Gandhi, in 1996 Chinese President Jiang Zemin visited India, the first visit to India by a Chinese head of state. The two countries signed the Agreement on Confidence Building Measures in the Military Field with regard to the India–China border areas. But this political advance was once again subject to a minor puncture, as in 1998 India conducted a successful nuclear test and in 2000 the Tibetan Buddhist leader Karmapa Ugyen Trinley Dorje fled China and joined the Dalai Lama in India. Beijing warned New Delhi that 'giving the Karmapa asylum would violate the Five Principles of Peaceful Coexistence' (Liu 2017). Nevertheless, India did not comply with the Chinese request, which it interpreted as Beijing's intrusiveness.

An Achilles' Heel?

Detectable from the above cursory history is a complex and sometimes highly frictional relationship. Underlying this is the fact that other BRICS countries generally have excellent relations with one another, as well as with India and China, on bilateral basis. The key issue, the apparent Achilles' heel in the BRICS association, so to speak, is the relationship between the Indians and the Chinese. Difficulties within the BRICS association are not confined to the China–India relationship, but no other frictions are of this magnitude and with the potential to give rise to consequences affecting other bilateral relations within BRICS. It is true that South Africa has sometimes voiced opposition to its trade deficit with China, and to Brazil over perceived dumping in the poultry market, and it is also true that Russia and China have somewhat competing interests in the Central Asia region (Kazak 2017), but there is no BRICS bilateral relationship quite as problematic and potentially destructive as that of India–China.

This section deals with the four core issues in the China–India relationship—the South China Sea and the two states' growing relations with one another's traditional rivals, as well as the multiple boundary disputes and resultant standoffs. An assessment follows of how determinative these will be for the bilateral relationship between India and China (and therefore for the BRICS association).

The South China Sea

In January 2015, the US President Barack Obama, who would later (16 April 2015) write a very laudatory *TIME* magazine Person of the Year article on Narendra Modi, became the first president to visit India for the second time, and the first to attend the Republic Day parade in Delhi. At their first meeting, Obama and Modi reportedly spent some 45 min talking about China, and both expressed concern about Beijing's expansionist stance, especially in the South China Sea (Gippner 2016). In the next twelve months India signed three military agreements with the US that gave its armed forces virtually unrestricted use of Indian base and supply facilities. This was followed by visits to Itanagar, the capital of Arunachal Pradesh (China claims Arunachal Pradesh as its own, and refers to it as 'southern Tibet'), by the US consul general in Calcutta, and to a monastery at disputed Tawang by the US ambassador Richard Verma in February and October of 2016. Indeed, in May 2016 India had gone a step further and sent four warships to join a US–Japan task force and cruise for three months through the South China Sea, calling on 'friendly' ports. This had not sat well with China, which considers the acts as an encroachment on its sovereign territory. Complicating matters further is India's commitment to Vietnam, another claimant on the South China Sea.

India's Japan-Allied Alternative to China's Belt and Road Initiative

The Maritime Silk Road is China's most ambitious initiative in history. Popularly known as One Belt and One Road (OBOR), this infrastructure project of gigantic proportions is an attempt by Beijing to bring under its sway more than 60 countries, from Scandinavia to the South Pacific islands, in its land and maritime versions (Madhav 2017). In a world of competing economic and trade alliances, OBOR has overtaken many others active in the region and beyond—by any reckoning this is singularly the biggest constellation of nations in the twenty-first century. But one prominent nation is missing in this mega show: India (Singh 2014). And that is no coincidence.

To counter OBOR, some scholars claim (Nair 2017), India and Japan proposed the Asia-Africa Growth Corridor (AAGC). The two governments launched the initiative during the 52nd annual general meeting of the African Development Bank (AfDB) held in the Gujarati capital of Gandhijinagar on 24 May 2017, with the hope that the project would be 'a cheaper option and leave a smaller carbon footprint than China's One Belt, One Road (OBOR) initiative' (Nair 2017). On 25 May, the two nations jointly presented a vision document for the project 'that is largely meant to propel growth and investment in Africa, by curtailing the ever-increasing presence of the Chinese on the continent' (Nair 2017). The AAGC is an attempt to create a 'free and open Indo-Pacific region' by rediscovering and creating new sea corridors that will link the African continent with India and countries in the South Asia and Southeast Asia subregions, as well as Oceania, through both public and private efforts, with joint ventures and consortiums to take up infrastructure, power and agribusiness projects in Africa. Bangladesh, Myanmar, Cambodia, Laos, Indonesia, Singapore and Australia are already on board, and on the African side Mozambique, Kenya, Djibouti and BRICS member South Africa have expressed interest, with plans being made to connect ports in Jamnagar, India with Djibouti in the Gulf of Aden (Nair 2017). Additionally, the ports of Mombasa and Zanzibar will be connected to ports near Mudarai, and Calcutta will be linked to the Sittwe port in Myanmar. India is also developing ports under the Sagarmala programme specifically for this purpose.

Does this signify a direct repost to China? An 'alternative to the Chinese alternative order', as it were? To begin with, the plan grew out of a November 2016 meeting between the Indian prime minister, Narendra Modi, and the Japanese prime minister, Shinzo Abe (*Times of India* 2017a). Furthermore, that India would choose to partner up with China's traditional rival is perhaps a response to China's own decision to prioritise its cooperation with India's own traditional enemy in the region, Pakistan (this is discussed further below).

The Pakistan Problem

The China–Pakistan Economic Corridor (CPEC) constitutes one of the largest foreign investments China has made in the framework of the OBOR initiative. The expenditures planned for the coming years, in the amount of approximately $46 billion, will further intensify relations between China and Pakistan as well as provide Beijing with access to the Arabian Sea, increasing its trade access to Europe, the Middle East and Africa. At the same time, Pakistan will assume a more prominent role in China's foreign policy. But CPEC also affects relations between India and Pakistan. The corridor runs through the region of Gilgit-Baltistan (GB) in northern Pakistan; this region belongs to Jammu and Kashmir, to which both India and Pakistan have asserted claims. Since the accession of the former princely state to the Indian Union in October 1947, India has claimed the entire area, and insists on resolving the dispute only with Islamabad, invoking the 1972 Shimla Agreement according to which disputes between the two countries are to be resolved through bilateral negotiation. Pakistan, by contrast, invokes a series of resolutions on Kashmir in the United Nations and views the former princely state as disputed territory the final status of which must be put to a referendum. The Kashmir dispute has been the cause of three of the four wars that India and Pakistan have waged against each other since 1947. 'China, by being aware of these sensitive and still to be concluded spots and averting them has essentially both undermined India, a fellow BRICS ally, and at the same time interfered in the Indo-Pak relationship on the side of Pakistan' (Wagner 2016: 2)—that in the Indo-Pakistani wars of 1965 and 1971 China took the side of Pakistan against India is still not forgotten in New Delhi and these recent moves refresh such memories.

China's friendship with Pakistan is interpreted negatively in India in particular because Pakistan and India have been at odds with one another, with India claiming that the Pakistani military dresses its troops in civilian clothing so that they can conduct 'terrorist' attacks on India. But whereas India has been unequivocal in condemning terror outfits and has identified Pakistan as the main source of terrorism, China has defended Pakistan at every single forum. China has blocked India's attempt at the UN for sanctions against Jash-e-Mohammad chief Masood Azhar (India has been campaigning for sanction against Masood Azar, who has allegedly masterminded several terror attacks in India). Lack of cooperation from China is therefore taken with offence in New Delhi.

Territorial Disputes

Since 1962, there have been numerous border incidents between the Indian and Chinese militaries, among them Nathu La in 1967 and Sumdrong Chu two decades later. Over the decades since the 1993 agreement there have been hundreds of similar face-offs between Chinese and Indian troops, none of which has led to a single bullet being fired (Jha 2017). In the recent past, too, the Depsang Plateau and the Chumar Demchok area witnessed face-offs in April 2013 and September 2014, respectively, with the latter occurring at the same time as President Xi Jinping's visit to India (Moreira 2016)—incidentally, the Chinese incursion in Bhutan happened around the time of Prime Minister Modi's visit to the US (Dwivedi 2017).

The Doklam face-off was triggered when a team of the People's Liberation Army (PLA) was prevented by Indian troops from extending a class-5 track in the Doklam Plateau area which falls into Bhutanese territory. The Indian Army acted in response to a request from the Royal Bhutan Army under the terms of the 2007 Bilateral Friendship Treaty. Moreover, the PLA's track building is in contravention of the 2012 agreement between the special representatives of India and China, whereby the status quo was required to be maintained in the said area until the resolution of the tri-junction in consultation with Bhutan (Dwivedi 2017). On 18 June, two days after construction began, 270 Indian soldiers with weapons and bulldozers entered Doklam to stop the Chinese troops from constructing the road. On 24 July, the Chinese foreign minister doubled down, stating that India knows the territory belongs to China. Soon thereafter, however, the US entered the fray on the Bhutanese-Indian side, with India further asserting that its retreat would be predicated on a Chinese retreat. On 28 August both sides withdrew their forces.

The implications for the bilateral relationship, and for BRICS, of these flashpoints and difficulties are discussed below.

Implications for BRICS?

When Lobsang Sangay, the head of the self-styled Tibetan government in exile, hoisted the Tibetan national flag on the shores of Pangong lake in Ladakh (a mountainous, semi-autonomous region in northern India, borders the Chinese autonomous regions of Xinjiang and Tibet), he hammered the last nail into the coffin of the most important budding

> alliance of the post-cold war period. This was BRICS, the association of Brazil, Russia, India, China and South Africa. He did so by bringing the two largest members of BRICS, both in terms of population and GDP, to the brink of war.

So wrote Prem Jha in a BRICS Business Council outlet (Jha 2017: 2).[1] And yet it did not come to be: as we have seen there has been no Sino-Indian war of 2017—despite, further, 72 per cent of Indians believing that border disputes between India and China could lead to an escalation and eventual war (Liu 2017). At one time it looked like the strained relations between China and India might jeopardise the BRICS summit in Xiamen (especially as India renewed cases against Chinese imports and levelled accusations of dumping). However, the decision by Modi to attend was a boost for the group. Speaking at the meeting, both Xi and Modi stressed the importance of the bloc to global development. Modi specifically called for coordinated action on counterterrorism at the plenary session, while the leaders' declaration also focused on counterterrorism, and for the first time condemned the Pakistan-based Haqqani network, Lashkare Taiba and Jaishe Mohammad—which have been blamed for several attacks in India—as terrorist groups. The declaration was hailed in the Indian media as a diplomatic victory for Modi, as Pakistan is a Chinese ally (Liu 2017).

The friendship between China and Pakistan, read billboards in Chinese and English dotting Islamabad 'is higher than mountains, deeper than oceans, sweeter than honey, and stronger than steel' (Tharoor 2015). But China views Pakistan, which it considers its 'all weather friend' (Lee 2016), also through the lens of counterterrorism: a number of extremist outfits allegedly linked to ethnic Uighur separatists within Xinjiang have training camps in Pakistan's rugged borderlands with Afghanistan (Tharoor 2015). However, China may not be expected to further compel Pakistan to cease its surgical operations into India, and neither should it be expected to, as the Pakistani attacks are motivated by Indo-Pakistani issues dating back as far 1947 when the two states, which had been part of the same colonial entity, became independent and saw millions killed on either side in the partition. Resolving these differences is up to India and Pakistan, and China cannot be expected to intervene, especially since it itself believes that India is harbouring a terrorist in the person of the Dalai Lama whom it views as participating in the 'three evils' of separatism, religious extremism and terrorism.

But at the same time there is reason to argue that China's aim is to contain India's rising power through strategic linkages with the country's neighbours, particularly Pakistan; 'it seeks to browbeat New Delhi in the hope that the latter will back down and defer to Beijing's growing might' (Basu 2017). India, however, has also been unusually tough and unrelenting in its stances, whether on the CPEC, Arunachal Pradesh or Sikkim, and both have ended up staring each other down while underlining that they are a 'different' country from the one that fought a war in 1962 (Basu 2017).

These flashpoints, and the rapidity with which they disappear and simultaneously linger, are perhaps a symptom of a Sino-Indian relationship that is based on an ability to 'agree to disagree'.

Agreeing to Disagree?

In December 1996, when then state president and Communist Party of China (CPC) general secretary, Jiang Zemin, visited Pakistan after a trip to India, he made a very significant statement before the Pakistan National Assembly. Speaking to Pakistani lawmakers, Jiang advised Pakistan to adopt the India–China template in their dealings with New Delhi, and not let contentious issues get in the way of the development of their relationship on other fronts, particularly trade and business, and people-to-people ties. 'If certain issues cannot be resolved for the time being, they may be *shelved temporarily* [italics added] so that they will not affect the normal state-to-state relations', Jiang said (Richards 2014).

The salience of this point has been revitalised once more in 2017. While any progress on the border issue was probably symbolic (the two remain unable to even agree on the Line of Actual Control (LAC) between their two armies), China is much more interested in making significant *investments* in India (Richards 2014). This was in spite of the fact that the numbers of face-offs are now steadily rising—up to July 2018 the number of transgressions was about 300 compared to about 200 in 2017, and it is likely to surpass 500 by the end of the year (Sen 2017). Nevertheless, border disputes have never been cause for China to cease trade relations. China has border disputes with most of its neighbours—over the years, it has resolved territorial disputes with Afghanistan, Kazakhstan, Myanmar, Pakistan, Russia and Tajikistan. At present, its biggest border disputes are with India and Bhutan, but China also shares maritime borders with four countries—Japan, South Korea, Vietnam and the Philippines (*Times of India* 2017b). Continued trade with these countries, in the face of precarious relations, is owed to the fact that there is a wide berth between military and commercial considerations. Further, the rising frequency of border incursions could be due to a disconnect between the sometimes autonomous and self-directed top-brass in the People's Liberation Army and the politicians in Beijing.

Prospects

Regional Responsibility and Trade –the Other Achilles' Heels?

As of 2015 there has been a slowdown in China's economic growth, and Beijing is anxious to avoid any major distraction from preventing the restoration of its economy so as to reach its projected aim of a moderately prosperous society by 2049, as well as to fund its OBOR grand plan. India's reluctance for conflict with China also revolves around the economical state of affairs in the country (Svls 2017). China's keenness for a partnership with India is because demography is its Achilles' heel, with the Chinese population ageing at an unprecedented pace. China's working-age population peaked in 2012 and median age will rise rather abruptly to 49 by 2050—with national debt at 300 per cent of GDP it has only a small window to achieve the 'national dream' of becoming rich before getting old. By contrast, India's working-age population will increase till 2050, enabling higher growth rates and eventually overtaking the US in terms of GDP (Sanwal 2017). For India, the fundamental question is that given the rise of protectionism in the US it cannot be a $10 trillion economy without integration into the growing Asian market and without benefiting from Chinese investment.

Additionally, both the Indian and Chinese governments recognise that 'their relations are a factor of stability in a multipolar world, and at a time of global instability', and that 'differences should not become disputes' (Sanwal 2017). Thus the India–China strategic convergence will need recognition that the Asian century is composed of two players.

The Nuclear Factor?

'The first Chinese nuclear test, coming two years after India's defeat in the 1962 Sino-Indian conflict, precipitated the Indian nuclear weapons program, which in turn first demonstrated its capacity in 1974' (Tellis

2015). New Delhi responded to the Chinese challenge with additional nuclear tests and in 1998 declared itself to be a nuclear weapon state and began to overtly develop its nuclear deterrent aimed at both China and Pakistan. India today is believed to possess an arsenal of some one hundred nuclear weapons, though this figure is highly uncertain. The country is thought to have produced close to 600 kilograms of weapons-grade plutonium, though it is unclear whether all this material has been machined into warheads.

> The total size of the Chinese nuclear weapons inventory today is widely believed to consist of some 250 nuclear warheads, but the accuracy of these or any other numbers is debatable. China has a substantial fissile material stockpile consisting of some 16 metric tons of highly enriched uranium and some 1.8 metric tons of weapon-grade plutonium, so there are no practical constraints on its ability to produce an arsenal of any size it chooses. Given the choices China makes in regard to delivery systems, it could deploy anywhere up to an additional 150 warheads over the next ten years. (Tellis 2015: 2)

China, which in 2016 vetoed India's membership to the Nuclear Supplier's Group of nations, did not oppose India's civilian nuclear deal with the US, but has on occasion argued for the same kind of nuclear exceptionalism to Pakistan that the US allowed for India. As both states are nuclear power states, the likelihood of a large-scale war is further reduced due to the notion of nuclear deterrence which holds that no war between two nuclear states is probable as they both are likely to engage in prudential pacifism for fear of the cost to be incurred in a relatively shorter period of time by the other's nuclear strikes (Fang 2014). Further, India's capability needs to be re-examined in light of its new strategic interactions with the nuclear powerhouse, the US, and US allies in the Asia-Pacific region (Yang 2016; Kugelman 2017; Madan 2017).

The Paradox

The strength of other bilateral relations within BRICS (China–Brazil, China–South Africa, China–Russia; India–Brazil, India–South Africa, India–Russia) means also that the tensions are circumnavigated and rendered obsolete—and, indeed, in seeking to compensate for the strained bilateral relationship with one another, China and India may aim to fortify their relations with the other BRICS members, thereby paradoxically fortifying the association.

To that degree, the BRICS association can be said to be relatively secure from unravelling on account of Sino-Indian strains.

Where to from Here?

A point in need of emphasis is the extent to which the BRICS association—unlike, say, the European Union, NATO or the African Union—is not predicated on, and does not aspire to, a dissolution of sovereignty and the propagation of a singular identity by the member states. Indeed, it is composed of independent nation states that are in association with one another for the purposes of individual growth through multilateral means. Therefore, we cannot expect New Delhi to subordinate itself to a 'globalisation with Chinese characteristics', and the reverse cannot be expected of Beijing in the region—that is not in the nature of states. Furthermore, the other BRICS members—South Africa, Brazil and Russia—do not, as China and India do, share thousands of kilometres of (historically problematic and colonially drawn) borders in a geographically intense part of the world. Indeed, the intriguing thing is the extent to which that India and China have managed to avoid more conflicts between them.

> Coexistence between India and China in this multipolar world order is possible, but their search for energy resources, quest to uphold their own identity ... and engagement in balance of power politics to exert authority on each other's presence, are some elements that guide their non-cooperative relationship (Panda 2017: 9).

One could remove 'India' and replace it with 'the US' or 'Japan' and this sentiment would carry just as much truth. That this can be said is telling; it particularly explicates Beijing's ability to pursue and deepen trade relations with states it partially resents and at the same time needs—whether Japan (its former coloniser, with whom it has numerous heated island disputes), the US (which it regards as encroaching on its Pacific vicinity) or the Philippines and Vietnam (with which it has disputes over the South China Sea). This is despite many predictions of looming and (especially vis-à-vis the US) seemingly 'inevitable' conflicts on account of historical patterns, which would seem to point towards conflict between a rising and an existent power. This chapter has found that the same kind of relationship exists between New Delhi and Beijing; that the two states engage in some intense strains that almost border on conflict but which do not hinder economic relations. And for that reason, these can, in the short- to medium-term (10 to 30 years), be said to offer no probable hindrance to the existence and growth of the BRICS association; nuclear deterrence, regional responsibility and mutual need of markets would seem to prevail over questions of territory and symbolism.

Notes

1. The 134-km long Pangong Lake is a particularly sensitive spot in China–India relations as half of it lies in Aksai Chin (both India and China claim the Aksai Chin area in its entirety), and the other half in Ladakh. Despite a 1993 agreement for peace and tranquillity signed by China and India, the Line of Actual Control in this area remains undemarcated. Patrol boats have therefore often faced each other on its waters.

Bibiography

Basu, T. (2017). India-China: A Game of Dangerous Brinkmanship. *Economic Times*, July. http://economictimes.indiatimes.com/news/defence/indiachinadangerousbrinkmanship/printarticle/59455674.cms.

Devadason, E. S. (2012). Enhancing China-India Trade Cooperation: Complementary Interactions? *China Review, 12*(2), 59–83.

Dwivedi, G. G. (2010). Doklam, China's Strategic Calculus and India's Policy Options. *Institute for Defence Studies and Analyses*, 11 August. http://www.idsa.in/idsacomments/doklamchinastrategiccalculusandindiapolicyoptions_.

Dwivedi, G. G. (2017). 'Doklam, China's Strategic Calculus and India's Policy Options,' *Institute for Defence Studies and Analyses*. https://idsa.in/idscomments/doklam-china-strategic-calculus-and-india-policy-options_ggdw.ivedi_110817 (Last accessed: 7 December 2020).

Fang, Tien-sze. (2014). *Asymmetrical Threat Perceptions in India-China Relations*. New Delhi: Oxford University Press.

Gippner, O. (2016). Antipiracy and Unusual Coalitions in the Indian Ocean Region: China's Changing Role and Confidence Building with India. *Journal of Current Chinese Affairs, 3*(1), 107–37.

Jha, Prem Shankar. (2010). India-China: Differences, Disputes and Deadlock. BRICS Business Council, 14 July. https://www.bricsbusinesscouncil.co.za/bricsopinion/indiachinadifferencesdisputesanddeadlock/.

Jha, Prem Shankar. (2017). 'The Bhutan Stand-Off Is an Opportunity, Not a Threat,' *The Wire*, https://thewire.in/diplomacy/bhutan-china-modiborder-opportunity. (Last accessed: 7 December 2020).

Jha, S. (2014). Xi Jinping in India: A Breakthrough in Relations? *The Diplomat*, 18 September. http://thediplomat.com/2014/09/xijinpinginindiaabreakthroughinrelations/?allpages=yes&print=yes.

Kazak, A. (2017). Russia's Ties with China, Pakistan Disturb India—Experts. *Russia Beyond The Headlines*, 5 April. https://www.rbth.com/international/2017/04/05/russiastieswithchinapakistandisturbindiaexperts_.

Keay, J. (2010). *India: A History: From the Earliest Civilisations to the Boom of the Twenty-First Century*. London: Happer Press.

Khatri, S. (2017). Events Leading to the Sino-Indian Conflict of 1962. *Institute for Defence Studies and Analyses*, September, Monograph No. 58: http://www.idsa.in/monograph/eventsleadingsinoindianconflict1962?.

Kugelman, M. (2017). Why the US-India Relationship is Headed for Big Things. *The National Interest*, 27 Jun. http://nationalinterest.org/feature/whytheusindiarelationshipheadedbigthings21335.

Lee, R. (2016). *The Strategic Importance of Chinese-Pakistani Relations*. Report, Doha: Al Jazeera Centre for Studies.

Liu Zhen. (2017). China, India Should Pursue Peace on Border, Move on from Dispute, Leaders Agree. *South China Morning Post*, 5 September. http://www.scmp.com/print/news/china/diplomacydefence/article/2109902/chinaindiashouldpursuepeacebordermovedispute.

Madan, T. (2017). When Modi Meets Trump: Where do US-India Relations Stand? Brookings Institute, 23 June. https://www.brookings.edu/blog/orderfromchaos/2017/06/23/whenmodimeetstrumpwheredousindiarelationsstand/.

Madhav, R. (2017). Turning Down China. *The Indian Express*, 17 May. http://indianexpress.com/article/opinion/columns/turningdownchinaonebeltoneroad4659155/.

Moreira, B. B. (2016). The Sino-Indian Border Dispute and Its CONsequences for Asian Security.' *Revista Mundorama*, 23 March. https://www.mundorama.net/?p=19035.

Nair, A. (2017). To Counter OBOR, India and Japan Propose Asia-Africa Sea Corridor. *The Indian Express*, 31 May: 1–2.

Panda, J. P. (2017). *India-China: Politics of Resources, Identity and Authority in a Multipolar World Order*. New York: Routledge.

Richards, C. (2014). Modi's Tokyo-Beijing Balancing Act. *The Diplomat*, 17 September: http://thediplomat.com/2014/09/modistokyobeijingbalancingact/?.

Sanwal, M. (2017). *A New Equilibrium with China: Near Simultaneous Rise of Neighbours is Not Unprecedented in Asia*. New Dehli: Institute for Defence

Studies and Analyses. http://www.idsa.in/idsacomments/anewequilibriumwithchina_sanwal_250817?q=print/.

Sen, S. R. (2017). Will Line of Actual Control with China Become Like Line of Control with Pakistan? *India Today*, 18 August. http://indiatoday.intoday.in/story/lineofactualcontrollineofcontrolindiachinapakistan/.

Singh, Z. D. (2014). Indian Perceptions of China's Maritime Silk Road Idea. *Journal of Defence Studies, 4*(8), 133–48.

Svls, A. (2017). The Deadlock at Doklam. *The Youth Journal*, 25 July. https://theyouthjournal.com/2017/07/25/thedeadlockatdoklam/.

Tellis, A. J. (2015). *Growing Nuclear Capabilities with no End in Sight*. Congressional Testimony, Washington, DC: Carnegie Endowment for International Peace.

Tharoor, I. (2015). What China's and Pakistan's Special Friendship Means. *Washington Post*, 21 April: 1–3.

Times of India. (2017a). Asia-Africa Growth Corridor Launched. *Times of India*, 25 May.

Times of India. (2017b). China Does Not Accept the McMahon Line Agreed on by Britain & Tibet. *Times of India*, 3 July. http://timesofindia.indiatimes.com/india/chinadoesnotacceptthemcmahonlineagreedonbybritaintibet/.

Wagner, C. (2016). 'The effects of the China-Pakistan Economic Corridor on India-Pakistan relations' (SWP Comment, 25/2016). Berlin: Stiftung wissenschaft und politik -SWP- Deutsches institut für internationale politik und Sicherheit. https://nbn-resolving.org/urn:nbn:de:0168-ssoar-46898-4 (Last accessed: 7 December 2020).

Yang, Xiaoping. (2016). *China's Perceptions of India as a Nuclear Weapons Power*. Washington, DC: Carnegie Endowment for International Peace. http://carnegieendowment.org/2016/06/30/chinasperceptionsofindiaasnuclearweaponspowerpub63970.

CHAPTER 8

Brics–Africa Cooperation in Perspective: The Case of Kenya

Westen K. Shilaho

Introduction

The relationship between Africa and Brazil, Russia, India, China and South Africa (BRICS) bloc is fraught with opportunities, suspicions and challenges. The question is whether Africa exercises agency in its partnership with BRICS, particularly China, the most ubiquitous member of this bloc in Africa. But what, in the first place, is African agency?[1]

African agency has been defined as 'a determined response by Africa's developmental states to the gains rather than the costs of discovery of Africa's potential by the BRICS, especially China' (Shaw 2015: 257). Africa's leading economies such as Nigeria, South Africa, Kenya and

[1] Sections of this chapter appeared in UJCI Africa-China Policy Brief, 5 March 2018, under 'Sino-Kenyan Cooperation: Whither the West?'

W. K. Shilaho (✉)
SARChI in African Diplomacy and Foreign Policy, University of Johannesburg, Johannesburg, South Africa

D. Monyae and B. Ndzendze (eds.), *The BRICS Order*, International Political Economy Series,
https://doi.org/10.1007/978-3-030-62765-2_8

Angola, however, are steeped in predatory politics, corruption, institutional dysfunction, pervasive mistrust and disconnect between governments and the people making it hard for the continent to design an African strategy to engage BRICS and other actors, particularly Western powers. The BRICS bloc aspires to tilt the global power equilibrium that is weighted in favour of the West, but could be militated by domestic incoherence, internal contradictions, deep fissures and rivalries (Bond 2018: 404). Sino-India border dispute is long standing. BRICS members betray right wing populism and nationalist politics similar to that which has burst in the open in the West. The bloc has some of the most autocratic leaders in the world. In India, since assuming power in 2014, Narendra Modi's politics thrives on Hindu nationalism which has exacerbated religious schism between Hindus and minority Muslims and often explodes into deadly interreligious violence. Controversial laws specifically the citizenship amendment bill of 2019 or 'anti-Muslim' law (that exclusively denies Muslim immigrants citizenship) and the anti-conversion law, evocatively referred to as 'love jihad' law (that criminalises interfaith marriages between Muslims and Hindus but in essence prohibits Muslim men from marrying Hindu women) have been enacted under Modi. These laws deligitimise minority Muslims and violate India's constitution that affirms securalism. Jair Bolsonaro is an unsavoury populist without regard for human decency and has encroached on the rights of citizens including indigenous Brazilians. Xi Jinping has tightened a grip on Chinese politics and is modelling the polity and society on his persona. Under his rule, basic rights, particularly of Uighur Muslim minorities and dissidents, are wantonly trampled upon. Beijing is also accused of pushing through draconian laws that curtail guranteed freedoms in Hong Kong and targeting pro-democracy activists. Russia's Vladimir Putin brooks no dissent, viciously hunts down opposition politicians, critics and is keen to elongate his stay in power in perpetuity. South Africa's credibility in Africa has taken a battering as political demagogues, nestled in autochthonous nativist politics and desperate to shore up sagging legitimacy among their respective constituencies, whip up populist anti-immigrant rhetoric, and xenophobia against African immigrants whom they scapegoat for social pathologies and governance deficits. This virulent bigotry trends almost daily on twitter locally under hashtags, #PutSouthAfricansFirst or #PutSouthAfricaFirst.

Pointedly, the BRICS bloc is not universally received enthusiastically in Africa since it is viewed as mercantilist and detached from Africa's well-being. In Africa, suspicions abound about the intentions of BRICS, including in South Africa, the last entrant into the bloc. Sceptics perceive

South Africa's BRICS membership only as symbolic because it is the 'small partner' on almost all indices, and they therefore regard South Africa as a conduit, 'gateway to Africa', through which the other BRICS countries strive to access the lucrative African market and its natural resources. The understanding is that, 'The essential power relationship that binds together the state leadership and large corporations, ranging across spaces from Western metropoles to the farthest African mine or agricultural field, is a nested hierarchy that includes imperialist and sub-imperialist relations' (Bond 2018: 404). Russia is richly endowed with natural resources and therefore Africa's minerals are of less significance but still Russia collaborates with Africa in natural resource extraction. Russia's new deposits are concentrated in far-flung regions of the vast country which makes exploitation prohibitive, while some such as manganese, chrome and bauxite are in short supply and the shortage has to be offset with imports (Daniel and Shubin 2018: 58).

South Africa's economic footprints are noticeable across the continent, and it attracts as much suspicion and is associated with imperialist inclinations as are the other countries within the BRICS constellation (Shaw 2015: 257). South Africa casts itself as the 'gateway to Africa' for the BRICS countries, being the continent's most industrialised country and the only African member of the Group of 20 (G20). These attributes enhance its arrogated leadership role in Africa, but also contribute to resentment by fellow African countries (Saunders 2014: 230). Thus Bond observes that 'multinational corporations (MNCs) and state firms based in the BRICS countries may find the so-called "gateway" function in Africa offered by South Africa of diminishing utility' (Bond 2018: 403). Individual African countries often engage external actors bilaterally in concert with the rubric of sovereignty sometimes in defiance of binding regional norms. South Africa's leadership in Africa is contested and even delegitimised.

For this reason, South Africa tried to downplay its special status during the first BRICS summit to be held in Africa that took place in Durban in 2013—hence the deliberately worded theme 'BRICS and Africa: Partnership for Development, Integration and Industrialisation'. Both the theme and the invitations extended to other African rulers were meant to accord the summit a continental appeal (Saunders 2014: 230). However, sceptics are not persuaded by diplomatic courtesies and flattery,

> I argue that the shifts declared by BRICS through its summits and other meetings only will not and/or cannot guarantee that through the membership of South Africa, Africa as a whole would likely change her place

> holistically within the liberal world economy and the existing nature of the international division of labour. For the BRICS' actions to be positively felt in Africa, there would first be a need for reforms prior to the BRICS' policy implementation. (Lumumba-Kasongo 2015: 80)

The close partnership between South Africa and China arouses tension among other African countries wary of this relationship, and themselves competing against South Africa for Chinese attention. Sino-sceptics are as much concerned about China's economic inroads into Africa as they are about South Africa's (Saunders 2014: 230). South Africa, like China and indeed the entire BRICS bloc, eyes Africa's economic opportunities in retail, telecommunications, agriculture and mining. The metropole economies, argues Bond, have drawn the BRICS into exploitative institutions such World Trade Organisations (WTO), Bretton Woods Institutions, United Nations Institutions and World Economic Forum (WEF) which effectively marks them out as accomplices in Africa's underdevelopment (Bond 2018: 404). South African companies such as Mobile Telephone Network (MTN), Digital Satellite Television (DStv) and Shoprite have flourished in Africa while others pulled out because of stiff competition and an unfavourable business environment. Shoprite has since decided to exit Nigerian market just like clothing firms, Mr Price, Truworths and Woolworths, that pulled out of the same market earlier owing to currency volatility, a struggling economy, corruption, poor infrastructure, the rule of law deficits and failure to appreciate Nigerians' tastes and cultures that influence their consumption habits. Amid this 'scramble for Africa', it is not tenable for Africa to separate allies from exploitative 'imperialists', and so,

'In the light of the new scramble, the question is not so much a choice between Europe, the USA, and China (or any other actor interested in the African resources). The challenge lies in setting a new course to make optimal use of the new scenario on the continent' (Melber 2008: 397). And this is what would constitute African agency.

China's role in revamping Africa's dilapidated infrastructure is mixed. It has endeared China to some and elicited criticism in equal measure. Whereas some have praised China's contribution in infrastructure development across Africa, critics have accused China of predatory lending, and propping up corrupt politicians in rogue states in exchange for Africa's natural resources, particularly crude oil and natural gas. Other commodities that China imports from Africa include timber, uranium, diamonds, fish, cotton and other farm produce (Alves and Draper 2007: 21). Some African countries had been drilling oil for decades before the arrival of Chinese investment in this sector. There are, however, substantial crude oil reserves in Sudan, Angola, Nigeria, the Gulf of Guinea and in many other parts of Africa that are yet to be exploited, latent resources, that China is investing in and exploiting (Alves and Draper 2007: 21). China's economic interests in Africa are not limited to natural resources, and Chinese companies are active in over 49 African countries not all of which are endowed with natural resources. In Sierra Leone, Seychelles and Senegal, for instance, China is involved in tourism-related construction work, wholesale and retail and the development of energy, transport, communications, health and education systems (Alves and Draper 2007: 22–23).

Western powers view China's 'principle of non-interference or the sovereignty doctrine' as opposed to their 'conditionality approach' (Pehnelt and Abel 2007: 16) as undermining their efforts to use conditional aid to combat corruption and improve governance in Africa (Pehnelt and Abel 2007: 1). China portrays itself as an anti-imperial, non-interventionist ally of Africa and 'Chinese businessmen seem to recognise Africa's challenges such as endemic corruption, political instability and the absence of the rule of law as opening economic opportunities rather than posing a threat' (Pehnelt and Abel 2007: 20). But Chinese foreign policy towards Africa masks the threat that China poses to nascent African industries, democracy and the lopsided geopolitical and economic relationship between China, the world's second largest economy, and Africa, the poorest continent. The benefits that Africa derives from this relationship are often overplayed and the impediments to a genuine partnership that do exist are glossed over or ignored outright (Alves and Draper 2007: 24). Thus,

> Potentially alternative choices – like new deals with China – do not necessarily improve governance. Chinese foreign policy is attractive for autocratic leaders and oligarchies still in power over societies which are run like the private property of cliques. Guided by the gospel of non-intervention, China provides grants and loans to kleptocracies with dubious human rights records and is not petty minded when it comes to funding modalities. (Henderson 2008: 12–13 in Melber 2008: 396)

This, in no way, implies that Western powers are lodestars of democracy, human rights and the rule of law since they have propped up allied autocrats since the Cold War period to date and expediently invoke good governance while upbraiding defiant ones.

The greatest threat that China poses to Africa, however, relates to governance, having become increasingly centralised under Xi Jinping verging on authoritarianism. Although, in and of itself, governance is not a sufficient prerequisite for economic growth and development, it is necessary for Africa's take-off and distribution of economic spin-offs. The role of external actors, especially Africa's former colonial masters, in the so-called resource curse phenomenon, cannot be denied. But Africa's inability to leverage its natural resources for the good of its citizenry is primarily a result of governance deficits, specifically paucity of leadership (Alves and Draper 2007: 25). Sham elections, politicisation of identity—ethnic, linguistic, cultural, religious and regional—for cynical power grabs, rampant corruption, absence of the rule of law and impunity contribute to Africa's poor governance record, and no amount of external intervention will remedy this state of affairs. Sustainable solutions to Africa's governance problems have to be home-grown but selective and careful appropriation, not mimicry, of exemplary practices from elsewhere is also required. Internal critics should not be generically dismissed as Western lackeys while regime apologists are not necessarily patriotic. External scrutiny should not be dismissed as interference in the sovereignty of African countries, which in any case, has been eroded by various treaties that African countries are signatories to. Civil strife and unresponsive governments have immensely chipped away at Africa's sovereignty. The tendency to shirk responsibility and wholly blame external actors, particularly former colonial masters, the US and their commercial entities, while absolving African rulers, for Africa's poor human development indices, is as spurious as the messiah complex that China is sometimes associated with. Almost all the African countries in which China invests (such as the Democratic Republic of Congo (DRC), Nigeria, Republic of Congo, Zimbabwe, Sudan, Ethiopia, Rwanda, Uganda, Angola and Kenya) have appalling human rights records and are plagued by corruption. Angola seems to have turned a corner with the ascendancy to power of Joao Lourenco in 2017, who immediately embarked on an anticorruption onslaught against his predecessor, Eduardo Dos Santos, his family and his corruption networks. If he sustains the momentum, Angola could redeem itself regarding the rule of law and governance requisite for stability and equitable distribution of national resources.

A contrary view, though, is that through trade, investment, foreign aid and project finance China has afforded Africa, home to some of the world's poorest, a chance to improve living standards. China's 'total package' (money, technology and political protection from outside pressures) is irresistible to African rulers in search of alternatives to the supposed consensus built around good governance, human rights and transparency (Alves and Draper 2007: 25). Whichever side one takes, what cannot be disputed is that China–Africa relations have contributed to Africa's infrastructure development (Pehnelt and Abel 2007: 1–2). Furthermore, the Chinese have invested in areas that Western countries have been unwilling to venture in, but China, like the West and other foreign actors, is not driven by altruism and humanitarian motives in Africa,

> Trade between China and Africa reproduces a classical skewed pattern; raw materials on the one side (Africa), in exchange for (value added) manufactured products on the other side (China). The global trade and exchange patterns have, despite new actors, not displayed any meaningful qualitative structural changes. Chinese trade and investment in African countries is not significantly different from other patterns. (Melber 2008: 394)

The relations between China and Africa during the Cold War may have been characterised by altruism and common ideologies when China competed with the Soviet Union for global influence and prestige, but not any longer (Alves and Draper 2007: 23). The pervasive official rhetoric encapsulated in China's Africa policy that speaks about 'sincerity, friendship, and equality', 'mutual benefit, reciprocity and common prosperity', 'mutual support, and close coordination' and 'continued learning from each other' (Alves and Draper 2007: 24) does not capture the reality of this relationship, which is fraught with suspicion, exploitation and inequalities.

Relations between Brazil and Africa date back to the colonial era and are deeply embedded in the transatlantic slave trade that saw movement of enslaved Africans to the Americas. Brazil, with the highest population of black people outside of Africa, has strong ancestral ties to Africa, and maintains economic cooperation through trade, infrastructure investment and technical cooperation with Africa (Abdenur 2018: 194). Brazilian evangelical churches have found a foothold in Africa, although in Angola, some of them have been accused of corruption (money laundering) and forced to close down by the Angolan government. Like the other BRICS members, Brazil is involved in peacekeeping and peacebuilding missions in Africa and has deployed boots on the ground in trouble spots (Abdenur 2018: 195–196). Africa–Brazil relations were at an all-time high during the era of the socialist President, Luis Inacio da Silva (2003–2010) but have waned over the years under his rather insular successors. In spite of the South-South cooperation, Brazil's mining and infrastructure projects in Mozambique were shrouded in opacity, and caused poverty, which evoked neo-colonialism, an accusation that is often levelled against China and the BRICS bloc generally (Abdenur 2018: 202). Brazil's ties with Angola, Cape Verde and Mozambique, are based on a common colonial heritage as, former colonies of Portugal and span over a range of interests including defence, construction, oil, mining and agriculture. Brazilian firms that operate in Africa tend to hire local workers to distinguish Brazil from Chinese companies that almost exclusively use Chinese workers (Abdenur 2018: 194). Africa–Brazil relations have waxed and waned in tandem with the regime in power. Brazil imports minerals and raw materials from Africa while Africa imports agricultural products, ethanol and car parts from Brazil (Begbie 2018).

Russo-Africa relationship is different from that which Africa has with colonisers—Belgium, Britain, France and Portugal. Since Russia did not colonise Africa and supported its anti-colonial movements, it has some credibility in Africa (Daniel and Shubin 2018: 55). During the Cold War, Russia supported allied African countries with diplomatic, economic and military assistance and was also in the forefront in supporting struggles against the vestiges of colonialism in Southern Africa. In the aftermath of the disintegration of the Soviet Union, the Russian Federation became economically weak which forced it to drastically disengage from Africa and explore closer ties with the West (Daniel and Shubin 2018: 51). For this reason, among the BRICS countries, Russia is the least present in Africa regarding trading relations and cultural exchanges (people-to-people relations). 'New Russia', since the 1990s, not only pulled out of Africa but also neglected it (Daniel and Shubin 2018: 55). Russia's trade with Africa constitutes food, beverages, tobacco, oil, mineral products and manufactured goods which happens mainly with North Africa—Algeria and Egypt. Its main investment in Africa is mining (Daniel and Shubin 2018: 58–59).

Military relations between Russia and Africa involve arms transfers, military training, UN peacekeeping operations and combating terrorism and piracy (Daniel and Shubin 2018: 60–61).

India and Africa share a longstanding history of trade, and were allies in anti-colonialism struggles. The Bandung conference, the first gathering of newly independent African and Asian states kicked off the South-South solidarity and inspired the quest by global South for a just and equitable world (Virk 2018: 246). India has expanded its trade interests with Africa that range from coal, oil, natural gas, and uranium. It has diversified its trading partners of which South Africa, Niger and Tanzania, are integral to India's nuclear power ambitions owing to uranium reserves (Begbie 2018). Africa exports raw materials to India and imports manufactured goods—petroleum products, pharmaceutical products, motor vehicles—and rice and frozen meat. India has been keen to distinguish itself from China in its engagement with Africa by trying to emphasise development (Virk 2018: 254–257). The maiden India-Africa forum, modelled on Forum on China-Africa Cooperation (FOCAC), was held in 2008 and underscored the rivalry between the two powers in competition for Africa's natural resources and investment opportunities. India is also involved in peacekeeping operations across Africa to secure its investments and Indian migrants concentrated in east and southern Africa. Intermittent incidents of racism, and racially motivated violence against African students in India, however, mar this relationship.

This chapter broadly analyses the cooperation between BRICS countries and Africa without minimising the role that Africa's traditional Western trading partners still play on the continent. It specifically zeroes in on the China-Africa partnership, using Kenya, the East African region and the Horn as entry points. China is the most noticeable among BRICS countries by investments in Africa, and so takes up a disproportionate space in the chapter. The chapter argues that unless Africa's poor governance is addressed, Africa cannot leverage its natural resources for the good of its people regardless of the external actor it engages. Therefore, a seemingly moral dichotomy between the West and BRICS, specifically China, in which the latter is portrayed as Africa's ally while the former, its foe, does not stand scrutiny. It only evokes a Cold War shibboleth.

China in the East African Region and the Horn of Africa

During the Forum on China-Africa Cooperation (FOCAC) conference in 2015, Ethiopia, Kenya, Tanzania and Republic of Congo were designated as the four 'industrial cooperation demonstration and pioneering' countries. Ethiopia is one of the African countries to have attracted massive Chinese manufacturing investment. It has financed and set up industrial zones such as the Eastern Industrial Zone and the Addis Ababa railway line that connects landlocked Ethiopia to the port of Djibouti and underwrote 83 per cent of the total cost of the project. This railway line has revolutionised transportation between the two countries, dramatically slashing the journey from Addis Ababa to the Djibouti port from three days by road to 12hours, which is a boost to export industries in Ethiopia (*China-Africa Research Initiative* 2018). Djibouti is a strategic port in the Horn of Africa and its status has been highlighted through a series of Chinese-funded infrastructure projects. A multipurpose port, a livestock port and an inland salt port for salt export are some of the new projects. The construction of a new free trade zone (FTZ) is ongoing as part of the port complex, that began in January 2017 and will be operated as a joint venture between the China Merchants Port Holdings Company (CMPH), Dalian Djibouti Ports and the Free Zone Authority (*China-Africa Research Initiative* 2018).

China loaned Djibouti US$492 million to finance the Djibouti section of Addis Ababa-Djibouti railway, for which Ethiopia is the guarantor. A Chinese loan of US$322 million also funds a water pipeline from Ethiopia, linking up the two countries in yet another major project. Djibouti is a geostrategic ally to China and many other foreign actors. It hosts China's first overseas naval base, which the Chinese euphemistically refer to as a 'logistics facility' for use by its peacekeeping and humanitarian operations in Africa. The base was also expected to help in anti-piracy operations in the Gulf of Aden. China's base adds to other military bases of the US, France, Italy and Japan that are already located in Djibouti (*China-Africa Research Initiative* 2018).

Kenya's 'Look East' Policy Amid Western Influence

Kenya demonstrates that in spite of the prominence of Chinese interests in Africa, Africa's traditional trading partners, its former colonial masters, are still influential. When the Al-Qaeda terrorist organisation bombed the US Embassy in Nairobi in 1998, it plunged Kenya headlong into the US-led 'war on terror', and substantively influenced its subsequent foreign relations. Kenya's foreign policy takes cognisance of the threat posed by terrorism, noting that 'with international terrorism now elevated into a foremost threat to global security, combating this scourge has become a crucial agendum of Kenya's external relations, and a subject of its strategic partnerships' (Republic of Kenya 2014). In 2002, the Al-Qaeda attack on an Israeli-owned hotel in Kenya's port city of Mombasa and the firing of two surface-to-air missiles at an El Al plane carrying Israeli tourists while taking off from Mombasa accentuated the terror threat to Kenya.

Kenya's successive governments have in one way or another been shaped by the 'war on terror', which betrays the US influence over these regimes that placed them on a collision course with Muslim communities, especially in the coastal region. A backlash ensued, and ramped up anti-American sentiment. Kenyan Muslims have accused security forces of religious profiling, and have blamed the brutality meted out to Muslims on the embrace of anti-terrorism laws at the behest of the US by former President, Mwai Kibaki (Barkan 2004). These draconian laws contravened basic human rights, and were therefore unconstitutional. While Kenya participated in the 'war on terror', Kibaki signed business agreements with China at the expense of Kenya's Western trading partners. Consequently, China funded numerous infrastructure programmes, specifically road construction, under the so-called Look East policy.

The central argument in this chapter is that despite Kenya's perceived shift to the East (a byword for China) the West still exerts significant influence over its domestic and international affairs. Besides the 'war on terror', the West exercises undue influence over Kenyan politics, as evidenced by US, British and EU interventions in the aftermath of the violently disputed presidential elections in 2007, 2013 and 2017 as they had done before. During the protracted electioneering period in 2017 characterised by annulment of presidential results and boycott of subsequent ones by the opposition, Western meddling was again evident. In 2008, Western powers piled pressure on protagonists to accept a power-sharing agreement following intercommunal violence after a stolen presidential election, resulting in the formation of a grand coalition government that did not address structural causes of recurrent violence during elections. They also threatened to impose sanctions such as travel bans on recalcitrant politicians on either side of the dispute which forced them to accede to the Western imposed roadmap out of the internecine violence that almost tipped into civil war.

Kenya's new Standard Gauge Railway (SGR) is one of China's most significant Belt and Road Initiatives in Africa (*China-Africa Research Initiative* 2018). Phase I from Mombasa to Nairobi, was funded through Chinese loans worth US$3.6 billion which is 90 per cent of the total contract. Kenya is a major destination for Chinese investment, including manufacturing and the establishment of industrial parks such as the Sino-Africa Incubation Park in Kenya's Export Processing Zone. Chinese loans have financed renewable energy projects in Kenya, including loans for geothermal drilling and power plants at Olkaria and for the Garissa solar power project as well as a US$900 million loan for a new coal plant in Lamu on the Kenyan coast (*China-Africa Research Initiative* 2018). Judges blocked the coal plant project following a campaign and petition by civil society activists. The court ruled that the government had failed to conduct an environmental assessment and public participation. Had it gone ahead, the plant would have contributed greenhouse gas emissions, affected fishing, the economic mainstay of the local community and affected the health of the people owing to pollution. It would also have affected the Lamu archipelago, a pristine United Nations Educational Scientific and Cultural Organisation (UNESCO) world heritage site (*The EastAfrican* 2019).

Uhuru Kenyatta, who has been in office since 2013, has maintained Kenya's alignment with the US-driven 'war on terror', kept Kenyan soldiers in Somalia under the African Union Mission in Somalia (AMISOM) ostensibly to stabilise Somalia. The Kenyan government and its military have been implicated in racketeering involving charcoal and sugar smuggling in cahoots with Al-Shabaab terrorists (*Foreign Policy* 2015; ISS [n.d.]). Here, the Kenyan government is also being driven by war economy benefits. Kenya's international relations during Kenyatta's first term in office were shaped by crimes against humanity charges that he, his deputy William Ruto and four other suspects faced at the International Criminal Court (ICC). Kenyatta signed a raft of bilateral agreements with China, and under his administration, the Chinese-funded Standard Gauge Railway (SGR) line from the port city of Mombasa to Nairobi was constructed. The SGR was initially conceived as a regional project to run into neighbouring Uganda and Rwanda, but Rwanda pulled out, citing high costs and opted to connect to a newly refurbished Tanzania-Zambia Railway (TAZARA) line instead, and argued that this route would be shorter and cheaper. Rwanda's minister of finance and economic planning, Claver Gatete, declared, 'We opted for the route transiting to Tanzania during the construction of our railway line because [building] the Kenyan route would be expensive and time-consuming' (*Sunday Nation* 2016b).

Rwanda took this decision despite a prior agreement with Uganda and Kenya to link all three countries to the Indian Ocean through the SGR at a cost of US$13 billion (KSh 1.3 trillion). Other than the three East African countries, SGR was also meant to connect Eastern Democratic Republic of Congo (DRC) to Kenya's Mombasa port to facilitate China's reach into the hinterland for natural resources but competition among multinationals and donors for lucrative infrastructure projects, endemic corruption, and a lack of shared norms among regional states upended the ambitious project and integration efforts in the East African region. Large-scale corruption in Kenya that massively raised the cost of constructing the Kenyan segment of the SGR influenced Rwanda's decision, the least corrupt country in the region according to Transparency International, to reconsider its partnership with Kenya. It was also claimed that the French Total petroleum company had helped to persuade Uganda to opt for the Tanzanian route, since it was also drilling for oil in Tanzania. China was ready to fund the Ugandan section of the SGR too, provided Uganda hired a Chinese contractor. In the event, the prohibitive cost of the Kenyan section, coupled with the influence of the French oil giant, put a damper on what had been billed as a major new transport corridor in the East African region.

In the meantime, the region had also launched another ambitious transport corridor, the Lamu Port South Sudan Ethiopia Transport Corridor (LAPSSET), intended to connect the East African hinterland to the Kenyan port of Lamu. Despite Uganda being a landlocked country, and Kenya's largest trading partner, it pulled out of LAPSSET, opting to export its crude oil through the Tanzanian port of Tanga rather than Kenya as was initially planned. Kenya's mercurial and combustible politics and endemic corruption influenced this decision too.

Uganda's economy was affected during violence witnessed in Kenya in 2007–08 following disputed presidential elections. Opposition protestors in Nairobi uprooted a section of the archaic Uganda railway line (Lunatic Express), while marauding tribal militias blocked roads, disrupted road transport which made it virtually impossible for Uganda to receive its imports from and through Kenya, its economic lifeline. The shortage of petroleum supplies crippled Uganda's economy, prompting a frantic effort by its President, Yoweri Museveni, to mediate in the conflict. This demonstrates that political instability in Kenya spills over into neighbouring Uganda as is the case with conflicts that often become regional.

Uganda's decision to divert its crude oil pipeline to Tanzania was informed by security concerns, which shows that for the viability and sustainability of LAPSSET and SGR projects, the East African Community (EAC) must become a cohesive and stable political and economic entity. The recurrent political impasse between Uganda and Rwanda with border closures over mutual accusations of each harbouring the other's dissidents thus interference in each other's internal affairs, is another impediment to efforts towards regional integration in East Africa. Transformative politics is indispensable to the viability of these projects.

But this is currently prevented by mutual suspicions, bad governance, corruption, political instability (South Sudan), normative incoherence and the resultant disparate regimes in the region, all of which are undemocratic, if not authoritarian. Unlike his predecessors, Tanzania's President, John Pombe Magufuli, in power since 2015, is as autocratic as fellow regional rulers. He clamps down on critical social media practitioners, and journalists, arbitrarily has his critics arrested, bans political activities and deploys state violence against opponents and critics—dictatorial attributes hitherto alien in Tanzania.

Kenyatta regarded the SGR as his flagship project, despite the fact that it was mooted by his predecessor. The SGR reinforced the perception of a shift towards China and a snub of the West, specifically US, Britain and France, among the Permanent Five (P5) members of the United Nations Security Council (UNSC), that endorsed crimes against humanity charges against Kenyatta and five other suspects before the ICC and opposed deferral of the cases for a year or referral to Kenya as provided for by the Rome Statute, options punted by the Kenyan government and the African Union (AU). The charges arose from egregious human rights violations committed during the violence in 2007–08, in which over 1300 people were murdered, and over 500,000 were displaced after a presidential election had been stolen (Republic of Kenya 2008: 345–352). Kenyatta was named one of the masterminds and accused of murder, deportation or forcible transfer of population, rape, persecution and other inhumane acts through the provision of 'institutional support' to a tribal militia *mungiki* that committed these crimes in concert with security elements (ICC 2015). This retaliatory violence against opposition-supporting tribes was in support of the then incumbent, Mwai Kibaki, a co-ethnic of Kenyatta's. Upon being indicted in 2010, Kenyatta resorted to verbal attacks against the ICC, the West, and opponents whom he stigmatised as Western stooges. He accused them of trumped up charges. Kenyatta further whipped up ethnic bigotry for political capital. Upon controversially ascending to power in 2013, he ramped up his tirade and dismissed Western powers as diminishing imperialists and only toned down this rhetoric, abandoned it altogether and embraced the West when the case against him collapsed. Kenyatta's campaign of calumny against the ICC and the West was self-serving. His aim was to discredit them before his local supporters and wriggle out of the ICC dragnet. The multi-billion-dollar infrastructure projects undertaken by China in Kenya are idiosyncratic, rather than evidence of Kenya's ideological shift. Kenya's politics are ethnic and personality in orientation, dominated by rent seekers, surrogates of Western capital, who have stakes in virtually the entirety of Kenya's economy including real estate, dairy, banking, energy, transportation, infrastructure, health, education, security and tourism. Corruption surrounding the SGR, the opacity of agreements between Kenya and China evidenced by inability by the former Auditor General, Edward Ouko, to audit the SGR project bear testimony to this (*Sunday Nation* 2019). The Chinese-funded projects in Kenya are marred by corruption and are significant not for their impact on the well-being of Kenyans but their high profitability value to wheeler dealers and political elite.

With the backing of Western capital, the most reactionary cohort among the country's political elite has monopolised economic power since 1963 that it exploits to consolidate their hold on politics. The mantra of human rights, democracy and good governance propagated by the West in the wake of the collapse of the Soviet Union has worn thin and finally fallen off. The West-Kenya relations are primarily for safeguarding Western interests in the country. Wary of losing out to China on mega projects, Western powers pay lip service to ideological, normative politics. Despite evidence of extrajudicial executions, persistent electoral fraud, exclusionary politics, a culture of impunity and state interference in the ICC cases, the West did not sanction Kenyatta. Instead, it embraced him in return.

In 2013, the then US President Barack Obama launched a legacy project, Power Africa, which was intended to provide electricity to 60 million new consumers and generate 30,000 megawatts of electricity in Africa by 2030, a continent where lack of access to electricity has contributed to underdevelopment. It was a public-private initiative, with US business moguls lurking on the fringes and angling for the much sought-after African market.

In July 2015, Obama made a historic two-day state visit to Kenya as the first sitting US president to do so. Other than ancestral ties to the country, the visit conferred a sense of legitimacy on Kenyatta that largely dispelled lingering credibility and illegitimacy questions—stemming from the ICC charges and the disputed elections in 2013. A barrage of calls within Kenya (specifically by Western envoys and sections of civil society) and internationally, had been made to dissuade Kenyatta from standing during the 2013 elections owing to the egregious charges he faced before the ICC. Significantly, the Obama visit underscored Kenya's strategic importance to international capital and the fight against terror.

Ultimately, in pursuit of its national interests, Kenya has initiated multilateral relations with emerging powers, in the global South, and in Africa under Pan-Africanism, for a multipolar world, as a counterpoise to Western hegemony. However, Kenya has no intention of turning its back on the West, or can hardly afford to, which it affirms through its foreign policy,

> In order to strategically place the country in the international arena, the architects of Kenya's foreign policy charted a pragmatic approach, informed by several principles; which have stood the test of time. This approach [has] ensured that Kenya successfully forges mutually beneficial alliances with the West while constructively engaging the East through its policy of positive economic and political non-alignment. (Republic of Kenya 2014)

China-Africa Lopsided Partnership: The Case of Sino-Kenyan Cooperation

China's relations with Kenya are as old as independent Kenya itself. China opened an embassy in Kenya in December 1963, but downgraded it to chargé d'affaires in 1965 in reaction to Kenya officially aligning itself with the West through the adoption of Sessional Paper No. 10 of 1965 on African socialism. The word 'socialism' is misleading. It does not connote an adherence to left-wing ideology as was the case among African countries that aligned with the Soviet Union. Instead, the paper definitively spelled out Kenya's Western orientation, in effect defining it as capitalist

(*Saturday Nation* 2014). A West-East polarity in the Kenyan government then boiled over and the Western leaning faction accused China of subversion by supporting the faction ideologically oriented towards the Soviet Union and China. The Kenyan government expelled China's first secretary in 1966 and China retaliated, expelled Kenya's charge d'affaires the following year which collapsed diplomatic relations. It took the exit of both Mao Zedong and Jomo Kenyatta for the relations to normalise.

China and Kenya have maintained economic, cultural and educational relations, although this bilateral relationship is heavily weighted in favour of China. In 2015 Kenya's imports from China totalled KSh320.8 billion, and exports to China a paltry KSh8.4 billion (*Business Daily* 2017). Imports from China increased during the construction of the Chinese-funded and managed SGR, with the first phase from Mombasa to Nairobi completed just two months prior to the 2017 elections.

The fanfare accompanying the project and the opening of this initial segment of the SGR pointed to political capital that Uhuru Kenyatta sought to derive from the investment. It is the first railway line to be built in independent Kenya, and construction of the second phase, from Nairobi to Naivasha, and the inland container depot in Naivasha were launched in December 2019. Kenyatta's family land in Naivasha marks the end point of the SGR after China declined to fund the third phase to Western Kenya over concerns about the viability of the entire SGR project. The inland container port is located in Kenyatta's family land (*The Standard* 2017). It prompted Kenyans to disparagingly refer to SGR as the 'railway to nowhere' since the area is remote and devoid of industrial activity, or other transport inks. SGR got the epithet the Lunatic Express 2.0. The metre gauge Uganda railway was named the 'Lunatic Express' because the cost was so prohibitive that even by the standards of the British Empire, it was a 'gigantic folly' (*The New York Times* 2017).

At the Beijing Forum on China-Africa Cooperation (FOCAC) summit in 2018, Uhuru Kenyatta's attempt to secure an agreement with China for the last phase of the SGR did not materialise. China declined to extend a loan to Kenya to the tune of KSh 380 billion that Kenyatta had requested because SGR no longer makes commercial sense to China given that it is not reaching Kampala as had been envisaged initially (*Sunday Nation* September 16 2018). Kenya had asked China to fund half of the cost so as to split it into a grant and loan. It was in reaction to a domestic backlash over Kenya's ballooning debt. Kenyatta suggested a shift to Public–Private Partnership (PPP) in financing other infrastructure projects to mitigate the debt burden (*Daily Nation* September 4 2018). Critics, however, cautioned that the projects might actually cost more as the financiers would have to operate the projects for some time to recoup their money. Kenya secured funding from China under the PPP initiative for the construction of a 30 km expressway from the main airport to Westlands district in Nairobi under the understanding that China would toll it until they recouped their money.

Kenyatta has been accused of overburdening Kenyans with loans, large chunks of which are looted. The SGR is arguably the highlight of Sino-Kenyan cooperation thus far, but it also reveals how skewed this relationship is. China comprises a staggering market of about 1.3 billion people, but is not among Kenya's top ten export markets (*Business Daily* 2017), and Kenya's inability to take advantage of the opportunities offered by China is concerning. Aly-Khan Satchu, chief executive of Nairobi-based investment advisory firm, Rich Management, has stated, 'This is the most lop-sided trade relationship in the world. In fact, if you stripped out titanium, the Kenya export pipe to China would read close to zero. Clearly, both governments need to re-energise their responses to this problem' (*Business Daily* 2017).

China is second to Uganda as Kenya's strategic trading partner, and Kenya's topmost investor and contractor. Kenya must develop its manufacturing sector to cater for its market and export the surplus instead of merely consuming Chinese goods. Culturally, Kenya is the headquarters of CGTN (China Global Television Network) Africa, the African bureau of China Global Television Network, the English-language news channel run by the Chinese state broadcaster China Central Television which covers the entire continent. Kenya is therefore a hub for China's cultural power projection in Africa. CGTN seeks to rival Western media giants such as British Broadcasting Corporation (BBC) and Cable News Network (CNN) as well as Al Jazeera, the equally influential Qatari media network. CGTN sets the Chinese agenda in Africa, dispels any adverse publicity about China's exploits in Africa by the Western media and tries to win the hearts and minds of its African audience, traditional consumers of Western media.

Kenya is a destination of choice for Chinese tourists, the second largest group of visitors after American tourists. The flip side of China's pervasive economic ventures in Africa is that Kenya's exports to its neighbours, Uganda and Tanzania, have declined because of a stiff competition from cheap imports from China. *Sunday Nation* has encapsulated the Chinese stranglehold on Kenya's economy as follows,

> A Kenyan today is likely to travel on a Chinese constructed road, buy Chinese goods from supermarkets, watch football in a Chinese built stadium, get treated in a Chinese built hospital, use a Chinese mobile phone and will soon travel (*travels*) *my emphasis* from Mombasa to Nairobi on the Standard Railway Gauge (SGR) funded and constructed by the Asian giant. (*Sunday Nation* 2016a)

Kenya is so indebted to China that the International Monetary Fund (IMF) raised a red flag, and warned that Kenya's insatiable appetite for borrowing both domestically and internationally, particularly from China, could affect its economic prospects, largely due to its large and growing repayment burden (*Sunday Nation* 2016a). In 2016, the World Bank raised similar concerns. But the Kenyan government ignored this advice, and continued to borrow money from China. In early 2018, Kenya's debt surpassed the globally accepted threshold of 50 per cent of gross domestic product (GDP) by 6 per cent, and no less than 40 per cent of national revenue was being diverted into offsetting public debts. This debt burden cancelled out the expected economic benefits of the SGR and other ventures funded by foreign direct investment (FDI). In fact, it threatened Kenya's long-term Vision 2030, under which it strove to become a middle-income and industrialised country.

Chinese Influence Through Education and Culture

China appreciates the centrality of culture and education—soft power—in the making of a hegemony. It understands that there is no better way of exerting influence in Kenya and Africa than spreading Chinese culture and providing educational opportunities in China to as many Africans as possible. This is an established approach by nations seeking to leverage their military and economic power over others. Africa's former colonial masters maintain influence and dominance over Africa, not through military might but education and culture. It has conditioned formerly colonised societies to aspire to be like the colonial master; etched in their collective psyche is the colonial master and Westernisation as the apogee of success and excellence. In this regard, China has set up four Confucius

Institutes in Kenya, at the University of Nairobi, Moi University, Egerton University and Kenyatta University, tasked—as elsewhere—with teaching Mandarin, spreading Chinese culture and promoting people-to-people exchanges.

The Chinese government has offered scholarships to Kenyan students since 1982, benefiting thousands of them over the years. At the time of writing, a total of 1400 Kenyan students were studying in China. China also plays a significant role in skills transfers to Kenya. So far, 45,000 Kenyans received professional skills training through the SGR, which officially opened on 1 June 2017 (*Daily Nation* 2017). Since 2006, a total of 1800 Kenyan officials, technicians, and other staff have received specialised training in China.

The Politics of Sino-Kenyan Cooperation

The China-Kenya partnership is political much as hardnosed politics seem to take a back seat compared to Kenya's ties with Western nations. Kenya supports the 'One China' policy, which insists that Taiwan is an alienable part of the People's Republic of China. Rejection of Taiwan as a sovereign state is often the only political condition that China imposes on its diplomatic relations with African countries (Pehnelt and Abel 2007: 8). In return, China backed a UNSC resolution calling for a deferral of the charges against Kenyatta and his deputy, William Ruto and others at the ICC. The resolution was, however, defeated in November 2013.

China has been supportive of successive Kenyan governments. In January 2018, Kenyatta invited the Communist Party of China to train members of Jubilee Party, that propelled him into power, on democracy and party management despite China not self-identifying as a democracy. In fact, China is autocratic. As a permanent member of the UNSC, China safeguards its economic interests in Africa, and its opposition to the trial of the six Kenyans at the ICC had less to do with justice than its interests in Kenya.

China tends to avoid overt involvement in the domestic politics of African states, and Kenya is no exception. Despite being Kenya's leading trading partner, China has hardly been visible during Kenya's tumultuous multiparty elections. It was absent during damaging violence in 2007–08, and the equally polarising elections in 2013 and 2017. It did not comment on the 2017 electoral dispute, other than congratulating Kenyatta on his contested victory in August 2017, which the Supreme Court subsequently annulled.

China is, however, involved in peace and security cooperation, anti-terrorism, counter-piracy and regional peacekeeping missions across Africa. Some think that China supports reform of the UNSC to reflect the current power equilibrium in the world, while others hold that it does not since it is wary of India, its nemesis in Asia, and ambitious to join an expanded UNSC were that to happen. China is also involved in issues surrounding climate change which, unless addressed, will affect Africa disproportionately. China's support for Africa's quest to resolve its own conflicts was manifested through cooperation on conflict areas such as Burundi, South Sudan and Somalia and its military base in Djibouti illustrates China's influence over African security. It seeks to secure its economic interests in Africa, and the establishment of this base marks it as a formidable global actor.

Cronyism, Rent Seeking and Politics of Extraversion in Kenya

Cronyism obtains where politically connected individuals control power, domestic monopolies and extractive industries. These people, whose business ventures are often dubious, are preoccupied with profits and do not invest in sectors of the economy that have the greatest benefit to the majority of the people. They are fixated on return on capital—profit—but not raising people's purchasing powers, delivering on public goods and job creation. Rent seekers portray mega infrastructure projects such as roads, ports, airports and railway lines, as indispensable to a functioning economy, but these amenities hardly contribute much to the economy in the absence of leadership and the manufacturing sector. van de Walle understood rent seeking as a political system in which the ruler, together with a group of allies, his clients, maintain the system in order to extract benefits referred to as prebends or illicit rents (van de Walle 1994: 133–134; Gyimah-Boadi 2007: 29; Widner 1994: 53).

Rent seekers keep the cost of doing business high for rent extraction and launch capital intensive projects that do not economically empower the poor since these projects are important to the extent that political elite and their cronies profiteer extensively. Rent seekers do not invest in the productivity of the labour force which in Kenya's context entails modernising the informal sector and agriculture so that tea, coffee, maize, sugarcane and dairy farmers get returns on their labour and efforts. Middle men and importers of contraband goods, however, profiteer at the expense of the informal sector that is hobbled down by bureaucratic red tape, high overhead costs in taxation and electricity bills and corruption. The bulk of Kenya's economy is informal and so fixation on foreign investors by the government hardly makes sense until one factors in rent seeking. The agricultural sector has all but collapsed owing to importation of superfluous produce by rent seekers.

In Kenya, political and economic power is concentrated within a tiny plutocracy adept at manipulating ethnicity to consolidate it Naturally, democratic tenets have been eroded thus perennially stolen elections marred by disputes, state and intercommunal violence, and pervasive tribalism resulting in an illegitimate state. Kenyan plutocrats, the core of rent seeking politics in the country, relate to the state through self-interest. Uhuru Kenyatta and his extended family has interests in hospitality, dairy, energy, healthcare, media, transportation, real estate, banking, tourism and construction. He has exponentially expanded these and other interests since 2013 when he assumed power starting from where his father left off in 1978. The privatisation of the state exemplified through fusion between public and private interests makes nonsense of the idea of conflict of interest (*The Elephant* 2018a). Kenyatta had no qualms about having the SGR dry port in Naivasha constructed in his family land. Kenya's plutocrats' guiding question during bilateral negotiations is: 'What is it for me? They are not driven by civic nationalism or national interests—the quest to strike the best deal for the citizenry while engaging either with the West, China or any other external actor but seek to extract maximum rents for self-aggrandisement.

The theory of extraversion, postulated by Jean-Francois Bayart, also describes ways in which Sub-Saharan African rulers, have actively participated in the processes that have created and maintained the continent's dependent position within the global system in return for rents they extract from this asymmetrical relationship be it through war, Foreign Direct Investment (FDI), elections, curricula, Structural Adjustment Programmes (SAPs), good governance and democracy industry, and poverty reduction strategy papers and even grandiose infrastructure projects (Bayart 2000). He discredits marginalisation as the cause of Africa's dire economic conditions as advanced by proponents of the dependency theory. Bayart argues that Africa's dependence on the West, and now China, should be analysed through the lens of extraversion. This theory disputes the notion that Africa has always played a passive role in world history and affirms Africa has agency.

Infrastructure Programmes

The SGR; the Mombasa portal terminal and Special Economic Zone; Thika Road, linking Nairobi to the formerly industrial town of Thika; the Kenya-Ethiopia highway; the southern, eastern and northern bypasses around Nairobi; the conversation of Lang'ata Road in Nairobi into a dual carriageway and the expansion of Outering road in Nairobi are some of the mega public projects that have demonstrated Chinese workmanship, and timely delivery in Kenya. Kenyan contractors lack the technical know-how and more acutely, professionalism and requisite work ethos, that militates against their undertaking such massive projects. China Communication Construction Company (CCCC) has built and now manages the SGR, further highlighting the lop-sidedness of this relationship. Controversially, the company was selected through single sourcing despite an open call for tenders an indication of corruption. The SGR was embroiled in corruption since inception. The Kenyan government bizarrely argued that it did not have to select a company through a competitive bidding because it cut costs and it was in the nature of government-to-government agreements to be sealed as such (Wissenbach and Wang 2017:12). Corruption exponentially raised the cost of the SGR,

> There is a widespread perception that established Kenyan political elites have pocketed large sums of kickbacks from the SGR. These perceptions overshadow the overall objectives of the project and its genuine contribution to filling the infrastructural gaps in Africa. (Wissenbach and Wang 2017: 12)

LAPSSET, the SGR and the discovery of oil in Turkana were expected to boost Kenya's GDP by some 9.5 per cent. These projects were in line with Kenya's Vision 2030. Kenya's ambition is to attain middle-income status by 2030, and for that to happen its economy must grow by seven per cent a year (*Sunday Nation* 2016b). LAPSSET has since gone cold, coupled with shrinkage of SGR from a regional to a Mombasa-Nairobi project have dented Kenya's economic projections. The discovered oil deposits are small by international standards and their commercial viability is in doubt. Kenya's ambitious infrastructure is also in line with the African Union's Agenda 2063, adopted in 2013. Divided into ten-year action plans, this blueprint is aimed at realising a united, prosperous and peaceful Africa by 2063.

China's strategic importance to Kenya and to Africa rests on a number of factors as articulated by the then Chinese ambassador to Kenya, Liu Xianfa. China's has been the world's fastest growing economy for the past 30 years, and been the second largest economy in the world since 2010. Besides being the leading trading nation in terms of goods, it holds the largest foreign exchange reserves in the world, and accounts for between a quarter and a third of global economic development. Many Western brands and products are manufactured in China, which has rightly earned the moniker, the World's Factory. It has the most advanced and longest high-speed train in the world, and a robust e-commerce sector, marked by widespread online shopping (*Daily Nation* 2017). These factors account for China's place in the world as a consequential trading and political actor.

The Kenyan government has been faulted over the SGR project. David Ndii, an economist, a public intellectual, civil society activist and political strategist, argues, inter alia, that the SGR was a bad investment since it is economically unviable, and that the Kenyan government should have concentrated on LAPSSET and upgraded the antiquated 'Lunatic Express' (Uganda railway line), thus ending up with two cheaper and more rapidly completed transport corridors (*Saturday Nation* 2017). The SGR cost $6 billion, equal to one third of Kenya's foreign debt, even after the extension to Western Kenya was shelved and epitomised Kenyan government's borrowing spree, ballooning the country's foreign debt to almost KSh 5 trillion at the time of writing.

Ndii, arguably the most unstinting critic of SGR project, further argues that the SGR has not resolved issues—including corruption—that rendered rail transport in Kenya lamentably inefficient. He argues that the colonial railway line became derelict because of endemic corruption that hollowed out the state, including parastatals such as Kenya Railways (*Saturday Nation* 2017). Politicians, influence peddlers and other well-connected individuals, collapsed these state entities, then invested in road transport and would therefore rather see railway transport grind to a halt, thus boosting the movement of goods from Mombasa to the hinterland and to neighbouring countries by road. This is why the Kenyan government, counterintuitively, intends to transport crude oil from Turkana to

Mombasa by road instead of the SGR or a pipeline. The SGR, contends Ndii, will not improve carrying capacity or reduce costs, because railway cargo does not have to move fast, and so increasing the speed from 60kph by the old railway line to 80kph by SGR is inconsequential and does not justify the colossal cost. The conclusion is that SGR is a bad investment because it cannot generate the revenue needed to offset the US$4 billion spent on building the line from Mombasa to Nairobi and additional KSh 6 billion for the extension to Naivasha. Ndii argues that investment should instead have been directed at LAPSSET on the basis of equitable development, as provided for in Kenya's 2010 Constitution that sought to dismantle centralisation of power and resources and the attendant divisive tribal politics since LAPSSET project would have benefited historically marginalised arid and semi-arid regions and coastal region of Kenya (*Saturday Nation* 2017).

Kenya is held captive by international capital and its local surrogate that is detached from the well-being and interests of the populace. The SGR project was informed by its high rents value to the ruling elite not strategic relevance to the well-being of Kenyan citizens—thus lack of public participation before implementation and disregard for views by critics who had dismissed it as unviable despite a favourable self-serving feasibility study by the contractor, China Road and Bridge Corporation (CRBC) (*The Elephant* 2018b). Although China declined to extend another loan for phase III to Western Kenya, it gave out a $400 billion loan for the rehabilitation of the 120-year-old colonial railway line from Naivasha to Kisumu yet revamping the entire line from Mombasa was the most economically viable option from the word go.

The SGR project perpetuates centralisation of power, resources and marginalisation in Kenya. This concentration of development projects in regions that successive governments historically favoured perpetrates inequalities and poverty that the Constitution sought to address (*Saturday Nation* 2017). This inland container depot in Naivasha threatens the economy of Mombasa city, and towns along the highway into the hinterland that rely on trucking. Workers at Mombasa port have protested incessantly against the government decree that all cargo must move by SGR and be cleared from Naivasha which is more prohibitive and takes away jobs from Mombasa to Naivasha. Ugandan importers defied this decree and threatened to explore other options which forced the government to back down and let them collect their imports from Mombasa as before. Kenyatta is opposed to devolution and the equitable distribution of national resources and favours allocation of revenue on the basis of population size as opposed to economic indices manifested in poverty or wealth. Disquiet among Turkana, a pastoralist community, over a skewed sharing of oil revenue is evidence. As the catchment community, it insists that 10 per cent of the oil revenue must be allocated to it, but the government intends to allocate only five per cent. There is currently no legislation that governs this issue (the devolution of resources and power is the subtext). Until the discovery of oil in Turkana in 2012, a semi-arid, sparsely populated and derelict area, Kenya's successive governments neglected it which has made its inhabitants, among the most marginalised in Kenya. Kenyatta's resistance to devolution is informed by his desire to maintain centralisation that enables him and his cohort to extract resources from the periphery for their benefit, as was the practice before the 2010 Constitution.

William Ruto, Kenyatta's deputy, led fellow Kalenjin co-ethnics in campaigning and voting against the Constitution during the referendum in 2010. Kenyatta was ambivalent—that was interpreted to mean he supported the status quo. Kenyatta habitually breaches the Constitution by ignoring court orders, makes appointments at variance with gender and ethnic provisions, tramples on basic rights such as freedom of assembly, freedom of information, freedom of the media, freedom of speech, and resists police reforms aimed at placing the police under civilian oversight. He has initiated an illegal constitution overhaul aimed at ensuring his tight grip on Kenya's politics and economy possibly in perpetuity. Fundamentally he trashes the doctrine of separation of powers. The government is mired in endemic grand corruption in which Kenyatta's political supporters and relatives are invariably implicated which punctures the misleading notion by his supporters that he means well but is under siege because of unsavoury allies.

China's Influence in Africa: Interests Versus Normative Politics

The 'war on terror' and China's commercial interests have relegated issues of constitutionalism and democracy in Kenya and Africa to the back burner. The US has abandoned all pretence as an agent of normative politics in Africa and across the world. Its mantra, 'the rule of law at home, and interests abroad' holds sway. China's pervasive economic interests in Africa, especially infrastructure, have forced the West to react. In August

2012, the then US Foreign Secretary, Hillary Clinton, embarked on an 11-day tour of Africa. In her first address in Dakar, Senegal, she characterised the US as committed to 'a model of sustainable partnerships that adds value rather than extracting it'. She further stated that 'America will stand up for democracy and universal human rights even when it might be easier to look the other way and keep the resources flowing'. These remarks were widely interpreted as a subtle criticism of China, which has been accused of exploiting Africa's natural resources, giving nothing in exchange and supporting dictators thus undermining democracy. The US and Western allies stand indicted for similar charges.

Obama's 2015 tour of Africa included Ethiopia, a country with an appalling human rights record, and whose jails hold political detainees journalists, and social media activists critical of the regime in power. Initially, Abiy Ahmed, Ethiopia's prime minister since April 2018, appeared less inclined towards authoritarianism that characterised his predecessors. It was hoped that he would safeguard the rule of law and human rights and sustain the reform process especially after he was awarded the Nobel Peace Prize in 2019. However, Ahmed's regime has continued a deeply entrenched culture of autocracy in Ethiopia marked by intolerance, brutality, extrajudicial executions, and political assassinations. Deadly ethnic divisions continue to blight Ethiopia fragile society much the same way as before. Ahmed declared war on Tigray region that he accused of defying his authority. Eventually Ethiopia tipped off into civil war, towards the end of 2020, pitting government forces and Tigray Region forces in which Eritrea and other neighbours were sucked. The armed conflict has brought into sharp focus the tension between ethnic federalism and political centralisation. It has also exposed the fragility of economic growth in the absense of the rule of law and social cohesion. As the seat of the AU, Obama could not bypass Ethiopia during this last tour of Africa as the US president, but his silence on human rights violations in Ethiopia rendered hollow Clinton's earlier attempt to favourably compare the US to China in respect of their exploits in Africa and Obama's rousing speech at the African Union headquarters that extolled democratic values. While in Zambia, Hillary Clinton threw all caution to the winds, and openly criticised China,

> We are however, concerned that China's foreign assistance and investment practices in Africa have not always been consistent with generally accepted international norms of transparency and good governance, and that it has

> not always utilised the talents of the African people in pursuing its business interest. (*Reuters* 2011)

Before embarking on an official five-nation visit to Africa, Rex Tillerson, Donald Trump's first secretary of state, also criticised China and cautioned Africa about China's intentions. While acknowledging China's role in improving Africa's infrastructure, he faulted China for burdening Africa with debt while creating few jobs. Although remarks by these two top US state officials could not be dismissed out of hand, the US was not doing any better, and its engagements in Africa are hardly underpinned by the interests of Africans. It has maintained diplomatic and commercial links with the most autocratic regimes in Africa, beginning with the dark days of single party and military dictatorship as long these dictators were allied to the US and opposed to the Soviet Union. Tillerson's visit was themed on counter-terrorism, democracy, governance, trade and investment (the accent on democracy and governance was meant to highlight that China does not care about these issues in its relationship with Africa and was not indicative of any such commitment by the US).

Not to be left behind, the US Construction Company signed a KSh300 billion contract with the Kenyan government to build the Mombasa-Nairobi highway. This agreement was sealed days before the 2017 general election, and replicated the SGR in that it was a single sourced project to be financed by the US government, backed by commercial loans. Opposition politicians cited this project when they accused the then US ambassador to Kenya, Robert F. Godec, of meddling in Kenya's political crisis in favour of Uhuru Kenyatta despite evidence of electoral fraud during the protracted conflict stemming from the 2017 elections.

The US and European countries have clearly abandoned their rhetoric about democracy and governance in Kenya. In October 2017, Ambassador Godec led fellow Western envoys in openly taking sides in Kenyan politics. In a public statement, they urged the opposition politician, Raila Odinga, to recognise Kenyatta following the (yet again) fraudulent 'fresh' elections that month that he and his supporters had boycotted despite having earlier urged the opposition to participate in those elections notwithstanding concerns about credibility, impartiality of state institutions and incompetence and biasness of the electoral body.

Kenya is a society deeply divided ethnically, and so it is difficult to organise politics around sound policy positions other than the ideology of tribalism. Cumulatively, the absence of issue based politics, a sense of nationhood, trust and the rule of law give Western countries the confidence and effrontery to intervene in Kenya's domestic affairs whereas China has long steered clear of local politics in African countries in which it has invested. It prefers back-room deals and has avoided taking sides in Kenyan politics, although its close relationship with Kenyatta and its investments in Kenya show that this cooperation is not apolitical. In August 2013, soon after being sworn in, Uhuru Kenyatta undertook an extended state visit to China, during which he signed numerous bilateral agreements. China's economic interests in and loans to Kenya are so extensive that Kenyatta's critics have accused him of mortgaging the country to the Chinese through predatory lending.

The Undercurrents of China–Africa Partnership

China seeks to define its partnership with Africa as a win-win one, based on mutual respect. It attempts to express this relationship outside Western paternalism that typifies relations between Africa and their former colonial masters, which is characterised by legacies of exploitation, oppression and racial superiority. Away from official rhetoric, China–Africa relations are also marred by paternalism. Chinese companies in Africa have been accused of exploiting local workers, propping up autocratic regimes through arms sales—and Africans are widely portrayed in stereotypical terms in Chinese media and literature. In Kenya, Chinese nationals have been accused of racism by running Chinese-only restaurants and other recreational facilities that local people are not allowed to patronise. A Chinese worker was deported from Kenya after a recording emerged in which he dismissed Kenyans, including Uhuru Kenyatta, as monkeys. Thus, like Westerners, the Chinese stand accused of denigrating black people. An expose by a Kenyan daily newspaper painted a grim picture of Kenyan workers on the SGR trains,

> But beneath this shiny veneer is a tale of pain, anguish and broken dreams for a multitude of Kenyans who feel trapped on the train that ably fits the moniker Orient Express, because on it, Chinese nationals have created a small kingdom in which they run roughshod over Kenyan workers who say they are experiencing neo-colonialism, racism and blatant discrimination as the tax payer foots a Sh30 million a day bill for the train, which loosely translates to Sh1 billion at the end of every month. (*Standard Digital* 2018)

But the government upbraided the workers for a 'bad mentality', praised the Chinese protestant work ethic and counterintuitively promised to investigate the allegations. This response underscored the failure by Kenya's successive governments to uphold basic human rights, including labour rights, the dignity of Kenyans and promote a sense of nationhood. Unresponsive politics, and deference to China leaves Kenyan citizens exposed to exploitation.

Early in 2018 there was an uproar when China's state television ran a prime-time skit laced with racial undertones in celebration of the Chinese New Year. An actor in blackface and dressed like a monkey lampooned black people, and portrayed China as Africa's messiah. The skit attracted condemnation for pandering to racial stereotypes and betraying a superiority complex by the Chinese (ironically, the skit was filmed in Kenya during the construction of the SGR, and in celebration Sino-African relations). In 2016, a Chinese laundry detergent company was forced to issue a public apology after running an advertisement in which a black male was stuffed head first into a washing machine and emerged a moment later transformed into a fair-skinned Asian male. In April 2020, Chinese authorities racially profiled and discriminated against black people in Guangzhou and barred them from hotels, residences, shops and restaurants under the guise of containing Covid-19 pandemic. At the time, videos circulated on social media depicting gratuitous violence against black people in China. It elicited rare protests by some African countries such as Nigeria and Ghana. Twitter was awash with trending hashtags such as #ChinaMustExplain through which users condemned China. The Chinese authorities denied accusations of racism and accused Western media of disinformation against China in effect downplayed concerns by African governments and the blight of the victims.

In 2018 it was reported that China had for five years been tapping into the servers at the Chinese-built AU headquarters in Addis Ababa. It was alleged that software had been installed on the AU computer system that automatically downloaded data onto servers in Shanghai late at night. China built and paid for this computer network. If these concerns are true, it is hardly evidence of a partnership of mutual respect. Accusations of racism, neo-colonialism, paternalism and betrayal, however, are expedient. It is easier for critics of China's surging influence in Africa to make these accusations than to focus on the crux of the matter: the failure, on the whole, by African rulers to exercise agency by leveraging their natural resources, and prioritising the interests of their citizens. African rulers' failure to dignify people does not mean these people have to be degraded but it enables it.

What is important is Africa's lack of agency in its partnership with China which is underscored by lack of strategy in engaging with China either by individual African countries or collectively under African Union. Quite a number of African rulers brutalise their citizens through extra-judicial executions, engage in grand corruption, are predatory, disregard participatory governance, promote exclusionary politics, fail to uphold the rule of law and exhibit a colonial hangover. A perverse belief that Westernisation, Westerners and everything from abroad (the West, from China or elsewhere is superior to what is local) weighs them down. It is therefore counter-intuitive to expect external actors (including China) to treat Africa and its people with dignity. It is axiomatic that local politics have a bearing on international politics. It therefore follows that a country mired in divisive domestic politics as Kenya is, is almost certain to have a poor international standing and perennially come short in its engagements with foreign actors.

African governments tend to uncritically portray China as an alternative to the West as if international relations are hinged on an 'either-or' binary. Neither is it tenable to assess the West and China on account of normative politics, as Hillary Clinton and Rex Tillerson tried to do. Both China and the West are inspired by similar interests which are to exploit Africa's natural resources. It is incumbent upon Kenya (and, by extension, Africa) to identify and safeguard its interests and to improve governance before it asserts itself internationally. It is important, however, to note that the dichotomy between democracy on one hand and development on the other is false. Some of the proponents of development dismiss agitation for human rights, stating that one cannot eat democracy. What they fail to understand is that,

> There is no sustainable development without institutionalised democratic norms and entrenchment of human rights and their corresponding values, one cannot eat an authoritarian ruler either, and as democracy movement in African countries has shown, people would at least like to have the right to say that they are hungry. There is need to implement both democracy and development for the benefit of the majority of the people. (Melber 2008: 399)

In Kenya, as in many other parts of Africa, local labourers often accuse Chinese companies of poor working conditions, low pay and racism. However, this is consistent with failure of the Kenyan government to uphold fundamental rights such as labour rights, the rule of law, to promote a sense of nationhood, national pride and trust among the citizenry. Chinese companies operating in Kenya encounter corruption and the absence of a legal and regulatory framework to undergird their activities and behaviour. And if there is one, it is not enforced. They meet a people balkanised into meaningless and primordial tribal enclaves and incapable of asserting themselves as a nation defined by binding norms and self-pride. As a result, these Chinese companies do as they please with impunity in sync with the political elite who have no regard for the dignity of the citizenry. China's conduct in Kenya is less a racial than a statutory and nation-building issue, compounded by endemic corruption and debilitating tribal politics.

China has played a major role in transforming Kenya's infrastructure but this process has not been problem-free. Chinese nationals have, for instance, been involved in illegal trade in wildlife trophies, particularly elephant tusks. Animal poaching is part of organised crime run by syndicates, some of which are based in East Asia. This has been a sore point in the relationship between China and Kenya, and has marred the former's otherwise unparalleled record in sprucing up Africa's dilapidated infrastructure. Of course, without local partners in government, the Chinese would not pull off this crime. The SGR has also been criticised as a blow to wildlife conservation in Kenya. With the backing of Uhuru Kenyatta and his security forces, the second phase of the SGR to Naivasha was diverted through Nairobi National Park. Conservationists protested to no avail. The relevant state bodies, including the National Assembly, the National Environmental Authority (NEMA), the Kenya Wildlife Service and the National Environment Tribunal, which are meant to promote and protect the public interest, conspired to defeat objections against running the SGR through the park. Apparently Kenya's power mandarins used the SGR to appropriate part of the parkland, which would otherwise not have been possible. The SGR locomotives have hit and killed wildlife along the Nairobi-Mombasa route contrary to the promise, during the construction, that measures would be put in place to ensure that this would not happen (*Standard Digital* 2018).

Conclusion

Africa–BRICS relations are laudable because they reinforce South–South relations and multi-polarity in global affairs whose locus of power has tremendously shifted in the recent years. This relationship is endowed with opportunities and fraught with hurdles too. Africa should not choose friends or identify enemies based on who has supposedly done more for it and who has not. As long as Africa does not get its act together particularly with regard to governance and inclusive politics, it is likely to be fair game in the global order. Global relations are ruthlessly self-interested and actors that are not technologically, economically, culturally and militarily strong come short which accounts for Africa's less than ideal status globally. Africa owes it to itself to exercise its agency, by leveraging its natural resources, population and landmass to extract the best possible deals from BRICS—its prominent member, China or the West to halt the current scramble for its resources.

China and Kenya have cooperated for quite a long time and while this has benefited both countries it has greatly favoured China. Kenya, therefore, needs to devise a strategy for getting more out of the partnership. Kenya may be the junior partner on account of the size of China's economy and population, but these attributes do not in themselves inevitably disadvantage Kenya or give China an edge. The main factors that have put Kenya in this disadvantageous position are its poor governance, exemplified by impunity and corruption and its inability to assert itself, to safeguard its interests and to take advantage of the opportunities offered by China.

China's role in developing Kenya's infrastructure has, however, come at a steep cost. Specifically, the debt burden or debt trap accompanying the projects undertaken by China has provoked the concern of international ratings agencies such as Moody's, as well as the Bretton Woods institutions and some Kenyan scholars and commentators. Continued borrowing and rampant corruption runs the risk of undermining the benefits of these brick and mortar developments by indebting Kenyans far into the future. Kenya needs to reap the benefits of educational opportunities and skills transfer schemes between the two countries, and to use them to develop its own capacity to undertake mega projects instead of outsourcing them to China and the West. This would curb capital flight, and boost local skills in the many areas of specialisation needed to grow the Kenyan economy.

Kenya should assert itself in this relationship. Crucially, Africa must forge a common approach, much as this has proved elusive as individual African states prefer engaging China on their own—to their own disadvantage. Africa should stop romanticising its partnership with China, and comparing it unfavourably with ties to the West. The partnership should be seen for what it is: an interest-based relationship among nations. Accusations of racism levelled at the Chinese media, Chinese contractors in Kenya, the spying debacle at the AU headquarters (when software was secretly installed that transmits data elsewhere) and racism by Chinese authorities against black people in China are issues that Africa has to condemn with the same vigour that racism in the West, denigration by Westerners, racially motivated police murders and extrajudicial executions in the US, evoke in Africa. #BlackLivesMatter hashtag must apply too when injustice is meted out to Africans by venal African rulers and allies in the global South.

In forging its relations with external actors, Kenya should be guided by the interests of its citizens instead of those of kleptocrats, and should also stop being preoccupied with whether it aligns itself with the West or China since international politics is hardly based on binaries. Africa must disabuse itself of the notion that being in a partnership with either amounts to snubbing the other. Despite an apparent shift to China, Kenya is still a Western ally. Western influence in Kenyans' social life, politics and economy is testament to this. It is not in Africa's best interests to choose between China and the West. Instead, it should constantly guard its own interests—regardless of which foreign power it is dealing with.

Bibilography

Adbenur, A. E. (2018). Brazil-Africa Relations: From Boom to Bust? In D. Nagar & C. Mutasa (Eds), *Africa and the World Bilateral and Multilateral International Diplomacy*. Cham: Palgrave Macmillan.

Alves, P., & Draper, P. (2007). Introduction: China's Growing Role in Africa. In G. Le Pere (Ed.), *China in Africa Mercantilist Predator or Partner in Development? Midrand*. Institute for Global Development: South Africa.

Barkan, J. (2004). Kenya After Moi. *Foreign Affairs, 83*(1), 87–100.

Bayart, J. F. (2000). Africa in the World: A History of Extraversion. *African Affairs, 99*(395), 217–267.

Begbie, Y. (2018). *BRICS: What is in it for Africa?* https://www.africa.com/brics-whats-in-it-for-africa/. Accessed 7 July 2018.

Bond, P. (2018). Can the BRICS Re-Open the "Gateway to Africa"? South Africa's Contradictory Facilitation of Divergent Brazilian, Russian, Indian and Chinese Interests. In D. Nagar & C. Mutasa (Eds), *Africa and the World Bilateral and Multilateral International Diplomacy*. Cham: Palgrave Macmillan.

Business Daily. (2017). Is Kenya Getting a Raw Deal From the Trade Ties with China? https://www.businessdailyafrica.com/news/Is-Kenya-getting-a-raw-deal-from-trade-ties-with-China/539546-3792806-15hc955z/index.html. Accessed 6 January 2020.

China-Africa Research Initiative. (2018). China in East Africa and the Horn: Ports, Trains and Industrial Zones. https://static1.squarespace.com. Accessed 7 July 2018.

Daily Nation. (2017, September 8). Education Key to China-Kenya Ties. Online: https://www.nation.co.ke/oped/opinion/Education-key-to-China-Kenya-ties/440808-4086492-rjq6c1z/index.html. Accessed 1 March 2018.

Daily Nation. (2018, September 4). Kenya Wants China to Pay Half the Cost of SGR Extension to Kisumu. Online: https://www.nation.co.ke/kenya/news/-kenya-wants-china-to-pay-half-the-cost-of-sgr-extension-to-kisumu-83872. Accessed August 20.

Daniel, R., & Shubin, V. (2018). Africa and Russia: The Pursuit of Strengthened Relations: In The Post-Cold War Era. In D. Nagar & C. Mutasa (Eds), *Africa and the World Bilateral and Multilateral International Diplomacy*. Cham: Palgrave Macmillan.

Foreign Policy. (2015, November 12). Report: Kenyan Military "in Business" with Al-Shabab. Online: https://foreignpolicy.com/2015/11/12/report-kenyan-military-in-business-with-al-shabab/. Accessed 26 August 2020.

Gyimah-Boadi, E. (2007). Political Parties, Elections and Patronage: Random Thoughts on Neo-Patrimonialism and African Democratiztion. In M. Basedau, G. Erdmann, & A. Mehler (Eds), *Votes, Money and Violence Political Parties and Elections in Sub-Saharan Africa*. Scottsville, South Africa: University of Kwazulu-Natal Press.

Henderson, J. (2008). *China and the Future of the Developing World: The Comong Global Asian Era and its Consequences*. Helsinki: UNU-WIDER.

International Criminal Court (ICC). (2015, March 13). *Situation in the Republic of Kenya: The Prosecutor v. Uhuru Muigai Kenyatta*. Online: https://www.icc-cpi.int/CaseInformationSheets/KenyattaEng.pdf. Accessed 31 October 2018.

Institute for Seurity Studies. (n.d.). *THINK AGAIN: Who Profits from Kenyan War in Somalia?* Online: https://issafrica.org/amp/iss-today/think-again-who-profits-from-kenyas-war-in-somalia. Accessed 26 August 2020.

Lumumba-Kasongo, T. (2015). Brazil, Russia, India, China, and South Africa (BRICS) and Africa: New projected developmental paradigms. *Africa Development, 40*(3): 77–95.

Melber, H. (2008). China in Africa: A New Partner or Another Imperialist? *African Spectrum, 43*(3): 393–402. Online: https://www.ssoar.info/ssoar/bitstream/handle/document/35328/ssoar-afrspectrum-2008-3-melber-China_in_Africa_a_new.pdf?sequence=1&isAllowed=y&lnkname=ssoar-afrspectrum-2008-3-melber-China_in_Africa_a_new.pdf. Accessed 26 August 2020.

Pehnelt, G., & Abel, M. (2007). *China's Development Policy in Africa*. South African Institute of International Affairs, China-Africa Policy Report No 1. www.saiia.org.za. Accessed 7 July 2018.

Republic of Kenya. (2008). *Commission of Inquiry into Post-Election Violence (CIPEV) or Waki Commission*. Nairobi: Government Printer. Online: http://www.dialoguekenya.org/docs/PEV%20Report.pdf. Accessed 10 August 2020.

Republic of Kenya. (2014). *Kenya Foreign Policy*. http://www.mfa.go.ke/wp-content/uploads/2016/09/Kenya-Foreign-Policy.pdf. Accessed 14 December 2018.

Reuters. (2011, June 10). Clinton Warns Africa of China's economic embrace. Online: https://uk.reuters.com/article/us-clinton-africa/clinton-warns-africa-of-chinas-economic-embrace-idUKTRE75962920110610. Accessed 1 November 2018.

Saturday Nation. (2014, May 10). Why China's "Soft Power" Appeals to Kenya. Online: https://www.nation.co.ke/kenya/news/why-china-s-soft-power-approach-appeals-to-kenya-982328. Accessed 25 August 2019.

Saturday Nation. (2017, September 22). How Business Rivalry Between USA and China is Undermining Our Constitution, Democracy and Sustainable Development. https://www.nation.co.ke/kenya/blogs-opinion/opinion/how-business-rivalry-between-us-and-china-is-undermining-our-constitution-democracy-and-sustainable-development-454132. Accessed 25 August 2020.

Saunders, C. (2014). Strengthening Governance in South Africa: Building on Mandela's Legacy. *The Annals of the American Academy of Political and Social Science, 652*, 222–237.

Shaw, T. M. (2015). African Agency? Africa, South Africa and the BRIC. *International Politics, 52* (2), 255–268. Online: https://link.springer.com/article/10.1057%2Fip.2014.48. Accessed 25 August 2020.

Standard Digital. (2018, July 8). Exclusive: Behind the SGR Walls. https://www.standardmedia.co.ke/kenya/article/2001287119/exclusive-behind-the-sgr-walls. Accessed 25 August 2020.

Sunday Nation. (2016a, April 24). Asian Giant's Local Links Tell of Growth, Debt and Suspicion. https://www.nation.co.ke/kenya/news/asian-giant-s-local-links-tell-of-growth-debt-and-suspicion-1192316. Accessed 6 January 2018.

Sunday Nation. (2016b, May 22). Why Kenya's Influence in East Africa is Under Threat. https://www.nation.co.ke/kenya/news/why-kenya-s-influence-in-east-africa-is-under-threat-1200834. Accessed 6 January 2018.

Sunday Nation. (2018, September 16). Questions on Viability of SGR Refuse to go Away after China Cuts Funding. https://www.nation.co.ke/business/Questions-on-viability-of-SGR-refuse-to-go-away/996-4761966-sgtqe5z/index.html. Accessed 12 October 2018.

Sunday Nation. (2019, January 13). Has Anyone Seen New Railway Audit? Online: https://www.nation.co.ke/kenya/news/has-anybody-seen-new-railway-audit–127370. Accessed 26 August 2020.

The EastAfrican. (2019, June 27). Big Win for Activists and Kenyan Court Blocks Coal Plant. Online: https://www.theeastafrican.co.ke/tea/news/east-africa/big-win-for-activists-as-kenyan-court-blocks-coal-plant-1421082. Accessed 26 August 2020.

The Elephant. (2018a, July 7). Crony Capitalism and State Capture: The Kenyatta Family Story. Online: https://www.theelephant.info/op-eds/2018/07/07/crony-capitalism-and-state-capture-the-kenyatta-family-story/. Accessed 25 August 2020.

The Elephant. (2018b, July 21). SGR by the Numbers—Some Unpleasant Arithmetic. https://www.theelephant.info/op-eds/2018/07/21/sgr-by-the-numbers-some-unpleasant-arithmetic/. Accessed 1 November 2018.

The Standard. (2017). The SGR Line will Stop at Kenyatta's Naivasha Family Land: Raila Odinga Claims. Online: https://www.standardmedia.co.ke/entertainment/local-news/2001245993/the-sgr-line-will-stop-at-kenyatta-s-naivasha-family-land-raila-odinga-claims. Accessed 26 August 2020.

The New York Times. (2017, June 8). Kenyans Fear Chinese-Backed Railway is Another 'Lunatic Express'. Online: https://www.nytimes.com/2017/06/08/world/africa/kenyans-fear-chinese-backed-railway-is-another-lunatic-express.html. Accessed 26 August 2020.

Van de Walle, N. (1994). Neopatrimonialism and Democracy in Africa, with an Illustration from Cameroon. In *Economic Change and Political Liberalization in Sub-Saharan Africa* (pp. 129–157). Baltimore, MD: John Hopkins University Press.

Virk, K. (2018). Africa and India: Riding the Tail of the Tiger. In *Africa and the World Bilateral and Multilateral International Diplomacy*. Cham: Palgrave Macmillan.

Widner, J. (1994). Political Reform in Anglophone and Francophone African Countries'. In J. Widner (Ed.), *Economic Change and Political Liberalism in Sub-Saharan Africa*. Baltimore. MD: The John Hopkins University.

Wissenbach, U., & Wang, Y. (2017). *African Politics Meets Chinese Engineers: The Chinese-Built Standard Gauge Railway Project in Kenya and East Africa* (China-Africa Research Initiative Working Paper 13). Washington, DC:

Johns Hopkins University School of Advanced International Studies. Online: https://static1.squarespace.com/static/5652847de4b033f56d2bdc29/t/594d739f3e00bed37482d4fe/1498248096443/SGR+v4.pdf. Accessed August 2020.

CHAPTER 9

African Perceptions of the BRICS: Optimistic, Pessimistic or Pragmatic?

Bob Wekesa

Introduction

Since its establishment in 2009, scholarship on the BRICS as geopolitical formation has generated great interest from wide-ranging academic disciplines, popular platforms such as the media and geographical viewpoints (Stuenkel 2015). The early inclusion of South Africa in December 2010 has served to ensure that perspectives on the implications, for Africa, of this relatively new bloc are explored. An anecdotal survey of literature indicates that the Africa–BRICS studies and commentaries peaked in 2011 and 2013, these being the years, respectively, when South Africa was formally admitted into the bloc and when it hosted the fifth BRICS summit. For the most part, however, much of the literature is focused on the BRICS in Africa rather than African responses to the BRICS.

This chapter moves away from the bulk of previous analyses that have zeroed in on the Africa–BRICS relations from the perspective of the

B. Wekesa (✉)
University of the Witwatersrand, Johannesburg, South Africa
e-mail: Bob.Wekesa@wits.ac.za

D. Monyae and B. Ndzendze (eds.), *The BRICS Order*,
International Political Economy Series,
https://doi.org/10.1007/978-3-030-62765-2_9

BRICS as they direct their policies and deal-making towards the continent. Instead, the chapter is interested in looking at perceptions on the BRICS from the continent—an understudied area in the fledgling field of BRICS scholarship and a potential contribution to Afro-based studies. As Y. Wu and C. Alden (2014) have argued, 'there is clear acknowledgement in BRICS research circles that the rapid expansion of the countries' trade and high-level engagement with the rest of the world is in contrast to ill-informed public perceptions of their policy intentions'. This is particularly true for and in Africa.

The question that the chapter seeks to shed light on is whether Africans are optimistic, pessimistic or pragmatic in their perceptions of the BRICS and, by extension, what this says about BRICS soft power capital on the continent. These perceptions, potentially leading to an assessment of the image of the BRICS in Africa, are tracked by undertaking a textual media content analysis of two leading business news and analysis publications, the *Business Day* of Nigeria and Kenya's *Business Daily*. Although the selection of only two newspapers from two out of 55 African countries is clearly problematic because it is unrepresentative of the continent, the point is that the analysis can be extrapolated to the rest of the continent as an indication of probable perceptions. Moreover, Nigeria and Kenya are considered economic powerhouses in the Western and Eastern reaches of the continent and, in addition, they, along with South Africa, have some of the most established media systems in Africa. Indeed, in discussions on the idea of South Africa as a gateway to Africa, not just for the BRICS but for other external players as well, scholars (for instance, Vickers and Cawood 2018) have pointed out that Kenya and Nigeria are also points of entry, along with Ghana, Rwanda, Angola and Egypt, for example.

With the common adage that media is the first draft of history (Shafer 2010) and even the 'fast' draft, media content can help us to understand perceptions in lieu of a more extensive survey of African public opinion on the BRICS. Apart from Wasserman's (2013) work on the BRICS in South Africa, where he found that perceptions are neither overly positive nor outrightly negative, there appears to be little if any literature on the BRICS in African media. Yet, how the BRICS as a collective is framed and therefore perceived in African media is a bellwether of this geopolitical formation's image on the continent. The media-based image of the BRICS in Africa in turn invites questions on the level of soft power—that is, the extent to which the BRICS formation is seen as attractive or unattractive to Africa from the point of view of culture, ideologies and institutions (Nye 1990a, b). By analysing media reporting, we can make provisional conclusions as to whether the BRICS are perceived in a manner that boosts their soft power (optimism) or in a manner that diminishes their soft power (pessimism).

The motivation is that analysis of the BRICS in Africa in terms of what the formation is doing or not doing on the continent misses a critical point by not taking cognisance of African agency in the engagements. African agency is essentially the ways and means by which Africa, as a collective and as individual states, pursues internal interests rather than being merely on the receiving end of external partners' agendas. In other words, from an African agency perspective Africa is an actor rather than only being acted upon (see Murithi 2014; Ndlovu-Gatsheni 2014; Tieku 2014). As Shaw (2015) has argued, 'African agency constitutes a determined response by the continent ... [for] gains rather than costs of the discovery of Africa's potential by the BRICS'. Positioned in an Africa-looking-out standpoint, the chapter argues that the successes and failures of the BRICS among themselves and in their engagements with Africa are first and foremost of concern to the BRICS nations themselves and of concern only secondarily to Africa. African scholarship should therefore be focused on the gains and/or losses that the BRICS portend for the continent's self-interest.

The bulk of analyses on the BRICS and Africa have bifurcated into individual BRICS countries' relations with the continent, with China claiming the larger portion of the literature. This is an extension of the argument that the BRICS are cohesive in certain respects such as challenging the West, but quite different and distinct in other respects such as their variegated economic statuses. Moving away from the asymmetries, convergences and divergences between Brazil, Russia, India, China and South Africa as individual parts of the whole, the chapter looks at the BRICS as a collective, convinced that such an approach can be productive in testing the concept informing the formation and sustenance of the 12-year-old geostrategic bloc. In so doing, South Africa is firmly placed within the BRICS category even though it is an African nation—to analyse South Africa outside of the BRICS would be to negate the idea of the BRICS as a collective. In any case, analyses on South Africa and the BRICS, including tropes such as the validity of its inclusion, its putative representation of Africa and as the ostensible gateway to the rest of the continent in the BRICS scheme of things have been appreciably ventilated in policy and academic literature (for instance Virk 2018; Kahn 2011; Stuenkel 2015).

Optimism, Pessimism, Pragmatism

Perceptions about the BRICS in Africa present a mixed picture. While some commentators see the engagements in a negative light, others see it positively while yet others take an in-between position, viewing the relations as positive in some aspects and negative in others. As terms that describe and analyse tropes in the relations, 'negative' and 'positive' are bipolar, polarised and antagonistic. Instead, we can use the labels of optimism and pessimism, which grasp the negativity and positivity without assuming that negative or positive perceptions are so distinct as to be considered cast in stone (see Wekesa 2017).

Optimistic discourses are based on areas where Africans' views are convergent with the BRICS' interests in Africa. For instance, the fifth BRICS Summit in 2013 in Durban, South Africa, under the theme 'BRICS and Africa' stands as the occasion when the BRICS attracted potentially optimistic views from Africans and with African leaders representing regional economic blocs in attendance (Virk 2018; Brand South Africa 2013). As a rule of thumb, optimism towards the BRICS is discernible in cases where the BRICS in Africa phenomenon is framed in positive, enthusiastic and alluring terms.

Whereas optimism would be good for the BRICS interests in Africa, pessimism would be bad for the interests of the BRICS in Africa. Take the case of national sovereignty. Contrary to the policies of active intervention in African affairs from the old powers, the non-interference foreign policies of emerging powers are seen as giving Africans room for greater ownership of their development paths (Vaes and Huyse 2013). Pessimism on the other hand, is looked at from the viewpoint that Africans may not be enthusiastic or, indeed, are critical of the formation—or when the BRICS are viewed through negative lenses. Misgivings have for instance been expressed about the rhetoric of non-interference and mutual benefits from the BRICS to Africa (Vaes and Huyse 2013). Moreover, as emerging economies the BRICS countries are seen as having deleterious effects on Africa by turning blind eyes to human rights, democratic principles, good governance and transparency (Vaes and Huyse 2013) and propping up undemocratic regimes on the continent (Bond undated).

Pessimistic discourses essentially and often cynically diverge from the view that BRICS portend well for Africa's economic, diplomatic and even cultural interests. As an example, although South Africa's presence in the BRICS may be seen as a good for the continent as a whole, in reverse it may be reason enough for some African countries to resist the BRICS. As Virk (2018) points out, competitors such as Nigeria and Senegal 'take umbrage at the fact that external powers look to South Africa as Africa's global representative'. Pessimism is discernible in cases where the BRICS in Africa phenomenon is framed in negative, unenthusiastic and sometimes blistering terms, with commentators turning sour and the discourse underlined by suspicion and mistrust by Africans.

Optimism is looked at from the perspective of Africa and Africans being bullish about the relations or vis-à-vis the relations, rather than the BRICS themselves being bullish about their formation in Africa. A key trope in the optimistic outlook on the BRICS in Africa is that the mere notion of 'emergence' portends a 'golden opportunity' for Africa (Vaes and Huyse 2013). Along the lines of the BRICS as a developmental opportunity for Africa, some argue that recent upward economic growth that touched off the 'Africa rising' mantra was a consequence of ramped-up engagements with emerging powers, especially in their purchase of African natural resources (Taylor 2014). However, the pessimistic view is that 'with the arrival of emerging economies in Africa alongside traditional [Western] trade associates, the historical process of under-development is in danger of being further entrenched' (Taylor 2014). While optimism can be seen in the impressive economic and trade flows between the BRICS and Africa (Deych 2015), their apparently ravenous appetite for African minerals ends up devastating ecologies and exploiting African workers (Bond undated). Africa's reliance on BRICS for development is considered dangerous, as is evident in the impact of the crash in commodity prices which slowed down Africa's economics (Bond undated).

While optimism with the BRICS in Africa is framed along the lines of global South solidarity, on the pessimistic end the continent may end up falling prey to a new scramble (Vaes and Huyse 2013; Virk 2018) not dissimilar to the European-led colonialism, especially with regard to trade imbalance in the disfavour of Africa as well as economic relations based on Africa's export of raw materials and the importation of finished products (Virk 2018). In fact, those who assess the BRICS as being different from the West are seen as gullible in not grasping the fact that at their core the BRICS are part and parcel of the global capitalist system (Bond undated; Taylor 2014).

It is for the reason that African optimism towards the BRICS can easily turn pessimistic and vice versa that the third perceptual category, pragmatism, becomes an important analytical strand. As Vaes and Huyse (2013) have argued, Africans have demonstrated nuance in assessing emerging powers' interests in Africa as thumbs up on the financial flows into their economies while thumbs down on the debt burden that arises out of access to cheap loans.

The pragmatic discourse is marked by equivocation, ambiguity and ambivalence, taking neither a too welcoming stance nor an overly dismissive attitude. The pragmatist's worldview is inclined towards cautious optimism with a dose of healthy scepticism. In the literature, titles such as 'BRICS in Africa: prizes and pitfalls of building a new global order' (Carmody 2013) or 'BRICS without straw, or the building blocks of a New World Order?' (Spector 2013) immediately imply a middle-of-the-road attitude of taking stock of the optimism towards Africa while being wary of the pessimistic dimensions in the relations.

Pragmatism denotes the discursive ways in which Africa or Africans strategise to lever the benefits that would accrue from the BRICS in any number of ways. As one South African analyst put it, Africa has to aggressively seek funding to address its infrastructure gaps with the New Development Bank (NDP) as one of the sources for funds. However, the capitalisation of the NDP at $100 billion is too low for the huge African infrastructure needs, thus, the need for Africans to seek assistance from the BRICS as well as other sources such as the World Bank, sovereign wealth funds and global pension funds (Mabanga 2015).

Pragmatism is when Africans, in a hard-nosed and business-like approach, seem to see the practical aspects in engaging with the BRICS. Seeing the glass as neither half full as would an optimist nor half empty as would a pessimist, a pragmatist seeks to seize points of benefit in the relations while attempting to minimise the drawbacks.

The mixed perceptual picture of African perceptions towards the BRICS thus falls into three discourse categories: optimism, pessimism and pragmatism. These three strands speak to the creation of a discourse to the extent that they have been repeated, reproduced and sustained since the emergence of the BRICS in such a manner as to forge perceptions. The three strands speak to creation of meaning in the Africa–BRICS engagement, notwithstanding the ideological, geographical or disciplinary positioning of the meaning makers. The three discourse planks therefore potentially provide the conceptual tools through which we can access popular African perceptions on the BRICS using African media as a source.

The optimistic discourse has it that the BRICS are altruistic towards Africa, being keen to co-opt the continent in a battle with the West on mutually equal terms. The BRICS countries never colonised Africa and have supported the continent's positions in the global system. However, on the pessimistic end, the asymmetry in status between African countries and their BRICS partners makes it impossible for Africa to be placed at par with the BRICS. At any rate, the fact that the Africa, at the African Union (AU) as well at the individual state levels, does not have a coherent policy towards the BRICS does not inspire confidence (Virk 2018). Labelling the BRICS countries as sub-imperialists aspiring for Western imperialism, Bond (undated: 25) leads to the conclusion that they have no qualms in exploiting Africa's weaknesses.

Analysis: Optimism, Pessimism and Pragmatism in the Media

Only 25 articles were available on the online platforms of Kenya's *Business Day* (September 2010–February 2015) and Nigeria's *Business Daily* (March 2013–January 2018) indicating that journalistic interest in the BRICS story in Nigeria and Kenya is quite low. It is understandable that the website of Nigeria's *Business Day* has 18 articles compared to *Business Daily* of Kenya's seven articles. Quite apart from its population size, Nigeria was seen as a candidate for the BRICS in competition with South Africa as a result of which its media would have higher levels of coverage than Kenya's, as Kenya has not harboured BRICS inclusion ambitions. It would have been expected that these specialised, niche market newspapers that serve elite readers in the corporate, financial and policy circles would have high frequencies of coverage of the BRICS. That the coverage of BRICS is miniscule stands as a general indicator of pessimism. A glance at general news newspapers from English-speaking African nations indicates that reporting on the BRICS is even more muted.

The quick conclusion of the BRICS attracting little coverage in Kenyan and Nigerian press may be a result of lack of interest in the BRICS formation, a form of pessimism. By contrast, the coverage of individual BRICS countries, particularly China and South Africa, is quite high in both publications. This trend is replicated in other newspapers from other countries based on anecdotal observation. The upshot is that there is a problem in seeing the BRICS as a collective, with most reporting and commentary ostensibly headlined as 'BRICS' essentially abandoning the label to focus on individual BRICS countries. We can therefore make the claim that African countries are more desirous of bilateral relations with Brazil, Russia, India, China and South Africa than relations on a multilateral scale—for instance, Nigeria and the BRICS or Kenya and the BRICS. If indeed the claim of African countries favouring bilateral over multilateral relations holds water, we can also conclude that African countries are more pragmatic than they are optimistic or pessimistic towards the BRICS.

Analysis at the level of headlines speaks to newsroom-level perceptions in which the BRICS are framed as the 'other'. The bulk of the headlines are framed weakly; that is, they do not persuasively fall into the optimistic, pessimistic or pragmatic categories (see Chong and Druckman 2007; Wekesa 2016), when analysed from the perspective of African perceptions. Focused on merely reporting developments in the BRICS bloc in the manner of dissemination news and information (what editors label as 'foreign news'), most of the headlines are not explicitly optimistic, pessimistic or pragmatic with regard to Kenyan and Nigerian interests, and this arguably applies even more to African countries with smaller economies. As an illustration, headlines such as 'Emerging nations voice concerns over slow IMF reforms' (*Business Daily* 29 March 2012) or 'BRICS bank set to launch next week' (*Business Day* 11 July 2014), reveal little with regard to direct African interests in Kenya and Nigeria. One article points to this 'other' perspective by explaining that the BRICS is 'a group of five newly industrialised or developing economies which sought to have closer economic, financial and political ties among themselves'. This sustains the view that African interest in the BRICS is low. Thus, if we consider pragmatism as equivocation, ambiguity and ambivalence, a conclusion can be made that Africans, by default, tend to be more pragmatic than optimistic or pessimistic towards the BRICS phenomenon.

Of the few headlines that are explicitly focused on African interests towards the BRICS, most are optimistic rather than pessimistic. In some of the headlines we see optimistic perceptions towards the BRICS, framed as the BRICS being exemplars or role models for Kenya and Nigeria, or these countries aspiring for inclusion in acronym-based formations. Illustrations include: 'Kenya joins 'Lucky Seven' successors of BRICS' (*Business Daily* 1 February 2015); 'Taxation: What Lagos has learnt from BRICS that Nigeria should!' (Olamilekan [*Business Day*] 26 January 2018); 'Nigeria lags the BRICS peers in 2017 university rankings' (Onyekwelu [*Business Day*] 2 May 2017). As explained elsewhere in this chapter, instances of media 'self-criticism' of their own countries in relation to the BRICS counts as optimism for the BRICS. The pragmatic perspective in these respects is the apparent counsel to authorities in the African countries to follow the example of BRICS countries, a perspective fleshed out below.

Because of the weak framing of the headlines, analysts would have to put themselves in the shoes of Kenyan and Nigerian journalists in order to determine optimism, pessimism or pragmatism. Thus, based on the assumptions that Kenyans and Nigerians are critical of the capitalistic policies of Western-dominated financial institutions, especially the World Bank (WB), the International Monetary Fund (IMF) and global economies more generally, it would be expected that the challenge posed by the BRICS to these global North institutions would be viewed optimistically, even though weakly framed. This can be seen in headlines such as 'Emerging nations voice concerns over slow IMF reforms' (*Business Daily* 29 March 2012), 'Emerging economies to bail out EU' (*Business Daily* 14 September 2011) and 'BRICS to create credit rating agency to rival Fitch, others' (*Business Day* 17 October 2016). In these respects, African optimism about the BRICS seems to be driven by a pessimistic narrative in respect of the Western institutions. The headline 'Emerging economies to bail out EU' essentially ridicules the West—it would have been unthinkable for the great powers of Europe to seek assistance from an institution of the global South.

However, the laudatory narrative of the BRICS as nations with fast-paced growth turns pessimistic in the wake of the slowdown in their economies. One article characterises this pessimism by saying that the glow surrounding the BRICS had faded, implying the need for cautiousness by Africans when dealing with the BRICS—a perspective that introduces pragmatism.

Most of the strongly optimistic are the two headlines from the Kenyan newspaper: 'Kenya gains as S. Africa joins BRIC economies' (*Business Daily* 15 April 2011) and 'Emerging economies renew investment interest' (*Business Daily* 7 December 2010). The most explicitly pessimistic are three from the Nigerian newspaper, 'The silence of the BRICS' (Singh [*Business Day*], 2 September 2014) 'Carmakers must look beyond BRICs' (Ochonma [*Business Day*] 30 October 2013), 'Crumbling BRICS' (*Business Day* 22 March 2013). A conclusion can therefore be drawn that perceptions about the BRICS vary from one African country to another, based on the engagements of the said countries with the BRICS generally and the specific BRICS nations individually.

In the case of Nigeria, as reflected in the coverage, expectations that this African economic giant deserved a place in the ranks of the BRICS may be a shaper of pessimism. One article in the Nigerian newspaper begins: 'In 2010, South Africa was invited to join BRIC and many wondered why Nigeria was not picked ahead of South Africa, considering its population size, abundant oil and gas resources and strong growth prospect' (Olamilekan, January 2018). On the other hand, Kenya, with apparently little in the way of ambition for inclusion in the BRICS, can find room for favourable consideration of the bloc, as seen in the two hopeful Kenyan headlines quoted above.

In the curious headline 'crumbling BRICS' we see idiomatic play on the idea of the BRICS as mortar and bricks or, as one South African analyst put it, 'BRICS without straw'. Pessimism is seen in the portrayal of the individual countries that form the building blocks of the collective as falling apart, rather than holding, that the problems the BRICS face—such as economic deceleration in the case of Brazil and China, and Russia's fall-out with the West—mean that they cannot be of much value to Africa. This re-emphasises the view that African countries should not always maintain 'starry eyes' towards the BRICS: the code for pragmatism.

It would appear that academics tackling the Africa–BRICS phenomenon fall more on the pessimistic than optimistic end of things, with very little in the way of explicitly pragmatic persuasions, as discussed above. Beyond the headlines, what is the picture that emerges from textual content analysis on the basis of African perceptions of the BRICS?

An interesting finding is that similar to academic analyses, the coverage of the BRICS often turns to individual countries even when treating them as a bloc. In some reported cases, the BRICS is even conflated with the whole of Asia and South America. Brazil and India are seen as potential partners in delivering generic medical drugs at prices affordable to Africans. South Africa's inclusion in the BRICS is seen as a boon for African countries (Kenya specifically), as South African companies with a strong presence could be conduits for increased capital flows, expertise and knowledge from the other BRICS countries into the continent. Instead of analysing the performance of the BRICS countries as collective in matters of tax-GDP ratios and tax compliance, the performances of Brazil, Russia, China and South Africa are compared separately to that of Nigeria, drawing attention to the fact that the BRICS nations are independent states with their own, rather than collective, tax regimes. The Chinese economy is reported as slowing down while the Brazilian economy faced a recession and India's remained cautiously stable. The investment strategies of the BRICS in African countries are covered not as a bloc but as individual countries. These and other instances further sustain media-based perceptions of the BRICS as forged separately rather than as a collective, giving vent to the idea that the BRICS are either ill-understood in Africa or not favourably considered.

The two newspapers present a mixed picture on the optimistic, pessimistic and pragmatic continuum captured by an article that says 'They [BRICS] promise huge potential for growth but also pose significant political, monetary, and social risks' (*Business Dictionary* 2018). In suggesting that Kenya is among seven other countries tipped to replace BRICS as new frontiers for investment, the perceptual implication is that the concept behind the BRICS formation is worth emulating. On the other hand, however, it suggests that interest in the BRICS as sites for global investment is waning—this is as new entrants into the ranks of fast-paced economies threaten the assumed prowess of the BRICS. Thus, the BRICS are seen as not being exceptional in the face of the emergence of countries labelled as NEXT-11 (Bangladesh, Egypt, Indonesia, Iran, Mexico, Nigeria, Pakistan, the Philippines, Turkey, South Korea and Vietnam) and MIKTA (Mexico, Indonesia, South Korea, Turkey and Australia); this is being pessimistic about the BRICS. As the *Business Day* reports, citing an IMF report, the Nigerian economy expanded at a faster rate than the combined average for BRIC (Brazil, Russia, India and China) countries, in the period 2012–2013. This would suggest that in some African countries, business elites see their economies through optimistic prisms and the BRICS economies through pessimistic lenses. Other articles question the value of a geopolitical organisation based on an acronym mooted by a global consulting firm.

For the most part, coverage of the establishment of the BRICS in 2010 is essentially perception-neutral insofar as perceptions are concerned, save for the refrain throughout the content suggesting that the BRICS was established to rival and check 'Western hegemony'. However, a whiff of optimism can be read in the formation of the BRICS bank, the New Development Bank (NDB) in 2014 in that it would rival Western-dominated institutions like the World Bank. This sliver of optimism is boosted by the argument that BRICS economies seek to forge 'symbiotic relationships' characterised by cheap loans focused on infrastructure development, unlike the stringent conditions and other governance baggage that comes with funding from Western-dominated financial institutions. Also optimistic in the context of 'BRICS versus the West' is the coverage of the announcement to set up a credit-rating agency that would assess the economies of developing nations in more favourable terms. The reverse however, is an argument that Africans should not be overexcited about the NDB because it is not the only global developmental finance institution: regional banks such as the Inter-American Development Bank, the Asian Development Bank and the African Development Bank are not only potential sources of funding for African projects but also have cooperative relations with the Bretton Woods institutions.

Cast in the rise of the BRICS narrative in the wake of the financial crisis begun in 2008, the upward looking articles simultaneously damp down on the West. In other words, the anticipated financial flows from the BRICS, along with technological transfer, will effectively weaken links between Africa and its traditional economic partners in the global North. The investments from the BRICS would target areas of investment in which Africa needs capital injection, such as real estate, telecommunication, agriculture and the manufacturing sectors. One article puts it succinctly: the BRICS countries are already part of the African infrastructure solution. Here, we can again see a subtle critique of the West, which has focused on the 'softer' developmental issues such as governance, democracy and human rights—an instance of optimism for the BRICS.

The theme of the need for African countries to learn from the BRICS as role models is well represented in the media data. Nigeria, a writer argues, is saddled by a tax regime burdened by obsolete laws leading to inefficiencies in tax collection. This pessimism towards Nigeria's—and by extension African—tax regime, suggests optimism towards BRICS nations which have more efficient tax administration systems that are continually being streamlined. The argument is that African countries should emulate the BRICS, essentially raising the BRICS into a potential exemplar for African countries on a score of good practices in economic spheres.

The role model theme as a shaper of optimism can be seen in a number of other examples. For instance, a commentator argues that Nigeria needs to invest in research at its universities to effectively compete with BRICS peers increasingly performing well in global university ranking indices.

Another article laments that the exclusion of Nigeria from the BRICS denied the country an opportunity to learn and benefit from membership of the bloc and thereby gaining 'critical insight and knowledge'. Nigerian optimism towards the BRICS as a role model can however also be read from a pessimistic viewpoint in the sense of Brazil, Russia, India and China having favoured South Africa, a geopolitical competitor for supremacy on the continent. Similarly, other African countries could view South Africa, and by extension the BRICS, with a measure of envy.

The optimistic view of South Africa as the intermediary of the BRICS on the continent bolsters the South Africa-as-gateway-to-Africa label as reported by Kenya's *Business Daily*. However, the 'South Africa and the BRICS in Africa' theme is not uniformly agreed upon. For instance, although the Nigerian paper hails the hosting of the fifth BRICS summit in South Africa in 2013 as optimistic of BRICS interest in Africa, the trope of South Africa beating Nigeria in the two African nations' courting of the BRICS in 2011 presents a pessimistic picture.

These mixed perceptions can be seen by one article having both optimistic and pessimistic sentiments. For instance, the article that laments the BRICS countries passing over Nigeria to co-opt South Africa is at the same time quite optimistic of the fifth BRICS summit: the theme was Africa friendly, advancing the African agenda, and reflected South Africa's dual objectives of benefiting itself as well as Africa more broadly.

Conclusion

Work on media-based African perceptions of the BRICS is necessarily a work in progress. As indicated in this chapter, perceptions differ from one country to another. Indeed, perceptions may differ from one media house to another based on the media platform's editorial bent, ownership and target audience. Still, we can cautiously conclude that by dint of not being a popular topic in African media coverage of the world, the BRICS is viewed as the 'other' and therefore much more pragmatically than optimistically or pessimistically. In soft power terms, therefore, the BRICS, as a collective, do not have much in the way capital. This simultaneously suggests at least two things about African agency: muted coverage of the BRICS as an indicator of poor analytical appreciation of its impact on the continent and poor coverage as dismissal of the BRICS acronym in favour of bilateral regions with individual BRICS. The sum of this is that, on the whole, the media-based image of the BRICS as a collective in Africa is, in the first place, unappreciable, to the extent that it is little understood. If African media cover the BRICS only in sporadic and ad hoc versions, then how much worse are everyday Africans?

Bibliography

Atuanya, P. (2014, April 21). Nigerian Economic Expansion Tops BRICs as Reforms Accelerate. *Business Day* [online]. http://www.businessdayonline.com/companies/article/nigerian-economic-expansion-tops-brics-as-reforms-accelerate/. Accessed 16 June 2018.

Bond, P. (Undated). *The Brics Re-scramble Africa*. http://www.iese.ac.mz/wp-content/uploads/2017/11/VConfIese_PBond.pdf. Accessed 22 June 2018.

Brand South Africa. (2013). *African Blocs to Attend BRICS Summit*. https://www.brandsouthafrica.com/investments-immigration/business/trends/global/summit-160113b. Accessed 26 June 2018.

Business Daily. (2010). Brazil Joins Brics Nations in Second Scramble for Pie of African Market. Available at: https://www.businessdailyafrica.com/economy/3946234-1173202-vwyra3z/index.html. Accessed 16 June 2018.

Business Daily. (2010, December 7). Emerging Economies Renew Investment Interest. *Business Daily* [online]. Accessed 16 June 2018.

Business Daily. (2011). *Emerging Economies to Bail Out EU*. Available at: https://www.businessdailyafrica.com/markets/Emerging-economies-to-bail-out-EU/539552-1236424-8w5cbbz/index.html. Accessed 16 June 2018.

Business Daily. (2011). Kenya Gains as S. Africa Joins BRIC Economies. Available at: https://www.businessdailyafrica.com/markets/Kenya-gains-as-S-Africa-joins-BRIC-economies/539552-1144746-9jw90q/index.html. Accessed 16 June 2018.

Business Daily. (2012). Emerging Nations Voice Concerns Over Slow IMF Reforms. https://www.businessdailyafrica.com/markets/Emerging-nations-voice-concerns-over-slow-IMF-reforms/539552-1376244-wm2m41z/index.html. Accessed 16 June 2018.

Business Daily. (2014, July 9). BRICS to Sign Deal Creating Development Bank. *Business Daily* [online]. https://www.businessdailyafrica.com/markets/BRICS-to-sign-deal-creating-development-bank/539552-2377548-nkgkvsz/index.html. Accessed 16 June 2018.

Business Daily. (2015, February 1). Kenya Joins 'Lucky Seven' Successors of BRICS. *Business Daily* [online]. https://www.businessdailyafrica.com/economy/Kenya-joins-successors-of-BRICS/3946234-2609408-7j5l8b/index.html. Accessed 16 June 2018.

Business Day. (2013, March 28). A Win-Win in Infrastructure—The Durban BRICS Summit. *Business Day* [online]. http://www.businessdayonline.com/

opinion/analysis/article/a-win-win-in-infrastructure-the-durban-brics-summit/. Accessed 16 June 2018.

Business Day. (2013, April 2). BRICS and Bangui. *Business Day* [online]. http://www.businessdayonline.com/columnist/article/brics-and-bangui/. Accessed 16 June 2018.

Business Day. (2013, March 22). Crumbling BRICS. *Business Day* [online]. http://www.businessdayonline.com/columnist/article/crumbling-brics/. Accessed 16 June 2018.

Business Day. (2013). What the World Needs from the BRICS. http://www.businessdayonline.com/opinion/analysis/article/what-the-world-needs-from-the-brics/. Accessed 16 June 2018.

Business Day. (2014). BRICS Bank Set to Launch Next Week. http://www.businessdayonline.com/companies/article/brics-bank-set-to-launch-next-week/. Accessed 16 June 2018.

Business Day. (2014). BRICS Sees Bali Trade Deal Implemented Despite India Concern. Available at: http://www.businessdayonline.com/world/article/brics-sees-bali-trade-deal-implemented-despite-india-concern/. Accessed 16 June 2018.

Business Day. (2015). BRICS Call on G20 to Work Harder on Economic Policy Cooperation. Available at: http://www.businessdayonline.com/companies/article/brics-call-on-g20-to-work-harder-on-economic-policy-cooperation/. Accessed 16 June 2018.

Business Day. (2015). *Goldman's* Next 11 Markets Are Sinking Faster Than the BRICs. Available at: http://www.businessdayonline.com/companies/article/goldmans-next-11-markets-are-sinking-faster-than-the-brics/. Accessed 16 June 2018.

Business Day. (2016). BRICS to Create Credit Rating Agency to Rival Fitch, Others. Available at: http://www.businessdayonline.com/news/article/brics-to-create-credit-rating-agency-to-rival-fitch-others/. Accessed 16 June 2018.

Business Day. (2016). China Backs BRICS Nations Despite Global Uncertainty. Available at: http://www.businessdayonline.com/world/china/article/china-backs-brics-nations-despite-global-uncertainty/. Accessed 16 June 2018.

Business Day. (2017). South Africa Eyes BRICS Partners to Build New $10 Billion Refinery. http://www.businessdayonline.com/news/article/south-africa-eyes-brics-partners-build-new-10-billion-refinery/. Accessed 16 June 2018.

Business Dictionary. (2018). Emerging Economies. http://www.businessdictionary.com/definition/emerging-economies.html. Accessed 5 March 2019.

Carmody, P. (2013, September 12). BRICS in Africa: Prizes and Pitfalls of Building a New Global Order. *The Guardian* [online]. Available from: https://www.theguardian.com/global-development/2013/sep/12/brics-africa-global-order. Accessed 26 June 2018.

Chong, D, & Druckman, N. J. (2007). Framing Public Opinion in Comparative Democracies. *American Political Science Review, 101*(4), 637–655.
Daily Maverick [online], March 27. https://www.dailymaverick.co.za/article/2013-03-27-brics-without-straw-or-the-building-blocks-of-a-new-world-order/#.WzHVJ6czbIU.
Deych, T. (2015). BRICS as an Important Actor in Africa. *Insight on Africa, 7*(2), 169–185.
Eichengreen, B. (2018, August 18). Banking on the BRICS. *Business Day* [online]. Available from: http://www.businessdayonline.com/exclusives/analysis-sub/article/banking-on-the-brics/. Accessed 16 June 2018.
Kahn, M. J. (2011). The BRICs and South Africa as the Gateway to Africa. *Journal of the Southern African Institute of Mining and Metallurgy, 111*, 493–496.
Mabanga, T. (2015, July 7). What BRICS Can Do for South Africa and Africa. *Mail & Guardian* [online]. https://mg.co.za/article/2015-07-07-what-brics-can-do-for-south-africa-and-africa. Accessed 26 June 2018.
Murithi, T. (2014). The Evolution of Africa's International Relations. In T. Murithi (Ed.), *Handbook of Africa's International Relations*. London: Routledge.
Ndlovu-Gatsheni, J. S. (2014). Pan-Africanism and the International System. In T. Murithi (Ed.), *Handbook of Africa's International Relations*. London: Routledge.
News Agency of Nigeria. (2016, October 15). BRICS Leaders Set for Goa Summit. *Business Day* [online]. http://www.businessdayonline.com/news/article/brics-leaders-set-for-goa-summit/. Accessed 16 June 2018.
Nye, J. (1990a). Soft Power. *Foreign Policy* (80), 153–171.
Nye, J. (1990b). The Changing Nature of World Power. *Political Science Quarterly, 105*(2), 177–192.
Ochonma, M. (2013, October 30). Carmakers Must Look Beyond BRICS. *Business Day* [online]. http://www.businessdayonline.com/politics/life/the-lead-story/article/carmakers-must-look-beyond-brics/. Accessed 16 June 2018.
Olamilekan, S. (2018, January 26). Taxation: What Lagos Has Learnt from BRICS That Nigeria Should! *Business Day* [online]. http://www.businessdayonline.com/exclusives/analysis-sub/article/taxation-lagos-learnt-brics-nigeria/. Accessed 16 June 2018.
Onyekwelu, S. (2017, May 2). Nigeria Lags THE BRICS Peers in 2017 University Rankings. *Business Day* [online]. http://www.businessdayonline.com/exclusives/article/nigeria-lags-brics-peers-2017-university-rankings/. Accessed 16 June 2018.
Shafer, J. (2010). *Who Said It First? Journalism Is the 'First Rough Draft of History'*. http://www.slate.com/articles/news_and_politics/press_box/2010/08/who_said_it_first.html. Accessed 26 June 2018.

Shaw, M. T. (2015). African Agency? Africa, South Africa and the BRICS. *International Politics, 52*(2), 255–268.

Singh, J. (2014, September 2). The Silence of the BRICS. *Business Day* [online]. http://www.businessdayonline.com/exclusives/analysis-sub/article/the-silence-of-the-brics/. Accessed 16 June 2018.

Spector, J. B. (2013). *BRICS Without Straw, or the Building Blocks of a New World Order?* https://www.dailymaverick.co.za/article/2013-03-27-brics-without-straw-or-the-building-blocks-of-a-new-world-order/.

Stuenkel, O. (2015). *The BRICS and the Future of Global Order*. Lanham, MD: Lexington Books.

Taylor, I. (2014). *Africa Rising: BRICS Diversifying Dependency*. Oxford: James Currey.

Tieku, K. T. (2014). Theoretical Approaches to Africa's International Relations. In T. Murithi (Ed.), *Handbook of Africa's International Relations*. London: Routledge.

Vaes, S., & Huyse, H. (2013). *New Voices on South-South Cooperation Between Emerging Powers and Africa: African Civil Society Perspectives*. Leuven: Hiva—Research Institute for Work and Society. https://lirias.kuleuven.be/bitstream/123456789/397152/2/R1507_New_Voices_on_South_Cooperation.pdf. Accessed 21 December 2016.

Vickers, B., & Cawood, R. (2018). South Africa's Corporate Expansion: Towards an 'SA Inc.' Approach in Africa. In A. Adebajo & K. Virk (Eds.), *Foreign Policy in Post-Apartheid South Africa*. London and New York: I.B. Tauris.

Virk, K. (2018). South Africa and the BRICS. In A, Adebajo & Virk, K (Eds.), *Foreign Policy in Post-Apartheid South Africa: Security, Diplomacy and Trade*. London and New York: I.B. Tauris.

Wasserman, H. (2013). South Africa and China as BRICS Partners: Media Perspectives on Geopolitical Shifts. *Journal of Asian and African Studies* 201X, *XX*(X), 1–15.

Wekesa, B. (2016). Building Blocks and Themes in Chinese Soft Power Toward Africa. In Z. Xiaoling, Wasserman, W & Mano, W (Eds.), *China's Media and Soft Power in Africa: Promotion and Perceptions*. Basingstoke, UK: Palgrave Macmillan.

Wekesa, B. (2017). New Directions in the Study of Africa-China Media and Communications Engagements. *Journal of African Cultural Studies, 29*(1), 11–24.

Wu, Y., & Alden, C. (2014). *BRICS' Public Diplomacy and the Nuances of Soft Power*. South African Institute of International Affairs. http://www.saiia.org.za/opinion-analysis/brics-public-diplomacy-and-the-nuances-of-soft-power. Accessed 25 June 2018.

CHAPTER 10

BRICS and Beyond: Some Principles of Educational Collaboration in the Global South

Maxim Khomyakov

BRICS Educational Collaboration: A General Introduction

The overall aim of this chapter is to discuss nascent educational collaboration between the BRICS countries. On the one hand, this collaboration is still very young: BRICS ministers of education met for the first time in 2014 and the first agenda-setting meeting was held in Brasilia in 2015. On the other hand, there are already a number of ongoing projects, including fairly large schemes such as the BRICS Network University or the evolving BRICS University League, but also smaller bilateral and multilateral summer schools, conferences and educational programmes. It is still not very clear, however, what real benefits this collaboration has brought or what, in general, is the added value of the joint projects

M. Khomyakov (✉)
University of Central Asia, Bishkek, Kyrgyzstan
e-mail: maxim.khomyakov@ucentralasia.org

D. Monyae and B. Ndzendze (eds.), *The BRICS Order*, International Political Economy Series,
https://doi.org/10.1007/978-3-030-62765-2_10

between these distant countries with such different educational systems. What kind of rationale can be thought of as underlying the collaboration of BRICS countries (or the global South in general) in education and research? What impact could it have upon the development processes—or even for the very understanding of development in the framework of the 'emerging economies' of the global South? This chapter will try to answer these and some other closely related questions.

In order to do so, however, a more general question should first be asked. What is the current state of international education worldwide, and how can the countries of the global South find a proper (and better) positioning in the global system? The chapter answers the first question in terms of describing a 'global academic revolution', and seeks to address the second through a review of excellence projects on one hand and 'horizontal' academic networks on the other. It argues that the very horizontality of the networks makes them more suitable for taking into account the shared problems and common challenges of the global South countries, while excellence projects are, rather, oriented towards the transfer of the global North model of the world-class research university, measured by the world academic rankings. These three issues are the main objectives of the first three parts of the chapter, devoted accordingly to the academic revolution, excellence projects and BRICS educational networks.

The main cases selected for the analysis are of the Russian '5/100' excellence project and of the BRICS Network University. The reasons for choosing them are simple and obvious; '5/100' is the most recent excellence project in BRICS countries and clearly oriented along the lines of the global academic revolution in its attempt to build several world-class universities on Russian soil; the BRICS Network University, on the other hand, is the most developed university association among the five nations, and focused upon 'facilitating sustainable developing of the BRICS countries' (Memorandum 2015).

In order for the network educational collaboration to make any sense, however, it should be considered in the context of the search for a comprehensive rationale behind global South collaboration in general: if 'developing' countries of the global South are merely recipients of the proper models and institutions to be transferred to them from global North, there is no place for any meaningful South-South collaboration. However, if these countries are to develop their own institutions based upon their unique experiences and interpretations of modernity, the models of horizontal South-South collaboration are of paramount importance. That is why the last part of the chapter pays close attention to the theories of multiple modernities and new concepts of development as the main theoretical frameworks for thinking about BRICS collaboration.

All these ideas, taken together, enable the chapter to address the main question of this book: whether BRICS is able to provide any meaningful alternative to the existing world order. It claims that horizontal educational collaboration is really critical here. BRICS clearly would not be able to become a viable alternative if it does not develop something valuable to offer to the rest of the world. Whatever this might be, education and research taken together are the only way to develop such an alternative model—and this new model would in its turn make sense only if it addressed the main modernity questions through the experiences of real men and women of the global South countries—or, in other words, is based upon shared understanding of the issues they have in common. Since the most of these issues seem to relate to development, elaboration of the new concept of development becomes really important.

The chapter does provide a detailed analysis of this logic, but has to leave the main question open. There is a clear need for an alternative world order which would better accommodate the claims and address the challenges of the global South countries. Whether BRICS would be able (or even really willing) to perform this role is, however, still far from clear. More time and effort are certainly needed, but the opportunity seems still to be available.

Academic Revolution: Towards Formation of Transnational Educational Capitalism

Everywhere in the world, higher education today is experiencing a period of radical transformation, with rapidly changing content and structure of education. These changes are so drastic that some attentive observers have even coined the term 'academic revolution' to describe what is happening in the sphere of higher education. There are four main processes which jointly determine radical change in today's university environment: massification, commercialisation, globalisation and internationalisation (Altbach et al. 2009).

These four processes are, however, not separate. They are so tightly interconnected and entwined that they seem to be only aspects of a single global transformation—of one general trend. On the one hand, the growing middle class in a number of global South countries is seeking access to tertiary education abroad, contributing to internationalisation and massification of the universities in the North. On the other hand, internationalisation almost inevitably leads to a higher degree of commercialisation, simply because it seems to be very difficult to persuade national taxpayers to support international students. As in any transnational corporation, in today's university nationally defined common good comes into conflict with internationally attracted resources and worldwide activity. Global presence, contributing to making the world a global campus—as in the 1984 David Lodge novel *Small World: An Academic Romance*—also transforms the university into a transnational commercial enterprise. Thus, the four elements of the academic revolution are interwoven, contributing together to the worldwide process of radical transformation.

It follows that this transformation is neoliberal in its essence (Khomyakov 2016). One of its obvious results is the treatment of higher education not as an important public good but, rather, as a product for international sale (Hazelkorn 2011; Rhoads et al. 2014; Dill and Soo 2005). The logic of the public good has been substituted by the logic of the private commercial brand, and the Humboldtian idea of individual development has given way to the educational services provided by the universities. The result is a phenomenon of educational capitalism, which threatens to wash away non-commercial values (Sandel 2012). As commercial enterprises, the universities stop performing some of their important social functions such as, for example, enhancing social equality through inclusive comprehensive education or providing moral education to future citizens (Sandel 2012).

Internationalisation is certainly one of the most prominent aspects of this global transformation. The explosive growth of the young population in such countries as Nigeria (median age 18.4), India (27.9), Ethiopia (17.9), Kenya (19.7), Philippines (23.5), Pakistan (23.8), Angola (15.9) and Nepal (24.1) make them potentially very attractive markets from which to recruit foreign students. The shortage of tertiary education institutions, combined with the gradual growth of the middle class, leads to an increasing number of young people from these countries seeking paid education abroad. It is very important to notice at this point that the academic neoliberal revolution thus further reinforces the gap between South and North. The first is treated as a source of potential students, bringing money to the economies of Europe and North America, which are increasingly attractive study destinations. This growing gap certainly reveals the neocolonial nature of the global educational market structure.

In the countries of the global North itself the resulting commercialisation of the universities is increasingly blurring the boundaries between public and private education. In many public universities in the US, for example, only one-fifth of the budget comes from public sources (Altbach et al. 2009). This makes us wonder in which sense education in the 'developed countries' still can be called public.

All these considerations mean that not only do both internationalisation and the academic revolution in general bring with them putative or real openness, inclusiveness or equality but they also lead to the consolidation of the global educational market; to fierce competition among both universities and national educational systems; to the substitution of nationally oriented approaches by transnational commercial education—as well as to the gradual disappearance of the concept of education as a public good and, consequently, to the growing struggle of the universities for material and human resources, both domestically and internationally. Internationalisation and the academic revolution in general also contribute to the ever-growing gap between South and North and, by the same token, to the condition of radical global inequality. In short, internationalisation and globalisation accompany the formative processes of the global educational capitalist system.

It is absolutely unsurprising, then, that the formation of the global educational market has led to the emergence of the new private business of academic rankings. The Big Academic Three, composed of the Academic Ranking of World Universities (ARWU, Shanghai ranking), Times Higher Education ranking and Quacquarelli Symonds (QS) World Academic ranking seem to have monopolised this business. Ostensibly meant to provide a reliable guide to the global landscape of the higher education, the rankings have in reality led to the intensification of global inequality and to the creation of a new neocolonial disciplinary practice, as well as to unprecedented pressure on both national governments and universities. This pressure has led, among other things, to the inclination of university leaders to use the results of the rankings in their strategic planning, even when they believe that the picture provided by the rankings distorts the reality gravely. Thus, E. Hazelkorn (2011) noted that while most leaders of higher education institutions (HEIs) believe that the university rankings favour old universities (89 per cent), that they establish a hierarchy of HEIs (82 per cent), and that they are open to distortion and inaccuracies (81 per cent), the leaders are at the same time also inclined to use the results of the rankings in setting goals for strategic planning (63 per cent) and to consider them as providing important comparative information (73 per cent). Only 40 per cent of these leaders, however, believe that the rankings provide a valid assessment of the quality of higher education (Hazelkorn 2011).

The very logic of the world university rankings seems to imply favouring those institutions which are already very powerful. Indeed, the concept of the world-class university (WCU) as it has been developed by a number of scholars is based upon understanding a WCU as an institution which attracts talents and resources globally and is effectively led towards this aim by a team of good professionals (Salmi 2009). This is clearly a circular way of defining a WCU since, of course, only the universities of *already existing* world repute are able to attract talent and resources. In other words, a WCU is one which is recognised as such globally. In turn, this implies, tautologously, that Harvard, Cambridge, Yale and Oxford represent world-class universities.

This vicious cycle of reputation in the rankings produces what Robert Merton has famously called a 'Matthew effect'—the situation where those who already have the reputation gain everything and those without established reputations continue to lose resources (Rigney 2010; Safon 2013; Hazelkorn 2011). What rankings produce, then, is a greater inequality in reputation and, therefore, in the resources the universities are able to attract. Rankings are almost always biased towards old, established, large traditional universities.

Inequality, fostered by these reputational gaps, is twofold. On the global scale, there is obvious inequality between the nations: rankings favour the British and American model of research university more than, say, the socially responsible highly autonomous institutions of some continental European countries (Safon 2013; Saisana and D'Hombres 2008; Jeremic et al. 2011; Altbach 2006; Li et al. 2011).

At the domestic level, the schools of inherited reputation usually perform better in all the main league tables. International rankings seem to favour the leading schools of particular nations such as, say, Moscow State University in Russia or Al-Farabi National Kazakh University in Kazakhstan, whose international reputation is very much inherited, while the other universities in the same country must build theirs—sometimes from scratch. It certainly makes the task of building world-class universities even more formidable for the higher education institutions which do not yet belong to this rather elite club. After all, the majority of the rankings elevate institutions 'with advanced reputation in both teaching and research, as historical bearers of state mission' (Pusser and Marginson 2013).

Domestically, international rankings reinforce the inequality between elite and mass higher education institutions, while globally they widen the gaps between perceived educational conurbations and the deeply provincial 'periphery'. That is why B. Pusser and S. Marginson describe the project of the world academic rankings as 'neoimperial' and argue that 'because the norms of ranking systems are mostly consistent with the world's strongest higher education institutions located in the United States, this disciplinary effect is especially invidious in nation-states outside the United States. Despite the global variations in resources, states of development, national histories, traditions, languages and cultures, institutions outside the United States are pressed into following the template of the globally dominant universities...' (Pusser and Marginson 2013: 558).

Thus, '... the state project being pursued here is not simply national but also neo-imperial, being most closely tailored to the interests of the nations traditionally dominant in the higher education sector: the Western nations and, above all, the English-speaking nations led by the United States and United Kingdom' (Pusser and Marginson 2013: 559).

The majority of universities from the global South countries lose in this competition. Those who abstain from the race lose from the very start; those who participate find it impossible to compete with the established centres of academic power, and eventually lose anyway. The arrival of new technologies resulting such as in MOOCS (Massive Open Online Courses) does not really make this world more open and equal. In the context of transnational educational capitalism, open courses lead to further exclusion and inequality. M. Zembylas and C. Vrasidas (2005) claimed that instead of helping to create a culturally neutral 'global village', digital networks helped Western countries to colonise the world again, to increase their opportunities and to expand their reach. S.A. Rye (2014) demonstrated how seemingly 'democratic' (meant to be inclusive and equality-based) Norwegian online courses in Development Management, which involved both Norwegian and African students, actually produced some important new inequalities and exclusions. African students, for example, had to deal with cultural peculiarities built into the very structure of the course and, as a result, were not always capable of demonstrating the same level of performance as the students from Norway. With all their democratic potential and the millions of students taking online courses in the best world-class universities, the MOOCs do not necessarily contribute towards narrowing the gap between North and South.

The growing gap makes the universities in the emerging economy countries seek an effective strategy for overcoming most serious differences. Arguably, there are two possible strategies here: the first is an attempt to gain a proper share of the global educational market through active participation in the worldwide excellence race, whereas the second is a quest for an alternative vision. In terms of the existing structure of academic power, the first strategy consists in active participation in educational neocolonialism as described above, while the second tries to implement anti-colonial principles of a more or less radical nature. By the same token, the first is about better integration into global academia whereas the second concerns the creation of additional alternative networks and consortiums. The best implementations of the first are national excellence projects, whereas in the second the main focus is on horizontal network programmes. Quite naturally, then, the integration strategy is totally in agreement with the current neoliberal transformation of global education; the networks, however, represent an ambitious attempt to find an alternative to transnational educational capitalism. Finally, integration to world academia today means orientation towards creating elite world-class universities, but the horizontal networks focus primarily on the peculiar problems of societies in the global South.

Many universities in the BRICS countries today (especially in China and Russia, with their extensive excellence projects such as 'project 985' in China and the '5-100' project in Russia) seem to play both games simultaneously, trying not too consistently to get their share of the neocolonial pie and to find alternatives to the dominant power structure. This is an unsustainable situation, because one suspects that it masks the neo-imperial fight for markets. In other words, it is still very unclear whether the BRICS countries are willing and able to find an alternative to the existing power distribution or whether they are simply fighting for a bigger share of the power. In the context of neoliberal *knowledge society discourse*, education and science are directly connected to these power structures.

It is still too soon to judge what in reality is going on in the higher education systems of the BRICS countries and of the global South in general. On the one hand, in their attempts to build WCUs many countries tend to reproduce external Northern models and play the old game of market competition in the global educational space. On the other hand, through forming horizontal university networks and enhancing South-South educational cooperation, BRICS countries do try to form an alternative vision of international education. The struggle between these two tendencies seems to reflect the general contradiction of BRICS policies between neocolonial and inclusive models of development. In any case, the future of the BRICS bloc seems to depend very much on which of these tendencies would finally win.

Excellence Projects: Paving the Way for Transnational Education

The impact of the new transnational higher education upon national systems of higher education is especially strong in the countries which are struggling for better representation in the global educational market. This struggle is strongly intensified by the obsession with academic rankings that can sometimes lead to compromising national goals and domestic traditions in higher education. There is, for instance, the example of Japan, where the government has recently recommended that universities not spend precious resources on humanities and social sciences and close the relevant departments (ICF Monitor 2015). Humanities are *national* in essence, and they naturally lose their place in the new *transnational* order of higher education.

This bias is natural for the rankings, which tend to favour hard sciences over humanities. Humanities do not produce new technologies and are not considered to be useful for generating revenues (Amsler and Bolsmann 2012). Moreover, with their focus on the development of national cultures, the research output of humanities cannot be properly measured by international citation indexes. Finally, both by tradition and their nature, humanities are still very much books-oriented rather than journals-oriented disciplines—and this also adds to the difficulties of the 'objective' measurement favoured by the world university rankings, since even world's top historians or philosophers very often have comparatively low h-indexes.

It does make sense, then, to agree with Rauhvargers (2013), who describes the rankings as (1) focusing on elite universities; (2) relatively neglectful of the arts, humanities and social sciences and (3) reliant upon such poor indicators as, for example, the faculty/student ratio in measuring teaching quality (Rauhvargers 2013). Those who want to secure higher positions in the academic rankings more quickly will have to support already rich universities, contributing to further inequality growth and to the sacrifice of certain disciplines (especially those focused in human development, such as humanities) for the sake of the developing technology-oriented knowledge.

Those who decide to actively participate in the global academic race must be ready to invest heavily in few elite institutions. For one thing, 'a world-class university is a $1–1.5 b[illion]-a-year operation' (Hazelkorn 2007) and, for another, building a new reputation is even more expensive than maintaining an existing one. That is why, among BRICS countries, China has since 1999 been spending in total about US$6 billion for programmes devoted to the creation of WCUs. In 2012–17, Russia invested US$878.5 million in its well-known 5/100 project, which supports enhancing the 'international competitiveness' of the 21 best Russian institutions of higher education.

Despite some interesting results, the performance of the universities in the BRICS countries in the world academic rankings is still not impressive. Even China, with all its huge investments had only seven universities in the top-200 of the 2016 Times Higher Education (THE) ranking and eight universities in top-200 of the QS World University Ranking. Russia had one university in both rankings; South Africa had two institutions in the THE top-200, and one in the QS top-200; India and Brazil are not represented in the THE top-200, and have two universities each in the QS rankings top-200. On the other hand, the UK is represented with 32 universities in the THE top-200 and with 30 institutions in the QS top-200. This is a good illustration of the huge gap in academic power and weight which emerging economy countries are so desperately trying to bridge with their excellence projects.

In the end, then, it would appear that the main goal of the excellence initiatives is better integration into the world academy rather than addressing the most pressing domestic issues. In the Russian case, the project is openly oriented towards enhancing the performance of Russian universities on the global scale and has initially set the educational system an utterly unrealistic task of bringing at least five universities into the top-100 of the rankings. In other cases, the goals could be expressed in more subtle ways, but all of them invariably promote transnational technological education, which has become the new educational normality of the twenty-first century. Thus, internationalisation becomes one of the most important goals of higher education development.

What is most important here is that in this quest for better integration into the world academy the universities are compelled to change according to external standards. Therefore, the negative impact of the rankings is far less 'on institutions at the top of the global ranking tables that can determine their own identities' (Amsler and Bolsmann 2012). In the emerging countries, however, sometimes even elite national institutions have been 'partly displaced' by the top global universities (Marginson 2007). In the countries which aspire for better positioning of their higher education systems in the main league tables, the impact of the rankings can become really disastrous.

The rankings become a powerful disciplinary tool because they define both external standards and the best performers, thus becoming an important instrument for benchmarking (Hazelkorn 2011; Proulx 2011). In the case of Russia, the main benchmarks for the best 5/100 universities are set according to the rankings. The Higher School of Economics (Moscow), for example, chose the London School of Economics and Political Science, Erasmus University Rotterdam, Humboldt University of Berlin, Hong Kong University of Science and Technology and the University of Warwick as its benchmarks (Programma HSE 2013). The Ural Federal University (Ekaterinburg), a large technical school, focused on attracting foreign students from Asia and compared itself with Aalto University (Finland), Sungkyunkwan University and Yonsei University (both in South Korea), City University of Hong Kong and TsinHua University (both in China). Interestingly, for the Ural Federal University the main elements of comparison were the current position and historical dynamics of these universities in THE and QS academic rankings (Programma UrFU 2013).

Another obvious feature of the excellence programmes is their orientation towards creating WCUs, elite institutions with a distinct mission and purpose and further increasing basic educational inequalities in their societies. Those institutions, recruiting the best students from the best high schools, receive additional support from public funds. Since the majority of the best high-school alumni belong to the upper middle class, the governments indirectly subsidise those who could by no means be called the least advantaged members of society. Excellence programmes, thus, indirectly reinforce social inequality.

It is not surprising, then, that the development programmes of most Russian university participants in the 5/100 project exhibit a neoliberal orientation towards *enhancing competitiveness* or *developing the national economy* (for example, Programma UrFU 2013). Integration to the academy is defined less in terms of joining the old good 'republic of letters' than entering fierce competition for material and human resources. Internationalisation is also used as a synonym for market competitiveness (see also a powerful critique of the concept of international by Paesi 2005).

The excellence projects have positive sides as well. They make the universities care about their reputation, set high standards and integrate research and education in global academia. The projects stimulate researchers to publish in respected journals and motivate professors to create educational programmes able to attract good students. The rankings become an interesting benchmarking instrument and do provide university management with some useful metrics. Undoubtedly, 'rankings are here to stay. Even if academics are aware that the results of rankings are biased … they also recognize that an impressive position in the rankings can be a key factor in securing additional resources …' (Rauhvargers 2013: 25).

The quest for better integration to the market-driven world academy, however, should not lead to the university forgetting the most pressing problems at home and compromising its own mission. The difficulty lies in finding a proper balance between orientation to international standards and national or regional commitment. This is not an easy task. In his welcome address to the participants of the Seventh QS-APPLE conference held on 16 to 18 November 2011 in Manila, Fr. Rolando V. Dela Rosa, O.P. Rector of the University of Santo Thomas, noted that his university would probably become a world-leading one if the rankings took into consideration the number of saints produced by particular institutions (QS Top Universities 2011). The seemingly joking nature of this remark should not obscure the obvious fact that many global South countries like the Philippines would probably need those aspiring to be saints more than those who prepare for the career of office manager. In any case, neoliberal world-class universities glorified by the world academic rankings do not seriously embody the domestic social role of the university—a role which is certainly important for the global South countries in general, and for the BRICS countries in particular.

There is no any evidence, moreover, that putative BRICS academic rankings would help the situation. On the one hand, there already exist some BRICS and 'emerging economies' academic rankings being issued by both THE and QS, although these rankings are almost identical to the world rankings as far as measurement and metrics are concerned, and the only real difference seems to be artificial geographical limitations. On the other hand, even if BRICS does create its own new university ranking mechanism it would inevitably retain the main drawbacks of the existing world academic rankings. The point is that it does not really make sense to take into account the needs of such different societies and educational systems with the aim of incorporating all of them into a unified ranking mechanism. Any unified ranking would necessarily be too abstract and would not take into consideration the real and different needs of the BRICS societies. One of the important points in this respect is that what most BRICS countries need is an inclusive quality education, which is very difficult to measure internationally and which, therefore, is not really measured at all by the main rankings which are focused instead upon research performance.

Horizontal University Networks: Addressing Common Problems

An answer to the misbalances of the obsession with the world academic rankings is given by the horizontal academic networks of the universities of similar position and status, which share general approaches to the common problems of their similar societies. These networks can be seen as an emerging alternative model of university collaboration and higher education development.

The still dominant model of university interaction is that of 'vertical' North–South collaboration, in which Northern expertise and standards are exchanged for the human (students) and material (funding) resources of the Southern nations. S.A. Rye (2014) discerns three main types of such collaboration for development. The first is to provide free places for the global South students at the universities of the global North (still, by the way, the main practice of the 'educational internationalisation' employed by the Russian government. The second is connected with establishing higher education institutions of high 'international' (that is, Northern) quality standards in the global South countries (either by supporting local universities or through creating foreign campuses of the best universities). Finally, the third type of vertical collaboration is online education, which provides the students with opportunities for international mobility without actually moving. Arguably, all these types of interactions involve a certain transfer of standards in the direction of South and transfer of the resources in a predominantly Northern direction. Even when these collaborations are supported by international donors, they promote further expansion of Northern standards and culture.

That is why developing horizontal South-South university cooperation is both new and important, because it brings a hope of overcoming the dependence of the Southern universities of the values, standards and cultures of their Northern partners. In the overwhelming majority of cases, however, this collaboration is still merely a weak addition to the predominantly hierarchical development-driven North–South collaboration.

BRICS is no exception. Quite naturally, BRICS is a club, based upon pragmatic rather than normative consensus. The overall goals and immediate tasks of BRICS were always pragmatic: overcoming the consequences of the global economic crisis, creating conditions for sustainable development, safeguarding security and so on.[1] That is why the creation of a common educational sphere has never been a proper task of BRICS interaction, and collaboration in research and education among BRICS countries has never been very intensive. The number of co-publications between researchers in any pair of the five countries does not exceed three per cent of the total number of publications of the particular BRICS nation (Khomyakov 2016a). Only China has an intensive international student exchange programme; the double degree programmes between universities in different BRICS countries are also very rare.

The number of international degree-seeking students from the BRICS countries in the best Russian universities differs greatly. Of 5 498 students from the BRICS countries in 12 Russian universities, participants in the BRICS Network University, 5 120 are from China, 191 from South Africa, 136 from India and only 39 from Brazil. The following diagram demonstrates distribution of these students in the participant universities. (Fig 10.1)

In any case, the situation does not resemble a developed intra-BRICS educational collaboration. In many respects it is still very much a plan rather than reality. One of the possible reasons is the difference between the educational systems of the BRICS nations (with the exception of

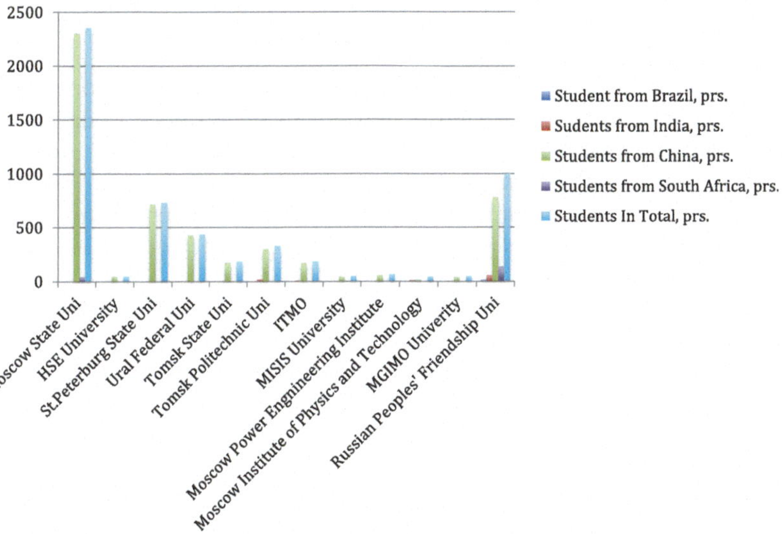

Fig. 10.1 Degree-seeking students from Brazil, **India, China and South Africa in Russian universities—participants in the BRICS Network University scheme in 2017**

China and Russia), which simply cannot be meaningfully compared with each other. All these facts allowed P.G. Altbach and R.M. Basset to claim that the concept of the BRICS block '... is actually of little relevance in understanding the complex higher education environment ...' (Altbach and Basset 2014: 2).

It can also be argued, however, that if BRICS is to develop and to provide a real *alternative vision* of world making, it is bound to have something to tell to the world not only in terms of sheer pragmatism but also in terms of values. To become really sustainable, BRICS (and, generally, other members of the global South) should obtain a normative dimension. Any real value-framework, however, arguably requires a common educational and research area as well as rich cultural interactions between countries—thus, if the BRICS project is to be considered seriously as a viable alternative to the existing model it has to eventually include all these aspects. If BRICS countries are to become real leaders of the consolidated global South, they should find their own way in education and research—otherwise the BRICS club would not live up to its own promise and will be more or less quickly substituted by more viable alternatives.

The most successful attempts to build international common educational and research areas are in the Bologna process, and other important European initiatives such as organising the Erasmus academic mobility programme or establishing the European University Institute in Florence. BRICS experts can certainly learn from these experiences when they try to create joint educational projects, but the possibilities of borrowing are very limited because the links between BRICS countries simply cannot be as tight—and their interrelations so intense—as those between European member states. The BRICS club does not aspire to establish political unity or a common market, so it cannot aim to develop a common educational and research area.

The normative framework for this collaboration is still to be developed, although I briefly discuss some possible candidates for this role in the last section of this chapter. In a general sense, the very concept of an emerging South with an inherent understanding of horizontally structured collaboration can be seen as a basis for such collaboration. In such an understanding BRICS is not simply an anti-globalist movement directed against the prevailing neoliberal world order, but an important attempt to provide an alternative vision of development, devoid of the remnants of imperialism and colonialism. The ideas of the global South, of development and of interpretations of modernity are really crucial for such collaboration. These ideas lie behind the most developed of the BRICS educational projects, the BRICS Network University (NU). The network consists of 56 universities from all five BRICS countries, jointly implementing Master's and PhD programmes in the six priority areas BRICS studies economics, water resources, IT, ecology and energy. Established by the memorandum of understanding signed by the ministers of education of the BRICS countries, the Network University involves a complex horizontal coordination mechanism, based upon the principles of what has been announced as a new concept of development. All efforts have been taken to ensure the equality and autonomy of the participants in the project, which should eventually become a basis for the sustainable university collaboration of the BRICS countries.

Unlike the European University Institute, this BRICS initiative is a network without its own developed infrastructure—that is, without buildings, libraries and computers. Unlike the Shanghai Cooperation Organization Network University (another network initiated by Russia), the BRICS NU does not imply the existence of a permanent secretariat or rector's office. Unlike the European Erasmus programme, it does not have—at least at the initial stage—any consolidated budget, so that each country is supposed independently to finance the participating universities.

The president of the BRICS NU is appointed annually by the current BRICS chair country, whereas the International Governing Board (IGB) collectively takes all strategic decisions. The board consists of 15 permanent members, representing universities and ministries of education of all five countries. Following the rules of the other BRICS bodies, all decisions are taken on the basis of consensus and do not imply a voting mechanism. On the national level, the activity of the BRICS NU is organised by certain national coordinating committees, composed of the representatives of the individual universities. Finally, all substantive issues are discussed in the six international thematic groups, organised in accordance with the six priority areas. The whole system of coordination is rather complex, and consists of national and international, formal and substantial, ministerial and universities-related bodies. The complexity of the system inevitably makes the decision-making process very long sometimes, and always quite difficult; there is, however, a shared understanding that only such a system really corresponds to the principles of equality and autonomy of the horizontal BRICS collaboration.

One of the most problematic and at the same time important issues in this context is how financial decisions are taken and through which mechanism the participating universities are supported. According to the MOU on the establishment of the BRICS NU, financial matters are the domestic responsibility of each BRICS country. Some of them (Brazil in 2015, South Africa in 2017) decided to allocate finances to individual institutions; Russia intends to support incoming students through the mechanism of subsidised places at the participant universities (starting at least from 2019, when the network is supposed to generate the first exchange students), while India considers supporting BRICS NU activity through the university grant commission which provides funding for all universities in the country. China had not decided on the mechanism at the time of writing, probably because it would first need to clearly define relations between the BRICS Network University on the one hand and the China-financed project of the BRICS University League. The differences in funding procedures, along with the absence of a consolidated budget, add difficulties to the project and reflect its complex nature.

Important aspects of BRICS NU activity are the Internet presence of the project and annual general gatherings (not to mention regular meetings of the individual international thematic groups). The face-to-face meetings of all participants are important for the success of the project, which is why the 2016 New Delhi Declaration of the BRICS ministers of education envisages holding annual BRICS NU conferences. Face-to-face interactions between researchers of the BRICS countries, situated physically far away from each other, are thus considered to be of high importance. They are especially significant because individual researchers and professors in the US or Europe still have better knowledge of relevant activity there than in BRICS or other Southern countries. Since real interactions between individual professors and researchers are considered to be the basis for successful networking activity, BRICS NU envisages extensive face-to-face work.

As for the Internet presence, apart from the project webpage (https://nu-brics.ru), several groups in the project are currently working on online courses in BRICS NU priority areas. In total, international thematic groups are at the moment working on 22 joint Master's and PhD programmes, six of which have already been opened for the students (four in computer sciences and two in ecology and climate change), and another 18 are going to enrol the first students in 2019. One additional programme in computer science, four programmes in BRICS studies, four programmes in economics, four programmes in energy, one programme in water resources and pollution treatment, and two additional programmes in ecology and climate change will be opened. It is clear that with all these programmes in place, the BRICS NU will become the largest, the most comprehensive and certainly the most ambitious project as far as South-South cooperation in education is concerned. That is why the BRICS NU is justifiably regarded as a flagship project of educational collaboration among emerging countries. However, difficulties with funding, uneven participation in the project and the complex mechanism of decision-making do make the development of these programmes a difficult and rather long process.

There is another, quite different, initiative which is usually also mentioned in the context of educational collaboration between the BRICS nations: the BRICS University League, a voluntary university association, regularly referred to by various BRICS declarations and statements. Officially initiated by five Russian and five Chinese universities in 2013, it is now coordinated by Beijing Normal University (China).

Unlike the Network University, the League is rather slow in developing its activities. It still lacks a signed charter, a developed plan of activities and a clear organisational structure. In a way, it is still to be established. The main difference between the League and the BRICS Network University project is its purely voluntary nature—it is independent of any official ministerial decision. The idea, thus, is that its activity would be complementary to the work of the BRICS Network University.

The BRICS: An Alternative Vision?

As has already been argued above, sustainable educational and research collaboration by the BRICS countries is impossible without a more comprehensive normative framework justifying its ambitions. If the BRICS club is just another neo-imperial gathering of countries trying to enhance their international standing and to get their share of the postcolonial market, it cannot be expected to provide a viable alternative to the existing world order and their collaboration will remain purely pragmatic—which, in the absence of strong common interest, will inevitably tear the club apart. We have already witnessed such processes in the conflict between India and China over the construction of a road in Bhutan. The Brazilian U-turn after Dilma Rouseff's impeachment is another example of the looming dangers which might threaten the very existence of BRICS (see Chapter 2 of this volume). After all, when established common institutions are absent, too much seems to depend upon the current political course and will of each of the BRICS countries.

It is not very clear, however, what the normative framework to help overcome such problems could be. After all, as has been already noted, the BRICS countries are so different and are situated so far away from each other that it would be really difficult to locate the longstanding interests and features they have in common. One thing, however, has been clear from the very beginning: the BRICS club is sustainable only as a leader of a consolidated global South. Even if it contains Russia, with its Arctic regions, Northern ambitions and rich imperial past, the BRICS makes sense only as an articulation of the interests of the global South. The idea is that through BRICS the South will participate in the alternative global governance. Only in this context is the participation of such small countries as South Africa justified: it takes part in BRICS projects as a leader of the whole African continent. Similarly, Brazil represents South

America, Russia leads Central Asia, China represents Far East and South-East Asia, while India expresses the interests of Southern Asia. One can, of course, ask whether these countries are able to represent the regions they are supposed to lead, whether they have the necessary moral and material power and whether they are credible and trustworthy. All these questions would not however change the fact that the only way for the BRICS to become sustainable is to inspire confidence and hope in the global South as a whole.

The idea of global South makes sense if there is a real possibility of an alternative vision of social development. In other words, consolidation of the global South is achievable if development (or progress) does not follow a straight line from one point to another. This means rejection of the modernisation theory, at least in its classical post-Second World War version. The problem is that 'theories of modernisation in the 1960s understood the combination of autonomy and rational control as realized solely and definitively in the institutions that emerged in Europe and the US … As a result, modernisation in newly developing countries was understood as an imitation of that which had occurred in more advanced countries' (Larrain 2007). Unlike the theory of modernisation as a single way of establishing a set of distinctly modern institutions, the new theory understands modernity as 'experience and interpretation' of the modern condition. We are now talking, then, of *plural modernities*, rather than the *s*ingle modernisation of different societies. How is this understanding possible?

After Johann Arnason's and Peter Wagner's seminal works on modernity (Arnason 1989; Wagner 1994) it has become almost commonplace to refer to Cornelius Castoriadis's characterisation of modernity as based upon a certain 'double imaginary signification'. The modern period, according to Castoriadis, 'is best defined by the conflict, but also the mutual contamination and entanglement, of two imaginary significations: autonomy on the one hand, unlimited expansion of 'rational mastery' on the other. They ambiguously coexisted under the common roof of reason' (Castoriadis 1997). Arnason thinks of these two principles (or, rather, 'significations') as having divergent, mutually irreducible logics so that 'the pursuit of the unlimited power over nature does not necessarily enhance the capacity of human society to question and reshape its own institutions, and a coherent vision of the autonomous society excludes an unquestioning commitment to the more or less rationalized phantasm of total mastery' (Arnason 1989). These logics, however, are not only divergent, but also 'entangled', and both are present in modernity from its very outset (Carleheden 2010). In short, 'modernity has two goals – to make man master and possessor of nature, and to make human freedom possible. The question that remains is whether these two are compatible with one another' (Gillespie 2008).

Importantly, these two pillars of modernity are not really definite principles but, rather, significations—in other words, 'multiform complexes of meaning that give rise to more determinate patterns and at the same time remain open to other interpretations' (Arnason 1989). The interpretations are given and the definite patters are formed, in their turn, in real historical situations by real people, and thus reflect a complex interplay of different elements, including other imaginary significations, pre-modern traditions, popular sentiments or political considerations. The question of how these patterns are formulated against a particular socio-historical background is, then, one of the most important and interesting questions arising in the study of modernity. These patterns represent what can be called different trajectories of modernity.

Without going into further details of the plural modernity theory, it is worth emphasising that, being based on experiences and interpretations, specific modernity constellations or trajectories are formed by real people in real time and space and therefore differ from place to place. This in its turn means that the global South is not an 'underdeveloped' region in need of modernisation according to Northern standards; it is not less 'modern', than the 'developed' countries of the North. However, it is alternatively modern.

The plural modernity theory thus opens up interpretative space for understanding the global South not simply as a competitor, but rather as an alternative to the global North. In education, the patterns of North–South collaboration as well as the activities of various excellence programmes most closely correspond to the classical idea of educational modernisation, whereas horizontal networks make sense as alternative ways of organising international collaboration in education only in the framework of the *plural modernity* theory.

Rejection of the classical modernisation idea has, however, some important consequences. One of them is abandonment of the traditional development concept, based upon aid and involving complex mechanisms of discipline and control. This development has always been a form of the colonial education of the underdeveloped barbarians. Such approach is best expressed in the famous J.S. Mill passage: 'Despotism is a legitimate mode of government in dealing with barbarians, provided the end be their improvement, and be justified by actually effecting that end. Liberty as a principle has no application to any state of things anterior to the time when mankind have become capable of being improved by free and equal discussion' (Mill 1977). Such development projects are quite justly questioned and criticised by many post-development scholars (Escobar 1995; Rahnema and Bawtree 1997).

However, as rejection of modernisation does not imply abandoning the concept of modernity altogether, the pitfalls of the classical development concept should not lead us to reject development theory as such. Of course, in the framework of plural modernity theory, development can no longer be treated as an effective transfer of good institutions from one place to another. As the experience of many former Soviet Union countries has recently demonstrated, such transfer is counter-productive in the majority of cases—in almost all the countries of the former Soviet Union, the deficiencies of the 'transferred' institutions are obvious (for democracy, for example, see Freedom House 2017; Fish 2005). Even if the exact causes of these deficiencies are not always completely clear, the efficiency of any institutional 'transfer' is really questionable. But if one recognises each country's possibility of being modern *in its own way*, the sought-after development can only be in growing its own institutions, based upon a particular constellation of modernity. In other words, to be effective the development has to fit the trajectory of the society in question.

The new concept of development as a basis for BRICS countries' interactions has been recently proposed by the scholars of the BRICS Studies Centre at Fudan University, Shanghai. The concept implies 'non-zero sum game', win-win development based upon principles of autonomy (independence), equality, inclusiveness and sustainability (green development) (Win-win Cooperation 2015; Fan 2016). Autonomy in this concept means independent choice of the development path, while equality refers to '… equal treatment of all economic actors internally and to equal participation in international economic competition externally' (Fan 2016). Both autonomy and equality are notoriously absent in traditional development instruments, where BRICS countries together have only 13 per cent of votes at the World Bank and 14.29 per cent at the IMF whereas the US alone, for example, has 15 per cent (WB) and 16.6 per cent (IMF) of the votes.

The inclusiveness means the balancing character of all instruments and channels of development, so that the BRICS New Development Bank, for example, does not substitute traditional instruments but, rather, complements their activity. In this sense, inclusiveness, according to Yongming Fan (2016), means inclusiveness in both cooperation and competition, and guarantees against the exclusivist approach. As, in late modernity, fast development almost always entails environmental issues, any new concept of development should be based upon the principle of the 'harmonious coexistence between human beings and environment and between individuals and society in the progress of development' (Fan 2016: 6). In a way, a new concept of development is still a general idea only. It has to be further developed, however, if BRICS is going to offer a valuable alternative to the existing structures of power, including academic power.

Collaboration by the BRICS countries thus makes normative sense if it is going to promote a new concept of development based upon the plural understanding of modernity for all the countries of the global South. Such understanding of BRICS cooperation is rather thick and, frankly speaking, far from what this collaboration looks like today; to make such cooperation sustainable the BRICS must seriously think of becoming a real leader of the global South—which, in its turn, is impossible without employing plural modernity theory and without elaborating a new concept of development, and this necessitates the creation of a common educational area. Joint educational projects are capable of bringing a normative dimension into the purely pragmatic BRICS bloc. Through various excellence projects, BRICS countries participate in the life of global academia and compete in the educational market according to the rules set by the dominating academic powers. However, to make the development sustainable they need to support the horizontal networks, which would further elaborate and implement the principles of the new theory of the development and would incorporate real experiences and interpretations of modernity. The most successful of these networks for the moment is the BRICS Network University, a unique and ambitious initiative of the BRICS ministries of education. The question, however, is the extent to which BRICS is really capable of becoming a speaker for the global South as a whole, since otherwise it would turn into another pragmatic international organisation, pursuing its own particular egoistic interests. What is also important is that education plays a pivotal role in all attempts to answer these questions.

Notes

1. There is some evidence supporting this claim, mainly, of course, the ten BRICS summit declarations. For an analysis of the primary aims of the BRICS groupings, see Stuenkel (2015).

Bibliography

Altbach, P. G. (2006). *International Higher Education: Reflections on Policy and Practice*. Boston College, MA: Center for International Higher Education.

Altbach, P. G., & Basset, R. M. (2014). Nix the BRICs—at Least for Higher Education Debate. *International Higher Education, 77,* 2–5.

Altbach, P. G., & Hazelcorn, E. (2017). Why Most Universities Should Quit the Ranking Game. *University World News,* 8 January 2017. http://www.universityworldnews.com/article.php?story=20170105122700949. Accessed 2 December 2018.

Altbach, P. G., Reisberg, L., & Rumbley, L. (2009). Trends in Global Higher Education: Tracking an Academic Revolution. A Report Prepared for the UNESCO 2009 World Conference on Higher Education. Paris, France: UNESCO.

Amsler, S. S., & Bolsmann, C. (2012). University Ranking as Social Exclusion. *British Journal of Sociology of Education, 33*(2), 283–301.

Arnason, J. P. (1989). The Imaginary Constitution of Society. In Giovanni Busino et al. (Eds.), *Autonomie et autotrasformation de la sociètè. La philosophie militante de Cornelius Castoriadis*. Genève: Librairie Droz: 32–37.

BRICS Ministries of Education. (2015). Memorandum of Understanding on Establishment of the BRICS Network University. https://nu-brics.ru/media/uploads/filestorage/documents/MoU_SU_BRICS.pdf. Accessed 29 October 2018.

Carleheden, M. (2010). The Imaginary Signification of Modernity: A Re-examination. *Distinktion: Scandinavian Journal of Social Theory, 21,* 51–70.

Castoriadis, C. (1997). *World in Fragments: Writings on Politics, Society, Psychoanalysis, and the Imagination*. Stanford: Stanford University Press.

Dill, D. D., & Soo, M. (2005). Academic Quality, League Tables, and Public Policy: A CRoss-national Analysis of University Ranking Systems. *Higher Education, 49*(4), 495–533.

Escobar, A. (1995). *Encountering Development: The Making and Unmaking of the Third World*. Princeton, NJ: Princeton University Press.

Fan, Y. (2016). New Concept for Development: The Logic Behind Emerging Economies' Cooperation. *BRICS Studies Centre Newsletter, 2,* 3–12. http://center-brics.urfu.ru/inbrics/issue-2/. Accessed 29 October 2018.

Fish, M. S. (2005). *Democracy Derailed in Russia: The Failure of Open Politics*. Cambridge: Cambridge University Press.

Freedom House. (2017). https://www.rbth.com/politics_and_society/2017/04/06/freedom-house-democracy-takes-a-hit-in-the-former-soviet-union_736506. Accessed 29 October 2018.

Gillespie, M. A. (2008). *The Theological Origins of Modernity*. Chicago and London: University of Chicago Press.

Hazelkorn, E. (2007). How Does Ranking Impact on Higher Education. *IMHE Info. Journal of the OECD Programme on Institutional Management in Higher Education*. http://www.oecd.org/edu/imhe/39802910.pdf. Accessed 12 February 2018.

Hazelkorn, E. (2011). *Rankings and the Reshaping of Higher Education: The Battle for World-Class Excellence*. Basingstoke: Palgrave Macmillan.

ICF Monitor. (2015). Japanese Government Asks Universities to Close Social Sciences and Humanities Faculties. http://monitor.icef.com/2015/09/japanese-government-asks-universities-to-close-social-sciences-and-humanities-faculties/. Accessed 11 February 2018.

Jeremic, V., Bulajic, M., Martic, M., & Radojicic, Z. (2011). A Fresh Approach to Evaluating the Academic Ranking of World Universities. *Scientometrics, 87*, 587–96.

Khomyakov, M. (2016). Building a World-class University and the Role of University Ranking: A Russian Case. In K. Downing & F. Ganotice (Eds.), *World University Rankings and the Future of Higher Education* (pp. 393–419). IGI-Global.

Khomyakov, M. (2016a). 'BRICS: New Horizons for Collaboration in Education?', in *BRICS. BRICS Studies Center Newsletter, 1*, 19. http://center-brics.urfu.ru/inbrics/issue-1/. Accessed 10 February 2018.

Larrain, J. (2007). Latin American Varieties of Modernity. In P. Wagner & N. Karagiannis (Eds.), *Varieties of World-Making Beyond Globalization*. Liverpool: Liverpool University Press.

Li, M., Shankar, S., & Tang, K. (2011). Why Does the USA Dominate University League Tables'. *Studies in Higher Education, 36*(8), 923–37.

Marginson, S. (2007). University Rankings, Government and Social Order: Managing the Field of Higher Education According to the Logic of the Performative Present-as-Future. In M. Simons, M. Olssen, & M. Peters (Eds.), *Re-reading Education Policies: Studying the Policy Agenda of the 21st Century*. Rotterdam: Sense Publishers.

Mill, J. S. (1977). *On Liberty: Collected Works of John Stuart Mill* (Vol. Xviii). Toronto and Buffalo: University of Toronto Press.

Paesi, A. (2005). Globalization, Academic Capitalism and the Uneven Geography of International Journal Publishing Space. *Environment and Planning*, A 37(5), 769–89.

Programma HSE. (2013). http://www.hse.ru/data/2015/01/23/1105522658/Программа%205-100%20ВШЭ%20рус%20(1).docx. Accessed 10 February 2018.
Programma UrFU. (2013). https://urfu.ru/fileadmin/user_upload/common_files/competition/Programma_povyshenija_konkurentosposobnosti_UrFU.pdf. Accessed 10 February 2018.
Proulx, R. (2011). Using World University Ranking to Inform and Guide Strategic Policymaking: A Case Study of a Canadian Research University. In K. Yu & A. L. Stith (Eds.), *Competition and Cooperation Among Universities in the Age of Internationalization*. Shanghai: Shanghai Jiao Tong University.
Pusser, B., & Marginson, S. (2013). University Rankings in Critical Perspective. *The Journal of Higher Education, 84*(4), 544–68.
QS Top Universities. (2011). *Which University has More Saints?* www.topuniversities.com/university-rankings-articles/world-university-rankings/which-university-has-most-saints.
Rahnema, M., & Bawtree, V. (Eds.). (1997). *The Post-Development Reader*. London: Zed Books.
Rauhvargers, A. (2013). Global University Rankings and their Impact. Report II, European University Association. http://www.eua.be/Libraries/Publications_homepage_list/EUA_Global_University_Rankings_and_Their_Impact_-_Report_II.sflb.ashx. Accessed 5 February 2018.
Rhoads, R. A., Li, S., & Ilano, L. (2014). The Global Quest to Build World-class Universities: Toward a Social Justice Agenda. *New Directions for Higher Education, 168,* 27–39.
Rigney, D. (2010). *The Matthew Effect: How Advantage Begets Further Advantage*. New York: Columbia University Press.
Rye, S. A. (2014). The Educational Space of Global Online Higher Education. *Geoforum, 51,* 6–14.
Safon, V. (2013). What do Global University Rankings Really Measure? *The Search for the X Factor and the X Entity, Scientometrics, 97*(2), 223–44.
Saisana, M., & D'Hombres, B. (2008). *Higher Education Rankings: Robustness Issues and Critical Assessment: How Much Confidence can we Have in Higher Education Rankings*. Luxembourg: European Communities.
Salmi, J. (2009). *The Challenge of Establishing World-Class Universities*. Washington, DC: World Bank.
Sandel, M. (2012). *What money Can't Buy: The Moral Limits of Markets*. London: Allan Lane.
Stuenkel, O. (2015). *The BRICS and the Future of Global Order*. London: Lexington Books.
Wagner, P. (1994). *A Sociology of Modernity: Liberty and Discipline*. London and New York: Routledge.

Wagner, P. (Ed.). (2017). *The Moral Mapping of South and North*. Edinburgh: Edinburgh University Press.

Win-win Cooperation: New Development Concept for BRICS Partnership. (2015). Shanghai: Fudan University, FDDI, Center for BRICS Studies.

Zembylas, M., & Vrasidas, C. (2005). Globalization, Information and Communication Technologies, and the Prospect of a 'Global Village': Promises of Inclusion or Electronic Colonization? *Journal of Curriculum Studies, 37*(1), 65–83.

CHAPTER 11

The Global South and Industry 4.0: Historical Development and Future Trajectories

Wynand Lambrechts, Saurabh Sinha, and Tshilidzi Marwala

Introduction

The notion of globalisation and digital supremacy (*Economist* 2018) accelerates trade between domestic markets and the international segment; in the modern information age, globalisation methods have evolved; not only do they gather information but they also use the information effectively and create value (Akcali and Sismanoglu 2015). Globalisation refers to the tendency of international trade, investments, information and communication technology (ICT), and outsourced manufacturing to interlink the economies of diverse countries. Socio-economic benefits are increased through innovation in science and technology, with the common goal of bringing about positive change. Innovation is essentially a combination of developing new products, or presenting products with enhanced capabilities, introducing new means of production, creating novel markets, acquiring new sources of raw

W. Lambrechts (✉) · S. Sinha · T. Marwala
University of Johannesburg, Johannesburg, South Africa
e-mail: wynand.lambrechts@vodamail.co.za

D. Monyae and B. Ndzendze (eds.), *The BRICS Order*, International Political Economy Series,
https://doi.org/10.1007/978-3-030-62765-2_11

materials, or developing unique organisational procedures of traditional economic processes. In the search for new industry standards and innovations, especially for the networked manufacturing paradigm that is enabled through the Internet, multiple industrial regions globally are facing similar challenges in the implementation of digitised and globalised industrial processes.

The Global South, and many emerging markets, inevitably have additional limitations and risks to mitigate, which will be identified in this chapter. International benchmarks, countries that thrive on innovation, provide future recommendations for action regarding industrial processes of the future, and the strengths and weaknesses of these champion countries can be closely studied as inputs to emerging markets and the ways they approach industrial processes based on technological advances. Four examples, outlined by the Plattform Industrie 4.0 programme, show how countries' abilities to adapt to changing environments, affecting historical and current performance, can be utilised to spearhead industrial change. Four key examples are:

- The United States (US), a country known for its abilities of radical innovation, a breeding ground for start-ups for the Internet of things (IoT) and manufacturing renaissance;
- Europe, especially Germany, known for engineering excellence and visionary concepts that integrate technology, society, and economy;
- China, the benchmark for speed and adaptability, with pragmatic application of quick wins and long-term strategy of mature technologies and strategic development of key technologies;
- Japan and South Korea, with their ability to scale innovation by application, with massive constructions of smart factories and large manufacturing plants to strengthen products and services through domestic demand.

As described in Akcali and Sismanoglu (2015), innovation is one of the most important factors for countries to drive employment growth, sustainable growth, social prosperity, and an enriched quality of life of their residents. External collaboration, both developed and emerging, between countries, as well as open innovation, play an increasingly central role in organisational innovation management and performance (Gkypali et al. 2017). The innovation paradigm is shifting towards the vital pursuit of external factors to access new ideas, technologies, and resources, or to commercialise internal ideas externally and implement intellectual property (IP) (Gkypali et al. 2017). The increasing speed of technological change is driving firms to carry out technological innovation continuously to maintain long-term competitiveness (Zhang and Tang 2017). Innovation is a cooperative and societal movement, and the promotion of diversified knowledge is increasingly affected by collaborative environments. The extremely competitive and fast-changing modern milieu makes innovation more challenging, expensive and precarious for organisations. If companies do not evolve with the industry, domestic and international markets suffer and economic growth slows down. This is especially worrying in emerging markets, where strong and continuous economic growth is crucial for long-term sustainability.

Artificial intelligence (AI) and technological innovation must be adopted in the Global South, where a general misconception among onlookers of digital trends is that consumers in emerging markets do not profit from developments in technologies (Kohli 2018). This is partly true when considering the application adopted by emerging markets. If one considers an automatic robotic cleaner, then, yes, the advances in technology are not relevant to poorer countries. However, considering advances in Internet distribution, a precursor for affordable Internet, advances are crucial in providing sustainable and cost-effective Internet solutions to emerging markets, as well as growing socio-economic development. As a result, technology has the ability to widen the global digital divide, but it also has the potential to mitigate it (Kohli 2018). AI, for example, can be integrated into far more than household appliances or non-critical applications, and has found practical uses in. for example, education, health care, disaster relief, finance, logistics, and business services. According to Kohli (2018), AI has already transformed developing countries through, for example:

- mapping and analysing post-earthquake reconstruction needs through machine learning in Nepal;
- AI tutors across Africa, which are helping students understand coursework better through remote access to crucial information;
- optimising and analysing the delivery of supplies for fleeing refugees in African countries, and
- improving crop yields in India by providing AI applications to rural farmers to boost profits.

All these innovations are relatable to the United Nations (UN) Sustainable Development Goals (SDGs) on issues such as eradicating poverty, mitigating health care inequality, access to education, and fighting global warming. The UN has launched the AI for Good global summit, a platform for global (and inclusive) dialogue on AI. The programme creates a platform to discuss opportunities for using technology for humanitarian work, accelerating the progress to the SDGs, specifically in emerging markets such as the Global South.

To encourage innovation further, bodies such as General Electric, NASA's Kennedy Space Center, and Samsung have adopted an approach called *open innovation*. The results of this initiative have been studied in academic journals, with varying results when implemented in developed countries or in emerging markets. The *open innovation* approach, therefore, requires tailored policies to support an ecosystem that benefits developing countries. Such an approach needs constant pursuit of external environments for novel concepts, information, and technologies. It also requires additional resources, typically difficult for SMEs to acquire, and 'significant internal knowledge and additional skills to turn externally acquired knowledge and technologies into commercially viable products' (Sag et al. 2016). Economic profits from *open innovation* in developing countries can be boosted by the broader innovation ecosystem and suitable policies initiated by the local government. Such policies, explicitly led by government, should include research into peripheral knowledge and technologies, industry tendencies, and the newest innovations, as well as the formulation of reports on worldwide, regional, and sectoral levels, and exploring open innovation intermediaries, establishing collaboration with external actors, and translating these initiatives into local culture, work ethic, and working environments (Sag et al. 2016).

The incipient fourth industrial revolution (Industry 4.0) is firmly reliant on modern technology, information transfer and smart solutions in the industrialised sector. Jeremy Rifkin, a leading originator of the European Union's (EU) long-term third industrial revolution economic vision, called Smart Europe, defines the enabling technologies of an industrial revolution as

> ... three defining technologies emerge and converge to create what we call in engineering a 'general-purpose technology' that forms an infrastructure that fundamentally changes the way we manage power and move economic activity across the value chain. And those three technologies are

> new communication technologies to more efficiently manage the economic activity, new sources of energy to more efficiently power the economic activity, and new modes of mobility, transportation logistics, to more efficiently move the economic activity. (Holodny 2017)

Innovative solutions for Industry 4.0, moving towards smart manufacturing, require solutions in two primary areas: technology and organisation. Technological advances are driven by innovative and skilled workers, whereas proficient organisation requires effective and relevant policies supported financially and legally by governments and the private sector.

The policies that manage and drive Industry 4.0 are specific in their affordability, accessibility, appropriateness, and integration. There is a fundamental requirement for appropriate and dynamic policies and technology scaling to take Industry 4.0 forward, with specific focus gradually being placed on emerging markets within the BRICS bloc (Brazil, Russia, India, China, and South Africa) and including the Global South (less developed countries in Africa, Latin America, and Asia). Current policies in developed markets such as Europe (particularly in Germany) and the US serve as reputable strategies that can and should be adopted by the BRICS countries. BRICS countries have several key advantages over many other emerging markets; advantages such as large workforces, abundant natural resources, and established infrastructure that empower these economies to potentially dominate the data space and effectively dominate the Industry 4.0 revolution. Change will not wait. Business leaders, entities with educational responsibilities (such as universities and governments) must be proactive in encouraging new skills and retraining people so that entire populations can benefit from the fourth industrial revolution. The Global South must play a significant role in Industry 4.0, not out of choice, but because of the necessity of positive and sustainable growth in the future. However, the gap for these emerging markets to establish dominance, or at least become integral players in the sector, is closing, as Europe and the US spearhead Industry 4.0 domestically and internationally. It has been observed (Nistor 2015) that the economies of the BRICS group have attracted large inflows of foreign direct investment (FDI), reaching a fifth of the FDI inflows from the global share in 2015 (Nistor 2015). The inexpensive labour force in China, the young (albeit ageing) population of India and natural resources in Brazil, Russia, and South Africa are among the advantages that attract FDI in these countries. Africa in particular has its own specific set of policy gaps that must be overcome to participate in Industry 4.0, whereas South Africa, despite being the smallest on most indices, can again become the economic hub it once was in Africa, if governmental support for strategies and initiatives is obtained without restrictions, as well as reduced bureaucracy in numerous sectors (see Chapter 12 in this volume). Applicable policy gaps and recommendations on investment volumes, leverage effects, and mechanisms to ensure continuous private investments are mentioned in this chapter, with a specific focus on the African continent and South Africa in particular.

The introductory paragraphs briefly mentioned the fourth industrial revolution, Industry 4.0, as the main driver of the changing industrial landscape for the future. This chapter explores the role that the fourth industrial revolution can potentially play in emerging markets. Industry 4.0 is essentially an evolution of the first, second, and third industrial revolutions. Developing countries have played extensive roles in the first three industrial revolutions, their associations being both good and bad, and the following section provides a brief history of these revolutions, with the focus on developing countries.

The Road to the Fourth Industrial Revolution (Industry 4.0)

A revolution, a noun stipulating *change*, defines a dramatic and wide-reaching transformation in conditions, attitudes, or operation. The current universal manufacturing setting is the consequence of consecutive spells of innovation and economic development, as well as geographical accrual. Although an industrial revolution is often considered a single, isolated event, such revolutions are typically defined by a series of successful innovations that drive economies and industries forward at a particular time. Each industrial revolution builds on the modernisations of the preceding one, leading to more progressive manufacturing. The following section presents a brief history of the four industrial revolutions that shifted paradigms in industry, leading to new manufacturing landscapes where production and distribution capabilities were significantly improved. In the fourth industrial revolution, the role of higher education and academia to train individuals to innovate future technologies and applications in the Global South is also described.

The first industrial revolution is the label bestowed on the period in the eighteenth and nineteenth centuries that transformed Britain from a primarily agrarian society into the manufacturing capital of the world. During this period, mainly small, agrarian, rural communities in Britain changed to urban, industrialised societies. Advances in the agricultural domain brought about increases in the supply of food and raw materials. Improvements in industrial organisation and continuous advances in technology further increased production rates, efficiency, domestic and foreign commerce and, consequently, profits. Production of food and manufacturing of clothing, furniture, and tools were not confined any longer to homes, rural shops, or simple machines. The textile industry initially served as the vehicle to develop new inventions to meet the growing demands of the industry (World Economic Forum 2017).

Britain's role as the birthplace of the industrial revolution was underwritten by various factors, the most important of which were a *politically stable society*, along with its status as a world-leading colonial power and of course its large deposits of coal and iron ore. For Britain, a small island between the north Atlantic Ocean and the North Sea, to become a major economic and military power with an empire that controlled trade networks and colonies across the globe, showed stellar examples of leadership, management, and influence—with a supportive government that encouraged commerce, provided patents to protect inventors, and offered financial aid (Neuss 2016).

The invention of the first efficient steam engine by a Scottish inventor, James Watt, spearheaded mechanisation in the first industrial revolution. Watt dramatically improved the efficiency of the existing steam engines (the Newcomen steam engine) by using a condenser separately from the main piston chamber and implementing rotary motion as opposed to oscillating beams. Watt introduced the notion of horsepower, and the International System of Units (SI-unit) of power, the watt, was named after him. Mechanisation leading to industrialisation should however not be viewed as a single, independent event, or invention (such as the Watt steam engine). Improvements and mechanisation of blast furnaces, smelting practices, and the invention of the mechanical loom for the textile industry also contributed to the important mechanisation that revolutionised industries.

Challenges in the transportation sector, specifically high transportation costs, incentivised manufacturers to establish their workshops close to the sources of raw materials, and provide services and products to local and regional markets. By the mid-eighteenth century, in many regions across Europe and North America, the equilibrium between agriculture and manufacturing had shifted towards increased manufacturing, with villagers relying on artisanal (mechanised) activities for their livelihoods (see South African History Online 2018). Labour-intensive agriculture was becoming more of a supplemental activity. Mass extraction of raw materials such as coal, in combination with the steam engine, followed by railroads, created a new type of energy that propelled economies, material exchanges, and human travel.

Industrialisation resulted in an increase in urbanisation, with some individuals becoming abundantly wealthy, a significant portion of individuals categorised as belonging to the middle class enjoying the benefits of the new prosperity, and an alarming percentage of people having to endure atrocious working and living conditions (see South African History Online 2018). These were the 'workhorses' of the population, hired solely for mundane tasks in the mechanised processes of the time. The upper and middle classes enjoyed a variety of factory-produced goods and new services, while the poor and the working class were forced to deal with other challenges and poor conditions. Long hours, tasks such as cleaning of operating machinery and hazardous environments beleaguered the poor during this time.

In southern Africa, the industrial revolution had a different bearing from Europe; the colonial rule of European countries over Africans transformed this period. In South Africa, the discovery of minerals, specifically diamonds (in 1867) and gold (in 1886), radically transformed the economic and political structure of the country. Foreign capital was invested in South Africa and large-scale immigration took place, but there was a great need for inexpensive labour to ensure profitability. This was specifically evident with the dawn of the second industrial revolution during the latter part of the nineteenth century, peaking around approximately 1870–1914.

The second industrial revolution was also known as the technological revolution, and was a period of very quick industrial development and growth for pre-existing industries (from the first industrial revolution), brought about by several key factors, primarily in countries such as Britain, Germany, France, Italy, Japan, and the US. Some of the identified key factors responsible for the second industrial revolution included:

- expansion and long-haul networks of railroads;
- high-volume and large-scale production and an exponential increase in demands for iron and steel components;

- increasing dependence on and higher efficiency of machinery used for manufacturing, replacing many activities previously performed by humans;
- a further increase in the use of steam power in a multitude of environments;
- development of chemical synthesis that introduced synthetic fabrics, dyes, and fertilisers used in agriculture;
- widespread telecommunication over long distances with the electrical telegraph; and
- the emergence of new sources of energy: electricity, gas (petroleum), and oil, which led to the development of the internal combustion engine.

The second industrial revolution enabled globalisation to new levels, an increase in interaction (socially, economically, and culturally) between people locally and internationally, and was a precursor of the world as we know it today. Social transformations from the second industrial revolution included characteristics such as urbanisation and the convenience of cost-effective housing near factories that employed individuals, a higher pace of work primarily driven by machines to produce commodities for an increasingly urban population and affordability of manufactured goods and services for a larger percentage of the population. The population is 'constantly changing due to births and deaths and the migration of families to find better sources of income' (Lambrechts and Sinha 2016). However, not all transformations were for the better; the overall health of the workforce declined because of poor working conditions, and families were separated as work obligations moved from the home towards factories. Artisans were less desirable and this led to a loss in livelihood for these craftsmen. Availability of work became unpredictable, with variations in the demand for goods. For women, specifically, initially drawn to cities to work in factories, the loss of jobs and an oversaturated market led to a sense of class, a rise in prostitution and the spread of disease (see South African History Online 2018).

In the 1860s, Indians were brought to the British colony of Natal as indentured labourers on five-year contracts. The indentured servants worked primarily on sugar plantations where the working conditions were harsh, cruel, and, in many circumstances, inhumane. Indian indentured labourers replaced traditional Zulu workers, since the Zulu culture did not agree with male workers being applied to agricultural work, and inexpensive Indian labour was already employed successfully in other British colonies (see South African History Online 2018). The colonial government of Natal assured the workers of grants of land on termination of their contracts in order to encourage them to renew their five-year contracts, but these commitments were rarely honoured. The workers were offered the opportunity to become independent workers after their initial contracts expired, which a large portion of the Indian labourers accepted, allowing them to explore the neighbouring states: the Cape Colony, the Orange Free State (only for a brief period, unless prior permission had been obtained), and the South African Republic (also known as the Transvaal Republic). By the 1870s and 1880s, diamond mining had taken over as the primary fortune-seeking activity after diamonds were discovered on the bank of the Orange River. Soon thereafter, 95 per cent of the world's diamonds came to be mined in Kimberley (see South African History Online 2018). Both the local Afrikaans-speaking white South Africans (known as the Boers) and the British aimed to take control of these rich resources, and were typically hostile and antagonistic towards one another. Under Act 25 of the Statute Law of the Orange Free State of 1891, settlement of Indians in the province was discouraged through a set of discriminatory legislation. Indian labourers were not allowed to obtain the burgher right of Transvaal, and they were not allowed to own fixed property except if assigned by the government, and they had to be inscribed in a register if they settled with the objective of trading.

Approximately a century later, during the second part of the twentieth century, more key inventions and technological improvements, primarily in energy generation and electronic components, led to another major economic paradigm shift, the third industrial revolution. Nuclear energy, the invention of the transistor (first demonstrated at Bell Labs at the end of 1947), and the rise of microprocessors are some of the defining technologies of the third industrial revolution. Communication became a radical influence of the third industrial revolution, evolving from the telegraph used during the second industrial revolution to the telephone, radio, television, and later the Internet, hence the paradigm shift occurring from the third industrial revolution towards communication, energy, and mobility, enabling manufacturers to computerise and automate machinery. The requirement for human intervention became smaller. This allowed production lines to run constantly without concern for human fatigue, resulting in lower production costs (by up to 97 per cent for various 3D printing case studies, according to [Stratasys 2019]) when labour cost increases and increased international trade. Communication across any distance around the world became virtually instant and cost-effective. Interplanetary travel and space research and biotechnology improved, and new medical equipment, commercially attainable mobile computing through miniaturisation and mass automation became commonplace.

These inventions and innovations are the most recent precursors to the next industrial revolution, termed Industry 4.0, which might still be in its infancy, but the rapid growth of this landscape is evident.

The Fourth Industrial Revolution (Industry 4.0)

The European Parliament defines Industry 4.0 as:

> the organisation of production processes based on technology and devices autonomously communicating with each other along the value chain: a model of the smart factory of the future where computer-driven systems will monitor physical processes, create a virtual copy of the physical world, and make decentralised decisions based on self-organisation mechanisms. (Gouarderes 2017)

Industry 4.0 (also called the industrial Internet in certain countries) is an effort of industrial companies to effect comprehensive transformation and revolution of their value chain in a technological age defined by AI. Industrial enterprises are digitising essential functions along the value chain, in both vertical operations processes and horizontal associates. Vertical sector-specific policies typically support specific industries, while horizontal policies do not target specific industries. Across the ideological spectrum, the relevance of industrial policies and strategies is acknowledged by economists and governmental leaders (Stiglitz et al. 2013). In addition, imperative to this transformation is the introduction of digital functionalities within the portfolios of industrial companies, introducing new data-oriented services, and moving towards becoming real digital enterprises. These enterprises will therefore offer physical products at their core, augmented by digital interfaces and innovative data-oriented services. The main features of Industry 4.0, as listed by the European Parliament, are:

- interoperability allowing human operators and smart facilities to link and communicate;
- virtualisation through linking simulated plant models to sensor data;
- decentralisation of technology where systems analyse decisions based on environmental inputs;
- real-time adaptive capabilities;
- service orientation; and
- flexibility and modularity to change or expand systems based on current requirements.

While the third industrial revolution concentrated on the automation of discrete machines, 'equipment and processes, Industry 4.0 focuses on the end-to-end digitisation of all physical assets and integration into digital ecosystems with value chain partners' (PwC 2016). Key terms that are typically associated with this movement into a new industrial era include:

- pattern-identification through big data;
- automation (and technologies such as 3D printing);
- cloud-based computing services;
- virtual reality (VR) and augmented reality (AR);
- AI;
- cyber-physical systems (CPS); and
- the IoT.

All these are considered technologies that drive the modern trends of automation, autonomy, and information transfer in manufacturing technologies. To define Industry 4.0 completely, several key technical aspects are discussed in the following subsection. These technologies play a significant role in the definition and integration of the fourth industrial revolution.

Technical Description of Industry 4.0

Technologies that play an indisputable role in facilitating digital trends are CPS, the IoT, Cloud computing, and Cognitive computing. A CPS involves the integration of computation and networking, as well as physical processes that are being monitored through these, typically, embedded computing devices. A CPS integrates dynamic changes in the physical environment with software and networking to provide abstractions and modelling, design and analysis of the data. CPSs have been applied to a variety of disciplines and practical applications, most notably in transportation, energy, health care, and environmental sustainability (Alur 2015). Importantly, a CPS is a control system that interacts with the physical world through a feedback loop, essentially measuring the environment using sensors and influencing it through actuators (Alur 2015). Figure 11.1 is a simplified representation of a CPS based on a feedback loop, sensing specific parameters and controlling actuating units to influence the immediate environment.

CPSs offer the groundwork of critical infrastructure development for Industry 4.0 and are essentially the foundation of emergent and forthcoming smart systems, with the intention of refining the quality of life in numerous areas. Furthermore, cyber-physical production systems that rely on modern developments in computer science, information and communication technologies, and manufacturing science and technology, are

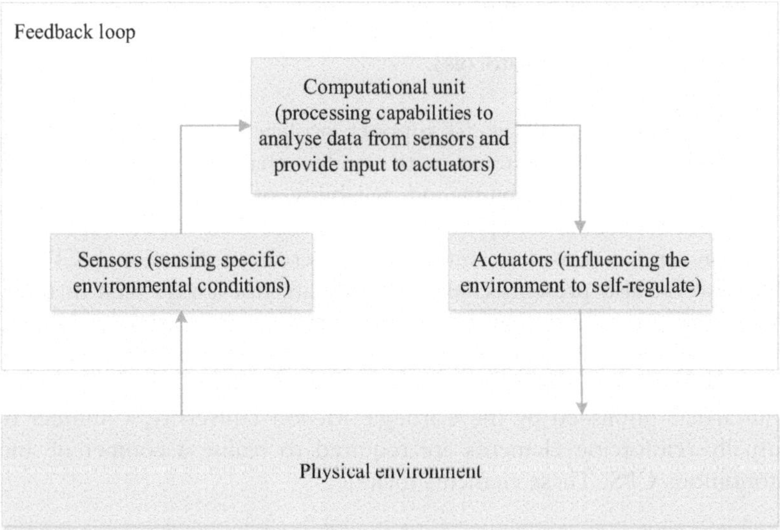

Fig. 11.1 A simplified representation of a CPS based on a feedback loop, sensing specific parameters and controlling actuating units to influence the immediate environment

featured as an enabling technology for Industry 4.0, where future industrial production will be described by the 'individualisation of products' through diverse and modular production techniques (Monostori 2014). A CPS is a structure, typically at the core of Industry 4.0 conversion, which links the physical environment through sensing devices and actuators with the cybernetic setting of information processing. It is where the real and virtual worlds seamlessly connect and transform manufacturing processes. These systems are built from, and depend on, unified incorporation of computational algorithms and physical modules. A commonly used architectural summary for a CPS comprises a (bottom-up approach):

- configuration level (self-configuring for flexibility, self-adjusting for environmental and device variations, and self-optimising for external disturbances);
- cognition level (remote visualisation for human interaction);
- cyber level (performance variation identification and data mining);
- data-to-information level (analytic degradation and device performance predictions); and
- smart connection level (effortless connection to multiple devices through standard protocols).

The objective of a CPS is to support proficient expansion of high-confidence pervasive systems with nodes that are functional and synchronous for predictability and reliability of an integrated system. A CPS often includes components and services from various manufacturers or service providers, integrated to create a functional CPS. A CPS however also presents challenges that are not always seen in traditional business information systems of previous industrial landscapes, often requiring a combination of engineering proficiencies that spans the technical domain, as well as new forms of systems engineering. According to an article published by the Carnegie Mellon University, a number of mutually reinforcing elements are required to realise a competent and autonomous CPS. These elements include:

- Accurate timing verification to ensure that tasks and responsibilities performed by real-time systems are completed within the allocated timeframes. The resilience and performance of such a system are determined by its ability to schedule tasks and events based on the inputs of various sensors and actuators. Critical systems, such as accident-avoidance in autonomous vehicles, depend largely on the successful implementation of timing verification, which includes memory governance and validations/invalidations of critical assumptions.

- Implementing a set of model-checking algorithms and functional authentication parameters to certify that software resources perform as necessary and produce logical correctness to mitigate undesired behaviour of distributed software.
- Maximising the probability that a CPS meets its anticipated objectives through effective probabilistic verification analysis systems to predict the likelihoods of realising a predetermined goal. This can be accomplished based on numerical methodologies such as Markov decision processes. Other methods include Monte Carlo simulations, sampling, and statistical model checking to verify estimations.
- Optimising modularity, performance, and scalability for autonomous structures through transferrable, open-sourced, and decentralised operational environments: a collaborative autonomy platform with accessible user interfaces to aid human workers to regulate and comprehend a diverse and large assortment of data from sensors, actuators, and other ubiquitous devices.
- Finally, the ability of self-adaptation of a variety of unplanned and unexpected changes in the environment, including operational malfunctions without human intervention. This technique includes control of short-term predictions of the immediate and remote environment to facilitate proactive adaptations.

A recent publication by CPSE Labs provides several practical application domains where CPS is deployed. CPSE Labs is a project that aims to accelerate the transfer of scientific findings, research prototypes, and development tools into innovative products and services that are equipped for commercial incorporation into the Industry 4.0 framework. These applications include:

- improved safety in homes and offices;
- improved comfort through automated temperature, humidity, and air quality;
- improving and automating production lines;

- monitoring the safety and activities of commuters;
- optimising crop yield and reducing the use of pesticides and fertilisers by identifying the need for them and applying them only when required;
- observing the well-being of livestock and issuing programmed fore-warnings of infection or injuries;
- accumulating environmental data for early warning systems of natural disasters; or
- monitoring the human health of admitted patients.

Closely related and mutually beneficial to CPS are the IoT, smart cities, and the smart grid. The IoT, a network of physical devices (things) embedded with electronic circuits, sensors and actuators, typically operating on open-source software, enables the transfer of data within a CPS. These IoT components essentially allow objects or environments to be sensed and/or controlled remotely across existing network infrastructures, such as the Internet (combined with local network topologies to facilitate inter-device communication). Cloud computing and ubiquitous computing are models that enable pervasive access to shared pools of configurable resources over the Internet. These resources include physical computer networks and access to high-powered servers for computing power, as well as storage resources, practical applications, and data-centred services. Through the definition of these services and the holistic paradigm towards data-oriented industrialisation, the essence of Industry 4.0 can be defined. In developing countries, the implementations and applications of IoT differ from that of developed countries, and is typically applied to alleviate issues and risks not associated with the developed world.

The IoT is earmarked to 'transform the way food, water, energy, and aid are distributed in developing countries' (Hasenauer 2017). Gartner, Inc.'s NYSE:IT predicts that 20.4 billion connected things will be used worldwide, and says that in 2017 consumer applications represented 63 per cent of the total applications (Van Der Meulen 2017). According to Fernández et al. (2017), the most recurrent use of IoT technologies to date in developing countries is addressing clean water distribution challenges and improving sanitary conditions. In developing countries, the Global South, and any emerging market, the price of technology is still an obstacle for pervasive use of, for example, the IoT. However, initiatives are already implemented in rural communities and emerging countries that utilise the IoT to improve the quality of life of millions of people; Fernández et al. (2017) gives examples:

- Bangladesh: A network of arsenic sensors has been implemented to monitor the quality of drinking water and prevent water pollution on a large scale.
- China (JiangSu province): A variety of IoT sensors is used to monitor drinking water in key points in the distribution network.
- India: Piramal Sarvajal has developed a low-cost reverse osmosis system coupled with smart controllers to efficiently distribute and monitor drinking water to certain rural areas in India.
- Kenya (region of Kyuso): The University of Oxford has piloted a programme that monitors the acceleration/movement of manual drinking water pumps through IoT sensors. Data are analysed (in real-time at Oxford) and potential failures at each pump can be detected.
- Indonesia: IoT water flow sensors and motion sensors assess the effectiveness of personal hygiene training delivered to parts of the rural population, for example monitoring if/how people wash their hands after using lavatories.
- China/India/Africa: Pervasively distributed weather stations in many regions control irrigation pumps according to the current weather, saving water, and improving crop yields.

According to Kreische et al. (2015), thousands of IoT sensors already monitor air quality, traffic, and water distribution in urban megacities in the Global South, including Rio de Janeiro in Brazil, Beijing in China, and New Delhi in India. Its uptake (albeit still limited in rural areas) is also evident in local governments that aim to increase the effectiveness of data analysis and drive economic growth through better resource management. There are also several factors, according to Kreische et al. (2015) that contribute significantly to the widespread implementation of IoT solutions, especially in urban areas in the developing world, which include:

- Technology prices have come down significantly since approximately 2010, with reported figures of 80 per cent to 90 per cent in sensor/actuator price reduction, leading to emerging markets now

being able to buy large numbers of IoT devices and distribute these across key areas.
- Albeit still far from an ideal situation, Internet penetration in developing countries has grown significantly, and the number of users that own Internet capable devices is also growing (as a result of lower technology prices).
- Local governments have started to realise the potential of IoT and have therefore started to adapt policies to support its growth locally, driving innovation in the ICT sector, and to develop IoT devices specific to a region's requirements.
- Collaborations, primarily through the Internet, between programmers in developed countries such as Singapore have accelerated software development for IoT devices specific to regions in emerging markets.

From the brief technical overview of Industry 4.0, it is evident that the fourth industrial revolution requires skilled workers, as opposed to historical revolutions that focused on high-volume, typically mundane, and repetitive tasks performed by workers not requiring an abundance of knowledge on industrial processes. As a result, formal education is crucial to ensure sustainability of growth in Industry 4.0 and innovative solutions of systems enhancing the quality of life for populations. The following section reviews areas of importance within the educational requirements of the imminent fourth industrial revolution with reference to countries of the Global South.

Global South's Competitiveness in Industry 4.0

Industry 4.0 is the next stage in the digitisation of the industrial sector, driven primarily by four patterns in the developed world. These trends or movements are not exclusively responsible for Industry 4.0; rather, they contribute to a paradigm shift in manufacturing superseding the third industrial revolution. These movements include:

- a momentous rise in sheer data volumes (big data), increasing processing power, access and reliability of connectivity, and the viability of using low-power wide-area networks, wireless sensor

networks, as well as the capability of these systems to operate solely on renewable energy or through energy harvesting;
- the advent of strategies and technologies used by organisations for the data analysis of the information industry—comprising business intelligence, scientific, technical, and medical, as well as educational and training content;
- a shift in human–machine interactions from knobs and buttons, towards technologies such as touchscreens, virtual reality, and augmented reality; and
- new technologies that promote the transfer of digital commands to the physical world, for example three-dimensional printing and advanced robotics (Baur and Wee 2015).

Industry 4.0 includes the generation, analysis, and remote communication of data to enable wide-ranging new technologies, services, and marketing strategies. Digitisation and integration of processes vertically across entire organisations have to be performed from 'product development and purchasing, through manufacturing, logistics and service delivery' (PwC 2016). Gathered data regarding operations processes, process efficiency and operations planning should be available for analysis in real time, and ideally supported by virtual or augmented reality and optimised in a cohesive network infrastructure. Horizontal integration should include automated tracking technologies and real-time integrated planning procedures and allow seamless and ubiquitous execution. Furthermore, according to PwC (2016), the process of digitising products and services must include the transformation of existing products by 'adding smart sensors or communication capabilities that can be used with data analytics tools. Organisations are furthermore encouraged to provide disruptive digital solutions such as data-oriented services and integrated platform solutions' to generate additional digitally driven revenue streams and optimise customer interaction and access. According to Baur and Wee (2015), examples of disruptive technologies, or disruptive trends, include big data, advanced analytics, modern human–machine interfaces, and efficient digital-to-physical transfers.

For emerging markets to be successful in Industry 4.0 as well, collaboration with private and public firms is crucial. Companies such as Bosch have presented eight manufacturing plants in India, with most being Industry 4.0 enabled (Ajaykumar 2018). The company provides custom solutions, for example manufacturing execution systems and energy analytics, as well as deploying and testing these solutions for the recipients in the emerging markets. To adopt a digital transformation in emerging markets, Bosch adopts four key philosophies:

- introducing a digital culture that facilitates an understanding of digital transformation within a company;
- providing solutions that are focused and contextualised for the specific region, in this case India;
- ensuring that training programmes for project management are in place, not only to execute project plans, but also to build infrastructure that is sustainable for the future; and
- protecting local start-up companies and small and medium-sized enterprises (SMEs) and building an ecosystem with hardware partners and cloud-based services (Ajaykumar 2018).

According to Ajaykumar (2018), companies in emerging markets must identify the factors and conditions that have the greatest impact on the transformation of their production systems as Industry 4.0 gains traction. Bosch additionally presents a proposal for emerging markets and SMEs on how to prepare for being competitive in Industry 4.0, which includes steps that each company could follow, such as:

- assessing the maturity of the company for Industry 4.0 in terms of leadership focus, customer data, and smart products and services;
- defining the vision of Industry 4.0 participation and identifying the growth, impact, and risks;
- setting up a pilot programme on a small scale to test and verify Industry 4.0 competitiveness;
- engaging the supply chain partners and implementing more dynamic purchasing models, adaptable as supply and demand varies; and
- preparing the workforce, assigning Industry 4.0 champions, and recruiting individuals with learning potential as opposed to basing selection purely on current skills and education.

With reference to the above-mentioned steps, it is evident that even though an economy or market is lagging in terms of automation of manufacturing facilities hampering it in terms of Industry 4.0 competitiveness, business operations can gradually improve and embrace the ongoing global trend towards Industry 4.0, and smart manufacturing (Ajaykumar 2018). Souza (2017) also explains what impact and risks Industry 4.0 will introduce to emerging economies, depending on the

- timeframe when advanced and smart manufacturing technologies will be widely adopted;
- public policies required to deal with new economic developments; and
- urgency and pace at which local industries in emerging markets will and can adopt new technologies and business models.

According to Souza (2017), although Industry 4.0 is still in its infancy, adoption thereof will be faster compared to previous industrial revolutions, and companies (and countries) should start putting policies and strategies in place to ensure a smooth transition. In emerging markets, especially, larger risks exist, since Industry 4.0 will specifically move away from competitive advantages of lower labour costs and the availability of natural resources, and move towards requirements of skilled workers on manufacturing systems and more sustainable operating procedures. Personal skills such as critical thinking and trainability, as well as adequate technical skills, will become priorities for recruiters, and there will be a definite risk of job losses if workers are unable to adapt, posing another more prominent risk in emerging markets with limited resources and financial backing to retrain workers. As a major advantage for emerging markets, rural areas, and generally poorer areas, Industry 4.0 opens up new market opportunities through digital tools, low-cost sensors (IoT and CPS applications), 3D printing, and numerous other digital infrastructures driven by the Internet.

Figure 11.2 represents the essential qualities that an organisation should either incorporate into its current business model, or use as planning for future undertakings, in order to be compatible and competitive with a new industrial revolution that is taking forward the way business is conducted globally.

According to Fig. 11.2, the core competencies of an organisation that aims to dominate Industry 4.0 are, especially, digitising its capabilities, from products and services, through customer access and the value chains.

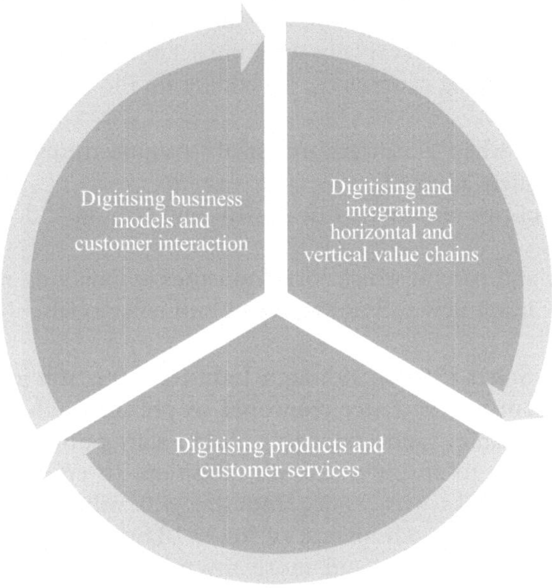

Fig. 11.2 The essential qualities that an organisation should incorporate to be compatible with Industry 4.0 in future (*Source* Adapted from PwC [2016])

In addition, PwC (2016) provides a list of contributing digital technologies to achieve full digitisation of core competencies, summarised in Fig. 11.3.

As seen in Fig. 11.3, various modern technologies are driving Industry 4.0 and organisations are able to incorporate these technologies, at relatively low cost, into their manufacturing business models to solidify their dominance in the fourth industrial revolution. Industries that combine large investments with advanced digitisation can achieve dramatic gains in revenue of both their top and bottom lines. Customers are the focus point of the modifications in value chains, products, and services, which are increasingly customised, focused, and adapted to customer needs. These digital industrial platforms can give an organisation a significant and crucial advantage over competitors that fail to implement such strategies, especially during the infancy stages of Industry 4.0. Fundamentally, Industry 4.0 requires a young, skilled, innovative, and financially backed

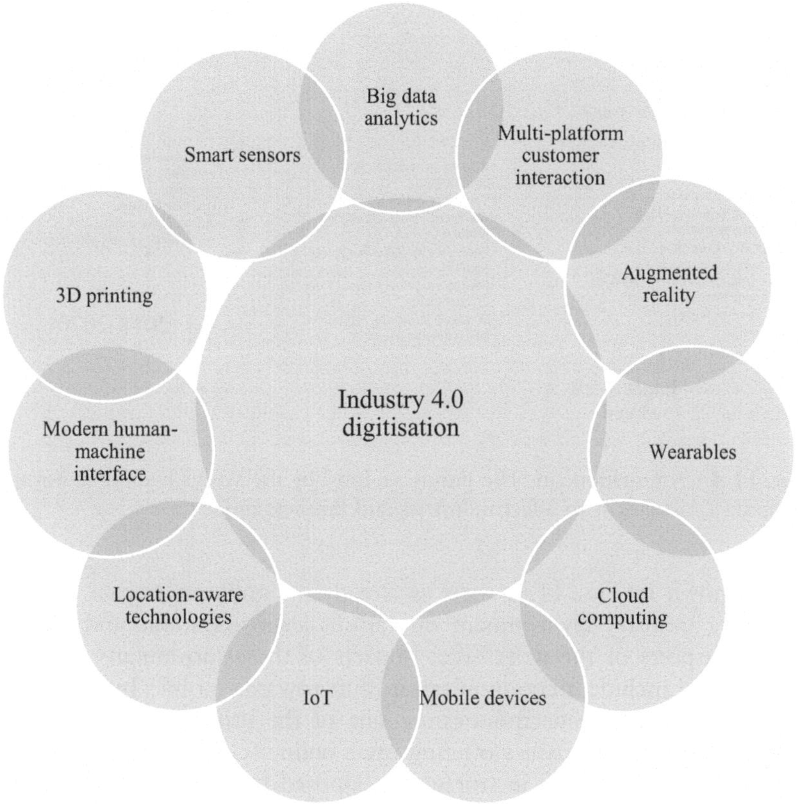

Fig. 11.3 A list of contributing digital technologies to achieve full digitisation of core competencies towards a compatible and competitive Industry 4.0 business model (*Source* Adapted from PwC [2016])

workforce to revolutionise the industrial sector into an automated, self-sustaining, dynamic, and financially viable dynamo. The impact that technological change has on business models, policies, and the internal structures of organisations are closely matched by demographic and socio-economic shifts. A timeframe in 'The Future of Jobs' by the World Economic Forum suggests a movement of the impacts of changing industrial landscapes on industries and business models, adapted and presented in Fig. 11.4.

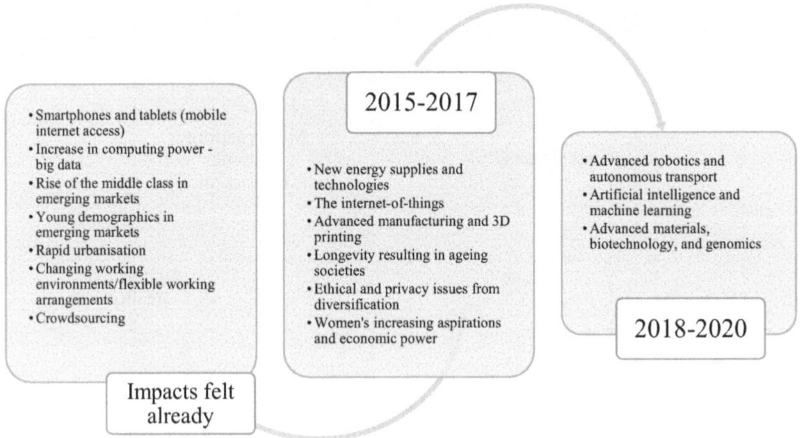

Fig. 11.4 A timeframe in 'The Future of Jobs' by the World Economic Forum suggests a movement to affect industries and business models

As shown in Fig. 11.4, there is already a significant impact from a changing industry environment on various socio-economic and demographic aspects of the workforce. Impacts of these movements that are experienced include a communication shift towards mobile Internet and Cloud computing. Smartphones are one of the primary drivers of this shift, with many companies offering users online (cloud) storage of their personal data. This shift in storage, as opposed to local storage on hard drives or flash storage, safeguards personal data in the event of hardware failure, simplifies data sharing and the transition between devices and reduces the cost requirements of investments in expensive hardware. Current technological solutions also offer multiple solutions to gather and process data, where the term big data is often used to describe trends of capturing, storing, analysing, and transferring large amounts of gathered data for various applications. In terms of the demographics of the current industrial scene, there is a definite rise in the middle class in emerging markets, representing a positive outlook for BRICS nations and other emerging countries. This shows that the change in how industrialisation is applied offers the workforce several socio-economic benefits that were not previously attainable. There is also a shift towards a younger and more skilled workforce in emerging markets, from which countries such as India and South Africa (among other African countries) can benefit, if this demographic group is proficiently educated and trained to contribute to Industry 4.0. Also evident in the current environment, with reference to Fig. 11.3, is rapid urbanisation where especially the younger demographic groups are moving away from rural and agricultural settings to live in cities, starting their education and professional careers in urban and densely populated areas. This is, of course, beneficial for innovation, since, as described in the introduction of this chapter, innovation is often a collaborative effort. Changes in working environments, compared to traditional hours spent in factories or offices, are also encouraged through innovations in communication, Voice over Internet, e-mail, and a large repository of online sources of knowledge.

Recent changes in the working environment, and aspects that will increase in popularity, include exploring new energy supplies and technologies, specifically renewable energy and energy harvesting for low-power sensors within the IoT. The fourth industrial revolution is also heavily focused on advanced manufacturing solutions, where 3D printing, for example, has become a large driver of future manufacturing. With respect to demographics and socio-economic consequences, societies are ageing, with longevity rising with medical advancements; and women are becoming even more capable of entering the skilled workforce, with technology assisting remote access in cases where women are taking care of children during their early development stages. There are however also challenges and uncertainty with respect to concerns about ethical and privacy issues, which are receiving increasing attention as the world moves towards fully automated digitisation.

Finally, with reference to Fig. 11.4, the entire Industry 4.0 is currently (as highlighted by the 2018–2020 time period) moving towards advanced robotics, autonomous transport, AI, machine learning, and advanced materials, biotechnology, and genomics. The technologies all have some degree of automation in common to assist humans with everyday tasks, providing effective implementation. Industry 4.0 offers 'new tools for smarter energy consumption, greater information storage and real-time yield optimisation' (Baur and Wee 2015). Traditional manufacturing models are changing and evolving and incumbents should be swift to identify this and react to new competitive challenges. As for the 2018–2020 time period in Fig. 11.4, since we are, at the time of writing, in the middle of this timeframe, several advances globally, as well as adaptations in emerging markets, are spearheading advanced robotics, autonomous transport, and advanced materials. Some examples of these are:

- In terms of advanced robotics, the Swiss robotic company ABB revealed at the end of 2018 that it is investing USD $150 million into an advanced robotics factory in Shanghai, China. This factory will use robots to build robots, eliminating to a large extent the need for human intervention. In additional, the factory aims to accelerate research into AI through its research and development centre. The factory is anticipated to be the most advanced in the world, and is expected to open by late 2020 (Moon 2018).
- Autonomous transport is becoming more commonplace, with companies such as Tesla, Uber, Lyft, and Google (which created Waymo specifically for autonomous vehicle research and development), as well as several key car manufacturers spearheading the movement. Waymo announced at the end of 2018 that it had reached 10 million miles of self-driving on public roads across the US (www.waymo.com) and Tesla's test fleet accumulated 1.2 billion miles of autonomous (autopilot) driving in 2018 (www.tesla.com). The data gathered by these companies could potentially be used by (shared with) emerging markets to develop further technologies and algorithms that improve autonomous driving, an opportunity presented through Industry 4.0.
- New and novel designs using nanomaterials, such as gallium nitride (GaN), used for example in light-emitting diodes (LEDs), are currently being researched, which could lead to brighter and more efficient displays (Hampson 2019). These LEDs, made from GaN nanowires, are already compact and efficient, but new vertical designs could take these devices to the next level. Technologies such as virtual reality and augmented reality could benefit from these advances, and with respect to training workers in emerging markets, there are numerous possibilities and applications in which this technology can be implemented. In addition, materials such as wood sponge (to clean up oceans), spider silk (a biomaterial that is stronger than steel), platinum-gold alloy (a material with characteristics comparable to diamond), and silicon X (leading to increased battery capacity compared to graphene) will all change technology for the better from 2019 onwards.

According to Baur and Wee (2015), in order to adapt to the changing environment of Industry 4.0, manufacturing industries should consider the following options to be deployed in business strategies as soon as possible:

- Modern and effective platforms that facilitate products, services, and information exchanges, such as open-source software in the industrial sector;
- Pay-by-use and subscription-based services that turn equipment and machinery from capital expenditure to operating expenditure for manufacturers (Baur and Wee 2015);
- Licensing of IP to generate value from expertise in product manufacturing and process development;
- Generation of measurable economic benefits, increased revenue or expense savings, from data sources, thus introducing capabilities to monetise data; and
- Preparation for digital transformation through researching strategies and methods to implement technology, sourcing skilled and educated digital talent, and investing a portion of business expenses into digital platforms, ideally replacing traditional means of manufacturing and earning revenue through sales and aftermarket support.

Of course, as with any emerging technology, industry, or shift in product or service delivery, inherent challenges will be faced throughout its life cycle. The primary challenges associated with Industry 4.0 can be summarised as pertaining to investment, workforce, standardisation, data security, and operational disruptions.

- Investment: This entails the difficult decision of where an enterprise should spend its capital investments with regard to Industry 4.0 to benefit from economic incentives obtainable through an updated business strategy.
- The workforce: In adapting to an environment where manufacturing is automated and smart factories are able to take advantage of high levels of efficiency and idea-to-market realisation, the workforce should be equipped to aid the process, as opposed to becoming obsolete in the process. This would force organisations either to

empower their current workforce and optimise talent, or replace it with skilled personnel within information technology disciplines.
- Standardisation: Successful implementation of Industry 4.0 necessitates deriving a standardised system that integrates well with both vertical and horizontal value chains and maximises value for both present and future investments.
- Data security: A caveat of Industry 4.0 is the publication and distribution of gathered data from open-source platforms, putting these organisations at risk of data in IP being breached, stolen, or unfairly practised by competitors. Securing the ubiquitous networks against cyber threats is important for an organisation to protect its reputation and its bottom line. This requires an up-to-date inventory of digital assets, authentication processes to guard digital and physical assets, as well as the ability to detect malicious and anomalous activity.
- Operational disruptions: This can be caused by various factors, including malfunctioning devices (especially with the large number of devices, or things, functioning at a particular time), process instabilities, and technical anomalies. Continuous monitoring of an integrated network of devices and assessing the current operational state of the network are key steps to indicate threats to operational continuity. High levels of reliability and long-term stability of the entire system are of paramount importance, often requiring high capital investments upfront.

Furthermore, and apart from technical challenges or the issue of a changing workforce, additional challenges of Industry 4.0 include adapting the culture and traditional sense of conducting business in a company, addressing any socio-economic factors that arise from changing the business culture, conducting successful pilots before implementing large capital investments, understanding and planning for shortened product life-cycles, encouraging sufficient health and safety planning to ensure machine safety, understanding the policies of the business case and the required business model/strategy, and adapting the management to support the transformation of an organisation fully. Table 11.1 summarises and lists the expected transitions across business models with the implementation of Industry 4.0.

Table 11.1 is a clear indication of a transformation from an era of rigid, efficiency-focused, and primarily manual manufacturing techniques

Table 11.1 The expected transitions across business models with the implementation of Industry 4.0

	Traditional manufacturing	*Industry 4.0 manufacturing*
Process	Rigid and manual	Dynamic and automated
Product	Standardised	Personalised and customised
Scale of factories	Large factories at centralised locations	Small factories at decentralised locations
Supply chain	Stock-based planning	Dynamic and predictive
Success metric	Low cost, high efficiency	High return on capital employment
Client relationship	Low and indirect	High and direct

Source Adapted from Aulbur et al. (2016)

to a more dynamic, agile, and ideally automated process of manufacturing. The key shift of focus from Table 11.1 is from mass production to mass customisation, facilitated by flexible production, shorter lead times of prototype development and open-source information sharing.

Conclusion

The Global South will be presented with numerous opportunities and innovations as a result of Industry 4.0 becoming more prevalent and maturing towards pervasive technologies globally. In developed countries, research and development towards preparing for Industry 4.0 are well under way, and emerging markets should also prepare for its imminent and inevitable rise. In this chapter, the road to the fourth industrial revolution is presented, with reference to the first, second, and third industrial revolutions and how each of these came about. Enabling technologies such as the IoT, CPS, VR, AR, 3D printing, Cloud networking, and automation in industry (including automated driving) all facilitate Industry 4.0, and the skills required from workers are shifting, where trainability and adaptability of workers are becoming the most important factors for recruiters to consider. Emerging markets are however still lacking some critical skills and services, including the availability and distribution of the Internet, and many obstacles must be overcome for these countries to participate successfully in Industry 4.0. Many urban areas and megacities in emerging markets in Brazil, Russia, India, China, and South Africa (BRICS) have started adopting smart technologies to improve on healthcare, water distribution, sanitation, and resource management, but rural areas, where a large portion of the populations still lives, are lagging behind in their implementation. This chapter has aimed to identify the technologies that can spearhead and sustain Industry 4.0 in developing countries, but also to identifies risks, policy changes, and limitations in these areas, and general techniques to increase the readiness of BRICS countries, and the Global South, for the fourth industrial revolution.

Under the Industry 4.0 umbrella, manufactured goods design and its development happen in simulated test beds and use digital production models, only tangible when all issues and problems have been addressed and corrected. This offers highly flexible, cost-effective, and quick-to-the-market solutions that open up various new opportunities for doing business, especially the trading of IP in open-source and *open innovation* environments. The fourth industrial revolution is therefore enabling all countries, developed and developing, to take part in the design and engineering of innovative new products and markets. Among the developing nations, the BRICS groups can take advantage of Industry 4.0 easiest, with changing economic, political, and social structures, a baseline infrastructure to work from, and the opportunity to access education and skills training from virtually anywhere in the world. Although technological infrastructure globally is still in its early stage with respect to adopting a revolutionised industry, it has already begun to transform manufacturing. Substantial cost savings in the manufacturing industry are realised largely from an increase in efficiency and technological integration. Revenue gains are essentially realised from proposing new digital features and components, such as offering analytics to customers and the availability of real-time data that offers tailored solutions to customers. This customisation is a worldwide tendency and is expected to spread even faster through the manufacturing industry in future. As more of these services are offered, customers are also increasingly demanding flexibility in how their products are designed and made, and are offered input into development and production processes at an early stage.

Digitisation also carries risks, especially with technologies in their infancy. The more information and data are placed in cyberspace, the higher the risk of cyberattacks. A general lack of standards and protocols associated with new implementations of technology is opening up these networks to malicious attacks, data breaching, and espionage. Cyberattacks and malicious viruses can have adverse impacts on technology-driven processes within Industry 4.0, potentially stifling networked and smart production systems, which are only repairable at a substantial cost. Sectors such as electronic warfare, earth observation, air and water pollution monitoring, cryptocurrencies, and autonomous vehicles are particularly vulnerable to cyberattacks if security is not treated with the utmost urgency. It is becoming a priority for both manufacturing companies and most individuals to protect themselves from cyberattacks, and to learn how to deal with such attacks when their security is breached. Companies are also becoming more vigilant in protecting their IP, to avoid competitors stealing sensitive information. Although this is not a new phenomenon, its repercussions have intensified, as big data from a variety of processes are being safeguarded online. Companies that embrace Industry 4.0 are beginning to track all of their products from idea to final product (Geissbauer et al. 2016), and are even providing users with upgrades and updates after the product is sold, either enhancing functionality or fixing errors that were not detected during production. This rapid addressing of consumer requirements also spearheads new products and services, since communication between manufacturers and their clients is becoming more commonplace, partly because of the introduction of software-as-a-service agreements. This display of rapid transformation is also beneficial to solving the demanding problems of the world, such as climate change, pollution, the increasing demand for energy, the pressures of urbanisation, and the problems related to ageing populations (Geissbauer et al. 2016).

In a follow-up chapter, BRICS and Industry 4.0, specific reference to BRICS countries and how they are preparing for Industry 4.0 is provided. Case studies are also presented in BRICS and Industry 4.0 to showcase some of the initiatives that already take advantage of advanced technologies to create sustainable technological innovations specific to the needs of emerging markets.

Bibliography

Ajaykumar, A. (2018). *Unleashing the Potential of Industry 4.0 in Emerging Markets*. http://arcweb.com. Accessed 22 January 2019.

Akcali, B. Y., & E. Sismanoglu. (2015). Innovation and Effect of Research and Development (R&D) Expenditure on Growth in Some Developing and Developed Countries. *Procedia—Social and Behavioral Sciences, 195*(3), 768–775.

Alur, R. (2015). *Principles of Cyber-Physical Systems*. Cambridge, MA: MIT Press.

Aulbur, W. (2016). *Skill Development for Industry 4.0 in BRICS Nations*. http://www.linkedin.com. Accessed 25 October 2017.

Aulbur, W., Arvind, C. J., & Bigghe, R. (2016). *White Paper: Skill Development for Industry 4.0: BRICS Skill Development Working Group*. http://www.globalskillsummit.com/. Accessed 13 October 2017.

Baur, C., & Wee, D. (2015). *Manufacturing's Next Act*. http://www.mckinsey.com. Accessed 11 October 2017.

Fernández, R. A., Zubelzu, S., & Martinez, R. (Eds.). (2017). *Carbon Footprint and the Industrial Life Cycle: From Urban Planning to Recycling*. New York: Springer International Publishing.

Geissbauer, R., Vedso, J., & Schrauf, S. (2016, May). A Strategist's Guide to Industry 4.0. *Strategy and Business*, 83.

Gkypali, A., Filiou, D., & Tsekouras, K. (2017, May). R&D Collaborations: Is Diversity Enhancing Innovation Performance? *Technological Forecasting & Social Change, 118,* 143–152.

Gouarderes, F. (2017). *Industry 4.0. Policy Department A: Economy and Scientific Policy*. Publications Office of the European Union. http://publications.europa.eu. Accessed 28 October 2017.

Hampson, M. (2019). *A Novel Design for Gallium Nitride LEDs Could Lead to Brighter, More Efficient Displays*. http://spectrum.ieee.org. Accessed 23 January 2019.

Hasenauer, C. (2017). *The Internet of Things in Developing Countries*. http://borgenproject.org. Accessed 16 January 2019.

Holodny, E. (2017). *A Key Player in China and the EU's 'Third Industrial Revolution' Describes the Economy of Tomorrow*. http://www.businessinsider.com. Accessed 14 October 2017.

Kennedy, S. (2015). *Made in China 2025*. http://www.csis.org. Accessed 7 November 2017.

Kohli, T. (2018). *AI and Technological Innovation Must Head to the Global South*. http://weforum.org. Accessed 18 January 2019.

Kreische, F., Ullrich, A., & Ziemann, K. (2015). *Internet of Things. Using Sensors for Good: How the Internet of Things Can Improve Lives*. Bonn: Deutsche Gesellschaft für Internationale Zusammenarbeit.

Lambrechts, J. W., & Sinha, S. (2016). *Microsensing Networks for Sustainable Cities*. Cham, Switzerland: Springer International Publishing.

Monostori, L. (2014, April 28–30). Cyber-Physical Production Systems: Roots, Expectations and R&D Challenges. In *Proceedings of the 47th CIRP Conference on Manufacturing Systems (CIRP)*. Ontario.

Moon, M. (2018). *Robots Will Build Robots in $150 Million Chinese Factory*. http://www.engadget.com. Accessed 23 January 2019.

National Economic Council (NEC). (2016). *Revitalizing American Manufacturing. The Obama Administration's Progress in Establishing a Foundation for Manufacturing Leadership.*

Neuss, L. (2016). *Why Did the Industrial Revolution Start in Britain?* (Working Paper). https://www.researchgate.net/publication/286017737_Why_Did_the_Industrial_Revolution_Start_in_Britain.

Nistor, P. (2015). FDI Implications on BRICS Economy Growth. *Procedia Economics and Finance, 32,* 981–985.

PwC Global. (2016). *Industry 4.0: Building the Digital Enterprise.* http://www.pwc.com/industry40. Accessed 11 October 2017.

Sag, S., Sezen, B., & Guzel, M. (2016, November). Factors That Motivate or Prevent Adoption of Open Innovation by SMEs in Developing Countries and Policy Suggestions. *Procedia—Social and Behavioral Sciences, 235,* 756–763.

South African History Online. (2018). *Lesson: The Industrial Revolution in Britain and Southern Africa from 1860.* http://www.sahistory.org.za. Accessed 17 January 2019.

Souza, M. (2017). *What Emerging Economies Can Teach Us About Designing Better Innovation Policies.* http://www.weforum.org. Accessed 22 January 2019.

Stiglitz, J. E., Lin, J. Y., & Monga, C. (2013). Introduction: The Rejuvenation of Industrial Policy. In J. E. Stiglitz, J. Y. Lin & C. Monga (Eds.), *The Industrial Policy Revolution I.* International Economic Association Series. London: Palgrave Macmillan.

Stratasys Ltd. (2019). *Case Studies: 3D Printing Resources.* http://stratasysdirect.com. Accessed 17 January 2019.

The Economist. (2018). *The Battle for Digital Supremacy.* http://www.economist.com. Accessed 27 January 2019.

United Nations Population Fund (UNFPA). (2016). *Demographic Dividend.* http://www.unfpa.org. Accessed 28 October 2017.

Van Der Meulen, R. (2017). *Gartner Says 8.4 Billion Connected 'Things' Will Be in Use in 2017, Up 31 Per cent from 2016.* http://www.gartner.com. Accessed 16 January 2019.

World Bank. (2017, January). *Global Economic Prospects. Weak Investment in Uncertain Times* (A World Bank Group Flagship Report). http://www.openknowledge.worldbank.org. Accessed 21 October 2017.

World Economic Forum. (2017). *Technology and Innovation for the Future of Production: Accelerating Value Creation* (White Paper). http://www3.weforum.org. Accessed 21 October 2017.

Zhang, G., & Tang, C. (2017). How Could Firm's [sic] Internal R&D Collaboration Bring More Innovation? *Technological Forecasting and Social Change, 125,* 299–308.

CHAPTER 12

BRICS and Industry 4.0

Wynand Lambrechts, Saurabh Sinha, and Tshilidzi Marwala

Introduction

For developing countries, specifically Brazil, Russia, India, China, and South Africa (BRICS), the fourth industrial revolution (Industry 4.0) poses significant challenges but also provides opportunities. The challenges, as reviewed in Chapter 11, are mainly categorised into three aspects:

- a labour force that is not regarded as highly skilled, as well as a general lack of industrial/vocational training;
- lack of (physical and cyber) infrastructure that is yet to be improved; and
- general exclusion from developed countries in terms of financial, capital, and human resources.

W. Lambrechts (✉) · S. Sinha · T. Marwala
University of Johannesburg, Johannesburg, South Africa
e-mail: wynand.lambrechts@vodamail.co.za

D. Monyae and B. Ndzendze (eds.), *The BRICS Order*, International Political Economy Series,
https://doi.org/10.1007/978-3-030-62765-2_12

This chapter reviews and discusses skills, policies, and challenges that developed countries and emerging markets require, and are faced with, to successfully integrate and participate in Industry 4.0. Emerging markets have several challenges to overcome before they are able to focus completely on Industry 4.0, but these markets have the advantage of learning from initiatives in developed countries and implementing similar strategies and policies.

In BRICS nations, there is a mismatch concerning the skills sets of job candidates and the skills sets expected of them to drive Industry 4.0 forward. In the 'The Future of Jobs' report by the World Economic Forum (WEF), the shift of employment, skills, and recruitment from 2015 to 2020 is summarised. The results are adapted and presented in Fig. 12.1.

As seen in Fig. 12.1, a clear shift towards individual skills, creativity, and critical thinking is projected by 2020, moving away from the management of employees, coordination with peers and active leadership on an individual basis, which were deemed most important during 2015. The type of transformation will be contingent on the type of industry, with entertainment and media distribution already undergoing substantial change in recent times. The financial sector and investment sector have yet to be drastically changed, often still relying on traditional means of conducting business, disregarding the importance of imminent digitisation. Technologically driven sectors such as mobile and cloud computing are already affecting the way people work, but AI and 3D printing are still in their infancy and only now presenting the advantages they will have for Industry 4.0. If drastic steps are not taken, specifically in the BRICS countries, this supply and demand gap will widen. 'Though the governments of the BRICS nations have undertaken independent initiatives to promote vocational education and skills development in the said countries, significant efforts are still required to focus on skills development for Industry 4.0' (Aulbur et al. 2016).

In 2015	#	In 2020
Complex problem solving	1	Complex problem solving
Coordinating with others	2	Critical thinking
People management	3	Creativity
Critical thinking	4	People management
Negotiation	5	Coordinating with others
Quality control	6	Emotional intelligence
Service orientation	7	Judgement and decision making
Judgement and decision making	8	Service orientation
Active listening	9	Negotiation
Creativity	10	Cognitive flexibility

Fig. 12.1 Changes in skills requirements between 2015 and 2020 across industries and geographies brought about particularly by the fourth industrial revolution (*Source* Adapted from the 'The Future of Jobs' report by the World Economic Forum)

Misguided Skills Development in BRICS Nations?

Industry 4.0, also considered an information revolution (Unnikrishnan and Aulbur 2016), is effectively the superposition of big data, connectivity, and information on top of industrial automation. The boundary between physical systems in the *real* world and cyber-physical systems (CPSs) in the virtual world is narrowing, and a primary appeal of Industry 4.0 is its ability to act as an economic game-changer that could open up numerous possible new business prospects (see also Chapter 11 of this volume).

Industry 4.0 is expected to minimise the cost of labour in terms of its location advantages, referring to the fact that work can be performed from anywhere in the world through networking and the Internet. However, significant changes to existing industrial models will have a major impact on the socio-economic factors in most countries (but especially in BRICS countries) and need to be addressed proactively. Through national strategies in BRICS countries (reviewed in this chapter), emerging markets have started to safeguard manufacturing competitiveness and have introduced the embracing of next-generation industrialisation. Unfortunately, progress is slow, with limited backing from government or private investors, and the general trend in manufacturing employment in BRICS nations show that it is in fact increasing, as opposed to the decrease in developed countries. Unnikrishnan and Aulbur (2016) present the statistics of employment in the manufacturing industry for the period between 2000 and 2015, and these statistics are adapted and presented in Fig. 12.2. Also presented, in Table 12.1, is the share of employment in manufacturing from 1973 through 2010, as reported by (Lawrence 2018), further confirming the general downwards trend of manufacturing employment in developed countries.

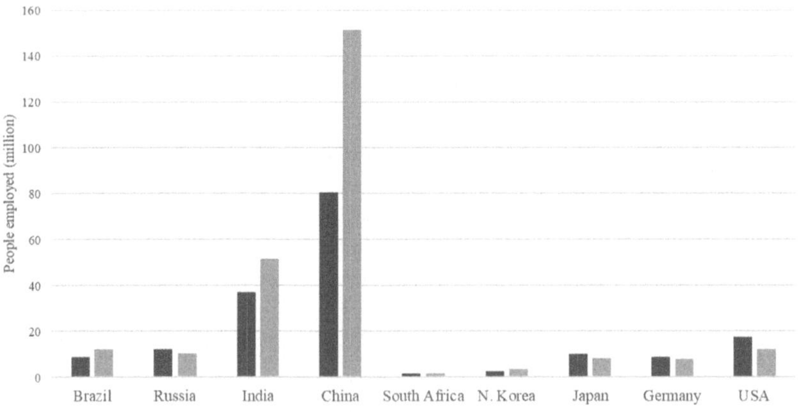

Fig. 12.2 Manufacturing employment for BRICS nations compared to developed countries for 2000 (dark grey) and 2015 (light grey)

Table 12.1 The share % of employment in manufacturing between 1973 and 2010, ranked according to share in 2010 (lowest to highest %)

Country	*1973*	*1990*	*2000*	*2010*	*% point change*
Australia	23.3	14.4	12.0	8.9	14.4
USA	24.8	18.0	14.4	10.1	14.7
Canada	22.0	15.8	15.3	10.3	11.7
Netherlands	25.3	19.1	14.8	10.6	14.7
Sweden	27.6	21.0	18.0	12.7	14.9
France	28.8	21.0	17.6	13.1	15.7
Japan	27.8	24.3	20.7	16.9	10.9
Italy	27.9	22.6	23.6	18.8	9.1
Germany	36.7	31.6	23.9	21.2	15.5

Source Adapted from Lawrence (2018)

As seen in Fig. 12.2 and Table 12.1, developed countries such as many European countries, Japan and the US, as well as Russia—which is in fact a BRICS nation—have shown a downward trend in manufacturing employment for the 2000–2015 period. This downwards trend is depicted in Fig. 12.3, a visual representation of the data in Table 12.1.

Manufacturing jobs are generally waning in developed countries. Workers are shifting from agricultural services and bypassing the manufacturing sector. Primarily in advanced economies, a rise in service sector employment usually reflects a departure from manufacturing jobs. A decline in manufacturing jobs is often met with concerns that a smaller manufacturing sector implies a decrease in economic growth, coupled with work scarcity for well-paying jobs, ultimately leading to worsening inequality. However, Gruss and Novta (2018) imply that a shift in economic activity is a natural part of structural transformation. They also specifically indicate that technology plays a large role in labour saving, leading to a general decline in manufacturing, and lower per capita income in this sector. This would additionally strengthen the perspectives of the trends seen in Fig. 12.3, where emerging markets are classically considered to lag behind in technological advances that ought to drive down the need for traditional labour in the manufacturing industry.

Additional areas, such as transport, telecommunications and commercial (financial) services, have higher levels of growth rates of output per worker than does modern manufacturing (Gruss and Novta 2018). Workers are therefore drawn towards jobs in these sectors, as the skills

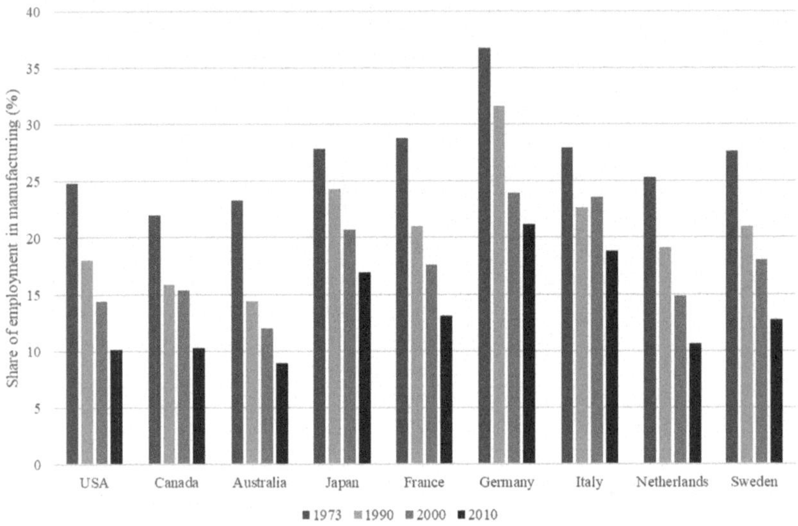

Fig. 12.3 The share (%) of employment in manufacturing between 1973 and 2010 (*Source* Adapted from Lawrence 2018)

required and daily stimulation (as well as general productivity) of working with technology-advanced and new developments are higher. Lawrence (2018) also highlights the economic and political importance of the decreasing manufacturing workforce, referring to the anger and resentment in the USA at the status quo that drove many voters to elect Donald Trump as president in 2016. For these voters, the (perceived) decline of manufacturing in the USA from its historical prevalence is the result of globalisation, digitisation, and robotics, combined with prejudice against countries (such as China) that have taken over these jobs. Lawrence (2018) points out that this viewpoint might be somewhat misguided, as manufacturing in the USA (and many other countries) had already started declining many years previously, as per capita income became less attractive in this sector.

Another curious fact pointed out by Lawrence (2018) is that developed countries are prematurely deindustrialising, since peak manufacturing employment historically shows higher levels of per capita income and total employment. Examples of peak manufacturing shares globally are given in Table 12.2, adapted from Lawrence (2018).

Table 12.2 Peak manufacturing years for several developed countries and emerging markets

Country	*Peak*	*Share (%)*	*Per capita income (2015 US $)*
USA	1953	25.0	17,977
UK	1961	32.0	15,214
South Africa	1981	17.0	11,776
Brazil	1986	15.4	11,492
China	2010	19.2	9876

Source Adapted from Lawrence (2018)

Table 12.2 shows that countries such as Brazil—currently an emerging market—reached a peak in manufacturing around 1986, when the equivalent per capita income was approximately US$11,400. Compared to an emerging and fast growing economy such as China's, whose peak in its manufacturing sector was reached in 2010, the per capita income was much lower. This is also true when compared to the historical data for the US, UK, South Africa, and also Brazil. The origins of this premature deindustrialisation are traceable to the same policies that have driven productivity increases and lowered the prices of manufactured goods globally (Lawrence 2018) through technology. Technological advances resulted in manufactured goods requiring far fewer (human) workers to manufacture them, compared to what was required historically, leading to workers looking for jobs and careers in other sectors.

As a result, the demand for core work-related skills and education levels between 2015 and projected towards 2020 has changed accordingly; Fig. 12.4 presents the demands in BRICS nations, as well as Japan, Germany and the USA (Unnikrishnan and Aulbur 2016).

According to Fig. 12.4, the embracing of Industry 4.0 will affect the eradication of lower-skilled occupations by the implementation of automation and robotic manufacturing, and the surge in throughput might result in a global drop in the number of jobs (specifically lower-skilled jobs) offered. Companies such as Tesla rely heavily on automation and robotic manufacturing on their production lines, and require a significant percentage of their workforce to have tertiary education. Noticeable from Fig. 12.4 is the demand for tertiary-level education in emerging countries compared to that in the developed countries Japan, Germany, and the US. Apart from Russia, the demand of BRICS nations for

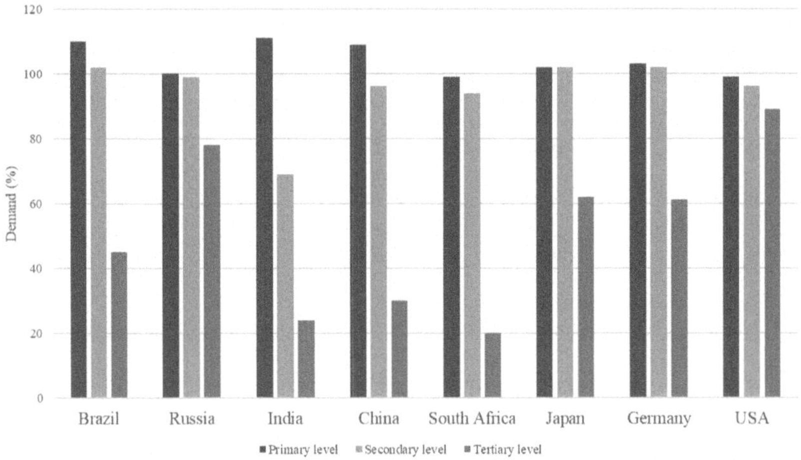

Fig. 12.4 Change in demand for core work-related skills between 2015 and projected towards 2020, in all industries

tertiary-level education is lower than 50 per cent—with South Africa having only a 20 per cent demand (pointing to its high dependence on lower-skilled manufacturing jobs). Japan, Germany, and the US demand 52 per cent, 61 per cent, and 89 per cent, respectively, showing that skilled workers who can take innovation in Industry 4.0 forward are in high demand.

Although many emerging markets are lagging behind in Industry 4.0 workforce development, this does not necessarily mean that they cannot participate in Industry 4.0. There are numerous methods, policies, and (multilateral) collaborative efforts that could accelerate their readiness for Industry 4.0.

The BRICS nations should take advantage of the opportunity to collaborate on skills development and prepare their workforces for Industry 4.0. (see also the arguments in Chapter 11 of this volume). There are numerous ways of addressing these opportunities. The primary appeal of Industry 4.0 is its ability to act as an economic paradigm shift and to provide companies with prospects of tailored and new offerings and business models in the digital domain. These new technologies provide a means for organisations to reduce their lead time and initial capital investment into prototype development, once the primary business model and capital goals have been achieved. This applies, for example, to technologies such as 3D printing, where initial machinery purchases, skills development, and software resources can be mitigated through continuous product development.

Industry 4.0 has recently become a geopolitical focus attracting greater attention from national governmental bodies aiming to become an integral part of the fourth industrial revolution. There is however another ongoing battle between emerging markets and the developed world, a battle for digital supremacy and strategic alliances to spearhead Industry 4.0 authority.

How Emerging Markets and Developed Nations Battle for (AI) Supremacy, While Dominating in Their Own Domains

There are, and have historically been, geostrategic rivalries between the West and the BRICS nations, specifically between the USA and China, and in modern times these rivalries are over AI and other enabling technologies of Industry 4.0. China has been lagging behind the USA (Horowitz et al. 2018) in terms of inventing disruptive technologies (Lee 2018). The USA still has a commanding lead in research, particularly as a result of its successful policies for universities to attract global scientific talent (Lee 2018). China, however, has the capability to implement and monetise current technologies on very large scale, and in terms of AI China has the advantage of a large market and vast resources to big data that could see them leading the AI revolution. Other countries that have also invested heavily in AI are Israel, Russia, and Singapore, as well as South Korea (Horowitz et al. 2018).

As specifically highlighted by *The Economist* (2018), the 'designed in the US, assembled in China' barcode on numerous products globally (such as Apple), is shorthand for the technological ***understanding*** between these global leaders, and competitors. This has however changed significantly in the last decade, and companies such as Alibaba and Tencent have market values of around US$500 billion, on par with that of Facebook (*Economist* 2018). Further, China is challenging the US's dominance in research and design by having:

- the third and fourth fastest supercomputers in the world (Sunway TaihuLight and Tianhe-2A);
- the first quantum satellite (Micius), launched into space in August 2016;
- a new US$10 billion, 37 hectare, quantum research supercentre in Hefei, Anhui Province, due to open in 2020; and
- a forthcoming satellite navigation system to compete with the US's global positioning system (GPS).

Unfortunately, there is also a pointing of fingers, and claims that China's theft of intellectual property has cost American companies in the region of US$1 trillion (*Economist* 2018). The competition for AI supremacy among all countries—not only China and the USA—will have substantial consequences for international politics. These consequences will have both military and economic/commercial implications, and countries that have the lead in either could have a foothold on the global economy through shifting the balance of power and international competition (Horowitz et al. 2018). This dominance will not only be felt within the AI sector, but in Industry 4.0 as a whole, and many developed countries have already initiated successful policies towards ensuring Industry 4.0 sovereignty.

Successful Policies that Drive Industry 4.0 in Developed Countries

At the end of the Second World War in 1945, and until the Great Recession of 2008, two phases in industrial policies in Europe were identified, each with completely different approaches and results. The first phase, which lasted until approximately 1980, was characterised by governments embracing selective targeted strategies to create leading industries that would be able to implement expansion in the domestic economy (a vertical approach). These selected industries were often technology-driven to overcome a gap evident between Europe and the USA and to spearhead international competitiveness. These interventions, however, tended to be generally unsuccessful and deindustrialisation of the newly industrialised countries (NICs) such as Hong Kong, South Korea, Singapore, and Taiwan during the 1970s and 1980s, and South Africa, Mexico, Brazil, China, India, Malaysia, the Philippines, Thailand, and Turkey in the early 2000s persisted. An NIC, also referred to as a newly industrialising economy or advanced developing country, describes a country that has an economy between developed and third-world categorisations. These countries have shifted from an agriculture-centred economy and into a more technologically advanced, urban economy. The second phase of industrial policies in Europe focused on a more horizontal approach designed to improve the operating environment for all corporations to create an environment where these organisations could be competitive. A surge in American productivity during the 1990s and the large-scale globalisation of industries threatened to derail these policies, and its consequences forced reconsideration after the Great Recession in 2008. Both these phases show that although a country is perceived as developed, governing policies and business models, at its core, determine the long-term growth and sustainability of transformation. Furthermore, and relevant today, the issues related to policies on industrial strategy can be summarised as follows:

- There is no single solution to address all industries, and solutions are typically specific to a country and/or sector.
- A choice between a horizontal policy versus more selective approaches must be made early, based on the requirements, capabilities, and support in a specific country.
- Flexibility to modify or improve policies must be encouraged.
- A fourth industrial revolution policy must at least emphasise digitised ecosystems and ubiquitous capabilities.
- Risks of '*government failure, policy capture, and protectionism*' must be addressed at all stages of proposed developments (Klitou et al. 2017).
- Subsequent and effective evaluation of strategies and policies must be performed by relevant and respected parties.

In Klitou et al. (2017), the essential flagship Industry 4.0 policies of Spain, the UK, France, Italy, Germany, the Czech Republic, Sweden, and the Netherlands are explored to identify how Europe aims to take advantage of digital opportunities presenting themselves from Industry 4.0. These enabling policies are useful to determine policy gaps that exist on the African continent and in other BRICS nations, which are deficient in Industry 4.0 development. Industry 4.0 policies might have a common goal to strive towards, but these policies typically vary greatly in their design, funding approaches and implementation strategies (Klitou et al. 2017). The majority of policies aim to strengthen industrial competitiveness and modernisation and ensure sustainable growth for future developments. Also evident when comparing many EU governmental policies for Industry 4.0, and pointed out by Klitou et al. (2017), is that economic objectives are typically combined with social and environmental objectives to ensure the sustainability of these programmes. EU governments, despite having tangible plans to develop fully into Industry 4.0 supremacy, have limitations in systematic cooperation between governments and means to exchange good (and bad) practices of the digital revolution. African countries can also learn from these shortcomings, as they plan to upgrade or replace their digital infrastructure.

Most countries in the EU, particularly Germany, are placing considerable focus on reaching higher productivity and increasing their manufacturing efficiency to deliver next-generation technologies, if appropriate funding can be secured. The development of new products, improving industrial processes, generous support to SMEs, and commercialisation is also emphasised as notable goals of these countries, explicitly visible in Italy, the UK, Germany, France, and Spain (Klitou et al. 2017). Certain initiatives also concentrate on market-based methodologies, providing loans to companies that participate in Industry 4.0 programmes. Combinations of wide-ranging resource backing are also evident in forerunner countries, with multiple funding instruments, tax incentives, and private investments all contributing to the bottom line of innovative start-ups and large industry players. In the UK, for example, facilitation of industrial-scale technology and expertise is provided to companies to de-risk innovation through technology centres (Klitou et al. 2017). Although most of the major Industry 4.0 policies rely fundamentally on public funding, a considerable leverage effect (the perceived predisposition of an asset's unpredictability to be negatively linked with the asset's return—therefore increased volatility after a downward price change [Bouchard et al. 2001])—can be achieved by relying on paired private investments with a likely high rate of return. Inherent challenges to these policies exist, primarily owing to the large difference in the volume of the multiplying leverage effect on investments.

Accordingly, the funding practices embraced might vary significantly in terms of type of action and extent. Generally, information on expected private leverage is not freely and widely available on all Industry 4.0 initiatives, and it becomes difficult to evaluate the success rate, but despite this it is evident that a wide range of methods is implemented. Tax incentives and strategic engagement with key industrial partners with dedicated support for SMEs have proven, as per the examples listed in Klitou et al. (2017), to be most effective. Importantly, each policy must be governed and therefore an effective and sustainable governance model should be put in place to support the policies over the long term.

Governance includes defining timelines and protocols that outline the intentions of the policy. To certify and discuss the validity and efficacy of a policy, routine practices such as calls for proposals, working groups, stakeholder consultations, and steering committees are necessary and typically implemented by EU Industry 4.0 initiatives (Klitou et al. 2017).

As outlined by the European Parliament, Industry 4.0 can only prosper if specific key requirements and policies are met. These key requirements are listed as standardisation of protocols, modifications reflecting innovative trade models, digital security, the availability of higher education for the workforce, investment in research and development, and a collective legal structure to back the distribution of Industry 4.0 which could collectively lead to productivity increases, growing revenue streams, and competitiveness. Essentially, the guidelines provided by the European Parliament are also applicable to emerging markets, where some of the listed key requirements are foreseeably more difficult to implement. These are evidently the requirements of the availability of higher education for the workforce, investment in research and development (public or private), and a collective legal structure, something that is very difficult to establish in an African context, for example. The EU policy approach is a dual strategy where, firstly, Industry 4.0 technology services could be sold (essentially an aggressive strategy aimed at developing and leading new markets) and, secondly, the benefits of increased productivity and competitiveness are advocated, making it easier to sell manufactured products (a defensive strategy aimed at maintaining competitiveness).

A Dual Strategy

A dual strategy in support of Industry 4.0 pools the principal market policy with a prominent dealer policy, placing equipment creators in a position to innovate and support the integration of ICT into production processes. The dual strategy as proposed by Germany in particular has three primary features that define it: developing horizontal inter-organisation value chains, end to end digitalisation (from product development to offered services), and vertical integration of modular and customisable industrialised systems.

Digitisation, Social Transformation, and Business Model Changes

In addition, according to the European Parliament, if this strategy is to succeed it is vital to integrate SMEs into international value chains. Three measurements of transformation, with respect to specifically the EU, are considered by the European Parliament related to the transformation of the economy for Industry 4.0: digitisation (technological transformation), social transformation, and a transformation in the organisational business model.

Digitalisation is the primary driver of technological transformation in the value chain on the way to Industry 4.0 and many organisations recognise and acknowledge the necessity to prepare for the change, but far fewer are actively implementing it. Although the importance of technological change might be more widely known and grasped in Europe, a similar trend is identified in African nations, where SMEs, especially, are least likely to have started implementing these changes. Importantly, inhibiting technology change, digital security poses risks for companies that are not yet willing to invest heavily in technology change and are afraid to undertake the associated risks and costs. The digital security concerns include IP protection, privacy and personal data protection, intuitiveness of systems, environmental protection, and personal health and safety implications.

In the EU there is increasing support for research into improving cybersecurity, but there is still a significant void in concrete contracts to support this, thus again showing the fundamental importance of financial backing for all areas of Industry 4.0. Africa/South Africa can consequently benefit from the experiences of international counterparts.

The second dimension of change refers to social transformation, where there is little evidence of its importance within Industry 4.0. Larger organisations are inclined to be more open-minded about social change than smaller firms and unions. The required skills to adjust to Industry 4.0 are still being developed, but if not addressed sooner rather than later the skills gap will widen and eventually become unbridgeable. This is a serious concern for African nations, as well as other BRICS nations, where political instability and poverty are rife and accessibility to education is lacking, something that must be addressed before undertaking Industry 4.0 transformation. The EU has addressed the current gap in skills, capabilities, and knowledge through sophisticated immigration strategies, although this could potentially create an uneven distribution of skills throughout the countries. A social change in education and its focus, at both school and tertiary levels, is required globally to accommodate the expected Industry 4.0 changes.

The third dimension of change is a transformation in the business paradigm such that the public sector assists in SMEs changing their policies to fit Industry 4.0. The challenges faced by SMEs can be mitigated through such an ecosystem, which will support them to participate in the value chain. This will lessen the burden of these enterprises with respect to costs, risks, decreased flexibility, and decreased strategic interdependence. The most promising intervention from the public sector appears to be (according to the European Parliament) to support research in the EU and in member states and to synchronise these activities in such a manner that others can follow, especially emerging markets that do not have the funding to conduct thorough research from first principles. By demonstrating good practice and feasible implementations, other countries can use the information and apply it based on their own requirements and environment. To maximise the value, research should not be limited to technological aspects and the manufacturing sector, but should include dissimilarities in economic structures as well.

Successful Policies That Drive Industry 4.0 in Developed Countries (Non-European Countries)

Singapore has long viewed manufacturing as a key pillar of growth, and as a result it accounts for nearly 20 per cent of the nation's GDP; however, the country is experiencing substantial pressure from both local competition and national restructuring and reindustrialisation. Mounting operating costs, a national labour crisis, and the dwindling Singapore dollar are forcing the local industry to spearhead its plans for Industry 4.0. To its credit, Singapore has acknowledged the need to overhaul its manufacturing infrastructure into one that offers more innovation-based and high-value production (Raman 2017). At its core, Singapore has recognised numerous key policies to implement in order to prepare for Industry 4.0. These changes, listed in Raman (2017), include reinventing the manufacturing industry, shifting towards new smart technologies, and discovering region-specific solutions.

Reinventing the manufacturing industry: Singapore has been improving its manufacturing base to enable digitisation and automation of its processes, aiming to enhance its efficiency and long-term competitiveness on the global stage. The Singaporean government has assigned substantial time and funds to investment in research and development projects in developing industry transformation and strengthening its workforce to move the industry forward more quickly. Singapore (the top-ranked country in the *Economist* Intelligence Unit's 2016 Asian Digital Transformation Index) already has an advanced smart-technology infrastructure, and skills in precision engineering, creative and technical design proficiencies, which will all benefit the manufacturers in the country in the transition from a value-added model to a value creation model.

Shifting towards new smart technologies: Singapore has invested in digital technologies that can line up with industry anticipations for ease, flexibility, and rapid turnaround times. Technologies such as 3D printing and augmented reality are key to redefining the existing production models and preparing the country for Industry 4.0. Importantly, Singapore is supporting the transition to Industry 4.0. In 2016, technology suppliers such as Siemens received positive interest and applications from customers in Singapore and the surrounding regions, indicating that the industry is starting to realise the importance of digitalisation to remain competitive. There is growing enthusiasm among Singaporean manufacturers for Industry 4.0 and many of these organisations are showing interest in acquiring the knowledge and expertise required to drive this transition.

Discovering region-specific solutions: since a single solution hardly exists for all manufacturers to prepare for Industry 4.0, companies need to contest both region-specific and industry-specific challenges with tailored methodologies. Many companies have already identified their position in

Industry 4.0, or at least determined what they need to strive for, but a large portion are still finding it difficult to optimise their manufacturing processes. The needs of the local industry must first be defined by organisations before they can invest heavily in Industry 4.0 processes that might be declared obsolete in the near future. Once this supply and demand chain has been identified, Singapore aims to scale up to larger regions and into the surrounding Asian regions. Successful technologies and business models will be able to scale relatively easily, since Industry 4.0 is scalable by design. Partnership platforms are important to enable industry players and manufacturers to collaborate, share resources, and achieve technology breakthroughs in more efficient and supportive ways. Advanced technology centres and multinational corporations are already working together to develop new applications for remanufacturing, with the aim of reducing cost and material use (Raman 2017). To summarise the policies listed above, Fig. 12.5 shows the steps that Singapore is taking

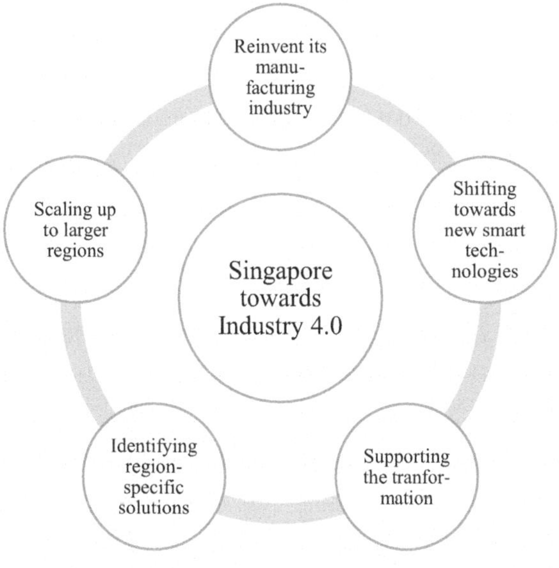

Fig. 12.5 The steps that Singapore is taking in order to revamp its industry and prepare for Industry 4.0, and to become a leader of this manufacturing model in its quest to become an innovation-based and high-value production state (*Source* Adapted from Raman 2017)

in order to revamp its industry and prepare for Industry 4.0, and to become a leader of this manufacturing model in its quest to become an innovation-based and high-value production state.

A total change to transform an economy to Industry 4.0 readiness should therefore firstly review present processes to certify that the most essential characteristics are considered, such as skills development and retention, business model changes, cross-border collaboration, cyber security, standards and implications for SMEs. Secondly, new measures should be adopted where policy gaps are identified to support a development infrastructure and play a coordinating role. As summarised in (Aulbur et al. 2016), various countries, both in the developed world and emerging BRICS nations, have national initiatives for advanced manufacturing. Examples are listed and described in the subsequent section of the chapter.

Initiatives from Developed Countries to Spearhead Industry 4.0 in BRICS

Plattform Industry 4.0

Industrie 4.0 (Germany) has been established as a collaborative effort and is already also active beyond the borders of Germany. It was a future project embraced in the Action Plan High-tech Strategy 2020 by the German Federal Government in 2010, encouraging the establishment of Plattform Industrie 4.0 in 2013, and expanded in 2015 with support from the Ministry for Economic Affairs and Energy and the Ministry of Education and Research.

According to the National Economic Council (NEC 2016), the Advanced Manufacturing Partnership 2.0 (AMP 2.0) is a 'national effort to secure US leadership in emerging technologies that will create high-quality manufacturing jobs and the global competitiveness of the USA'. AMP 2.0 is built on the pillars already established in 2012: 'i) empowering innovation throughout, ii) safeguarding talent, and iii) cultivating the corporate climate' (NEC 2016). The goal of this initiative is to carry out the vision set out for the private sector and recommend paths that could generate future innovation within the country, specifically in emerging manufacturing technologies.

The Japan Revitalisation Strategy (Japan) encourages Japan's Robot Revolution by promoting three primary pillars. These are:

- a major improvement in Japan's robot-construction and development capability;
- deployment and distribution of robots across Japan in a purpose to demonstrate its robots globally; and
- formulating business guidelines on the foundation of interconnection between robots and autonomous gathering and analysis of collected (big) data.

Japan's New Robot Strategy

Japan's superiority in the arena of robotics has been predominantly observed in the area of industrial robots (METI 2018). Japan's prime minister since 2012, Shinzo Abe, said that Japan would create a new industrial revolution through the use of robots (METI 2018) and utilise robots in a variety of fields, including nursing care. The New Robot Strategy is set to make Japan a pioneer at the global level, becoming a showcase for the use of robots. The intensive strategy started in the fiscal year 2015, and the initiatives that are promoted, include:

- an investment in a relevant project of 100 billion yen from government and the private sector;
- expansion of the robot market annually by 2.4 trillion yen;
- construction of a new robot test field in Fukushima, which provides testing areas for robots and drones;
- facilitating the innovation and acceleration of public participation through the World Robot Summit; and
- reducing the cost for the initial introduction of robots by 20 per cent and doubling the number of human resources to assist the introduction of robots to 30,000 by 2020.

The New Robot Strategy of Japan's vision for 2020 is that a comprehensive collection of products that are used regularly, such as motor vehicles, household appliances, and mobile (smart) phones, will have some robotic characteristics and will above all be permanently connected to the Internet (METI 2018). The vision is furthermore for an extensive array of information generated from these robots to be accrued, studied, and applied as big data through systems such as machine-to-machine systems and the IoT, further expanding possibilities of robots in the future. These visions are clearly in line with those of Industry 4.0, and Japan has actively started pursuing them through significant government and private backing.

Alliance Industrie du Futur

Alliance Industrie du Futur (France) closely shares the common goal of Plattform Industrie 4.0, of assisting its industrial companies to transform more rapidly and adopt principles of an economy based on the evolution of consumer behaviour and the rapid development of new manufacturing and digital technologies. A key objective of Alliance Industrie du Futur is to develop approaches and mediate digitisation projects for each target group of enterprises, from large multinational industrial players to small emerging local and international companies. The initiative implements its approach by a framework called competitiveness drivers, six core drivers each representing the different transformational challenges that the New Economy imposes on industry. These six drivers include connected devices and the industrial IoT (IIoT), advanced production technologies, new human–machine collaboration approaches, driven and optimised lines and factories, integrated customer–supplier relationships, and new social and business models.

Intelligent Factories Clusters is sustained by the Italian Ministry of Education, University and Research. This programme focuses on sustainable production with the Smart Factory project, involving collaboration with several scientific universities and the National Research Council in Italy. The cluster works on a programme of technological innovation to offer new manufacturing, added sustainability and production models, paying particular attention to environmental and economic improvements. Additional European Industry 4.0 initiatives include Smart Industry in the Netherlands, Produktion 2030 in Sweden, Connected Industry 4.0 in Spain, HVM Catapult in the UK, and Průmysl 4.0 in the Czech Republic.

Manufacturing USA (Advanced Manufacturing Partnership 2.0 (AMP 2.0))

Manufacturing USA (initially called Advanced Manufacturing Partnership 2.0 (AMP 2.0)) is a national effort introduced by the former president, Barack Obama, and the Massachusetts Institute of Technology to secure

US leadership in emerging technologies. It aims to bring together industrial partners (both private and governmental), the academic world and federal associates in a network of advanced manufacturing institutes to increase the manufacturing competitiveness of the US. The programme also aims to promote strong and maintainable national industrial research and development infrastructure. Unfortunately, the funding for a portion of the federal government expired on 21 December 2018 and a shutdown of the programme was initiated owing due to a lapse of congressional appropriations.

Emerging markets obviously have numerous additional challenges to deal with, such as initiatives aimed at spearheading Industry 4.0.

BRICS Nations' Challenges in Terms of Industry 4.0

To the credit of emerging markets, they have also been actively pursuing national strategies to facilitate Industry 4.0 growth and development. Key missions of national focus within the BRICS nations function as a lever and a considerable prospect to drive symbiotic geopolitical partnerships and collaborations. Each BRICS nation has its own opportunities and challenges in preparing for Industry 4.0. Several common factors can also be identified in these emerging markets. Table 12.3 lists the most prominent opportunities and challenges of the BRICS nations in preparation for Industry 4.0.

It is also evident that the BRICS nations have implemented strategies and initiatives to establish and drive Industry 4.0 forward in each country. These initiatives have quantifiable and measurable outcomes, both in short- and long-term goals. The most notable initiatives, as summarised by Aulbur (2016), are presented in the following.

Table 12.3 Opportunities and challenges of BRICS nations in preparing for Industry 4.0

Country	*Opportunities*	*Challenges*
Brazil	A potential high rate of return is expected for foreign investors willing to explore expansion opportunities	A general lack of awareness of digitisation technologies and the impacts of these solutions
	A favourable currency exchange rate for investors entering or expanding international markets	Low productivity and competitiveness indirectly resulting from economic instability (Feijoó 2016)
	A diversified and attractive domestic market that will create vast opportunities to develop Industry 4.0 in Brazil	Lack of skilled workers and a low drive from government to address these concerns
Russia	Russian specialists are traditionally in the vanguard of software, mathematics, intelligent algorithms, and associated fields—a head start in Industry 4.0	Insecurity in the Russian education system and particularly its higher education institutions
	The Russian school of engineering is highly developed, and growing, producing talented young individuals willing to grow their careers in Russia	Decisions made by its government to reduce financing of education in Russia Moving to bottom-up innovation approach during its emergence from recession (Koshkin 2016)
India	Governmental support initiatives such as Make in India are promoting Industry 4.0	Historically many crippling regulations and underdeveloped infrastructure that must first be addressed by government
	The IoT is already one of the most important aspects of Industry 4.0, and expected to capture a 20 per cent global share by 2020 (Chouhan et al. 2017) India has a large potential supply of skilled technical labour and typically low cost of manufacturing	India is known for its low value/high volume focus on commodity products utilising low cost/low skilled labour—Industry 4.0 productivity in manufacturing requires the opposite

(continued)

Table 12.3 (continued)

Country	*Opportunities*	*Challenges*
China	Governmental support initiatives such as Made in China 2025 is promoting Industry 4.0	A shrinking labour force and strengthening currency against the US dollar push investors to consider cost-effective alternatives of neighbouring countries
	China already has a firm foothold in industrial enterprises producing a wide range of consumer and industrial goods	China relies on imported key components in its industrial production activities; it has weak research and development strategies
	There is increased interest from foreign collaborations (such as from Germany) to spearhead Industry 4.0 in China	A shift from low value-added business to high-end manufacturing is needed
South Africa	'South Africa has an established and diversified manufacturing base that has shown its resilience and potential to compete globally' (Maponya 2015)	In comparison, current adoption of Industry 4.0 on the African continent is low. Low accessibility and availability of connectivity in the many rural areas across the country
	Manufacturing in South Africa remains a major player in the economy, aimed to make a larger impact on the GDP	Outdated policies, increased bureaucracy, and political instability are stifling early adoption of digitisation
	Willingness to train and retrain skilled workers in South Africa, specifically by higher education institutions	General hesitance for SMEs to invest in Industry 4.0

BRICS Initiatives Towards Industry 4.0

Brazil

In Brazil, the importance of the use of digital technologies for industrial competitiveness is not as widespread as would ideally be required to thrust forward Industry 4.0 development. According to a survey conducted by the National Confederation of Industry of Brazil, in all industries, 58 per cent of companies are aware of the importance of digitisation in the modern industrial revolution, with fewer than half of these companies truly implementing such strategies. Germany is working closely with Brazil to underscore the importance of partnership among countries in several aspects of manufacturing. The collaborative proposal for Industry 4.0 in Brazil highlights five strategic topics:

- the technologies to be used for fast, real-time, and low initial capital investments,
- configuration techniques of value chains,
- appropriate human resource training,
- regulatory frameworks, and
- planning for necessary infrastructure development.

Brazil additionally needs to focus on reducing bureaucracy in all priority areas to succeed in playing a dominant role in Industry 4.0 among the BRICS nations.

Russia

Technet (Russia) aims to define the boundaries of the market for the factory of the future and develop model-driven architecture requirements for institutional conditions, requirements, and infrastructure projects. Technet assesses the market size in general and its individual segments or technology areas and their importance for the development of the factory of the future. Assessment is conducted of the development potential of the scientific and technological groundwork for the implementation of the roadmap by the following groups of advanced manufacturing technologies:

i. digital modelling
ii. additive technologies
iii. industrial sensors and photonics
iv. industrial Internet
v. new materials
vi. robotics technology
vii. hybridisation technology for computer numerical control milling technology
viii. other technologies used to manufacture modern multifunctional machine tools.

India

Make in India encourages national and multinational firms to design, develop, and manufacture their products locally, in India. The programme was launched in September 2014 and its major objectives are job creation and skills development in 25 segments of the economy, including electrical machinery, electronic systems, renewable energy, and IT and business processes. It represents a comprehensive renovation of outdated procedures and policies. Most importantly, it signifies a change of the mindset of India's government towards moving from imposing authority towards stimulating business partners.

China

Made in China 2025 is an initiative to elevate Chinese commerce, drawing inspiration from Industrie 4.0 in Germany. The Chinese version of this initiative is, however, far broader in its extent, since Chinese producers are exceedingly inconsistent in quality, and numerous challenges have to be mitigated in a relatively short period to compete with advanced industrialised economies. 'Its guiding principles are to have manufacturing be innovation-driven, emphasise quality over quantity, achieve green development and optimise the structure of the Chinese industry' (Kennedy 2015). It emphasises the complete manufacturing system and not only innovation, endorses development of less complex industries to provide modern services, and focuses on state involvement.

South Africa

The biggest challenges preventing rapid growth of Industry 4.0 progress in Africa/South Africa remain the accessibility and availability of connectivity. This is a key topic in South Africa at manufacturing conferences (such as the annual Manufacturing Indaba), with dedicated sessions focusing on the implementation of Industry 4.0 and its implications for South African manufacturers. The Manufacturing Indaba is the largest manufacturing event in sub-Saharan Africa and adds value in introducing business connections and assisting manufacturers to innovate and grow. South Africa has established a diversified manufacturing base presented with resilience and prospects to participate globally. For South Africa and other sub-Saharan countries to be successful in Industry 4.0, an enabling environment is necessary, encompassing key elements such as funding and providing access to enabling technologies, encouraging adoption of new technologies, focusing on the youth to drive changes in ICT, and developing relevant skills both technical and essential human skills.

Although the African continent has a relatively low adoption of Industry 4.0, combined with a lack of understanding of the impact of digitisation (as is true in many countries worldwide), industry leaders as well as policymakers are increasingly discussing its future. Smart technologies can make a large impact at a socio-economic level, an important talking point among political leaders and governments. The future of South Africa might currently be somewhat difficult to predict, but it remains imperative for a new generation of workers (and a retrained current generation) to be technologically well informed and to have a considerably diverse set of skills (Ziady 2017).

The Social, Political, and Economic Position of Africa

Over the past 15 years, according to *The Economist*: Africa Rising, in 2010 'six of the world's ten fastest-growing countries were African' (AEO 2017). The availability of valuable commodities is partly responsible for this; between 2000 and 2008 approximately 25 per cent of Africa's development was derived from increased revenue from natural resources. Advantageous demography is also a significant reason for growth in African nations. As fertility rates in Asia and Latin America are declining, up to 50 per cent of the rise in the global population over the next four decades is expected to be in Africa. The third noteworthy source of growth in Africa has to do with the emerging manufacturing and service economies that African countries are starting to cultivate. The question must however also be posed: will African economies be able to keep up with demand as the demand for and price of commodities fluctuate?

Before discussing the positive changes in the social, political, and economic fortunes of Africa, placing these in an optimistic light with the intensification of Industry 4.0, it is important to indicate that there are still several alarming facts about Africa that threaten its development. A large percentage of Africans, most notably in the DRC, Mozambique, and Uganda, still live on less than US$2 per day (FocusEconomics 2018). This equates to a GDP per capita of less than approximately

US$700. Food production per person has collapsed since independence was obtained in the 1960s, the average lifespan in some countries is under 50, drought and famine continue, the climate is worsening, and deforestation and desertification are still on the rise, according to *The Economist*.

Sturdy growth and an enhancement in living circumstances for many Africans were witnessed in recent history, especially during and directly after the Great Recession, although conditions started to deteriorate again around the end of 2014. Frailer international growth and a decline in product prices (commodities) battered economic growth in several countries, with the consequence of a rise in unemployment and another decrease in living standards, leading to an increase in famine, crime, and corruption. 'Low growth was largely driven by external factors, particularly oil prices, which meant two of the three largest economies in sub-Saharan African, Nigeria and Angola had to accept lower earnings for their exports' (Ernst & Young 2017). As a result, both economies fell into recession, with Nigeria hit particularly hard, as the nation dealt not only with reduced terms of trade, but also with lower production levels as a result of domestic insurgency (Ernst & Young 2017). Slowing economies transformed into weaker exchange rates that resulted in higher consumer price inflation.

An economic indicator gauging an average citizen's economic well-being, a metric that relates unemployment rate, interest rates, and the annual inflation rate of a country, called the misery index, shows that African countries are still in much despair. Adapted from Hanke (2017) with data from the Economic Intelligence Unit, the 2016 misery index calculations of the first 50 countries (ranked from worst to best) are summarised in Table 12.4.

As seen in Table 12.4, listing the highest misery index to the lowest misery index, with the exception of China (98th), all BRICS countries are within the first 20 results of most miserable. Brazil and South Africa, rated third and seventh, respectively, are both bursting with corruption and incompetence that run to the very highest office, the presidency. Argentina (fourth) and Egypt (fifth) are also on the South American and African continents, and comparable with Brazil and South Africa. As a result, the outlook of both these countries is currently grim, and this has a knock-on effect on unemployment, inflation, interest rates, and crime. Such countries have many issues to resolve to attract foreign investments and boost an already suffering economy towards the next

Table 12.4 The 2017 misery index was first constructed by economist Art Okun, modified by Robert Barro, and later by Steve H. Hanke—his version, published on 28 February 2018, is supplied in this table. The misery index is the sum of the unemployment, inflation, and bank lending rates, minus the percentage change in real gross domestic product (GDP) per capita (as defined by Hanke). The table is ranked from worst (highest 'misery') to best (lowest 'misery')

Rank	*Country*	*Misery index*	*Rank*	*Country*	*Misery index*
1	Venezuela	573.4	26	Algeria	12.5
2	Syria	83.8	27	Paraguay	11.8
3	Brazil	75.0	28	Kazakhstan	11.7
4	Argentina	44.9	29	Honduras	11.5
5	Egypt	43.9	30	Saudi Arabia	11.3
6	Nigeria	36.0	31	Barbados	11.3
7	South Africa	35.9	32	Sri Lanka	10.1
8	Bosnia and Herzegovina	30.7	33	Costa Rica	10.9
9	Ukraine	29.3	34	Trinidad and Tobago	10.0
10	São Tomé and Príncipe	28.7	35	Spain	10.0
11	Iran	28.1	36	Russia	9.8
12	Jamaica	27.4	37	Guatemala	9.6
13	Azerbaijan	24.2	38	Moldova	9.4
14	Turkey	24.1	39	Nicaragua	9.4
15	Macedonia	23.0	40	Bolivia	9.3
16	Palestine	22.1	41	Mauritius	9.2
17	Jordan	19.1	42	Indonesia	8.7
18	Armenia	18.4	43	Croatia	8.6
19	Colombia	17.5	44	India	8.4
20	Greece	17.1	45	Mexico	7.9
21	Dominican Republic	15.5	46	Papua New Guinea	7.8
22	Serbia	14.8	47	Italy	7.6
23	Uruguay	14.7	48	Albania	7.1
24	Georgia	14.4	49	El Salvador	6.8
25	Peru	14.4	50	Chile	6.4

industrial revolution. In addition, all African countries (with a significant GDP with respect to the listed countries in Table 12.3) are within the top 13 of the highest misery ratings. Russia (36th) and India (44th) (both BRICS nations) are also among the 50 worst overall economies, although both these countries are showing tremendous economic growth, especially India. In Russia, economic recovery has been witnessed in the second quarter of 2017, with flourishing fixed investments pursued and increases witnessed in household spending that drove the GDP to increase at the highest pace since the third quarter of 2017. This is partly due to large infrastructure projects, primarily in the energy and transportation sectors, accelerated industrial production, a minor decline in unemployment, growth in domestic and international investments and low inflation with improving confidence.

The period between 2010 and 2014 witnessed a mean international economic growth of approximately 3.2 per cent per annum (2017). This growth drove investment into, and exports from, Africa. The International Trade Centre disclosed that the African continent showed increased export revenues from US$325 billion during 2009 to US$665 billion in 2012. Collectively, Africa experienced improving economic conditions (3.6 per cent per annum), relating to a general decline in the misery index, in the period between 2010 and 2014. Only the politically troubled North Africa experienced a decline in economic growth during this time. Viljoen's study (2017) provided records on 25 African countries and showed that 18 of these countries showed general improvement between approximately 2009 and 2014. The remaining countries that did not show overall improvement were Cape Verde, Egypt, Equatorial Guinea, Gambia, Libya, Malawi, and Morocco. However, as discussed in Viljoen, (2017), first reported by the World Bank (2017), 'emerging markets and developing economies experienced notably lower growth during 2015 and 2016', with a tentative recovery expected in 2017 (from a global growth of 2.3 per cent to an estimated 2.7 per cent). Stagnant global trade, subdued investment, and heightened policy uncertainty led to a challenging year for the world economy (World Bank 2017), which also influenced economic growth in African nations negatively. Global political, economic, and investment factors that contributed to worldwide investor uncertainty include the UK's withdrawal from the European Union (Brexit), insecurity about the appointment of Donald Trump as president of the USA in 2016, intensified political insecurity in Europe, China heading into a stage of relaxed economic growth, and the 2000s commodities boom (or commodities super cycle) ending around 2014 (Ernst & Young 2017).

In Africa, the economic growth in South Africa in 2016 was only marginally positive, at 0.3 per cent, the economic growth of

Angola during the same period was flat, and both countries' recovery depends on a spectrum of external factors, such as the regaining of global commodity prices and structural economic reform. Cote d'Ivoire remains 'one of the fastest growing countries globally, but again, it is highly dependent on commodity prices (cocoa) and its ability to manage internal conflict' (Ernst & Young 2017). Ghana also shows prospects of a recovering economy, with a new administration encouraging restored economic management. The African Development Bank, the Organization for Economic Cooperation and Development, and the United Nations Development Programme (UNDP) indicate that Africa's economic growth will rise following its 2016 plummet. This growth is influenced by a number of factors, including the current rebound in global commodity prices. However, these predictions assume that the regaining in product prices is persistent, global economies are strengthened, and national macroeconomic transformations are fixed. Ernst & Young's Attractiveness Program Africa 2017 shares the optimistic views on Africa post-2017, stating that African economies are in a much better position than they were one or two decades ago. The attractiveness report provides an executive summary of key civic investors as a vital source of discernment on FDI in Africa, investigating the desirability of a specific region/country as an investment target. According to Ernst & Young, the FDI patterns in Africa hold steady despite growing global uncertainty, with South Africa remaining the largest FDI hub, among the other key hub economies of Nigeria, Kenya, Egypt, and Morocco. Importantly, Ernst & Young state that digital transformation (interpreted as Industry 4.0) remains a potential game-changer for inclusive growth in Africa. This inclusive growth can only be achieved with increases in connectivity and collaboration.

In addition, according to the African Economic Outlook (AEO) report of 2017, entrepreneurship is an important factor in growing the economies of the continent. The UNDP Africa regional director specifically mentioned, 'The key to successful development in Africa is to nurture the emerging culture of entrepreneurship … a path that can unleash high-octane creativity and transform opportunities into phenomenal realisations'. The annual AEO monitors the state of affairs on the African continent using a collaborative approach. It evaluates the latest economic and social conditions in Africa, estimates expected advances for the near future, and reviews the structure of African economies. Specific focus is placed on entrepreneurship and industrialisation in Africa, with over 150 contributors to the report (AEO, 2017). A summary of Africa's economic growth suggests that it is affected by the liabilities of the international economy. The real GDP growth of the region slowed down to 2.2 per cent in 2016, mainly, as mentioned earlier, because of the continual decline in commodity prices and frail international economic growth. Regionally, the following summary is presented:

- East Africa showed the fastest growth, with 5.3 per cent real GDP growth.
- North Africa had the second fastest real GDP growth, at 3 per cent.
- Southern Africa showed a paltry 1.1 per cent growth, with its largest economy, South Africa, only showing 0.3 per cent real GDP growth.
- Dragged down by the recession in Nigeria, West Africa only posted 0.4 per cent growth.

The report (AEO 2017) also informs that the economic growth of Africa in 2017 should post increases all-round, estimating a 3.4 per cent real growth in GDP (0.7 per cent higher than the World Bank (2017) estimate), again assuming that the recovery in product prices is persistent, global economies are strengthened, and national macroeconomic transformations are fixed.

The Changing Social, Political, and Economic Fortunes of Africa

There are fortunately changing social, political, and economic fortunes in Africa that count towards Africa posting significant growth in the near future, and enabling countries to take advantage of industrialisation, to innovate, attract foreign investment, and improve the quality of life of their residents. The four primary aspects that drive this change in Africa are:

- Resilience from a strong domestic demand is encouraging positive economic growth;
- Africa's growth has become 'less dependent on natural resources and is progressively favoured by improvements in the business environment and macroeconomic governance' (AEO 2017);

- The continent is better adapted to withstand external and international setbacks due to increased structural diversification;
- As macro-fundamentals are weakening, policy certainty is becoming imperative to alleviate external setbacks, and the regions have acknowledged this and have started implementing policy changes.

Stimulating industrialisation in Africa ranks high on the policy agendas of many governments. The primary objective here is to create new labour-intensive industries, and in order to ensure successful implementation new industrialisation strategies are being explored. It is imperative for Africa to study the reasons for previous industrialisation policies that failed, and to address new opportunities and challenges brought about by Industry 4.0 and the current global economic environment, especially promoting growth in entrepreneurship. It is known that in many African nations (more than in South America and Asia), small businesses and firms are driving employment and entrepreneurship; however, it must be ensured that these firms have more potential to grow and contribute to the new wave of industrialisation (AEO 2017). At least 26 African countries have industrialisation strategies in place for 2017 going forward (AEO 2017). The main objective for African governments is to create conditions that allow their economies to adopt a higher, more inclusive and more sustainable growth path. Economic transformation will however not be possible without industrialisation through convergence with more advanced economies.

Competitiveness in Industry 4.0 can be achieved if successful and inclusive policies are established in African countries. These policies should be a combination of learning experience from developed countries such as Germany (which has implemented various successful policies), and through collaboration with other BRICS nations. The following section reviews potential policies to drive Industry 4.0 forward in Africa, and to endorse emerging countries as significant role players in the fourth industrial revolution.

Case Study: Enabling Access to Clean Water and Sanitation Through Sensing

As India (a BRICS nation) is moving towards the smart cities concept, a discernible improvement in solid waste management (SWM) is needed to provide a clean and hygienic environment to city residents (Dhaya et al. 2016). By combining technologies that drive Industry 4.0, such as the IoT, is has become possible to create smart SWM systems, which are dynamic and adaptable, sustainable, and more efficient. Under the umbrella of the Clean India Mission, spearheaded by the government of India, it has become important to control and analytically approach waste management in the country, especially in view of the large population and high poverty rates. The Clean India Mission (or Swachh Bharat Abhiyan campaign officially launched in October 2014) is intent on cleaning up the roads of cities in India, including smaller rural developments and towns. Essentially, the goal of this campaign is eliminating unsanitary practices in the country, and establishing accountable, sustainable, and semi-autonomous mechanisms for monitoring waste management. Its ultimate aim is to boost tourism in India, attract FDI, develop rural areas and improve the health of the population as well as that of foreign visitors and people working in India.

These projects link up rural sanitation and maintenance via IoT sensors virtually, and ensure access to maintained sanitation facilities. In India alone, up to 100,000 tons of municipal solid waste is generated daily (Dhaya et al. 2016). Waste management is therefore nearly impossible to maintain manually and has traditionally been a challenge. Public waste management services have been around for a long time in India, but limited innovation and low operational efficiency have forced the government to reconsider this strategy. Using smart technologies, efficient waste management is possible, reducing the amount of time and energy required to provide waste management services. Effectively, smart SWM systems are implemented using a specific set of rules, created by human operators, and performed by sensors, networks, and data gathering. Examples of smart waste management systems implementation include frequently sending the trash/waste content details to a control centre, locating the nearest waste removal collector with respect to the distance from the source, determining the shortest distance between the waste removal collector and the source, determining the least congested times that will be most efficient for the procedure to be performed, and guiding the collector to the nearest dumping site using global positioning satellites.

Implementation of these smart systems aims to automate several sectors such as waste management in countries with large populations. However, challenges are faced when considering implementation of these systems. A primary challenge is the cost to incorporate it in a vast geographical area, the logistics of maintaining the system and the requirement for skilled workers to both integrate and maintain the system. Given the low labour cost in India, implementing smart systems has economic benefits, since the overall cost of such a project will be reduced. Socio-economic benefits include upgrading the skills of informal sector workers already involved in waste management. In view of the high level of economic, social, and cultural diversity in urban areas in India, and for all countries, it is vital that sanitary services are effective to ensure minimal waste accumulation. Challenges with governance additionally complicate such initiatives, with weak institutions, slow governmental support, underresourced and short-staffed firms, and further rapid urbanisation among the problems that need to be addressed for sustained successful execution.

In September 2015, the survey results of the Clean India Mission were posted, and the following conclusions in terms of techno-economics and social implications were drawn. First, the largest encouraging result accomplished in one year of the Clean India Mission was the change in outlook and community sense positioning of children, confirmed by over 51 per cent of respondents. The largest adverse finding was the absence of commitment of metropolitan resident bodies—over 72 per cent of the people surveyed suggested that their municipality was not engaging residents in sanitation or a civic consciousness. Almost 13 per cent believed that the accessibility of communal lavatories had improved in their town. Inclusively, 21 per cent of the residents believed that their city had become cleaner because of the Clean India Mission. This accounted for more than one-fifth of the citizens, and indicated that the campaign had an impact.

Second, a key problem recognised by residents was the contribution of municipalities in the Clean India Mission and engaging citizens in the effort. Almost 95 per cent of those surveyed believed that it was crucial for the city and civic leadership to participate together with citizens on such an undertaking. In addition, 94 per cent of the citizens said that their municipality 'needed a major upgrade on all fronts, including skills, processes, systems, equipment, people and leadership'. The community also believed that the campaign ambassadors were 'under-utilised in the first year'; with over 82 per cent of respondents suggesting that ambassadors can 'motivate citizens and municipalities to work together'. In addition, 87 per cent of the respondents believed that a city's ability to reach Clean India Mission milestones should be a 'critical requirement before any smart city funds are released to the city'.

Case Study: Water 4.0

The first revolution in water distribution (Water 1.0) was the Roman invention of tubing drinkable water in, and manure out, of populated areas. The second revolution was to treat potable water to eradicate contagious microorganisms, thus protecting urban residents from diseases such as cholera. The third revolution, Water 3.0, witnessed pervasive implementation of sewage treatment plants. In modern times, a rising urban population and a change in climate are leading to chronic water shortages, such as experienced in Cape Town, South Africa, during 2017 and 2018. This calls for a fourth revolution in water, Water 4.0: managing resources efficiently.

Among the most important and indispensable services necessary in all communities are water services (Katko and Hukka 2015). These services consist of drinking water, gray water, industrial water, and sewage. Water plays an important role in community and societal development. In a developed and urbanised area, such as in the city of Singapore, buildings alone account for 25 per cent of water consumption (Fernández et al. 2017). This stresses the importance of accessible water to sustain urban developments. The importance of digitisation in modern society has been increasing for some time and people have started to address new trends that could change value creation chains and evolve into a new industrial revolution (Bufler et al. 2016). Both the municipal and the industrial water industry are facing challenges from decades of continuous population growth, to build and expand the water infrastructure in their countries. Germany has deemed it necessary—as should emerging nations and specifically the BRICS group—to participate in the emergence of Industry 4.0 and play a leading role, and to maintain further developments and their competitiveness. The German Water Partnership (GWP) has made significant contributions in establishing the working group Water 4.0, through interpreting digitisation on various levels of the value chain and in complex integrated systems.

Globally, the water industry (which includes drinking water and water designated for irrigation) is looking for ways to adapt and find efficient and effective solutions for global challenges. Climate change and rapid urbanisation are among the driving forces of such initiatives, as the scarcity of water resources is increasing in most countries. Water shortages are becoming more common, for a variety of reasons, including deficits in raw water supply (as a result of global warming, or other localised reasons), inadequate and outdated distribution systems in areas of rapid urbanisation and growing economies, improper operating policies of management agencies and lack of skilled workers to oversee operations, pollutants in water supply from urban runoff entering large bodies of water (Fernández et al. 2017), a sudden (unplanned) growth in demand, or damage to facilities.

Comparable to other industry sectors, the water industry is also in a position to strengthen its future competitiveness using automation and smart grids, as a holistic approach to Industry 4.0. The increased integration of the IoT, sensors, and modelling/simulation applications are creating new opportunities to increase the complexity (data dependability) of networking infrastructure and to illustrate them in production as well as early warning and decision-making processes. Operational improvements of this initiative are recorded in the areas of increases in quality of water and water accessibility, transformation and upgrading of services offered, and ensuring resource efficiency for the future, which are all key objectives of most digitisation technologies. The classification of developmental advances in water management has different possible interpretations and chronological spans (Bufler et al. 2016). Water 4.0 uses CPS to merge real and virtual worlds, through simulation and big data, to identify these developmental advances. Through linking of sensors, computer models, and real-time controllers with real water systems, participation of intelligent networks to and from the Internet is possible. Cross-sectional technologies allow complete consideration of water, regardless of whether it is falling as precipitation, supplied as drinking water or used for wastewater. Water 4.0 evaluates digital data and inputs it into forecasts, allowing complete consideration of sustainable decisions with respect to water usage.

As stated by Dr. Michael Prange, the general manager of the GWP, the German water sector benefits from 150 years of experience in technology, application, and management. Especially in developing countries and emerging markets, the demand for innovative technological expertise and qualified water management is rising rapidly, and German companies can use their knowledge and their standards to make an important contribution to the sustainable management of water resources. The opportunities for digitisation within the water industry and in other sectors have presented various benefits. Among these is the energy demand of water, especially in pumping stations. By linking water supply data with information provided from renewable energy sources, the supply of and demand for water can be coordinated better, thus saving energy for pumping water that might be squandered at a particular time when demand is low. The Water 4.0 campaign is also developing sustainable solutions to conserve resources using advanced technology and digitisation, especially in cities.

Conclusion

Industry 4.0 is a 'combination of several major innovations in digital technology, all currently maturing, and poised to transform the energy and manufacturing sectors' (Geissbauer et al. 2016). These technologies include AI, advanced robotics, sensors, and actuators within the IoT space, cloud computing, remote digital manufacture such as 3D printing, automation, autonomous vehicles, and cryptocurrencies, among other technologies such as software-as-a-service. Their goal is implanting all these features in an international value chain, rationed by numerous corporations from several countries (Geissbauer et al. 2016). If combined, these technologies incorporate the real (physical) and cyber worlds, enabling potent new ways of unifying universal procedures and passing the swiftness of software operations to large-scale instrument manufacture, eliminating the need for vast real-estate requirements and costly capital investments.

Talent management and skills development for Industry 4.0 remain challenging, especially in emerging BRICS countries, where political and economic instability is high. Furthermore, organisations should know exactly which skills to develop that would be beneficial and sustainable, during the early adoption of Industry 4.0. BRICS countries must embrace collaboration in research by universities to reduce dependence on the West.

Digital transformation is presenting new challenges for many employers, and their current and future workforces should be adaptable in this regard. New business models and strategies of cooperation and collaboration constitute added value to Industry 4.0, but space must be created for creativity and innovation. The emphasis should be placed on developing new technical skills, especially in operating activities and mechanical processes, purchasing and warehouse logistics. These new demands are becoming a major challenge for existing employees, often requiring retraining or further skills development.

BRICS countries can cooperate to effect expansion in the fourth industrial revolution, and these nations can learn from one another, and from developed nations, to implement best practices and effective infrastructure. The changing political, economic, and social fortunes of these countries are creating space for innovative urban environmental practices in cities. Collaboration among BRICS nations, also in higher education, will strengthen ties between countries as well, and improve the appreciation of different cultures, labour practices, and socio-economic improvements. Governments must make skills development a top priority and engage with partners, such as the private sector and universities, to widen the skills sets of young individuals.

Bibliography

African Economic Outlook (AEO). (2017). *Special Theme: Entrepreneurship and Industrialization*. African Development Bank Group. https://www.afdb.org/fileadmin/uploads/afdb/Documents/Publications/AEO_2017_Report_Full_English.pdf.

Aulbur, W. (2016). *Skill Development for Industry 4.0 in BRICS Nations*. http://www.linkedin.com. Accessed 25 October 2017.

Aulbur, W., Arvind, C. J., & Bigghe, R. (2016). *White Paper: Skill Development for Industry 4.0: BRICS Skill Development Working Group*. http://www.globalskillsummit.com/. Accessed 13 October 2017.

Bouchard, J., Matacz, A., & Potters, M. (2001). The Leverage Effect in Financial Markets: Retarded Volatility and Market Panic. *Physical Review Letters, 87*(22), 228701.

Bufler, R., Clausnitzer, V., Vestner, R., Werner, U., & Ziemer, C. (2016). *Water 4.0—An Important Element for the German Water Industry*. Published by German Water Partnership.

Chouhan, S., Mehra, P., & Dasot, A. (2017). India's Readiness for Industry 4.0: A Focus on the Automotive Sector. *Grant Thornton*. http://www.grantthornton.in. Accessed 7 November 2017.

Dhaya, R., Pattabiraman, P., Shahrukh, S., & Aravindh, J. (2016). Smart Waste Management Using Internet of Things. *Middle-East Journal of Scientific Research, 24*(10), 3358–3361.

Ernst & Young Attractiveness Program Africa. (2017). https://www.ey.com/za/en/issues/business-environment/ey-attractiveness-program-africa-2017.

Feijoó, R. T. (2016). *Brazil's Productivity and Competitiveness: Challenges and Opportunities*. http://www.linkedin.com. Accessed 6 November 2017.

Fernández, R. A., Zubelzu, S., & Martinez, R. (Eds.). (2017). *Carbon Footprint and the Industrial Life Cycle: From Urban Planning to Recycling*. New York: Springer International Publishing.

FocusEconomics. (2018). *The Poorest Countries in the World*. http://www.focus-economics.com. Accessed 20 January 2019.

Geissbauer, R., Vedso, J., & Schrauf, S. (2016, May). A Strategist's Guide to Industry 4.0. *Strategy and Business*, 83.

Gruss, B., & Novta, N. (2018). *The Decline in Manufacturing Jobs: Not Necessarily a Cause for Concern*. http://www.blogs.imf.org. Accessed 26 January 2019.

Hanke, S. (2017). *Misery Index: The World's Saddest (And Happiest) Countries*. http://www.forbes.com. Accessed 30 January 2019.

Horowitz, M. C., Allen, G. C., Kania, E. B., & Scharre, P. (2018). *Strategic Competition in an Era of Artificial Intelligence*. Washington, DC: Center for a New American Security.

Katko, T. S., & Hukka, J. J. (2015). Social and Economic Importance of Water Services in the Built Environment: Need for More Structured Thinking. *Procedia Economics and Finance, 21,* 217–223.

Kennedy, S. (2015). *Made in China 2025*. http://www.csis.org. Accessed 7 November 2017.

Klitou, D., Conrads, J., & Rasmussen, M. (2017, May). Key Lessons from National Industry 4.0 Policy Initiatives in Europe. *Digital Transformation Monitor*. http://www.ec.europa.eu. Accessed 7 October 2017.

Koshkin, P. (2016). *Russia's Take on Innovation: Top-Down or Bottom-Up?* http://www.russia-direct.org. Accessed 7 November 2017.

Lawrence, R. (2018). *The Future of Manufacturing Employment*. http://www.hsrc.ac.za. Accessed 26 January 2019.

Lee, G. (2018). *China and US Set for Arms Race in AI That Will Lead to Respective Spheres of Dominance, Says Expert*. https://www.scmp.com/business/article/2171630/china-and-us-set-arms-race-ai-will-lead-respective-spheres-dominance-says. Accessed 27 January 2019.

Maponya, C. (2015). Manufacturing Sector Can Drive South Africa's Global Competitiveness. http://www.sanews.gov.za. Accessed 9 November 2017.

National Economic Council (NEC). (2016, October). *Revitalizing American Manufacturing. The Obama Administration's Progress in Establishing a Foundation for Manufacturing Leadership*. National Economic Council.

Nistor, P. (2015). FDI Implications on BRICS Economy Growth. *Procedia Economics and Finance, 32,* 981–985.

Raman, S. (2017). Singapore's Advanced Manufacturing Avatar 'Industry 4.0'. http://www.futurereadysingapore.com. Accessed 14 October 2017.

The Economist. (2018). *The Battle for Digital Supremacy*. http://www.economist.com. Accessed 27 January 2019.

The Ministry of Economy, Trade and Industry (METI), Government of Japan. (2018). *Japan's New Robot Strategy*. http://www.djw.de. Accessed 26 January 2019.

Unnikrishnan, M.S., & Aulbur, W. (2016). *Skill Development for Industry 4.0*. http://economictimes.indiatimes.com. Accessed 23 January 2019.

Viljoen, C. (2017). *The Economic Index That Suggests a Change in Fortunes for Africa*. http://www.weforum.org. Accessed 21 October 2017.

World Bank. (2017, January). *Global Economic Prospects. Weak Investment in Uncertain Times*. A World Bank Group Flagship Report. http://www.openknowledge.worldbank.org. Accessed 21 October 2017.

Ziady, H. (2017, October 12–18). Work and the Future. *Financial Mail*.

CHAPTER 13

BRICS and FOCAC: Challenging or Supplementing Bretton Woods Institutions?

David Monyae and Emmanuel Matambo

Introduction

The multilateral organisation leading the global South's new counter to the West's domination of global financial markets and subsequent aid is the organisation of cooperation between Brazil, Russia, India, China and South Africa known as BRICS. BRIC, as it was known before South Africa's inclusion, was prompted by the astronomical economic growth of China and India and their informal partnerships with Brazil and Russia, driven by their collective influences in their respective regions. This collaboration culminated in fringe meetings between the member states' foreign ministers in New York in 2006 during a UN General Assembly which laid the foundation for the first diplomatic BRIC meeting in Russia in June 2009. The objective of the cooperative organisation was to change the global economic status quo and to improve the state of development

D. Monyae (✉) · E. Matambo
University of Johannesburg Centre for Africa-China Studies, Johannesburg, South Africa
e-mail: dmonyae@uj.ac.za

D. Monyae and B. Ndzendze (eds.), *The BRICS Order*, International Political Economy Series,
https://doi.org/10.1007/978-3-030-62765-2_13

financial institutions. The World Bank and the International Monetary Fund (IMF), otherwise known as the Bretton Woods institutions, are the global standard in developmental finance since their inception in 1944. Together with the General Agreement on Tariffs and Trade (GATT)—the founding agreement on which the World Trade Organisation (WTO) is based—they have arguably repackaged the chains of dependence that existed to move resources from the developing countries in the global South to the West during colonisation. The Bretton Woods international financial institutions (IFIs) have been criticised for using development needs of developing countries to keep them indebted to financiers by enforcing structural adjustment policies (SAP), usually accompanied by austerity measures. This obvious dependence and the governing of the institutions by Western ideology and American influence caused the global South's dissatisfaction and distrust of traditional IFIs.

With the emergence of the Chinese and the Indian economies in the early 2000s, an alternative to the IMF in China's foreign direct investment (FDI) has been realised. From a largely agriculturally based economy in the late 1980s and 90s, China has industrialised, and continues to industrialise, at a fast rate. In the 2000s China's economic prowess has seen Chinese companies competing with the West. This is a result of Chinese companies' ability to provide equivalent technical products and services at a fraction of the cost charged by Western companies (Lam 2018). India, Russia and Brazil saw similar growth projections in their economies in the 2000s and a financial collaborative partnership was forged. China's inroads in maintaining meaningful relationships with African states and the African Union (AU) meant that China enjoyed the significant influence in Africa that both the United States and Western Europe were grappling with for a large part of the twentieth century. China's renewed strength in politics, military and economy ostensibly challenges the United States' hegemony in global relations (Demchak 2019).

The British referendum of 23 June 2016 on whether to leave the European Union (EU) (the departure is known as Brexit) indicated a change of ideology by the British. Globalisation was making way for nationalistic protectionism. A mere five months later, in a shocking result, the United States elected Donald Trump as its forty-fifth president. More nationalistic than the majority of the Republican Party he represents, Trump's message leading up to the elections was of US protectionism and a relook at the global partnerships that the United States shares with the rest of North America, Europe and Asia (Nguyen 2017). His foreign policy was fuelled by exclusionist rhetoric aimed at marginalising foreign migrants for the benefit of American nationals. This antipathy to immigration was in tandem with the concerns of those who voted to leave the EU. Brexit and Trump have come to signal a shift in the focus of the champions of globalisation, to more insular political and economic policies.

Brexit has reverberated around the world. Financial markets have been jittery. In the UK, the centre of the storm, the pound sterling is in a precarious state and the FTSE fell sharply in the immediate aftermath of Brexit. Moody's quickly downgraded the UK's credit rating from stable to negative, and a number of US banks in London have initiated the process of relocating to other European capitals. The Bank of England announced a 250-billion-pound sterling contingent facility. 'Contagion' effects of Brexit have been felt worldwide. In the United States, the Dow Jones plunged by more than 500 points. Asian markets also crumbled, with Tokyo's Nikkei falling by 7.9 per cent—its worst fall since March 2011. Hong Kong's Hang Seng fell by 2.9 per cent and Singapore's benchmark Strait Times index by two per cent. A flurry of high-level meetings had to be held in the UK and in various European capitals on how to deal with the first exit from the EU by a sovereign country.

Leaders of the EU are worried about the demands from populist anti-EU parties in France and the Netherlands for referendums of their own on EU membership. Scotland could pull out of the UK, and Northern Ireland could reunify with the Republic of Ireland. The accession of Boris Johnson, an avowed champion of Brexit, to the British premiership attests to how inward-looking nationalism is taking hold of the West.

Amid these currents, non-Western players seem to have found timely solidarity with each other. Since its inception in 2009 the BRICS association has intended to create a currency repository that would act as a development bank to offset the shortcomings of the IMF and World Bank, especially considering the unequivocal influence that the United States enjoys in terms of who gets aid and how the aid is structured. The New Development Bank was born out of need, and serves to focus on projects as opposed to policies. South Africa, especially, campaigned for 'key initiatives such as the BRICS New Development Bank (NDB)' (Sitas 2018: 7). The NDB came into existence in 2014 with the BRICS nations as its member states. Its primary aim is to support projects through loans, guarantees, equities participation and other financial tools to promote inclusive economic growth, environmentally sustainable growth and regional integration, a far cry from the polarised heavily capitalised structure of the IMF and World Bank. The NDB has been said to mark a fundamental change in global economic and political power.

The remainder of this chapter will delve into detail on the current economic and political climate that led to the creation of the NDB, and what possible changes this landscape will undergo. It starts by outlining the IMF, its structure and how it conceitedly dictates policy to the developing world. This will form the foundation on which BRICS, FOCAC and China–Africa relations—with their motives and implications and the financial strategies from these emerging trends—will be based.

The IMF

At the 1944 Bretton Woods conference 29 countries agreed to establish a development institution to rebuild West European infrastructure that had been destroyed during the Second World War. This was only to be realised in 1947, when the IMF came into existence and started operating. More than a mere lender of money for state infrastructure development, the IMF was to also play a regulatory role in the functions of the world economy. This means that the institution could and would influence currencies and exchange rates, depending on global (read Western) needs.

As stated in Article I of the original Articles of Agreement (IMF 1990), the objectives of the IMF were:

1. To promote international monetary cooperation through a permanent institution which provides the machinery for consultation and collaboration on international monetary problems;
2. To facilitate the expansion and balanced growth of international trade, and to contribute thereby to high levels of employment and real income and to the development of the productive resources of all members as primary objectives of economic policy;
3. To promote exchange stability, to maintain orderly exchange arrangements among members, and to avoid competitive exchange depreciation;
4. To assist in the establishment of a multilateral system of payments in respect of current transactions between members and in the elimination of foreign exchange restrictions which hamper the growth of world trade;

5. To give confidence to member governments by making the general resources of the Fund temporarily available to them under adequate safeguards, thus providing them with the opportunity to correct maladjustment in their balance of payments without resorting to measures destructive of national or international prosperity;
6. In accordance with the above, to shorten the duration and lessen the degree of disequilibrium in the international balances of payments of members (Peet 2009).

On paper, the IMF is a non-partisan financial service provider for the global fiscal system. The organisation is supposed to be the custodian for the international monetary system and is responsible for correcting the anomalies that cause financial crises that stem from incorrect economic policies of member states. It is a repository for these member states to use when the said policy errors result in undesirable socio-economic conditions and can then be rectified. But the reality was much more complex and biased.

IMF Structure

The IMF has five major partner countries, namely the United States, Japan, the UK, Germany and France. Russia, China and Saudi Arabia have permanent seats on the board but do not possess the influence of the five major countries. The rest of the member countries are made up of creditor countries. The United States is the biggest contributor to the fund, followed by Japan and Germany, then France and the UK, and then Saudi Arabia, China and Russia. Collectively, the IMF has a fund of $290 billion, but also has contingency funds available to it such as the General Arrangements to Borrow (GAB) and the New Arrangements to Borrow (NAB) which collectively can contribute $46 billion in case of emergencies (IMF 2002a).

The percentages shared are as follows:

- USA—17 per cent.
- Japan and Germany—6 per cent.
- France and the United Kingdom—5 per cent.
- Saudi Arabia, China and Russia—3 per cent.

The IMF's main area of concern is economic policy, as indicated by its founding statements, meaning that it requires to know how the member and borrower economies are structured before any exchange of resources can be approved. This indicates that, with the influence the United States enjoys at the IMF, it could spread its capitalist ideology under the guise of the IMF and use the institute's resources as collateral for its own foreign policy objectives. The IMF includes SAPs in its agreements with developing nations, based on Article V ('Operations and Transactions of the Fund'), Section 3 of the Fund's Articles of Agreement, which broadly present the conditions governing use of the Fund's resources. Briefly, Section 3(a) states that the Fund 'shall adopt policies on the use of its general resources [...] and may adopt special policies for special balance of payments problems, that will assist members to solve their balance of payments problems in a manner consistent with the provisions of this Agreement and that will establish adequate safeguards for the temporary use of the general resources of the Fund' (Peet 2009). This is to ensure that the developing nations repay their loans. But these SAPs are detrimental to the very economies that they are meant to assist. William Easterly's (2005: 1) analysis found that 'none of the top 20 recipients of repeated adjustment lending over 1980–99 were able to achieve reasonable growth and contain all policy distortions. About half of the adjustment loan recipients show severe macroeconomic distortions regardless of cumulative adjustment loans'.

The debt repayment comes at a heavy cost to some countries where spending on health, transportation and education must be cut to ensure repayment of the loans. Countries have had to privatise national resources and reduce basic minimum wages to attract foreign investment to pay the very countries this investment comes from. Mark Weisbrot et al. (2009) have argued that 'the IMF is still prescribing inappropriate policies that could unnecessarily exacerbate economic downturns in a number of countries'. They further suggest that 'the re-establishment of the IMF as a major power in economic and decision-making in low-and-middle income countries, with little or no voice for these countries in the IMF's decision-making, could have long-term implications for growth, development, and social indicators in many countries'. It is this posture of the IMF towards the developing world that has caused disenchantment and a simultaneous commitment to emerging structures. Devalued currencies, privatised national assets and cheap labour resulting from SAPs seem to herald neocolonialism. Developing states are caught in a cycle of debt and are in a worse position than before the IMF-sponsored economic reforms.

The following are some of the loan facilities and their conditions set by the IMF under Article V:

- *Stand-by Arrangements* assure member countries that they can draw up to a specified amount, usually over 12–18 months, to deal with short-term balance of payments problems.
- *The Extended Fund Facility* provides assurance that member countries can draw up to a specified amount, usually over three to four years, to make structural economic changes that the IMF thinks will improve balance of payments.
- *The Poverty Reduction and Growth Facility* (replacing the Enhanced Structural Adjustment Facility in 1999) provides low-interest loans to the lowest-income member countries facing protracted balance of payments problems, with the cost to borrowers subsidised by funds raised through past sales of IMF-owned gold, together with loans and grants from wealthier member countries.
- *The Supplemental Reserve Facility* provides additional short-term loans at higher interest rates to member countries experiencing exceptional balance of payments difficulties because of sudden loss of market confidence reflected in capital outflows.
- *Contingent Credit Lines* provide precautionary IMF financing on a short-term basis when countries are faced by a sudden loss of market confidence because of contagion from difficulties in other countries.
- *Emergency Assistance* helps countries coping with balance of payments problems arising from sudden and unforeseeable natural disasters or, since 1995, emergency conditions stemming from military conflicts (IMF 2002b).

IMF borrowers are usually poor, underdeveloped nations, transitioning from either postcolonial turmoil or post communist financial crises. Either way, they are fragile governments incapable or too desperate to negotiate favourable conditions for their loans. The result is unsustainable economic policy reforms that prioritise export production over driving domestic activity. Multinational organisations are offered preferred conditions for the sake of foreign investment while local companies requiring governmental support fail and employment falls. The multinational organisations that have preyed on developing countries desiring aid have been mostly from the top five nations in the IMF. With the IMF electoral system proportional to each country's contribution, it is clear that the IMF objectives have shifted from aid to manipulating developing economies for capital gain. The industrialisation of traditional societies has in retrospect been an exercise to reimagine the chains of dependence that existed during colonisation. It is partly from these skewed realities that emerging powers are charting what could be termed alternative structures such as BRICS with their attendant financial institutions.

BRICS

The BRIC thesis, developed by Jim O'Neill, recognises that Brazil, Russia, India and China have changed their political systems to embrace global capitalism. Together, the BRICS account for more than 40 per cent of world population, and the voting share of these countries in the World Bank and IMF has increased by 13.19 per cent and 14.84 per cent respectively (Lin 2019: 74). In its report (O'Neill 2007), Goldman Sachs predicts China and India to be the dominant global suppliers of manufactured goods and services respectively, while Brazil and Russia would become similarly dominant as suppliers of raw materials. Cooperation is thus hypothesised to be a logical next step among the BRICs because Brazil and Russia together would form the commodity suppliers to India and China and thus the BRICs have the potential to form a powerful economic bloc to the exclusion of the modern-day G6 status. Brazil is dominant in soy and iron ore while Russia has enormous supplies of oil and natural gas. Goldman Sachs's thesis thus documents how commodities, work, technology and companies have diffused outward from the United States across the world.

Following the end of the Cold War (though early signs were there in the late Cold War), many of the governments comprising the BRICs initiated economic or political reforms to allow their countries to enter the world economy. In order to compete, these countries have simultaneously stressed education, foreign investment, domestic consumption and domestic entrepreneurship. India, arguably, has the potential to grow the fastest among the four original BRIC countries over the next 30–50 years. A major reason for this is that the decline in working-age population will happen later for India and Brazil than for Russia and China. The BRICs have continued to increase their contributions to the ever globalising markets. From 2001 to 2007, BRIC members enjoyed remarkable increase in their equity markets. Brazil's rose by 369 per cent, India's by 499 per cent, Russia's by 630 per cent and China's by 201 per cent, using the A-share market, or 'by a stunning 817 per cent based on the HSCEI' (O'Neill 2007: 5). One of the leading investment firms in the United States, Goldman Sachs Investment Company, speculated that by 2030 Brazil, Russia, India and China (the so-called BRIC economies) will eclipse the rich economies of Europe and North America.

Additionally, intra-BRIC trade increased to eight per cent of their total trade compared with five per cent in 2000, according to Goldman Sachs. With 30 per cent of world reserves and a threefold increase of FDI within their borders, to 15 per cent since 2000, the role of the BRICs in the world economy today and into the future cannot go unnoticed. As their productivity increases, their currencies will appreciate, further contributing to their GDP growth. By 2019, BRICS' total GDP grew by 179 per cent in a decade (Lin 2019). Because the BRICs have the scale and trajectory to challenge today's major developed economies in terms of their impact on the world economy and the evolution of globalisation, it is worthwhile to study their economies to gain a better understanding of the world economy today and the world economy in the future (see Wilson and Purushothaman 2003; Cheng et al. 2007).

While the BRICS countries are not on a sure path to economic hegemony in the world economy, the interplay between them and those of the G6 and Canada (the G7) is viewed by the investment community as a critical aspect of globalisation and interdependence. However, there are many obstacles to be overcome to ensure their success today and into the future. The key to further progress is improving long-term conditions to promote growth including macroeconomic stability, political institutional development, trade and investment openness and education. BRICS members are yet to make many of the necessary steps to establish these conditions. The synergies between economic well-being, sustainability and macroeconomic fundamentals, and on the proper functioning of a country's financial markets in general—and the stock markets in particular—are still an open question; further research is needed to disentangle the effects of specific institutional channels on growth and to understand the impact on advancement of institutional change. This has to take place against an inauspicious backdrop of incipient Western protectionism.

The New Development Bank

In March 2012 finance ministers from the BRICS countries were enjoined to assess

> '... the feasibility and viability of setting up a New Development Bank for mobilising resources for infrastructure and sustainable development projects in BRICS and other emerging economies and developing countries, to supplement the existing efforts of multilateral and regional financial institutions for global growth and development... We have agreed to establish the New Development Bank. The initial contribution to the Bank should be substantial and sufficient for the Bank to be effective in financing infrastructure'. (BRICS 2013: paragraph 9)

After feasibility studies by finance ministers from the BRICS, the New Development Bank (NDB) was formed by BRICS heads of states and governments in Fortaleza, Brazil with authorised capital of US$100 billion and initial subscription capital of US$50 billion which was to be shared among member states. That capitalisation of the NDB is shared equally among the five BRICS members sets it apart from the World Bank and the IMF (Lin 2019: 75). Because Bretton Woods institutions come with value-laden or conditional finances, the NDB will be a 'bank of projects' and not a 'bank of policies'. This is reminiscent of China's non-interference policy in the affairs of other countries. The NDB is a substantial addition to the existing efforts of the World Bank and the Asian Development Bank—the two main multilateral lenders—as well as bilateral development assistance extended mostly by Organisation for Economic Cooperation and Development (OECD) countries. Seen from this perspective, the NDB does not intend to supplant existing multilateral and regional financial institutions that are designed to promote global development and economic growth.

BRICS countries have carefully divided their influence over the bank. Each country was given a concession: the headquarters will be in Shanghai but speculation that this decision denotes China's dominance among the BRICS members is dispelled by the fact that the first president came from India, the first chair of the board of governors from Russia, the first chair of the board of directors from Brazil and the bank has its Africa Regional Centre in Johannesburg, South Africa. Jiejin Zhu (2018: 1) argues that the thrust for equality as the main feature of the bank was the consequence of 'competition between India and China for leadership'. The

NDB will represent an alternative source of finance for developing countries and a political response to institutions that have failed to adapt to the new economic order.

China's Growth and Appeal in Africa

Emerging trends from the non-Western world are understandably interpreted as attempts to create other centres for global economics. But these moves, while alternatives to the old order, are still not fully fledged harbingers of the new era. This is an illustration of the transition Africa is in (both politically and economically): from the previous age marked by colonial exploitation and imperialist institutions like the IMF that did not end the systematic poverty of the African continent, to current renewed Africa–China partnerships that undertake to 'respect each other's development path' so that no party should try to impose its will on the other (Xi 2017: 496). The partnerships with China are not forged by naive statesmen who believe in an altruistic Beijing foreign policy, but by seasoned campaigners who have learned from the iniquities of the past and the detrimental lasting effects of those decisions. Additionally, the support provided by the regional bodies, such as the African Union (AU) and the Southern African Development Community (SADC), informs regional African policies against exploitation or unfavourable organisations but in favour of industrialisation and regional integration. China's role in Africa is to promote industrialisation, as it is perceived as the foremost authority on reinvigorating African economies and modernising society through aggressive and robust manufacturing and industrialisation, which Africa is hoping to emulate.

Sino-Africa relations in their current form have raised criticism from the West. Paul Wolfowitz, the American diplomat who also served as president of the World Bank, remarked that Chinese unrestricted lending had 'undermined years of painstaking efforts to arrange conditional debt relief' (cited in Campbell 2008). The control of global South policies in exchange for loans was dwindling because China was offering African states loans without conditions. The development monopoly that the Bretton Woods institutions enjoyed was being challenged by China, and with its focus on sustainable partnerships instead of neoimperialist economic policy it was the obvious choice for development aid. During his first visit as president to Africa, Xi Jinping (2018: 337) vowed that China would 'continue to firmly support Africa's just position on regional and international affairs, and uphold the common interests of developing countries'. This rhetoric scarcely rhymes with the perceived attitude of Bretton Woods institutions. The IMF feared it was becoming obsolete, but more importantly, its influence was being eroded by Chinese deals. In a rant to the media Wolfowitz claimed that the Chinese partnership deals in Africa weaken IMF and World Bank governance structures and thus foster corruption—and then the head of the World Bank was removed because of charges of corruption. This was a reminder that the West, with its perceived moral high ground, is by no means immune to problems and also faces governance and corruption issues.

In 2008, Horace Campbell stated that the volume of Chinese trade with Africa had risen from US$81.7 million in 1979, to US$6.84 billion in 1989, to US$39.75 billion in 2005 (Campbell 2008). The increase in Chinese aid to Africa is indicative of the robust positive change the Chinese economy was itself going through. Between 2004 and July 2006 China's GDP grew by one-third. China's fixed investment tripled from US$400 billion in 2000 to an expected US$1.3 trillion in 2006. The Chinese State Administration of Foreign Exchange announced that foreign exchange holdings from foreign trade had been expanding at the rate of US$18.8 billion a month during 2006. These figures were revised upwards in 2007 and, by accumulating reserves of more than US$100 billion per quarter, the Chinese were expected to overtake Japan as the largest holder of US dollar reserves by the end of 2007. At the end of 2000, China's forex reserves stood at US$165.6 billion, but by 2006 its aggressive economic and commercial activities had placed China in a position where it held 20 per cent of the world's foreign exchange with about 70 per cent of its holdings in dollars.

In contrast, US debt had risen to over US$9.5 trillion. The National Bureau of Statistics raised its estimate of China's 2006 growth rate from 10.7 per cent to 11.1 per cent. China's huge domestic market, with over 1.5 billion citizens, insulates the economy from drastic global capitalist cycles of recessions and booms. It was totally impervious to the 1997–1998 Asian financial crisis. The Chinese economy is unusual: a booming capitalist economy controlled by a communist party that is still guided by the dictum of democratic centralism. On the other hand, the opening up of China led to difficult conditions for workers, with low wages in sweatshops. The company Walmart is emblematic of the kind of corporation that has invested heavily in China.

Low wages and low production costs underpin the manufacturing industries of textiles, automobiles, television sets, steel, chemicals, pulp and paper and plastics. It is this low-wage economy that enables China to flood the world market with cheap commodities. The environmental consequences of this model have deepened issues of desertification, pollution and the poisoning of water supply systems—it has not been possible to develop capitalist enterprises without the consequences: the destruction of the environment. The thirteenth Five Year Plan (2016–2020) has expressly acknowledged the urgency of arresting pollution in China. Xi conceded that Chinese consumption of steel, rubber, glass, oil and other raw materials has increased the global demand for raw materials and led to increased competition and higher prices, but in some places this placed a higher premium on 'development far above environmental protection' (Xi 2017: 423).

FOCAC and Its Impact on Africa–Chinese Relations

The Forum on China–Africa Cooperation (FOCAC) is the overarching platform for Sino-Africa relations. It was established in 2000 'in order to further strengthen the friendly cooperation between China and Africa under the new circumstances, to jointly meet the challenge of economic globalization and to promote common development' (FOCAC 2009). The inaugural FOCAC meeting was held in China in the year 2000 and was attended by fewer than ten African heads of government and Salim Ahmed Salim, at the time secretary general of the Organisation of African Unity (OAU) (later to be transformed into the AU) (Wekesa 2015: 1). The second FOCAC meeting was convened in Addis Ababa, Ethiopia in 2003 (Cissé 2012). It is noteworthy that Addis Ababa, often referred to as the capital city of Africa, is where the headquarters of the AU is found. The decision for FOCAC II was thus symbolic. In addition, there was an increase in the number of representatives from Africa governments, with 44 countries represented. This betokened Africa's espousal of FOCAC, and the choice of an African venue signified FOCAC as a joint Afro-Chinese initiative rather than an exclusively Chinese brainchild (Wekesa 2015: 3).

If the first FOCAC was about determining whether an Africa–China forum was feasible and the second about convincing Africa that FOCAC was a collective initiative, the events of 2006 were a clear demonstration that Africa was not a mere appendage to China's international relations.

For the first time, China crafted a white paper, its Africa Policy, which outlined China's strategic engagement with Africa.

Undeniably, FOCAC was also part of China's diplomatic offensive. One of China's long-term ambitions is to wean African countries away from Taiwan. This has been very successful—Malawi and Burkina Faso have renounced relations with Taiwan in favour of China, leaving Eswatini (formerly Swaziland) as the only African country that has such relations. China's incursions into Africa have demonstrated its 'go out' policy which encouraged overseas investment and, where possible, the physical movement of Chinese nationals from China to seek opportunities elsewhere. These movements have been carried out through state-owned enterprises (SOEs) that are becoming ubiquitous in African countries that have relations with China. Portfolios such as Ministry of Foreign Affairs (MFA) and Ministry of Commerce (MOFCOM), and financial institutions (China Exim Bank, China Development Bank and China Africa Development Fund) have been instrumental in deepening China's involvement in overseas economies and simultaneously boost trade, investments and aid. The impact in Africa has been massive. In 2011, trade between China and Africa reached US$160 billion and investments totalled more than US$13 billion. A plethora of Chinese SOEs has been vital in augmenting this increase in Sino-African economic ties.

Challenging or Supplementing Bretton Woods Institutions?

The main question posed in this chapter is difficult to answer because of the temptation to conflate the Bretton Woods institutions with one power, the United States, and then BRICS and FOCAC with China. Henry Kissinger (2011) and Michael Pillsbury (2016) understandably look at the United States and China as the two most important shapers of the ensuing international political system. The United States is explicably loath to cede, or even to share, its tenancy at the top of the global pecking order to a power whose values can seem like anathema at worst but also one that was a third-world backwater within living memory. Pillsbury argues that after what is termed 'a century of humiliation', after 1949 China has always had designs of supplanting the United States as a dominant global power. Given its illustrious history as a powerhouse of civilisation, China takes umbrage at the fact that for so long it was considered a power of no consequence and at the onset of the twentieth century was called 'the sick man of Asia' (Wang 2015). However, aside from this titanic strife between the world's two biggest economies, what is the motive of BRICS and FOCAC with regard to Bretton Woods institutions?

This chapter argues that BRICS and FOCAC do not, as multinational institutions, seek to challenge Bretton Woods institutions. BRICS countries are representatives of the developing world and the countries involved are juggernauts in their respective regions. BRICS is in tandem with the niche for regional powers that was opened with the dissolution of the Soviet Union and the effective end of the Cold War. The emerging world order ordained regional powers with the task of providing public goods for their regions. BRICS also offers a panacea to initiatives such as the structural adjustment programmes that did not take into stock the insights of the countries they were supposed to serve. Through initiatives such as the New Development Bank, the five members of BRICS have noted that infrastructure deficit is a major hurdle in the development of the developing world. It was thus thought imperative to build an institution that could remedy this deficit.

FOCAC was a formal framework through which Africa and China could conduct their growing political, economic and diplomatic relationship. It cannot be gainsaid that China was the main driver of this initiative. It is also noteworthy that China has bilateral agreements with individual African countries that seem not in accord with FOCAC ideals regarding whether African countries should collectively engage China. However, FOCAC does not, in its ideal form, seek to challenge the World Bank and IMF. One of the fundamental differences between FOCAC and Bretton Woods institutions is that FOCAC is not primarily a money-lending or financial body but merely a platform through which China can engage, in myriad ways, with the African countries with which it shares diplomatic recognition. Thus, neither China nor its African partners have to choose between FOCAC and Bretton Woods institutions. They all serve different purposes, purposes that are not mutually exclusive.

The foregoing does not rule out the possibility that individual players within BRICS, FOCAC and the Bretton Woods institutions could have intentions to challenge each other. This is the pith of the argument that while China and the United States could be locked in a battle for global dominance, their individual ambition need not be the preoccupation of their respective partners. BRICS and FOCAC serve the developing world in a manner that the developed world cannot. Members of these institutions supplement the value-laden policies of Bretton Woods institutions with the lived experiences and practical needs of the developing world. This is what creates differences in terms of ethics, politics and touchy issues such as democracy and human rights. A good combination of these different worldviews could prove pivotal in bolstering the fortunes of the developing world without its having to choose between the emerging and Bretton Woods institutions. Xi Jinping is keenly aware that through Chinese initiatives such as the Belt and Road Initiative (BRI), the Asian Infrastructure Investment Bank (AIIB) and the Silk Road Fund, some quarters of the international system are uncomfortable. However, he is quick to mention that 'these new financial mechanisms and traditional multilateral financial institutions such as the World Bank complement each other' (Xi 2017: 558). In sum, if BRICS and FOCAC are perceived as threats to Bretton Woods institutions, it is China that is often the target of such anxiety, rather than the entire developing world. Secondly, from the Western perspective, apprehension about emerging sources of economic and political cooperation seem to be driven by America's reluctance to share its prominent place in the global pecking order.

Conclusion

In the immediate aftermath of the Second World War the United States emerged as the most powerful global power, dominating international structures such as the United Nations (UN), the IMF and the World Bank. The Soviet Union tried to mount a countervailing force against the United States-led capitalist bloc during the Cold War, but this did diminish the dominance of the United States in influencing IMF, UN and World Bank policies. After the implosion of the Soviet Union, Russia emerged as one of the emerging powers that were finding a niche between the previously colonised players and the developed world.

The post-Cold War trends were characterised by the victory of liberal democracy over socialism, and even countries such as China that once exuded doctrinaire leftism were won over to market economics. Socialist Africa was smarting after the Soviet dissolution as it was forced by Western donors to implement foreign-bred structural adjustments which meant drastic reductions in subsidies and the privatisation of parastatals that were formerly publicly owned. Under such circumstances, the continent is understandably jubilant that the rise of China, BRICS, FOCAC and non-Western development banks are offering economic and financial alternatives that are considerate of the third world situation and hence not haughty towards the developing world. This chapter has traced these dynamics while posing the question of whether the non-Western structures that have been so well received in Africa are a replacement of or a supplement to the Bretton Woods institutions. In their current form, the emerging structures do not rival the Bretton Woods institutions, but if the ultra-nationalism that threatens to engulf the West—as seen through the leadership of Donald Trump and Boris Johnson—will be the norm, then the non-Western world will visibly reduce its allegiance to the West. The Sino-American trade war, ignited by the current US government, only works to enhance China's image as a more open and agreeable power.

We argue, finally, that China is Africa's biggest manifestation of change in international trends. It also represents Africa's new-found power to choose who it wants to court. However, Africa has to admit that its relations with China are still not relations among equals, and they follow the disturbing logic of Africa's regrettable relations with the West. The responsibility to craft and implement policies beneficial to Africa resides with the continent, for as long as Africa does not increase its fortunes, the current euphoria that defines its relations with non-Western powers will give way to despair and resentment.

Bibliography

Ahya, C., Xie, A., Roach, S. S., Sheth, M., & Yam, D. (2006). *India and China: New Tigers of Asia, Special Economic Analysis*. New York: Morgan Stanley Research.

BRICS. (2013). *Fifth BRICS Summit Declaration and Action Plan*. Available at http://www.brics5.co.za/fifth-brics-summit-declaration-and-action-plan/.

Campbell, H. (2008). China in Africa: Challenging US Global Hegemony. *Third World Quarterly, 29*(1), 89–105. https://doi.org/10.1080/01436590701726517.

Cheng, H. F., Gutierrez, M., Mahajan, A., Shachmurove, Y., & Shahrokhi, M. (2007). A Future Global Economy to Be Built by BRICs. *Global Finance Journal, 18*(2), 143–156.

Cissé, D. (2012). *FOCAC: Trade, Investments and Aid in China-Africa Relations*. Centre for Chinese Studies: Policy Briefing. http://hdl.handle.net/10019.1/21429.

Easterly, W. (2005). What Did Structural Adjustment Adjust? The Association of Policies and Growth with Repeated IMF and World Bank Adjustment Loans. *Journal of Development Economics, 76*(1), 1–22.

Demchak, C. C. (2019). China: Determined to Dominate Cyberspace and AI. *Bulletin of the Atomic Scientists, 75*(3), 99–104.

Forum for China-Africa Cooperation (FOCAC). (2009). *The Creation of FOCAC*. www.focac.org. Accessed 4 August 2019.

IMF. (1990). *Articles of Agreement of the International Monetary Fund*. www.imf.org/external/pubs/ft/aa/aa01.htm.

IMF. (2002a). *The General Arrangements to Borrow (GAB); the New Arrangements to Borrow (NAB): A Factsheet*. www.imf.org/external/np/exr/facts/gabnab.htm.

IMF. (2002b). *How Does the IMF lend? A Factsheet*. www.imf.org/external/np/exr/facts/howlend.htm.

Kissinger, H. (2011). *On China*. New York: Penguin.

Lam, K. T. (2018). *Chinese State Owned Enterprises in West Africa: Triple-Embedded Globalization*. London: Routledge.

Lin, S. (2019). *A Collection of Articles and Remarks by H. E. Ambassador Lin Songtian of China to South Africa*.

Nguyen, H. (2017). Donald J. Trump and Asia: From Campaign to Government. *Asian Affairs: An American Review, 44*(4), 125–141.

O'Neill, J. (2007). *BRICs and Beyond*. New York: Goldman Sachs.

Peet, R. (2009). *Unholy Trinity: The IMF, World Bank and WTO*. New York: Palgrave Macmillan.

Pillsbury, M. (2016). *The Hundred-Year Marathon: China's Secret Strategy to Replace America as the Global Superpower*. New York: St. Martin's Griffin.

Sitas, A. (2018). *Keynote Address: South Africa's BRICS Presidency 2018: An Inclusive Path Towards Global Development*. Johannesburg: IGD, UNISA and SABTT.

Wang, X. (2015). *Exploring the Miracle: The Truths Behind China's Modernization*. Beijing: Foreign Languages Press.

Weisbrot, M., Cordero, J., & Sandoval, L. (2009). *Empowering the IMF: Should Reform Be a Requirement for Increasing the Fund's Resources? (No. 2009–15)*. Center for Economic and Policy Research (CEPR).

Wekesa, B. (2015). Looking Back at FOCAC: 2000 to 2009 in Review. *The Emerging Powers: The FOCAC Series*, 2.

Wilson, D., & Purushothaman, R. (2003). *Dreaming with BRICs: The Path to 2050* (Global Economics Paper 99). New York: Goldman Sachs.

Xi, J. (2017). *The Governance of China*. Beijing: Foreign Languages Press.

Xi, J. (2018). *The Governance of China*. Beijing: Foreign Languages Press.

Zhu, J. (2018). Borrowing Country-Oriented or Donor Country-Oriented? Comparing the BRICS New Development Bank and the Asian Infrastructure Investment Bank. *International Organisations Research Journal [2019], 14*(2), 150–172.

CHAPTER 14

Conclusion

David Monyae and Bhaso Ndzendze

The BRICS phenomenon came about due to the failure of the post-1945 world order (led by the US and the Western powers) to both address concerns of the developing world in general and accommodating the emerging markets in particular. BRICS countries therefore came at the backdrop of the 2008 global financial crisis. Since its inception, BRICS have sought to assume the role of being the voices of the Global South. It has nonetheless been unable to either disrupt the hegemonic position of the West or fully unify the developing world. In its first decade of existence, BRICS has rather shown an incremental strength to establish a formidable development financial institution (DFI), namely, NDB, which will no doubt play a critical role in complementing the existing DFIs dominated by the West. By and large, BRICS formation remains trapped in its formative phase of being big on declarations and runs short on

D. Monyae · B. Ndzendze (✉)
Centre for Africa-China Studies, University of Johannesburg, Johannesburg, South Africa
e-mail: bndzendze@uj.ac.za

D. Monyae
e-mail: dmonyae@uj.ac.za

D. Monyae and B. Ndzendze (eds.), *The BRICS Order*, International Political Economy Series,
https://doi.org/10.1007/978-3-030-62765-2_14

implementation of its noble ideals. The main reasons for BRICS' lack of assertiveness are many. First, there are huge internal contradictions within and among member states. The differences among BRICS states in the sheer size of their population, economy and ideology bring more discords than unity of purpose. Although the volume does not deny BRICS' original conception from its market analyst/inventor Jim O'Neill, it however, takes a more developmental approach in relations to core matters raised within the BRICS formation.

This edited volume has therefore attempted to critically examine the cooperation of BRICS countries particularly in key sectoral areas. It specifically examined major thematic areas that brought BRICS countries together. The chapters covered a wide range of thematic areas under BRICS' purview. Although painstaking effort was taken in ensuring that no stone was left unturned and that the present book was as comprehensive as it could be, there were perhaps always bound to be some loose ends, and these serve as important areas for future research.

One of the principal areas which were glossed over is that of climate change. Despite some passing treatment in the work—especially by Lambrechts et al. in Chapter 12, in the discussion of Water 4.0—this aspect of BRICS growth merits more discussion from at least two angles. The first would stem from the environmental costs of the BRICS countries' ascendency to middle-income status (study here could go as far back as the Soviet era, the Great Leap forward, South Africa's industrialisation-mining nexus, India's multiple pollution sagas, and Brazil's deforestation dilemma at the behest of the Trans-Amazonian Highway). Secondly, the topic is especially interesting currently, in 2019, as the baton of environmental responsibility and championing of environmental protocols appears to have been abdicated by the USA and picked up by the BRICS countries, with China investing in renewable energy and India making commitments to manufacturing completely electric cars by 2030 (Goyal 2017). Some bold predictions have already been made in this regard:

> Projected declines in coal use in China and India are likely to reduce growth in global carbon emissions by roughly 2-3 billion metric tons (2.2–3.3 billion US tons) by 2030 compared to forecasts made a year back. Coal-fired power stations are increasingly uneconomical compared to solar power. In May [2017], India abandoned planned investments in coal-fired power stations with a combined capacity of 14 gigawatts, equivalent to the whole of the United Kingdom. Both countries are likely to achieve national climate emissions reductions ahead of target, potentially serving

> as a significant contributor to reduced net global emissions. (Robinson 2017)

Yet the reversal of US federal efforts against climate change need not mean lack of cooperation with US subnational entities and the broader West, which boasts some punctilious and motivated combatants against climate change including some states within the USA itself, and Germany in the EU. On the first point, Shuo (2018) observes that in September 2018 Xie Zhenhua, China's Special Representative for Climate Change Affairs, 'spearheaded a large Chinese delegation at the Global Climate Action Summit (GCAS) in San Francisco, [California]'. It is also not lost on Shuo that

> … at the birthplace of the idea of non-state climate action, the Chinese demonstrated they learn and adapt fast – Chinese local officials, business executives, academicians, philanthropists, and NGOs were all galvanised, and ready to put resources toward not just domestic environmental issues, but global action.

Xie's message to the world was clear: China is ready to engage, contribute and lead, at all levels. In the absence of federal climate action in the USA, Xie was translating Xi's grand vision into concrete terms in a manner that was cooperative with his US subnational host.

On the second point, Robinson (2017) argued that

> in pursuing these ambitious climate and energy policies, India and China have an opportunity to lend visible support to the German G20 Action Plan on Climate and Energy Growth, which was discussed at the [2017] G20 Summit in Hamburg. In a summit declaration, 19 of the 20 members, excluding the United States, agreed that the Paris climate accord was irreversible and reaffirmed their commitment.

Despite some discussion of military standoffs and interstate disputes between India and China in Chapter 7, this book's theme ('assertive or complementing the West?') also lends itself to being studied along the dimension of BRICS countries' collective security efforts. Case studies here could include nuclear capacity, joint exercises, sites of contestation involving the West and the BRICS (including the South China Sea and the Crimea) as well as the prospects of a common BRICS security outlet. The Shanghai Cooperation Organisation (SCO), now including the three

Asians of the five BRICS countries, could form an entire chapter—if not, indeed, an entire volume. This is made particularly pertinent by discussions of a 'new Cold War', and rising populism. There is also to be investigated the degree to which the BRICS countries' response to terrorism is akin to or different from the response mechanisms thus far pursued by the West.

Additionally, BRICS countries constantly raise matters of global peace and security in all of their summits. These countries often adopt common positions within UNSC concerning global hotspots such as Syria, Iraq and Afghanistan. In numerous occasions, however, BRICS countries demonstrate sharply divergence views and disagreements on matters of global peace and security. For instance, South Africa broke ranks with fellow BRICS members voting as a non-permanent member of UNSC (Resolution 1973) in 2011 in favour of the use of force in Libya. China and India have unresolved border dispute that constantly cause frictions between the two BRICS members states. Russia on the other hand, violated international law by invading Ukraine taking over Crimea. Brazil has also departed from BRICS' common position in the Israel–Palestine conflict. It has recently openly defied BRICS' position by siding with the USA in moving its Embassy from Tel Aviv to Jerusalem.

Three BRICS countries—South Africa, Russia and China—have at different points taken a common position in relation to the International Criminal Court (ICC). Notably, India is not a member of this judicial body. Scholarly interest in this issue could assess the extent to which the anti-ICC posture is an early example of BRICS assertiveness, whether dissatisfactions with the ICC is a BRICS-wide overlap in some way, and whether the BRICS could realistically prop up their own BRICS-led alternative legal structure—whether they would even be motivated to pursue such a transnational judicial endeavour—is interesting in its own right.

On the heels of Shilaho's chapter on the BRICS and Africa, greater and more case-specific study could be given to the BRICS countries' platforms for engaging Africa (such as the Forum on China–Africa Cooperation, the 2018-announced Russia–Africa Forum and the India–Africa Forum) and whether they bolster or undermine cooperation there. This would greatly complement the work done in this present volume as it would be conducted in the explicitly comparative method which always produces fascinating results.

Importantly, the outbreak of communicative diseases such as Ebola in parts of Africa and Covid-19 in China warrant further studies. Although health matter features prominently in BRICS' communiques, concerted efforts remain to be taken, which could strengthen the health infrastructure of members states. In this regard, insights generated could serve as proxies and speak not only to the determinants and inhibitors of cooperation, including the political economy of global healthcare, differential capacities, but also to matters of people-to-people movement, and the character it takes among these countries. Thus, another aspect which merits investigation is that of human movement. This is true of migration among the BRICS countries, including the presence of diasporas such as Indians in South Africa (home to the largest single Indian diaspora, owing to colonial legacies of indentured servitude), Chinese in Russia (especially in the Russian Far East), Chinese in South Africa (the largest on the continent, with histories of Chinese diaspora dating back to the nineteenth century), as well as BRICS citizens among the countries of the West, and the implications they could carry. Maxim Khomyakov's meta-analysis of BRICS countries' educational cooperation may close the gap in this regard, but curriculum-related work is also very relevant as we look into the idea of a future defined by a BRICS epistemological order.

Bibliography

Goyal, M. (2017). India Is Betting Big on Electric Vehicles, but Where Does That Leave the Makers of Hybrids? *Economic Times*. Read more at: https://economictimes.indiatimes.com/industry/india-is-betting-big-on-electric-vehicles-but-where-does-that-leave-the-makers-of-hybrids/articleshow/59195648.cms. Accessed 28 February 2019.

Robinson, M. (2017). Will China and India Lead on Global Climate Action and Environmental Protection? *World Resources Institute*. Read more at: https://www.wri.org/blog/2017/07/will-china-and-india-lead-global-climate-action-and-environmental-protection. Accessed 28 February 2019.

Shuo, L. (2018). Does China Still Want to Be a Global Environmental Leader? *The Diplomat*. Read more at: https://thediplomat.com/2018/10/does-china-still-want-to-be-a-global-environmental leader/. Accessed 28 February 2019.

Index

D. Monyae and B. Ndzendze (eds.), *The BRICS Order*, International Political Economy Series,
https://doi.org/10.1007/978-3-030-62765-2

U

V

W

X

Z

The manufacturer's authorised representative in the EU is Springer Nature Customer Service Centre GmbH, Europaplatz 3, 69115 Heidelberg, Germany. If you have any concerns regarding our products, please contact ProductSafety@springernature.com

Printed and bound by CPI Group (UK) Ltd, Croydon, CR0 4YY
30/09/2026
02225700-0011